TRANSVAAL CRICKETERS

1889/90 - 1993/94

compiled by

Robin Isherwood and Philip Bailey

Published by the Association of Cricket Statisticians and Historians, West Bridgford, Nottingham
1995
Typeset by Limlow Books
Printed by Peartree Printers, Derby
ISBN: 0 947774 42 4

INTRODUCTION

The first matches accepted as first-class in South Africa were the two Test matches of 1888/89. Transvaal's initial first-class match against Kimberley the following season was also the first ever Currie Cup match. Transvaal 'B' first played in the 'B' section of the Currie Cup in 1959/60, and since then 'B' teams for other South African provinces have been admitted to first-class status. Statistics for Transvaal 'B' are shown separately from Transvaal matches.

Special thanks are due to Hayward Kidson for obtaining many of the biographical details of the players. A who's who of first-class players first appeared in the *South African Cricket Annual* for 1956, then edited by Geoffrey Chettle, and has continued ever since, subsequent editors being Denys Heesom, Eric Litchfield, Peter Sichel, Ted Partridge, Michael Owen-Smith and Frank Heydenrych. The assistance of the following is also acknowledged: Dr. Ali Bacher, Brian Bassano and Philip Thorn.

Robin Isherwood
Philip Bailey
January 1995

Any additions or corrections to the biographical details will be gratefully received by Hayward Kidson, 25 June Avenue, Bordeaux, Randburg, 2194, Transvaal (Tel: 011 787 2767) or c/o Transvaal Cricket Board, PO Box 55309, Northlands, 2116, Transvaal.

CRICKETERS WHO HAVE PLAYED FIRST-CLASS CRICKET FOR TRANSVAAL BETWEEN 1889/90 AND 1993/94

ABERNETHY Terence Fitzgerald. b Pretoria 23.8.1930. lb.
ACOCK Mark George. b Cape Town 25.11.1956. rhb, ob.
ADAMS Frederick Charles. b Hofmeyr, CP 19.2.1947. rhb, rm.
ADAMS Vivian B. b Cape Town 18.1.1933. rhb, lm.
ADAIR Robin William. b Johannesburg 25.1.1957. rhb, ob.
ADCOCK Neil Amwin Treharne. b Sea Point, Cape Town 8.3.1931. rhb, rf. Natal. Tours (2), Commonwealth to New Zealand. South Africa (26).
ALDWORTH Derick Peter. b Pretoria 26.2.1936. rhb, rf.
ALLPASS George Lawrence. b Oudtshoorn, CP 3.8.1901. d Johannesburg 27.5.1954. rhb, wk.
ALLSOP George. b Houghton, Hampshire, UK 4.1.1864. d Johannesburg 27.3.1927. rhb.
ANDERSON Douglas Ian Evans. b Cape Town 26.1.1910.
ANDERSON Keith. b Johannesburg 1.11.1938. rhb.
ANDREW John Paul. b Johannesburg 24.5.1929. d Johannesburg 18.5.1960. sla.
ARGYLE John Robert. b Johannesburg 26.11.1950. rhb, ob.
ATFIELD Alfred John. b Ightham, Kent, UK 3.3.1868. d Caterham, Surrey, UK 1.1.1949. rhb, rm. Natal, Gloucestershire, London County.
ATKINSON Richard John. b Johannesburg 27.8.1955. rhb, rf.

BACHER Adam Marc. b Johannesburg 29.10.1973. rhb. Nephew of A. (Transvaal).
BACHER Aron (Dr). b Johannesburg 24.5.1942. rhb, lb, wk. Tour (1). South Africa (12). Uncle of W.Kirsh (Transvaal, Northern Transvaal), A.M. (Transvaal), M. (Northern Transvaal, Transvaal).
BACHER Michael. b Johannesburg 11.11.1959. rhb, rm. Northern Transvaal. Nephew of A. (Transvaal).
BAILEY Abaham (Sir). b Cradock, CP 6.11.1864. d Muizenberg, Cape Town 10.8.1940. rm. Father of D.T.L. (Gloucestershire).
BAILEY Charles Edgerton. b Ballarat, Victoria, Australia 21.10.1876.
BAILLIE John Hardie. b Johannesburg 20.6.1938. rhb, lb.
BAILLIE Trevor Nicholas. b Bloemfontein 2.10.1937. rhb, rm. Orange Free State.
BAINES Threlfall Werge Talbot. b Johannesburg 20.6.1908. rhb, lb. Eastern Province, Cambridge University.
BALASKAS Xenophon Constantine. b Kimberley 15.10.1910. d Hyde Park, Johannesburg 12.5.1994. rhb, lb-g. Griqualand West, Border, Western Province, North-Eastern Transvaal. Tours (2). South Africa (9).
BAM Ivan. b Cape Town 29.8.1885. Western Province.
BARKER Clifford M. b 1917. d El Alamein, Egypt (War) 27.7.1942.
BARLOW Edgar John. b Pretoria 12.8.1940. rhb, rm. Eastern Province, Western Province, Boland, Derbyshire. Tours (2), South Africa Fezela to England, Rest of the World to England (4). South Africa (30).
BARLOW Keith Alastair. b Johannesburg 2.2.1954. rhb, rm. Orange Free State.
BARNARD Llewellyn Jamieson. b Johannesburg 5.1.1956. lhb, ob. Northern Transvaal.
BARNES Abdullatief. b Kimberley 29.4.1941. rhb, ob.
BARRACLOUGH Alfred Dennis. b Cape Town 4.2.1917. wk.
BARRON Richard John. b Zeerust, Transvaal 1.10.1946. rhb, wk.
BARROW Alan. b Umtata, CP (Transkei) 23.1.1955. rhb, rm, ob. Natal, Northern Transvaal.
BATH Brian Francis. b Johannesburg 16.1.1947. rhb, ob,
BAUMGARTNER Harold Vane. b Henley-on-Thames, Oxfordshire, UK 17.11.1883. d Accra, Gold Coast 8.4.1938. rhb, sla. Orange Free State. South Africa (1).
BAYNE Shaun Wells. b Johannesburg 11.4.1955. rhb, rm.
BEAUMONT Rolland. b Newcastle, Natal 4.2.1884. d Berea, Durban 25.5.1958. rhb. Tour (1). South Africa (5).
BECKER Danzel Frank. b Pretoria 21.1.1948. rhb, rm. North-Eastern Transvaal.

BECKETT Ernest Edward. b Johannesburg 22.9.1893. d Pietermaritzburg 10.10.1992. rhb, wk.

BEGBIE Denis Warburton. b Middelburg, Transvaal 12.12.1914. rhb, lb-g. Tour (1). South Africa (5).

BEGG Yaseen. b Cape Town 8.5.1959. rhb, wk.

BELL Theodore Wilfred. b Smithfield, OFS 24.2.1874.

BENNET Harry James Graham. b 1886. d Johannesburg 22.7.1945.

BENNING Ian David. b Pilning, Bristol, Gloucestershire, UK 14.11.1963. rmf.

BENSE Brian David. b Dar-es-Salaam, Tanganyika 27.8.1931. rmf.

BERRY Albert Victor. b 1887. d Durban 3.5.1959. wk. Natal.

BERRY Robert William. b Salisbury, Rhodesia 17.6.1947. rhb, wk.

BEVES Gordon. b Brighton, Sussex, UK 15.3.1862. d Auckland Park, Johannesburg 22.3.1927. rhb. Nottinghamshire.

BISSETT George Finlay. b Kimberley 5.11.1905. d Botha's Hill, Natal 14.11.1965. rhb, rf. Griqualand West, Western Province. Tour (1). South Africa (4).

BLEWETT Joseph Warwick. b Johannesburg 25.9.1925. rhb, rfm. North-Eastern Transvaal.

BLOOM Max Leonard (Dr). b Johannesburg 7.11.1926. lb-g.

BOA Peter Macrae. b Windhoek, South-West Africa 18.12.1972. rhb.

BOCK Ernest George. b Kimberley 17.9.1908. d Springs, Transvaal 5.9.1961. rm. Griqualand West, North-Eastern Transvaal. South Africa (1).

BOND Kenneth Jackson. b Johannesburg 16.10.1941. rhb, wk. Eastern Province.

BOONZAAIER Neil Richard. b Cape Town 30.4.1956. rhb, lb. Border. Brother of A.D. (Natal).

BOOYENS William Andrew. b Edenvale, Transvaal 6.7.1956. lhb, sla.

BOTHA Paul Christopher. b Vereeniging, Transvaal 12.5.1963. rhb, lm. Northern Transvaal.

BOTHA Peterus Johannes. b Vereeniging, Transvaal 28.9.1966. rhb, rfm. Border.

BOWDEN Montague Parker. b Stockwell, Surrey, UK 1.11.1865. d Umtali Hospital, Southern Rhodesia 19.2.1892. rhb, wk. Surrey, Vernon to Australia, Warton to South Africa. England (2).

BRAIN Douglas McKenzie. d Paul Roux, OFS 14.2.1954.

BREAKEY Cyril. b Salisbury, Rhodesia 20.3.1912. d Johannesburg 10.1.1989. Father of J.C. (Transvaal).

BREAKEY James Cyril. b Johannesburg 31.12.1950. rhb, wk. Son of C. (Transvaal).

BRISCOE Arthur Wellesley. b Johannesburg 6.2.1911. d near Dessie, Ethiopia (War) 22.4.1941. rhb. South Africa (2).

BRISSENDEN Stanley Wilfred. b Germiston, Transvaal 10.4.1909. d Johannesburg 19.11.1960. rf.

BROCKETT Walter Blyth. b Johannesburg 27.7.1935. rf.

BROMHAM Charles George. b Hlobane, Natal 29.2.1916. d Pietermaritzburg 17.2.1987. wk. North-Eastern Transvaal.

BROTHERS Edward Malam. b Johannesburg 1.2.1907. d Johannesburg 13.1.1980.

BROWN Lennox Sidney. b Randfontein, Transvaal 24.11.1910. d Durban 1.9.1983. rhb, rfm, lb-g. North-Eastern Trannsvaal, Rhodesia. Tour (1). South Africa (2).

BRUORTON Derek Russell (Dr). b Grahamstown, CP 5.11.1928. rhb, lab.

BULL Kenneth Edward. b Johannesburg 29.8.1908.

BUNYARD Graham Stuart. b Port Elizabeth 17.10.1939. rhb, rf. Rhodesia. South Africa Fezela to England.

BUSSELL Edmund Peter. b Kimberley 9.8.1928. d Krugersdorp, Transvaal 10.6.1988. rmf.

BUTLER Benjamin Castor Hicks. b Middelburg, Transvaal 1.4.1935. rhb. Western Province.

BYNG John Anstruther. b 15.9.1877.

CAMERON Horace Brakenridge. b Port Elizabeth 5.7.1905. d Joubert Park Hospital, Johannesburg 2.11.1935. rhb, wk. Eastern Province, Western Province. Tours (3). South Africa (26).

CAMPBELL Henry Howie. b Johannesburg 30.9.1906. d Durban 5.9.1987.

CAMPBELL Thomas. b Edinburgh, Mid-Lothian, Scotland, UK 9.2.1882. d Milnedale Railway Siding, Natal 5.10.1924. rhb, wk. Tours (2). South Africa (5).

CARLISLE Alistair McDougall. b Salisbury, Rhodesia 16.4.1944. rhb. Father of S.V. (Zimbabwe Board XI)

CARLSTEIN Peter Rudolph. b Klerksdorp, Transvaal 28.10.1938. rhb, lb, wk. Orange Free State, Natal, Rhodesia. Tours (2). South Africa (8).

CARR Ronald Bernard. b Johannesburg 12.1.1938. rhb, lb-g. Essex.

CARTER Claude Pagdett. b Durban 23.4.1881. d Addington Hospital, Durban 8.11.1952. rhb, sla. Natal. Tours (2). South Africa (10).

CATTERALL Robert Hector. b Port Elizabeth 10.7.1900. d Kempton Park, Transvaal 3.1.1961. rhb, rm. Rhodesia, Natal, Orange Free State. Tours (2). South Africa (24).

CAWOOD Carey Hobson. b Graaff-Reinet, CP 30.12.1918. rhb, wk. Eastern Province. Brother of W.A. (Eastern Province).

CAWSE Charles Edward. b Cape Town 16.10.1908. d Johannesburg 26.6.1966. rmf.

CHAPMAN Peter Douglas Malcolm. b Beira, Mozambique 27.8.1922. rhb.

CHAPPELL Charles Stanley. b Kimberley 16.12.1895. d Johannesburg 7.6.1979. lhb, wk.

CHARNAS Morris. b Johannesburg 17.10.1930. d Glenmore, Durban 14.4.1991. rhb, sla. Western Province.

CHATTERTON Elton Valentine. b Benoni, Transvaal 27.2.1942. rhb, wk.

CHEETHAM John Richard. b Cape Town 23.8.1947. lhb. Western Province. Son of J.E. (Western Province), brother of R.S. (Transvaal, Natal).

CHEETHAM Robert Spencer. b Cape Town 24.7.1949. lhb, sla. Natal. Son of J.E. (Western Province), brother of J.R. (Transvaal, Western Province).

CHOTHIA Suleiman. b Nigel, Transvaal 10.8.1941. rhb, rm.

CHRISTY James Alexander Joseph. b Pretoria 12.12.1904. d Brighton Beach, Durban 1.2.1971. rhb, rm. Queensland. Tours (2). South Africa (10).

CHUBB Geoffrey Walter Ashton. b East London 12.4.1911. d East London 28.8.1982. rhb, rmf. Border. Tour (1). South Africa (5). Brother of A.P.A. (Border).

CLACK Thomas George. c King William's Town 6.2.1876. b Johannesburg 5.8.1951. Border.

CLARK Bryan John. b Johannesburg 13.5.1935. rhb.

CLARK Derek Alan. b London, UK 28.5.1928. lb.

CLARKE Sylvester Theophilus. b Lead Vale, Christ Church, Barbados, West Indies 11.12.1954. rhb, rf. Orange Free State, Northern Transvaal, Barbados, Surrey. West Indies Tours (3). West Indies XI to South Africa (2). West Indies (11). Half-brother of R.O.Estwick (Transvaal, Barbados).

CLAYTON Lewis Henry. b Kroonstad, OFS 6.6.1899. d Johannesburg 24.4.1976. wk.

COCHRAN John Alexander Kennedy. b Johannesburg 15.7.1909. d Johannesburg 15.6.1987. rmf. Griqualand West. South Africa (1).

COEN Stanley Keppel. b Heilbron, OFS 14.10.1902. d Durban 28.1.1967. rhb. Orange Free State, Western Province, Border. MCC (in South Africa). South Africa (2).

COETZEE Frederik Johannes. b Johannesburg 25.3.1942. rhb, rm.

CONNERTY James William. b Pretoria 29.3.1904. d Durban 27.7.1988. Eastern Province.

CONTE Myles Cusack. b Johannesburg 4.4.1947. rhb.

CONYNGHAM Dalton Parry. b Durban 10.5.1897. d Durban 7.7.1979. rm. Natal, Western Province. South Africa (1).

COOK Arthur Eyre. b King William's Town, CP 28.7.1889. d Benoni, Transvaal 25.9.1970. lhb, lm. Border. Leveson-Gower to Rhodesia. Brother of G.H. (Border), father of T.E. (North-Eastern Transvaal).

COOK Stephen James. b Johannesburg 31.7.1953. rhb, ob. Somerset. Tour (1). South Africa (3).

COOK Vincent Neale. b Harrismith, OFS 25.9.1907. d Durban 20.11.1983.

COOKE Gavin Peter. b Johannesburg 7.9.1971. rhb, rfm.

COOPER Alfred Edward. b Cape Town 10.8.1869. d Port Shepstone, Natal 15.8.1960. Griqualand West. Father of A.H.C. (Transvaal).

COOPER Alfred Henry Cecil. b Johannesburg 2.9.1893. d Johannesburg 18.7.1963. rhb, rm. South Africa (1). Son of A.E. (Griqualand West, Transvaal).

COOPER Frederick William. b Kimberley 5.5.1881. d Pretoria 30.8.1954. Grandfather of P.A. (North-Eastern Transvaal).

COPE David Gill. b Kimberley 14.8.1877. d Mostert's Hoek, CP 16.8.1898.

CORBETT Peter Llewellyn. b Vryburg, CP 24.8.1940. rhb. North-Eastern Transvaal, Natal. Brother of J.A. (North-Eastern Transvaal).

CORIN Richard Henry Maton. b Wynberg, Cape Town 5.9.1930. rhb, wk.

CRADOCK Thomas Tressillian. b Durban 25.5.1877. d Durban 25.6.1948. Natal.

CREESE William Henry. b Usk, Monmouthshire, Wales, UK 15.1.1870. d Belgium (War) 23.10.1918. MCC (in South Africa). Father of W.L.C. (Hampshire).

CRESSWELL Vernon George. b Pretoria 15.9.1958. rhb, wk. Eastern Province, Border, Northern Transvaal.

CREWS Basil (Dr). b Robertson, CP 15.3.1926. rhb, lb. Western Province, Border, Eastern Province.

CULLINAN Daryll John. b Kimberley 4.3.1967. rhb, ob. Border, Western Province. Tours (3). South Africa (8). Brother of R.E. (Border, Orange Free State).

CURNOW Sydney Harry. b Benoni, Transvaal 16.12.1907. d Perth, Western Australia, Australia 28.7.1986. rhb. Tour (1). South Africa (7).

DACEY Lawrence Stanley. b Johannesburg 28.5.1913. d Johannesburg 20.8.1993. rhb.

DAVIES Douglas David. Border, Western Province.

DAVIES Eric Quail. b King William's Town, CP 26.8.1909. d Port Alfred, CP 11.11.1976. lhb, rf. Eastern Province, North-Eastern Transvaal. South Africa (5).

DAVIES George R. b Calcutta, India 30.4.1933. rhb.

DAVIES Richard Edwyn. b 1900. d Cape Town 4.1.1960. Natal.

DAY Noel Trevor. b Johannesburg 31.12.1953. rhb, wk. Northern Transvaal.

DEANE Hubert Gouvaine. b Eshowe, Natal (Zululand) 21.7.1895. d Lower Houghton, Johannesburg 21.10.1939. rhb. Natal. Tours (2). South Africa (17). Son of H.P. (Natal).

DE VAAL Peter Derek. b Cathcart, CP 3.12.1945. lhb, sla. Northern Transvaal, Eastern Transvaal.

DEVITT Vincent Patrick. b Johannesburg 14.3.1905. d Johannesburg 30.6.1970.

DICKENSON Frank O.

DIFFORD Archibald Newcombe. b Cape Town 9.4.1883. d Palestine (War) 20.9.1918. Western Province. Brother of I.D. (Transvaal).

DIFFORD Ivor Denis. b Glastonbury, Somerset, UK 29.1.1873. d Johannesburg 5.2.1949. Brother of A.N. (Western Province, Transvaal).

DINDAR Nazier. b Lenasia, Transvaal 12.2.1966. rhb, rm.

DINSDALE Stephen Charles. b Buckhurst Hill, Essex, UK 30.12.1948. lhb, lm. Rhodesia, Essex.

DIXON Cecil Donovan. b Potchefstroom, Transvaal 12.2.1891. d Illovo, Johannesburg 9.9.1969. rhb, rm. Tour (1). South Africa (1).

DIXON Thomas James (Dr). b Shoreditch, London, UK 6.10.1847. d Potchefstroom, Transvaal 23.4.1915.

DODDS Peter Michael. b Durban 26.11.1933. lhb, sla. Natal.

DOIG James George Eric. b Cape Town 1873.

DONALDSON Ian Charles. b Johannesburg 3.4.1954. rmf.

DOUGLAS William Harvey.

DRAKE Anthony Herbert. b Johannesburg 14.9.1956. lhb, sla. Nephew of D.J.Drake (North-Eastern Transvaal, Orange Free State).

DRUMMER Francois T M. b Cape Town 20.9.1938. rhb, rm. Western Province. Brother of D. (Western Province).

DUFF William Dick. b Pietermaritzburg 19.9.1890. d Johannesburg 7.10.1953. lb-g.

DUFFUS Louis George. b Melbourne, Victoria, Australia 13.5.1904. d Johannesburg 24.7.1984. rhb, wk.

DUMBRILL Richard. b Wandsworth, London, UK 19.11.1938. rhb, rmf. Natal. Tour (1). South Africa (5).

DUMINY Jacobus Petrus. b Bellville, CP 16.12.1897. d Groote Schuur Hospital, Cape Town 31.1.1980. lhb, sla. Western Province, Oxford University. Tour (1). South Africa (3).

DUNLOP Drummond William. b Johannesburg 8.7.1952. lhb, rm.

DU PLESSIS Stephen James. b Durban 24.1.1967. rhb. Brother of J.H. (Western Province).

DU PREEZ Andre Louis. b Rustenburg, Transvaal 7.4.1954. rhb, lb. Brother of V.F. (Northern Transvaal, Transvaal).

DU PREEZ Vernon Francois. b Rustenburg, Transvaal 6.9.1958. rhb, lb. Northern Transvaal. Brother of A.L. (Transvaal).

DURING Albert Andre. b Strand, CP 7.6.1946. rhb, ob. Nephew of P.B. (Western Province).

DURING John Peter. b Robertson, CP. d Bloemfontein 18.9.1930. lhb. Western Province. Father of P.B. (Western Province), grandfather of J. (Western Province).

DU TOIT Jacobus Daniel. b Worcester, CP 8.9.1959. lhb, lm. Western Province, Boland, Northern Transvaal.

DU TOIT Sydney Daniel. b Parys, OFS 4.7.1919. rhb, rfm. Eastern Province.

DYER David Dennis. b Berea, Durban 3.12.1946. rhb, sra, wk. Natal. South African Universities to England. Son of D.V. (Natal), brother of G.D. (Western Province, Natal).

DYKE-POYNTER Robert Edgar John. b Pilgrim's Rest, Transvaal 7.6.1907. d Newlands, Cape Town 7.12.1966.

EASTERBROOK John Wilfred. b Durban 7.6.1892. d Durban 6.11.1969. lhb. Natal.

EATON David Penfold. b Cape Town 26.3.1934. ob.

EDWARDS David Neville. b Pretoria 15.2.1954. rhb. Northern Transvaal. Son of R.A. (North-Eastern Transvaal).

EHRET Brian Wally. b Johannesburg 29.7.1966. lhb, rfm.

EKSTEEN Clive Edward. b Johannesburg 2.12.1966. rhb, sla. Northern Transvaal. Tour (1). South Africa (1).

ELLIS Andrew Gray. b Pretoria 11.5.1947. d The Wilds Nature Reserve, Johannesburg 26.6.1971. rhb, rm.

ELLIS John Reid. b Leicester, Leicestershire, UK 1.7.1919. rhb. Natal.

ELWORTHY Frank William. b Cambridge, Cambridgeshire, UK 11.6.1893. d Johannesburg 15.3.1978. lhb, lb.

ELWORTHY Steven. b Bulawayo, Rhodesia 23.2.1965. rhb, rfm. Northern Transvaal.

EMSLIE Owen David. b Grahamstown, CP 12.9.1935. rhb. Orange Free State. Brother of H.G. (Eastern Province).

ENDEAN William Russell. b Parkview, Johannesburg 31.5.1924. rhb, wk. MCC. Tours (3). South Africa (28).

ENGELBRECHT Helmut. b Johannesburg 30.9.1966. rhb. Northern Transvaal.

ESTERHUIZEN Derek. b Boksburg, Transvaal 29.11.1939. rfm.

ESTWICK Roderick Orville. b Christchurch, Christ Church, Barbados, West Indies 28.6.1961. rhb, rfm. Barbados. Young West Indies to Zimbabwe. Half-brother of S.T.Clarke (Transvaal, Orange Free State, Northern Transvaal, Surrey, Barbados).

EUSTICE Raymond. b Johannesburg 11.11.1927. rhb.

FAIRCLOUGH John. b Grimsby, Lincolnshire, UK 23.7.1941. rhb, lm. Western Province.

FAIRON Gavin Peter. b Springs, Transvaal 19.12.1941. rhb, ob.

FARQUHARSON Reginald Arthur. b Mafeking, CP 31.10.1898. d Pretoria 10.11.1957.

FAULKNER George Aubrey. b Port Elizabeth 17.12.1881. d Walham Green, London, UK 10.9.1930. rhb, lb-g. MCC. Tours (4). South Africa (25).

FEATHERSTONE Norman George. b Que Que, Southern Rhodesia 20.8.1949. rhb, ob. Northern Transvaal, Middlesex, Glamorgan.

FELLOWS-SMITH Jonathan Payn. b Berea, Durban 3.2.1932. rhb, rm. Oxford University (Blue 3), Northamptonshire, MCC. Tour (1). South Africa (4). Son of H. (Natal).

FERNLEY David Leo. b Murree, India 29.5.1934. rhb. Eastern Province, Western Province.

FIELD Graham Eric. b Johannesburg 14.1.1953. rhb, rf.

FIELD Samuel. wk.

FINLASON Charles Edward. b Camberwell, London, UK 19.2.1860. d Surbiton, Surrey, UK 31.7.1917. rhb. Griqualand West. South Africa (1).

FINLAY Ian William. b Woking, Surrey, UK 14.5.1946. lhb, lm. North-Eastern Transvaal, Surrey.

FITZGERALD Peter Hamilton. b Pretoria 8.10.1955. lhb, rfm.

FLANAGAN Franklin Frederick. b Kimberley 16.2.1918. d Johannesburg 30.10.1968. Griqualand West. Father of J.P.D. (Transvaal).

FLANAGAN John Patrick Douglas. b Sandringham, Johannesburg 20.9.1947. rhb, rm. South African Universities to England. Son of F.F. (Griqualand West, Transvaal).

FLEISCHER Frederick. b Dordrecht, CP 16.6.1868. d Johannesburg 31.7.1938.

FLOQUET Bertram Harold. b Cathcart, CP 12.10.1883. d Johannesburg 16.6.1953. Brother of C.E. (Transvaal).

FLOQUET Claude Eugene. b Aliwal North, CP 3.11.1884. d Port Elizabeth 22.11.1963. rhb, rm. South Africa (1). Brother of B.H. (Transvaal).

FOLEY William Bernard Henry. b Cape Town 3.10.1906. d Bergvliet, Cape Town 13.8.1963. rhb. Western Province.

FOLSTER John Hasson. b Sydney, New South Wales, Australia 5.2.1892. d Johannesburg 8.5.1954.

FORBES Alan. b Johannesburg 27.10.1927.

FORREST James Edward. b Ipswich, Suffolk, UK 14.12.1921. rhb, rm.

FOSTER Neil Alan. b Colchester, Essex, UK 6.5.1962. rhb, rfm. Essex. England Tours (6), England XI to South Africa. England (29).

FOTHERINGHAM Henry Richard. b Empangeni, Natal (Zululand) 4.4.1953. rhb, ob. Natal.

FOX John Stephen. b Durban 4.7.1929. rhb, rm. Western Province, Orange Free State, Eastern Province.

FRAMES Algernon Sidney. b Jagersfontein, OFS 7.1.1891. d Johannesburg 12.10.1975. rhb.

FRANK Charles Newton. b Jagersfontein, OFS 27.1.1891. d Johannesburg 25.12.1961. rhb. South Africa (3).

FULLER James Herbert Frederick. b Bulawayo, Rhodesia 10.4.1916. d Bulawayo, Rhodesia 26.1.1967. rhb, rm, wk. Rhodesia.

FULLERTON George Murray. b Kensington, Johannesburg 8.12.1922. rhb, rm, wk. Tours (2). South Africa (7). Brother of I.R. (Transvaal).

FULLERTON Ian Ramsay. b Kensington, Johannesburg 24.9.1935. rhb. South Africa Fezela to England. Brother of G.M. (Transvaal).

FUNSTON Kenneth James. b Pretoria 3.12.1925. rhb. North-Eastern Transvaal, Orange Free State. Tour (1). South Africa (18). Father of G.K. (North-Eastern Transvaal, Griqualand West).

FURNISS Albert Douglas. b Johannesburg 6.10.1921. lhb, sla.

FUSSELL Basil John. b Johannesburg 21.10.1935. d near Brits, Transvaal 13.10.1991. rhb.

GAMBLE Mark Andrew. b Pretoria 4.10.1947. rhb, lb.

GARDA Ismail. b Johannesburg 24.5.1946. lhb, sla.

GARDNER Walter Thorne. b Barkly East, CP 13.6.1888. d Johannesburg 22.11.1931.

GARTLY John Devitt Elrick. b Johannesburg 8.1.1908. d Sidi Rezegh, Libya (War) 22.11.1941. wk.

GAYDON Claude Brian. b Johannesburg 28.9.1909. d Johannesburg 2.5.1966. Orange Free State.

GEORGEU George. b Cape Town 27.6.1913. rhb. Western Province.

GIBB Peter John MacKenzie. b Johannesburg 17.10.1931. rhb, wk.

GIBBS Keith Lawley. b Bloemfontein 30.12.1933. rhb, rfm. Orange Free State.

GOLDSMITH Mervyn Harold. b Johannesburg 12.3.1948. rm.

GOLDSTEIN Frederick Steven. b Bulawayo, Rhodesia 14.10.1944. rhb, ob. Western Province, Oxford University (Blue 4), Northamptonshire.

GORDON Norman. b Boksburg, Transvaal 6.8.1911. rf. South Africa (5).

GORDON-CAMPBELL Ryves John. b Harrismith, OFS 30.10.1914. d Durban 29.8.1988.

GRAHAM James Mackay. b Cape Town 8.8.1879. d Cape Town 6.1.1941. Brother of R. (Western Province), father of D.K. (Western Province).

GRAINGER Chad. b Johannesburg 23.9.1972. rhb.

GREVE Vivian Stanley. b Johannesburg 27.7.1946. rhb, lb.

GRIESSEL Lloyd Wayne. b Kroonstad, OFS 7.6.1960. rhb. Orange Free State.

GRIEVESON Ronald Eustace. b Johannesburg 24.8.1909. rhb, wk. South Africa (2).

GRIFFITHS Edward A.

GRINAKER Ola Wilhelm. b Durban 8.5.1923. d Knysna, CP 5.8.1985. rhb. Natal.

GYNGELL Anthony Hubert. b Johannesburg 1.4.1914. Griqualand West.

HALL Alfred Ewart. b Bolton, Lancashire, UK 23.1.1896. d Hospital Hill, Johannesburg 1.1.1964. lhb, lfm. Lancashire. South Africa (7).

HALL Norman. b Jeppe, Johannesburg 15.12.1901.

HALLIWELL Ernest Austin. b Drayton Green, Ealing, Middlesex, UK 7.9.1864. d Hillbrow, Johannesburg 2.10.1919. rhb, wk. Middlesex, MCC, London County. Tours (2). South Africa (8). Son of R.B. (Middlesex).

HAMILTON Eric Peter. b Johannesburg 5.5.1913. d over Sicily (War) 15.7.1943.

HAMMOND H W.

HAND Cecil Ridges. b 1890. d Pinetown, Natal 20.9.1934. Natal.

HANDFIELD C R. d Gibeon, South-West Africa (War) 6.5.1915.

HANKEY Stanley Edward. b Johannesburg 24.11.1935. rhb, sla.

HANLEY Rupert William. b Port Elizabeth 29.1.1952. rhb, rf. Eastern Province, Orange Free State, Northamptonshire. Son of A.W.D. (Border).

HANSEN Eldred Thomas Edwin. b Piet Retief, Transvaal 27.1.1930. rhb, ob. Orange Free State, North-Eastern Transvaal.

HARRIS Louis Ronald. b Johannesburg 15.2.1933. lhb.

HARRIS Terence Anthony. b Kimberley 27.8.1916. d Plettenberg Bay, CP 7.3.1993. rhb. Griqualand West. Tour (1). South Africa (3).

HARRISON John Spranger. b Ellel, Lancaster, Lancashire, UK 29.6.1857. wk.

HARRISON Ronald Felix. b Johannesburg 11.8.1921.

HATHORN Christopher Maitland Howard. b Pietermaritzburg 7.4.1878. d Johannesburg 17.5.1920. rhb. London County. Tours (4). South Africa (12).

HAYSMAN Michael Donald. b North Adelaide, South Australia, Australia 22.4.1961. rhb, ob. Northern Transvaal, Leicestershire, South Australia. Australian XI to South Africa (2).

HAZELHURST William Colin. b Transvaal 31.5.1881. d Johannesburg 3.2.1927.

HEANEY Llewellyn John. b Mossel Bay, CP 14.8.1914. lhb, sla.

HEATHER Percival Jackson. b Emerald Hill, Victoria, Australia 6.10.1882. d Melbourne, Victoria, Australia 29.6.1956. rhb. Natal, Victoria. Son of E.D. (Victoria).

HECTOR Alan Roy. b Springs, Transvaal 26.10.1939. d Durban 13.3.1986. rhb, rm. Eastern Province. Brother of R.G. (North-Eastern Transvaal).

HEELEY Henry Norman. b Pietermaritzburg 1.2.1879. b Johannesburg 14.1.1953.

HEINE Peter Samuel. b Winterton, Natal 28.6.1928. rhb, rf. North-Eastern Transvaal, Orange Free State. Tour (1). South Africa (14).

HELFRICH Dudley George. b Kimberley 17.5.1912. d Witbank, Transvaal 13.6.1980. wk. Griqualand West, North-Eastern Transvaal. Brother of C.D. (Griqualand West), B.A. (Griqualand West) and K. (Griqualand West, North-Eastern Transvaal).

HENNING Mark. b Johannesburg 26.3.1934. lhb, rmf.

HEPKER Victor Norman. b Bulawayo, Rhodesia 15.9.1908. d Johannesburg 20.2.1982.

HERBERT Sidney Ralph. b Johannesburg 16.8.1904. d Eshowe, Natal (Zululand) 15.12.1982. rhb.

HESTER Harold Carl. b Warmbaths, Transvaal 8.4.1940. rhb, wk. North-Eastern Transvaal.

HEWITT Glen Michael. b Johannesburg 16.4.1973. rhb, ob.

HICKSON John Arnold Einem. b Hornsey, Middlesex, UK 22.12.1864. d Surbiton, Surrey, UK 2.1.1945. wk. Middlesex.

HINGS John Thomas. b Leicester, Leicestershire, UK 27.12.1872.

HOAR Hilton Robert Vivian. b Johannesburg 27.10.1907. d Johannesburg 27.3.1972.

HOBSON Malcolm Ralph. b Graaff-Reinet, CP 5.6.1966. rhb, rfm. Natal, Eastern Province, Border.

HOLMES Neville Chamberlain McLean. b Barberton, Transvaal 3.9.1939. rhb, wk. North-Eastern Transvaal.

HOOPER Justin James. b Johannesburg 11.6.1958. rhb, rfm. Western Province.

HORAK Donald J. b Pretoria 1.8.1946. rhb.

HOWELL David Hugh. b Port Elizabeth 20.5.1958. rhb, wk. Western Province, Eastern Province, Border. Twin brother of I.L. (Eastern Province, Border).

HUBBARD Alistair Nugent. b Johannesburg 1.1.1951. rhb, rfm.

HUDDY Michael Edward. b Kroonstad, OFS 25.6.1940. rhb.

HUGHES Gary Philip. b Johannesburg 3.5.1958. rhb, rm.

HUNTER Bryan Leonard. b Witbank, Transvaal 10.3.1935. rhb.

HUTTON Richard Anthony. b Pudsey, Yorkshire, UK 6.9.1942. rhb, rfm. Cambridge University (Blue 3), Yorkshire. MCC U25 to Pakistan, Swanton to India, Rest of World to Australia. England (5). Son of L. (Yorkshire).

INCE Reginald Goodman. b 1902.
INCHBOLD Swithin John. b Pietermaritzburg 29.6.1911. wk.
INNES Gerald Alfred Skerten. b Cape Town 16.11.1931. d Cape Town 11.7.1982. rhb, ob. Western Province. Tour (1).
IRONSIDE David Ernest James. b Lourenco Marques, Mozambique 2.5.1925. rhb, rfm. South Africa (3).
IRVINE Brian Lee. b Durban 9.3.1944. lhb, rm, wk. Natal, Essex. South Africa (4).

JACK Steven Douglas. b Durban 4.8.1970. rhb, rf.
JACKSON Dirk Cloete. b Wynberg, Cape Town 21.4.1885. d Pretoria 17.9.1976. Western Province.
JACKSON Ian Matthew. b Johannesburg 12.5.1949. rhb, rm.
JACOBS Stefan. b Virginia, OFS 11.3.1966. rhb, rfm.
JAMES John William. b Johannesburg 24.9.1925. d Springs, Transvaal 4.6.1983. rhb, wk.
JAMES Michael. b Johannesburg 18.4.1960. rhb, ob.
JARDINE Allan James. b Johannesburg 8.2.1903. d Johannesburg 29.7.1958.
JENNINGS Raymond Vernon. b Vanderbijlpark, Transvaal 9.8.1954. rhb, wk. Northern Transvaal. Brother of K.E. (Northern Transvaal).
JOHNSON Clement Lecky. b Co.Kildare, Ireland 1871. d Maraisburg, Transvaal 31.5.1908. rhb, rmf. South Africa (1).
JOHNSON Graham William. b Beckenham, Kent, UK 8.11.1946. rhb, ob. Kent. Robins to South Africa.
JOHNSTON Mark O'Neill. b Pretoria 11.4.1971. rhb, wk.
JONES Charles Henry Kingsley. b Johannesburg 31.5.1909. d Winston Park, Gillitts, Natal 31.1.1985. rhb.
JORDAAN Lucas Cornelius Rudolph. b Johannesburg 20.7.1963. rhb, sla. Eastern Transvaal.
JOUBERT Frank Edwards. b Bloemfontein 9.5.1952. rhb, rfm. Northern Transvaal. Brother of A.R. (SAU).
JURGENSEN Neill. b Johannesburg 28.2.1957. rhb, rm.

KAHN Harry Michael. b Cape Town 30.1.1908.
KALLICHARRAN Alvin Isaac. b Paidama, British Guiana 21.3.1949. lhb, ob. Orange Free State, Guyana, Warwickshire, Queensland. West Indies Tours (8), Rest of World to Pakistan, West Indies XI to South Africa (2). West Indies (66).
KATZ Solly Joel. b Port Elizabeth 13.10.1942. rhb, wk. Eastern Province.
KEIGHTLEY-SMITH Arthur Walter. b Port Elizabeth 19.6.1911. d Randburg, Transvaal 7.5.1993. rhb, rfm.
KEMPIS George Stephen. b Port Elizabeth 25.11.1871. d Scottburgh, Natal 17.3.1948. rab. Brother of G.A. (Natal).
KENNEDY Archibald Benjamin. b Vryburg, CP 31.12.1886. d Somerset West, CP 30.4.1957.
KERBY Jack Colin. b Johannesburg 16.12.1935. rhb, rfm. Western Province.
KERR John F M.
KERR Kevin John. b Airdrie, Lanarkshire, Scotland, UK 11.9.1961. rhb, ob. Warwickshire.
KERR William Robert. b Johannesburg 23.4.1948. rhb, lm.
KIDD William David Bennie. b Durban 28.4.1931. rhb, wk.
KIMBER Sydney Ronald. b Germiston, Transvaal 9.1.1924. rhb.
KINSLEY Peter Howard. b Pietermaritzburg 2.10.1938. rhb.
KIRSH William. b Johannesburg 17.11.1960. rhb, rm. Northern Transvaal. Nephew of A.Bacher (Transvaal).
KLETTE John Edward. b Cape Town 8.2.1949. lhb. Western Province.
KLINCK Frederick Gordon. b Port Elizabeth 1865. d Doornfontein, Johannesburg 11.8.1893. lhb, rab.
KNODELL Terence Edward. b Luanshya, Northern Rhodesia 12.1.1956. rhb, wk.
KOTZE Johannes Jacobus. b Hopefield, CP 7.8.1879. d Rondebosch, Cape Town 7.7.1931. rhb, rf. Western Province, London County. Tours (3). South Africa (3).
KOURIE Alan John. b Johannesburg 30.7.1951. rhb, sla.

KUHN Sean Anthony. b Bulawayo, Rhodesia 18.2.1959. rhb, wk. Rhodesia.

LACEY Henry Stanley. b Johannesburg 31.5.1920. rhb, wk. Border.

LAING Dean Ralph. b Durban 18.9.1970. rhb, rm. Nottinghamshire.

LAMB C.

LANCE Herbert Roy. b Pretoria 6.6.1940. rhb, rm. North-Eastern Transvaal. Tour (1). South Africa (13). Son of W.P. (North-Eastern Transvaal), brother of A.P. (North-Eastern Transvaal).

LANGEBRINK Alfred Cecil. b Johannesburg 1.3.1902. d Merrivale, Natal 9.7.1983.

LANGTON Arthur Chudleigh Beaumont. b Pietermaritzburg 2.3.1912. d Accra, Gold Coast (War) 27.11.1942. rhb, rfm, rm. Tour (1). South Africa (15).

LAWRANCE J.

LE ROUX Frederick Louis. b Durban 5.2.1882. d Durban 22.9.1963. rhb, rm. Eastern Province. South Africa (1).

LEVICK Frederick Owen. b Johannesburg 28.12.1911. d Uvongo Beach, Natal 7.7.1986. wk. Griqualand West. Twin brother of R.P.O. (Transvaal).

LEVICK Robert Philip Owen. b Johannesburg 28.12.1911. d St Michael's-on-Sea, Natal 25.7.1983. Twin brother of F.O. (Transvaal, Griqualand West).

LEVY Clarence. b Johannesburg 24.1.1923. sla.

LEWIN Leo. b Johannesburg 26.1.1903. d Johannesburg 26.4.1961. rhb, lab. Natal.

LEWIS David Wyndham. b Roath, Cardiff, Glamorgan, Wales, UK 18.12.1940. rhb, lb. Glamorgan.

LEY Thomas.

LILLEY Aubrey Roy. b Grahamstown, CP 26.8.1950. d Greytown, Natal 10.8.1979. rhb, lm. Natal.

LINDSAY Denis Thomson. b Benoni, Transvaal 4.9.1939. rhb, wk. North-Eastern Transvaal. Tours (2), South Africa Fezela to England, Rest of World to England (2). South Africa (19). Son of J.D. (Transvaal, North-Eastern Transvaal).

LINDSAY John Dixon. b Barkly East, CP 8.9.1908. d Benoni, Transvaal 31.8.1990. rhb, wk. North-Eastern Transvaal. Tour (1). South Africa (3). Father of D.T. (North-Eastern Transvaal, Transvaal).

LINDSAY Nevil Vernon. b Harrismith, OFS 30.7.1886. d Pietermaritzburg 2.2.1976. rhb. Orange Free State. South Africa (1).

LINDSAY-SMITH Duncan. b Johannesburg 17.10.1946. rhb.

LISTER-JAMES Christopher Mark. b Durban 16.8.1960. rhb, rm. Natal. Brother of G.N. (Natal, Orange Free State).

LLOYD Edgar Llewellyn. b Grahamstown, CP 15.7.1902. d Johannesburg 2.7.1961. rhb.

LODWICK John Robert. b Johannesburg 19.8.1937. rhb, rf.

LOESER Paul Sydney. b Johannesburg 16.2.1914. wk.

LOHMANN George Alfred. b Campden Hill, Kensington, London, UK 2.6.1865. d Worcester, CP 1.12.1901. rhb, rmf. Western Province, Surrey. Lillywhite, Shaw and Shrewsbury to Australia (2), Sheffield to Australia, Hawke to South Africa. England (18).

LOMAS George Edward. b Burnley, Lancashire, UK. d Armadale Farm, near Umzumbe, Natal 12.3.1921. rhb.

LOSPER Henry. b Germiston, Transvaal 20.1.1956. rhb, rm.

LUCKIN Maurice William. b Romford, Essex, UK 22.10.1876. d Johannesburg 8.3.1937.

LUNDIE Eric Balfour. b Willowvale, CP (Transkei) 15.3.1888. d near Passchendaele, Belgium (War) 12.9.1917. rf. Eastern Province, Western Province. South Africa (1).

LUNDIE Paul Grant. b Johannesburg 24.7.1940. rhb, rmf.

LURIE Steven Alan. b Johannesburg 30.5.1964. rhb, rfm.

McADAM Sibley John. b Broken Hill, Northern Rhodesia 9.3.1948. rhb, rf. Eastern Province, Western Province. Grandson of S.J.Snooke (Border, Western Province, Transvaal), brother of W.J. (Western Province, Eastern Province).

McALPINE Neil Munro. b Maraisburg, Transvaal 1.8.1913. d Sandton, Transvaal 6.6.1976.

MACAULAY Michael John. b Durban 19.4.1939. rhb, lmf, sla. Western Province, Orange Free State, North-Eastern Transvaal, Eastern Province. Tour (1). South Africa (1).

McBRIDE Bruce. b Pietermaritzburg 21.10.1959. rhb, wk. Northern Transvaal.

McCARTHY J.

McCUBBIN George Reynolds. b Cape Town 18.1.1898. d Johannesburg 9.5.1944.

McDONALD Edward Gavin. b Grahamstown, CP 5.4.1879. d Johannesburg 15.1.1951.

McKAY Charles Donald. b Douglas, CP 21.5.1902. d Sterkfontein, near Krugersdorp, Transvaal 1970. lhb, wk. Griqualand West. Brother of A. (Griqualand West).

MACKAY James Rainey Munro. b Kentucky, near Uralla, New South Wales, Australia 9.9.1880. d Walcha, New South Wales, Australia 13.6.1953. rhb. New South Wales.

MACKAY-COGHILL Donald. b Kimberley 4.11.1941. lhb, lmf.

McKENZIE Kevin Alexander. b Pretoria 16.7.1948. rhb, rm. North-Eastern Transvaal.

McKEOWN Allen Charles. b Rondebosch, Cape Town 16.1.1925. d Durban 2.6.1960.

McKINNON Atholl Henry. b Port Elizabeth 20.8.1932. d Durban 1.12.1983. rhb, sla. Eastern Province. Tours (2). South Africa (8). Father of G.P. (Eastern Province).

MacLAREN Norman. b Johannesburg 31.1.1916. rhb, wk.

McMILLAN Brian Mervin. b Welkom, OFS 22.12.1963. rhb, rmf. Western Province, Warwickshire. Tours (3). South Africa (13).

McMILLAN Gordon Eric. b Germiston, Transvaal 18.11.1953. rhb, lm. Northern Transvaal.

McMILLAN Quintin. b Germiston, Transvaal 23.6.1904. d Randfontein, Transvaal 3.7.1948. rhb, lb-g. Tours (2). South Africa (13).

MacNAB Guy Neil. b Gwelo, Southern Rhodesia 4.11.1956. lhb, sla.

MAILE John Brian Roland. b Johannesburg 15.10.1926. rhb, rfm, ob. Western Province.

MALRAISON William Henry de Rockstro. b Wepener, OFS 4.12.1876. d East Africa (War) 31.5.1916.

MANACK Abdulhack. b Vereeniging, Transvaal 21.8.1967. rhb, rfm.

MANACK Hussein Ahmed. b Pretoria 10.4.1968. rhb, rm.

MARE Brett Lester. b Johannesburg 13.6.1959. rhb, lfm.

MARITZ Colin. b 14.3.1892. Griqualand West, Orange Free State, Eastern Province. Brother of G. (Griqualand West).

MARSHALL E.

MARTIN Gavin John. b Florida, Roodepoort, Transvaal 19.10.1946. rhb, rfm.

MARTIN Hugh. b Enkeldoorn, Southern Rhodesia 3.8.1947. rhb, rm. New South Wales. Son of S.H. (Natal, Rhodesia, Worcestershire).

MARVIN Edward William. d France (War) 24.3.1918.

MARX Ian Brandt. b Johannesburg 22.3.1930. rhb, rf.

MARX Waldemar Frederick Eric. b Johannesburg 4.7.1895. d Durban 2.6.1974. lhb, rm. South Africa (3).

MATTHEWS Brett Anthony. b Cape Town 5.7.1962. rhb, lm. Western Province, Eastern Province. Brother of C.R. (Western Province).

MATTHEWS John Peter. b Johannesburg 3.4.1950. rhb, rfm. Northern Transvaal.

MEINTJES Douglas James. b Pretoria 9.6.1890. d Johannesburg 17.7.1979. rhb, rfm. Tour (1). South Africa (2).

MELLE Basil George von Brandis (Dr). b Somerset West, CP 31.3.1891. d Orchards, Johannesburg 8.1.1966. rhb, rm, lb. Western Province, Hampshire, Oxford University (Blue 2). Father of M.G. (Transvaal, Western Province).

MELLE Michael George. b Forest Town, Johannesburg 3.6.1930. rhb, rf. Western Province. Tours (2). South Africa (7). Son of B.G.von B. (Western Province, Transvaal, Hampshire).

MELVILLE Alan. b Carnarvon, CP 19.5.1910. d Sabie, Transvaal 18.4.1983. rhb, lb-g, ob. Natal, Sussex, Oxford University (Blue 4). Tour (1). South Africa (11).

MEYER Jonathan Reid. b Kroonstad, OFS 23.6.1965. rhb, rfm. Eastern Province, Northern Transvaal, Eastern Transvaal.

MILTON John Griffith. b Cape Town 1.5.1885. d 14.6.1915.

MINNAAR Neil. b Cape Town 7.9.1953. rhb, rm. Natal.

MITCHELL Bruce. b Ferrierer Deep Gold Mine, Johannesburg 8.1.1909. rhb, lb. Tours (4). South Africa (42).

MITCHELL David Haddon. b Johannesburg 3.9.1933. rhb, rfm, lb. Eastern Province.

MITCHELL Frank. b Market Weighton, Yorkshire, UK 13.8.1872. d Blackheath, Kent, UK 11.10.1935. rhb, rm, wk. Yorkshire, London County, Cambridge University (Blue 4). Tours (2),

Mitchell to North America, Warner to North America, Hawke to South Africa, Bosanquet to North America. England (2), South Africa (3).

MITCHELL James Clarence. b Johannesburg 14.4.1947. rhb, sla. Rhodesia.

MITCHLEY Cyril Douglas. b Johannesburg 25.7.1960. rhb, rfm. Northern Transvaal, Eastern Transvaal. Son of C.J. (Transvaal), brother of M.J. (Transvaal, Northern Transvaal) and S.E. (Eastern Transvaal).

MITCHLEY Cyril John. b Johannesburg 4.7.1938. rhb, wk. Father of C.D. (Transvaal, Northern Transvaal, Eastern Transvaal), M.J. (Transvaal, Northern Transvaal) and S.E. (Eastern Transvaal).

MITCHLEY Mark John. b Johannesburg 15.3.1967. lhb, rm. Northern Transvaal. Son of C.J. (Transvaal), brother of C.D. (Transvaal, Northern Transvaal, Eastern Transvaal) and S.E. (Eastern Transvaal).

MOORE Barry Peter. b Uitenhage, CP 11.7.1951. rhb, rfm.

MORKEL Jan Willem Hurter. b Somerset West, CP 13.11.1890. d East Africa (War) 15.5.1916.

MORRISON Ian. b Johannesburg 11.9.1931. rhb. Brother of A. (SAU).

MORTON Henry. wk.

MOSENTHAL Herbert Francis. b Sydenham, London, UK 8.6.1866. d Sidmouth, Devon, UK 12.10.1904.

MOSES Eric Claude (Later changed name to Murray E C). b Johannesburg 18.7.1893. d Durban 10.7.1971. rhb, ob. Derbyshire.

MOSSOP Dennis Neil. b Salisbury, Rhodesia 1.10.1951. lhb, lm.

MOTLEY Arthur William. b Johannesburg 9.8.1931. rhb, rm. Father of K.G. (Northern Transvaal, Transvaal).

MOTLEY Kevin George. b Kensington, Johannesburg 5.7.1958. rhb, rm. Northern Transvaal. Son of A.W. (Transvaal).

MOULDER John Hardie. b Richmond, Surrey, UK 29.9.1881. d Johannesburg 13.10.1933. rhb, ob. Surrey, London County.

MULLER Granville A Bruce. b Cape Town 4.11.1943. rhb, rf.

MULLER Hendrik Stephanus Johannes. b Johannesburg 1.4.1932. rmf.

MURRAY Eric Claude see Moses E C.

MUZZELL Robert Kendal. b Stutterheim, CP 23.12.1945. rhb, lb. Western Province, Eastern Province. South African Universities to England. Son of J.K. (Border), brother of P.J. (Border).

NEEDHAM Peter Graham. b Johannesburg 17.7.1932. rhb, lb.

NEILSON Douglas Ralph. b Johannesburg 17.12.1948. rhb, rmf.

NEL John George. b Johannesburg 17.8.1914.

NELSON Thorwald Douglas. b 1893. d Johannesburg 24.10.1954.

NESER Vivian Herbert. b Klerksdorp, Transvaal 16.6.1894. d Pretoria 22.12.1956. rhb, wk. Oxford University (Blue 1).

NEUSTETEL Charles Maurice. b Kensington, London, UK 21.3.1873. d Johannesburg 26.4.1944. wk.

NEWBERRY Claude. b Port Elizabeth 1889. d France (War) 1.8.1916. lb. South Africa (4).

NEWBY William Crawford. b Stockton-on-Tees, Co.Durham, UK Oct.1856. d Thornton-le-Dale, Yorkshire, UK 2.8.1921.

NEWNHAM Lewis Cyril Ashby. b Jansenville, CP 13.9.1881. d Pretoria 20.11.1932. lhb, lab. Border.

NEWSON Edward Serrurier. b Sea Point, Cape Town 2.12.1910. d Durban 24.4.1988. rhb, rf. Rhodesia. South Africa (3).

NICKEL Aaron. b Johannesburg 31.5.1923. rfm.

NIEMEYER Walter Emanuel. b Boshof, OFS 30.7.1877. d Pretoria 27.11.1936. rm.

NIMR-SPRINGER Mark Christian. b Bulawayo, Rhodesia 3.3.1956. rhb, rfm. Rhodesia, Natal.

NORDEN Richard Watts. b Cape Town 4.1.1879. d Johannesburg 20.2.1952. sla.

NORRIS Craig Reginald. b Johannesburg 11.9.1963. lhb, lfm. Northern Transvaal, Eastern Transvaal.

NOURSE Arthur William. b Thornton Heath, Surrey, UK 26.1.1879. d Port Elizabeth 8.7.1948. lhb, lm, sla. Natal, Western Province. Tours (4). South Africa (45). Father of A.D. (Natal).

NUPEN Eiulf Peter. b Johannesburg 1.1.1902. d Hospital Hill, Johannesburg 29.1.1977. rhb, rfm. Tour (1). South Africa (17).

NUPEN Norman Robert Prang (Dr). b Johannesburg 14.10.1922.

OCHSE Arthur Edward. b Graaff-Reinet, CP 11.3.1870. d France (War) 11.4.1918. rhb. South Africa (2).

O'LINN Sidney. b Oudtshoorn, CP 5.5.1927. lhb, wk. Western Province, Kent. Tour (1). South Africa (7). Birth registered as S.Olinsky.

ONTONG Rodney Craig. b Johannesburg 9.9.1955. rhb, rfm, ob. Border, Northern Transvaal, Glamorgan.

OXENHAM Hereward Athelstone.

PAGE Hugh Ashton. b Salisbury, Rhodesia 3.7.1962. lhb, rfm. Essex.

PARK Michael. b Salisbury, Rhodesia 23.10.1957. rfm.

PARKER Gerald Clarkson. North-Eastern Transvaal.

PARKIN Durant Clifford. b Port Elizabeth 20.2.1873. d Sangster's Farm, (Eagle's Crag) Albany, CP 20.3.1936. rhb. Eastern Province, Griqualand West. South Africa (1). Father of D.H.C. (Transvaal), brother of L. (Eastern Province).

PARKIN Durant Herbert Clifford. b Grahamstown, CP 10.2.1910. Son of D.C. (Transvaal, Eastern Province, Griqualand West).

PARKYNS Sydney Charles. rhb, lab.

PARRYMORE Thomas Henry. b Johannesburg 1.3.1962. rhb, rfm.

PATEL Mohamed Farouk. b Johannesburg 19.12.1950. rhb, lb.

PATRICK William Ellison. b Cape Town 24.8.1934. rhb.

PEENS Andre. b Durban 1.8.1960. rhb.

PEGLER Sidney James. b Durban 28.7.1888. d Plumstead, Cape Town 10.9.1972. rhb, rm, lb. MCC. Tours (3). South Africa (16). Uncle of J.W.Bristow (Natal, Western Province, Griqualand West) and K.L.Bristow (Orange Free State).

PERRING John Baxter. b Kimberley 14.7.1893. d Johannesburg 14.9.1965.

PETERSEN Roy N E. b 1.6.1910. d 1988.

PHILLIPS John Glanville. b East London 8.11.1910. d Amanzimtoti, Natal 20.6.1985. lhb, lab. Border. Brother of R.R. (Border).

PICKERILL James Henry Maxwell. b Benoni, Transvaal 19.8.1918. d Johannesburg 27.6.1984. rhb, lab. North-Eastern Transvaal. Son of V.J. (Transvaal).

PICKERILL Vincent James. b Nottingham, Nottinghamshire, UK 28.11.1889. d Benoni, Transvaal 26.7.1964. Father of J.H.M. (Transvaal, North-Eastern Transvaal).

PIENAAR Roy Francois. b Johannesburg 17.7.1961. rhb, rm. Western Province, Northern Transvaal, Kent.

PINKERTON Anthony Donovan. b Calcutta, India 12.6.1930. rhb, rm.

PISTORIUS Donald Ivan. b Johannesburg 22.7.1933. rhb, rf.

PITHEY David Bartlett. b Salisbury, Rhodesia 4.10.1936. rhb, ob. Rhodesia, Western Province, Natal, Oxford University (Blue 2), Northamptonshire. Tour (1). South Africa (8). Brother of A.J. (Rhodesia, Western Province).

PITON John Henry David. b La Motte, Groot Drakenstein, CP 20.4.1865. d Johannesburg 20.7.1942. rhb, sr lob. Natal.

PLINT Arthur James. b Johannesburg 18.10.1955. lhb, sla. Northern Transvaal.

POLLOCK Andrew Graeme. b Port Elizabeth 14.11.1969. lhb, rfm. Grandson of A.M. (Orange Free State), son of R.G. (Eastern Province, Transvaal), brother of G.A. (Transvaal).

POLLOCK Graeme Anthony. b Port Elizabeth 7.4.1973. lhb, ob.. Grandson of A.M. (Orange Free State), son of R.G. (Eastern Province, Transvaal), brother of A.G. (Transvaal).

POLLOCK Robert Graeme. b Durban 27.2.1944. lhb, lb. Eastern Province. Tour (2), Rest of World to England (4), Rest of World to Australia, International Cavaliers to England. South Africa (23). Son of A.M. (Orange Free State), brother of P.M. (Eastern Province), father of A.G. (Transvaal) and G.A. (Transvaal).

PORTER Frank Wools. b Cape Town 9.4.1882. Border, Eastern Province.

POTHAS Nic. b Johannesburg 18.11.1973. rhb, wk.

QUINN Neville Anthony. b Tweefontein, OFS 21.2.1908. d Kenilworth, Kimberley 5.8.1934. lhb, lmf. Griqualand West. Tours (2). South Africa (12). Brother of M.H. (Rhodesia).

RADFORD Neal Victor. b Luanshya, Northern Rhodesia 7.6.1957. rhb, rfm. Lancashire, Worcestershire. England Tours (1), Worcestershire to Zimbabwe (2). England (3). Brother of W.R. (Orange Free State, Boland, Eastern Transvaal) and G. (Eastern Transvaal).

RAEL Lawrence C. b Johannesburg 7.10.1943. rhb, rm.

RALPH William Walter. b Johannesburg 29.5.1926.

RALPHS Harold. b Johannesburg 11.2.1915. rhb, wk. North-Eastern Transvaal.

RANKIN George Kenneth. b Potchefstroom, Transvaal 24.2.1907. d White River, Transvaal 24.11.1985.

REDICK Arthur William. b Beaufort West, CP 21.3.1886. d Johannesburg 8.1.1974. lb.

REICH Wilfred. b Pietermaritzburg 21.4.1940. rhb, rf.

REID Richard Bruce. b Lower Hutt, Wellington, New Zealand 3.12.1958. rhb. Wellington, Auckland. New Zealand (One-Day Internationals only). Son of J.R. (Wellington, NZ).

REID W O.

REILLY Neville Maxwell Donald. b Bloemfontein 21.2.1933. rhb, lb-g. Orange Free State. Son of C.M. (Orange Free State).

REX Artheo Charles. b Johannesburg 7.5.1939. d Johannesburg 16.5.1986. rhb.

RHODES Nikolas Richard. b Mufulira, Zambia 26.5.1965. rhb.

RICE Clive Edward Butler. b Johannesburg 23.7.1949. rhb, rfm. Natal, Nottinghamshire. South Africa (One-Day Internationals only). Grandson of P.S.S.Bower (Oxford University).

RICHARDS Barry Anderson. b Morningside, Durban 21.7.1945. rhb, ob. Natal, Hampshire, Gloucestershire, South Australia. Rest of World to England (2). South Africa (4).

RICHARDSON John Henry. b Pretoria 8.5.1935. rhb, wk. North-Eastern Transvaal. Father of D.J. (Eastern Province, Northern Transvaal) and R.P. (Western Province).

RIDGWAY Richard Kingsley. b Durban 9.8.1934. rhb, rfm.

RILEY James Robert. b Kidderminster, Worcestershire, UK 14.8.1964. rhb, rfm.

RINDEL Michael John Raymond. b Durban 9.2.1963. lhb, lfm. Northern Transvaal.

RIPPON Warne Victor. b Grahamstown, CP 31.8.1966. rhb, ob. Orange Free State, Border.

RITCHIE Gerald George. b Johannesburg 16.9.1933. rhb, rm.

RIVETT Colin Wilmot. b Zeerust, Transvaal 11.6.1929. rm.

ROBERTS Bruce. b Lusaka, Northern Rhodesia 30.5.1962. rhb, rm, wk. Derbyshire.

ROGERS Stanley. b Germiston, Transvaal 25.9.1937. rhb.

ROOTHMAN John Beresford. b Johannesburg 20.4.1926. rhb, rm. Rhodesia.

ROSE Albert.

ROSE Russell Spencer Kennedy. b Kimberley 17.4.1910. d Welkom, OFS 23.11.1988. rmf. Griqualand West, Natal.

ROSE-INNES Albert. b Port Elizabeth 16.2.1868. d East London 22.11.1946. rhb, sla. Griqualand West. South Africa (2).

ROSHOLT Aanon Michael. b Johannesburg 13.11.1920.

ROUTLEDGE Thomas William. b Liverpool, Lancashire, UK 18.4.1867. d Billingham, Co. Durham, UK 9.5.1927. rhb. Western Province. South Africa (4).

ROWAN Athol Matthew Burchell. b Kensington, Johannesburg 7.2.1921. rhb, ob. Tours (2). South Africa (15). Brother of E.A.B. (Transvaal, Eastern Province).

ROWAN Donald Alan. b Johannesburg 10.5.1922. ob.

ROWAN Eric Alfred Burchell. b Johannesburg 20.7.1909. d Edenvale Hospital, Johannesburg 30.4.1993. rhb, lb. Eastern Province. Tours (2). South Africa (26). Brother of A.M.B. (Transvaal).

RUBIDGE Yusuph. b Johannesburg 30.9.1952. rhb, ob.

RULE Kevin John. b Johannesburg 28.3.1963. rhb, wk. Northern Transvaal.

RUSH William Rolande Gerrard. b Kuruman, CP 22.1.1904. d Durban 3.3.1968. Western Province. Brother of E.D.B. (Griqualand West, Western Province).

RUSHMERE Mark Weir. b Port Elizabeth 7.1.1965. rhb, rm. Eastern Province. Tour (1). South Africa (1). Son of C.G. (Eastern Province, Western Province).

RUTHERFOORD John Henry Hugh. b Standerton, Transvaal. d Bramley, Johannesburg.

SACCO Desmond. b Johannesburg 22.9.1940. rhb, ob.

SADLER Leslie Allan. b Johannesburg 3.10.1913.

SANSBURY Derek John. b Brakpan, Transvaal 30.7.1945. rhb, ob.

SAUNDERS R O.

SCHUURMAN Dirk Jan. b Oudtshoorn, CP 1863. d Johannesburg 1941. rhb.

SCHWARZ Reginald Oscar. b Lee, London, UK 4.5.1875. d Etaples, France (War) 18.11.1918. rhb, g. MCC, Middlesex. Tours (4), Bosanquet to North America, MCC to North America, Leveson- Gower to Rhodesia. South Africa (20).

SCOTT Michael. sla.

SCOTT Malcolm William Llewellyn. b Pretoria 17.5.1947. rhb, rf. Border.

SECCOMBE David Thorne. b Johannesburg 14.4.1949. rhb, lm. Son of J.T. (Transvaal, North-Eastern Transvaal).

SECCOMBE John Thorne. b Johannesburg 10.2.1920. d Johannesburg 5.3.1985. rhb. North-Eastern Transvaal. Father of D.T. (Transvaal).

SECCULL Arthur William. b King William's Town, CP 14.9.1868. d Johannesburg 20.7.1945. rhb, rm. Griqualand West, Western Province. South Africa (1).

SEEFF Lawrence. b Kensington, Johannesburg 1.5.1959. rhb, lb. Western Province. Brother of J. (Western Province).

SELSICK Peter Lee. b Johannesburg 16.11.1963. rhb. Northern Transvaal.

SERRURIER Louis Roy. b Sea Point, Cape Town 7.2.1905. d Hermanus, CP 16.1.1990. rhb, rm. Western Province, Oxford University, Worcestershire.

SHALDERS William Alfred. b Kimberley 12.2.1880. d Cradock, CP 18.3.1917. rhb. Griqualand West, London County. Tours (3). South Africa (12).

SHAW Basil Philip. b Johannesburg 20.5.1918.

SHEPSTONE George Harold. b Pietermaritzburg 9.4.1876. d Springkell Sanatorium, Germiston, Transvaal 3.7.1940. rhb, rf. MCC. Tour (1). South Africa (2).

SHERWELL Percy William. b Isipingo, Natal 17.8.1880. d Bulawayo, Rhodesia 17.4.1948. rhb, wk. MCC. Tours (2), Leveson-Gower to Rhodesia. South Africa (13).

SIEBERT Kenneth Henry. b Johannesburg 29.10.1932.

SIMON Allan. b Bloemfontein 7.2.1943. rhb.

SINCLAIR Donald McIntosh. b Cape Town 3.9.1878. d France (War) 11.7.1916. rhb. Brother of J.H. (Transvaal).

SINCLAIR James Hugh. b Swellendam, CP 16.10.1876. d Yeoville, Johannesburg 23.2.1913. rhb, rm, lb. London County. Tours (4). South Africa (25). Brother of D.M. (Transvaal).

SKJOLDHAMMER Kevin Peter. b Johannesburg 30.3.1958. rhb, ob.

SKOTTOWE Arthur Brittiffe. b Mooi River, Natal 29.8.1891. d West Ealing, London, UK 28.1.1983.

SLATEM John James. b Graaff-Reinet, CP 1872. d Johannesburg 20.3.1941. wk.

SMITH Charles Aubrey (Sir). b City of London, UK 21.7.1863. d Beverly Hills, California, USA 20.12.1948. rhb, rf. Sussex, Cambridge University (Blue 4). Lillywhite, Shaw and Shrewsbury to Australia, Warton to South Africa. England (1).

SMITH C A.

SMITH Charles James Edward. b Gamtoos River, CP 25.12.1872. d Johannesburg 27.3.1947. rhb. South Africa (3). Brother of H.E. (Transvaal).

SMITH Frank Ernest. b Bury St Edmunds, Suffolk, UK 13.5.1872. d Sedbergh, Yorkshire, UK 3.12.1943. lhb, sla. Surrey, London County.

SMITH Frederick W. d 1913. wk. South Africa (3).

SMITH Frederick William (Later Attwood-Smith F W). b Johannesburg 17.11.1917. rhb.

SMITH Harold Edward. b Cradock, CP 21.4.1884. d Johannesburg. rhb. Tour (1). Brother of C.J.E. (Transvaal).

SMITH Paul Edward. b Durban 12.7.1963. rhb, rfm. Natal, Western Transvaal.

SMITH Steven Barry. b Sydney, New South Wales, Australia 18.10.1961. rhb, rm. New South Wales. Australia Tours (2), Australian XI to South Africa (2). Australia (3).

SNELL Richard Peter. b Durban 12.9.1968. rhb, rfm. Natal, Somerset. Tours (4). South Africa (4).

SNOOKE Stanley de la Courtte. b St Mark's, CP (Tembuland) (Transkei) 11.11.1878. d Wynberg, Cape Town 6.4.1959. rhb. Western Province. Tours (1). South Africa (1). Brother of S.J. (Border, Western Province, Transvaal).

SNOOKE Sibley John. b St Mark's, CP (Tembuland) (Transkei) 1.2.1881. d Humewood, Port Elizabeth 14.8.1966. rhb, rfm. Border, Western Province, MCC. Tours (4), MCC to North America. South Africa (26). Brother of S.de la C. (Western Province, Transvaal), grandfather of S.J.McAdam (Eastern Province, Transvaal, Western Province) and W.J.McAdam (Western Province, Eastern Province).

SNYMAN Otto Jeppe Andrew. b Prieska, CP 11.5.1946. rhb, ob. Western Province.

SOLOMON William Rodger Thomson. b Fort Beaufort, CP 23.4.1872. d Cradock, CP 12.7.1964. rhb. Eastern Province. South Africa (1).

SOMERS VINE Robert Edward. b Johannesburg 2.6.1912. d Johannesburg 6.6.1989. rhb.

SPENCER-YOUNG Russell. b Cape Town 12.4.1939. lhb, ob. Western Province.

SPRENGER Arthur Hermann. b King William's Town, CP 31.8.1889. d Johannesburg 20.7.1966. wk. Border.

SPRINGER M C (See Nimr-Springer M C)

STANLEY Sidney. b Pretoria 14.12.1933. rhb, lb. North-Eastern Transvaal.

STEIN Gerald Harold. b Durban 29.9.1927. rhb.

STEPHENS Christopher George. b Cape Town 8.1.1948. rhb. Western Province.

STEVENSON Graham Donald. b Johannesburg 15.10.1969. rhb, rfm.

STEWART Donald Adam Clark. b Johannesburg 1.3.1929. rhb, rmf.

STEYN Godfrey E. b Pretoria 23.8.1934. rhb, sla. Western Province, North-Eastern Transvaal.

STEYN Stephen Sebastian Louis. b Cape Town 11.3.1905. d Cape Town 14.10.1993. lhb. Western Province. Tour (1).

STOLL William A. b Cape Town 12.12.1884.

STRANGER Thomas. b 1894.

STRICKER Henry Bernard. b Johannesburg 1888. d East Africa (War) 15.2.1917. Brother of L.A. (Transvaal).

STRICKER Louis Anthony. b Beaconsfield, Kimberley 26.5.1884. d Rondebosch, Cape Town 5.2.1960. rhb, wk. Tours (2). South Africa (13). Brother of H.B. (Transvaal).

STRYDOM Jan Joubert. b Bloemfontein 8.9.1962. rhb, ob. Orange Free State, Northern Transvaal. Son of S. (Orange Free State).

STURGEON Eric Homer. b Durban 2.11.1900. d Louis Trichardt, Transvaal 27.11.1969.

SUSSKIND Manfred John. b Johannesburg 8.6.1891. d Johannesburg 9.7.1957. rhb, wk. Middlesex, Cambridge University. Tour (1). South Africa (5). Brother of B.V. (Orange Free State).

SUTHERLAND Harold John. b Johannesburg 16.2.1904. d Johannesburg 20.8.1963.

SWEET Norman L. b Johannesburg 22.3.1947. rhb.

SYLVESTER Malcolm William. b Johannesburg 13.12.1939. Border.

TAGG Victor. b Randfontein, Transvaal 20.12.1938. rhb, ob.

TALIADOROS George Demosthenes. b Johannesburg 17.9.1954. rhb, ob.

TALIADOROS Zenon. b Johannesburg 15.12.1932. rhb, lb.

TANCRED Augustus Bernard. b Port Elizabeth 20.8.1865. d Maitland, Cape Town 23.11.1911. rhb, rm. Griqualand West, MCC. South Africa (2). Brother of L.J. (Transvaal) and V.M. (Transvaal).

TANCRED Louis Joseph. b Port Elizabeth 7.10.1876. d Parktown, Johannesburg 28.7.1934. rhb. MCC, London County. Tours (4). South Africa (14). Brother of A.B. (Transvaal, Griqualand West) and V.M. (Transvaal).

TANCRED Vincent Maximillian. b Port Elizabeth 7.7.1875. d Florida, Roodepoort, Transvaal 3.6.1904. rhb, wk. South Africa (1). Brother of A.B. (Transvaal, Griqualand West) and L.J. (Transvaal).

TANDY John Hubert. b Pietermaritzburg 12.11.1882. d Cape Town 26.8.1954.

TAYFIELD Arthur. b Durban 21.6.1931. lhb, ob. Natal, North-Eastern Transvaal. Brother of C. (Transvaal, Griqualand West) and H.J. (Natal, Rhodesia, Transvaal).

TAYFIELD Cyril. b Durban 24.11.1932. rhb, rfm. Griqualand West. Brother of A. (Natal, North-Eastern Transvaal, Transvaal) and H.J. (Natal, Rhodesia, Transvaal).

TAYFIELD Hugh Joseph. b Durban 30.1.1929. d Hillcrest, Natal 24.2.1994. rhb, ob. Natal, Rhodesia. Tours (4). South Africa (37). Brother of A. (Natal, North-Eastern Transvaal, Transvaal) and C. (Transvaal, Griqualand West).

TAYLOR Alistair Innes. b Johannesburg 25.7.1925. rhb, lb. South Africa (1).

TAYLOR Herbert Wilfred. b Durban 5.5.1889. d Newlands, Cape Town 8.2.1973. rhb. Natal, Western Province, MCC. Tours (4). South Africa (42). Son of D., sen. (Natal), brother of D.,jun. (Natal).

TAYLOR James G. lab.

TEEGER James Andrew. b Johannesburg 11.8.1967. rhb, wk.

THOMPSON David Stuart. b Johannesburg 29.12.1959. rhb, rf.

THOMPSON Raymond Alfred. b 1881. d Nairobi, Kenya 31.10.1955.

THORP Brian Dunscombe. b Johannesburg 4.1.1934. rhb, lm.

TILLIM Anthony Frank. b Johannesburg 8.4.1938. rhb, lb. Natal.

TOMLINSON Oliver William. b Grahamstown, CP 18.2.1881. d Johannesburg 3.6.1938. rm.

TOWNSEND Frank Norton. b Clifton, Bristol, Gloucestershire, UK 16.9.1875. d Kimberley (War) 25.5.1901. rhb, wk. Gloucestershire.

TROSS S D.

TUCKER Gregory Brett. b Johannesburg 15.1.1957. lhb.

TUDHOPE Henry.

TURNER Frederick George. b Port Elizabeth 18.3.1914. rhb. Eastern Province.

TURNER Graeme John. b Bulawayo, Rhodesia 5.8.1964. lhb, ob. Western Province, Northern Transvaal, Oxford University (Blue 2).

ULYATE Clive Anthony. b Johannesburg 11.12.1933. rhb, rfm. Eastern Province.

UPTON Anthony Howard. b Johannesburg 11.4.1941. rhb. Father of P.A.H. (Western Province).

VAN BEUGE Terence William. b Pilgrim's Rest, Transvaal 14.5.1951. rhb, wk.

VAN BOECKEL Peter Henri. b Richmond, Yorkshire, UK 3.9.1964.

VAN DER BIJL Vintcent Adriaan Pieter. b Rondebosch, Cape Town 19.3.1948. rhb, rfm. Natal, Middlesex. Grandson of V.A. (Western Province), son of P.G.V. (Western Province).

VAN DER KNAAP David Saunders. b Johannesburg 7.9.1948. rhb, ob. Lancashire.

VAN DER LINDEN Wynand Johan (Dr). b Johannesburg 3.12.1955. rhb, lb.

VAN DER MERWE Deon. b Potchefstroom, Transvaal 4.10.1963. rhb, ob. Orange Free State.

VAN DER MERWE Edward Alexander. b Rustenburg, Transvaal 9.11.1904. d Emmarentia, Johannesburg 26.2.1971. rhb, wk. Tours (2). South Africa (2).

VAN DER WESTHUIZEN Johannes Petrus. b Vanderbijlpark, Transvaal 16.10.1964. lhb, sla.

VANDRAU Bruce Mather. b Johannesburg 31.5.1942. rhb, rm. Father of M.J. (Transvaal, Derbyshire).

VANDRAU Matthew James. b Epsom, Surrey, UK 22.7.1969. rhb, ob. Derbyshire. Son of B.M. (Transvaal).

VAN DUYKER Jan Coenraad. b Pretoria 10.8.1960. rhb, rfm. Northern Transvaal.

VAN VELDEN Adriaan Dirk (Dr). b Johannesburg 7.10.1922. d La Lucia, Durban 28.7.1986. rf.

VAN WEZEL Alfred William. b Kimberley 2.11.1908. d Florida, Roodepoort, Transvaal 23.7.1994.

VAN WYK Marinus. b Roodepoort, Transvaal 28.1.1950. d Roodepoort, Transvaal 6.9.1992. rhb, rm.

VAN WYK William Herman. b Roodepoort, Transvaal 25.10.1960. rhb, rfm.

VARNALS George Derek. b Durban 24.7.1935. rhb. Eastern Provinee, Natal. South Africa (3).

VARTY John Boyd. b Johannesburg 27.11.1950. rhb, lb.

VENN H.

VENTER Jacobus Francois. b Bloemfontein 1.10.1969. lhb, ob. Orange Free State. Brother of E.J. (Orange Free State).

VENTER Mark Stephen. b Johannesburg 19.4.1959. rhb. Northern Transvaal.

VERMEULEN Victor Ben Ned. b Johannesburg 16.7.1973. lhb, ob.

VIDEGAUZ Anthony. rhb.

VILJOEN Andrew. b Dunnottar, Transvaal 22.2.1955. lhb, lfm.

VILJOEN Kenneth George. b Windsorton, CP 14.5.1910. d Krugersdorp, Transvaal 21.1.1974. rhb. Griqualand West, Orange Free State. Tours (3). South Africa (27). Brother of S.F. (Griqualand West, Transvaal).

VILJOEN Sidney Frank. b Windsorton, CP 31.5.1908. d Klerksdorp, Transvaal 26.12.1959. rfm. Griqualand West. Brother of K.G. (Griqualand West, Orange Free State, Transvaal).

VINCENT Cyril Leverton. b Johannesburg 16.2.1902. d Mayville, Durban 24.8.1968. lhb, lm, sla. Tours (3). South Africa (25).

VINTCENT Charles Henry. b Mossel Bay, CP 2.9.1866. d George, CP 28.9.1943. lhb, lmf. South Western Districts. South Africa (3).

VOGLER Albert Edward Ernest. b Swartwater, near Queenstown, CP 28.11.1876. d Fort Napier Hospital, Pietermaritzburg 9.8.1946. rhb, rfm, rm, lb-g. Natal, Eastern Province, MCC, Middlesex. Tours (2). South Africa (15).

VON MENGERSHAUSEN Hubert Methley (Dr). b Howick, Natal 7.3.1892. d Umkomaas, Natal 7.8.1933. wk. Natal.

VORSTER Louis Phillippus. b Potchefstroom, Transvaal 2.11.1966. lhb, ob. Northern Transvaal, Worcestershire, Matabeleland Invitation XI.

VORSTER Louis William. b Krugersdorp, Transvaal 21.10.1942. rhb, lb.

WAITE John Henry Bickford. b Johannesburg 19.1.1930. rhb, wk. Eastern Province. Tours (5). South Africa (50).

WALKER Peter Michael. b Clifton, Bristol, Gloucestershire, UK 17.2.1936. rhb, lm, sla. Western Province, Glamorgan. Glamorgan to West Indies, Swanton to West Indies, Commonwealth to Pakistan. England (3).

WALLACH Benjamin. b Queenstown, CP 18.9.1873. d Troyeville, Johannesburg 25.5.1935. rhb, wk. MCC, London County. Tour (1).

WALLERS William Donald. b Johannesburg 30.12.1936. rhb, lb.

WALSH Frank Arthur. b Napier, CP 13.10.1905. d Kloof, Natal 7.10.1989. lhb, lab.

WALSHE Albert William Patrick. b Mile End, London, UK 25.8.1872. d Johannesburg 15.1.1949. Griqualand West.

WALTER Kenneth Alexander. b Johannesburg 5.11.1939. rhb, rf. South Africa (2).

WARD John Howell. b Germiston, Transvaal 28.12.1925. rhb. Rhodesia.

WARD Thomas Alfred. b Rawalpindi, India 2.8.1887. d East Springs Gold Mine, Transvaal 16.2.1936. rhb, wk. Tours (2). South Africa (23).

WARNE Frank Belmont. b North Carlton, Melbourne, Victoria, Australia 3.10.1906. d Edenvale, Transvaal 29.5.1994. lhb, lb-g. Worcestershire, Victoria, Europeans (India). Australia to India. Son of T.S. (Victoria).

WASHINGTON William Arthur Irving. b Mitchell Main, Wombwell, Yorkshire, UK 11.12.1879. d Wombwell, Yorkshire, UK 20.10.1927. lhb. Griqualand West, Yorkshire.

WATCHAM Dudley Griffith. b Cathcart, CP 10.11.1910. d Johannesburg 23.1.1985.

WATSON Gary Lancelot George. b Durban 3.10.1944. rhb, rf.

WEBSTER Trevor Craig. b Johannesburg 4.10.1969. rhb, rfm.

WEIDEMAN Izak Francois Nel. b Johannesburg 19.9.1960. rhb, rfm. Northern Transvaal.

WEIGHTMAN Norman Robert. b Pretoria 23.11.1942. rhb, rm.

WEINSTEIN Leonard Jack (Dr). b Oudtshoorn, CP 19.6.1940. rhb. Western Province, North-Eastern Transvaal.

WEIR Robert Stephen. b Coventry, Warwickshire, UK 4.12.1966. rhb, rfm.

WELTHAGEN Anthony John. b Port Elizabeth 5.9.1950.

WHITE Brad Middleton. b Johannesburg 15.5.1970. lhb, rm.

WHITE Gordon Charles. b Port St Johns, CP (Transkei) 5.2.1882. d Gaza, Palestine (War) 17.10.1918. rhb, lb-g. Tours (3). South Africa (17).

WHITE Raymond Christopher. b Johannesburg 29.1.1941. rhb, rm. Cambridge University (Blue 4), Gloucestershire.

WHYTOCK Leonard John. b Johannesburg 5.3.1897. d Johannesburg 19.12.1955. wk.

WICKHAM Frederick James. b Kimberley 25.9.1910. d Pietermaritzburg 30.7.1983. rfm. Griqualand West.

WIENAND George Victor. b East London 27.4.1910. Border.

WILLIAMS M G. Griqualand West.

WILSON Archer Sutherland. b Johannesburg 9.2.1938. rhb.

WILSON Joseph C. b 11.2.1869. lhb, lab. New South Wales.

WIMBLE Bentley Skelton. b Graaff-Reinet, CP 9.6.1864. d Johannesburg 2.9.1927. Eastern Province. Brother of C.S. (Transvaal) and P.S. (Transvaal).

WIMBLE Clarence Skelton. b Graaff-Reinet, CP 22.4.1861. d Johannesburg 28.1.1930. South Africa (1). Brother of B.S. (Transvaal, Eastern Province) and P.S. (Transvaal).

WIMBLE Percy Skelton. b Graaff-Reinet, CP 10.12.1865. d Johannesburg 30.5.1923. Brother of B.S. (Transvaal, Eastern Province) and C.S. (Transvaal).

WINSLOW Paul Lyndhurst. b Johannesburg 21.5.1929. rhb, lb. Rhodesia. Sussex. Tour (1). South Africa (5).

WITTE Ernest Victor. b East London 15.8.1912. d Durban 23.8.1989. rf. Western Province. Brother of R.C. (Border, Transvaal).

WITTE Reginald Charles. b Queenstown, CP 28.9.1913. rhb. Border. Brother of E.V. (Western Province, Transvaal).

WOOLER Robert Clifford. b Johannesburg 23.5.1920. d Hopetown, CP 1.9.1973. rhb, wk. Brother of C.R.O. (Leicestershire), uncle of D.G.W.Alers (Eastern Province, Border).

WRIGHT Neville Elliston. b Durban 8.4.1957. rhb, lb. Griqualand West, Natal.

WRIGHT Vincent McDowel Finlay (Dr). d Johannesburg 25.7.1982. wk. North-Eastern Transvaal.

WYNNE Owen Edgar. b Johannesburg 1.6.1919. d at sea, False Bay, CP 13.7.1975. rhb. Western Province. South Africa (6).

YACHAD Mandy. b Johannesburg 17.11.1960. rhb, lb. Northern Transvaal.

YATES Graeme Clive. b Johannesburg 23.11.1970. rhb, lf.

ZULCH Johan Wilhelm. b Lydenburg, Transvaal 2.1.1886. d Umkomaas, Natal 19.5.1924. rhb. Tour (1). Leveson-Gower to Rhodesia. South Africa (16).

Notes:

1) *Some Johannesburg and Cape Town suburbs have since become part of the municipalities of Johannesburg and Cape Town respectively whilst others have become separate or part of other municipalities in their own right. The Johannesburg suburbs which are identified as Transvaal are: Lenasia, Randburg and Sandton. The Cape Town suburb which is identified as Cape Province (CP) is: Bellville.*

2) *Since Zimbabwe's independence a number of place names have been changed. The place names stated are those that were in use at the time. The places affected are given as Old Name (New Name): Gwelo (Gweru); Que Que (Kwekwe); Salisbury (Harare); Umtali (Mutare).*

3) *In May 1963 Transkei became a self-governing territory within the Republic of South Africa but it reverted to being part of South Africa after the first multi-racial elections were held on 27/4/1994.*

4) *For identification purposes on the Register (apart from Bulawayo and Salisbury which were both in Southern Rhodesia) either Northern Rhodesia or Southern Rhodesia is stated until 24/10/1964. Southern Rhodesia is stated after this date until it became Zimbabwe on 18/4/1980.*

5) *Batsmen, bowler and wicket-keeper abbreviations used: g (right arm googly bowler); lab (left arm bowler - type unknown); lb (right arm leg break bowler); lb-g (right arm leg break and googly bowler); lf (left arm fast bowler); lfm (left arm fast medium bowler); lhb (left hand batsman); lm (left arm medium bowler); lmf (left arm medium fast bowler); lob (right arm under-arm bowler); ob (right arm off break bowler); rab (right arm bowler - type unknown); rf (right arm fast bowler); rfm (right arm fast medium bowler); rhb (right hand batsman); rm (right arm medium bowler); rmf (right arm medium fast bowler); sla (left arm slow bowler); sra (right arm slow bowler - type unknown); wk (wicket-keeper - includes players who kept wicket either occasionally or in an emergency).*

6) *The number of tours by South African teams abroad involving first-class matches are shown, and number of Test matches, e.g. South Africa (16). Other tours and first-class teams played for are noted separately.*

7) *The following played for South Africa in matches against 'rebel' touring sides in the 1980s, but never appeared in a Test match: H.R.Fotheringham, R.W.Hanley, R.V.Jennings, A.J.Kourie, K.A.McKenzie, H.A.Page, R.F.Pienaar, C.E.B. Rice, L.Seeff, V.A.P.Van Der Bijl and M.Yachad.*

8) *F.W.Elworthy played for South Africa v A.I.F. in 1919/20, W.D.Duff and V.H.Neser for South Africa v S.B.Joel's XI in 1924/25, but never appeared in a Test match.*

TRANSVAAL CAREER RECORDS 1889/90 TO 1993/94

		First	Last	M	I	NO	Runs	HS	Avg	100	50	Runs	Wkts	Avg	Best	5i	10m	ct	st
Abernethy TF	(T)	1949/50	1952/53	3	5	2	17	10	5.66	0	0	75	2	37.50	2/44	0	0	1	
Acock MG	(TB)	1993/94		1								67	2	33.50	2-67	0	0	0	
Adair RW	(TB)	1977/78	1987/88	18	32	7	784	161*	31.36	1	4	178	9	19.77	2/28	0	0	9	
Adams FC	(T)	1974/75		4	5	3	1	1*	0.50	0	0	291	11	26.45	3/37	0	0	0	
	(TB)	1973/74	1975/76	6	9	2	83	32*	11.85	0	0	465	19	24.47	5/57	1	0	4	
		1973/74	1975/76	10	14	5	84	32*	9.33	0	0	756	30	25.20	5/57	1	0	4	
Adams VB	(TB)	1963/64		1	2	0	17	16	8.50	0	0	100	2	50.00	2/70	0	0	0	
Adcock NAT	(T)	1952/53	1959/60	30	37	16	154	41	7.33	0	0	2217	130	17.05	8/39	7	2	7	
		1952/53	1962/63	99	117	35	451	41	5.50	0	0	6989	405	17.25	8/39	19	4	23	
Aldworth DP	(T)	1968/69	1970/71	6	7	1	5	2	0.83	0	0	443	15	29.53	5/75	1	0	1	
	(TB)	1965/66	1970/71	20	21	11	58	14*	5.80	0	0	1586	78	20.33	6/35	2	0	8	
		1965/66	1970/71	26	28	12	63	14*	3.93	0	0	2029	93	21.81	6/35	3	0	9	
Allpass GL	(T)	1939/40		1														1	
Allsop G	(T)	1890/91	1897/98	10	18	2	242	33	15.12	0	0	93	3	31.00	1/1	0	0	3	
Anderson DIE	(T)	1929/30	1936/37	5	8	1	140	63	20.00	0	1							9	
Anderson K	(TB)	1963/64		1	2	0	9	7	4.50	0	0							1	
Andrew JP	(T)	1951/52		2	3	0	49	24	16.33	0	0	180	3	60.00	2/84	0	0	0	
Argyle JR	(T)	1978/79		1	1	1	2	2*		0	0	60	2	30.00	1/24	0	0	0	
	(TB)	1977/78	1978/79	4	5	0	73	34	14.60	0	0	273	12	22.75	4/20	0	0	2	
		1977/78	1978/79	5	6	1	75	34	15.00	0	0	333	14	23.78	4/20	0	0	2	
Atfield AJ	(T)	1906/07		1	1	1	6	6*		0	0							0	
		1893	1906/07	8	13	2	137	45	12.45	0	0	102	3	34.00	3/102	0	0	5	
Atkinson RJ	(TB)	1978/79		1								81	6	13.50	4/37	0	0	0	
Bacher A	(T)	1960/61	1973/74	88	158	8	6133	235	40.88	15	31	82	2	41.00	1/8	0	0	87	1
	(TB)	1959/60	1960/61	3	5	0	191	101	38.20	1	1							3	
		1959/60	1973/74	120	212	10	7894	235	39.07	18	45	87	2	43.50	1/8	0	0	110	1
Bacher AM	(TB)	1993/94		2	4	0	23	18	5.75	0	0							3	
Bacher M	(TB)	1983/84		2	4	0	24	13	6.00	0	0	1	1	1.00	1/1	0	0	3	
		1983/84	1984/85	7	12	1	144	47*	13.09	0	0	1	1	1.00	1/1	0	0	5	
Bailey A	(T)	1893/94	1897/98	3	5	0	16	8	3.20	0	0	201	11	18.27	4/51	0	0	4	
Bailey CE	(T)	1904/05		1	1	0	36	36	36.00	0	0							1	
Baillie JH	(T)	1960/61	1964/65	3	6	0	19	11	3.16	0	0							0	
	(TB)	1959/60	1965/66	27	47	1	1445	85	31.41	0	9	287	10	28.70	3/28	0	0	17	
		1959/60	1965/66	30	53	1	1464	85	28.15	0	9	287	10	28.70	3/28			17	
Baillie TN	(TB)	1963/64	1970/71	9	9	5	106	45*	26.50	0	0	589	15	39.26	4/45	0	0	6	
		1956/57	1970/71	11	13	7	150	45*	25.00	0	0	712	16	44.50	4/45	0	0	7	
Baines TWT	(T)	1931/32	1936/37	12	19	0	719	96	37.84	0	8	347	1	347.00	1/22	0	0	11	
		1925/26	1936/37	20	33	1	1045	96	32.65	0	10	453	2	226.50	1/8	0	0	17	
Balaskas XC	(T)	1936/37	1946/47	16	18	4	358	84	25.57	0	1	2015	85	23.70	8/60	6	4	10	
		1926/27	1946/47	75	107	13	2696	206	28.68	6	12	6656	276	24.11	8/60	20	9	47	
Bam I	(T)	1913/14		1	2	0	41	34	20.50	0	0	44	7	6.28	5/16	1	0	2	
		1906/07	1913/14	3	4	0	61	34	15.25	0	0	125	16	7.81	5/16	1	0	2	
Barker CM	(T)	1937/38		1	1	0	13	13	13.00	0	0	87	2	43.50	2/83	0	0	1	

		First	Last	M	I	NO	Runs	HS	Avg	100	50	Runs	Wkts	Avg	Best	5i	10m	ct	st
Barlow EJ	(T)	1960/61	1967/68	30	53	7	1855	212	40.32	5	9	1693	56	30.23	4/28	0	0	26	
	(TB)	1959/60		6	10	0	227	72	22.70	0	1							9	
		1959/60	1982/83	283	493	28	18212	217	39.16	43	86	13785	571	24.14	7/24	16	2	335	
Barlow KA	(T)	1974/75	1977/78	10	10	4	74	32*	12.33	0	0	557	13	42.84	3/55	0	0	5	
	(TB)	1973/74	1980/81	23	34	8	616	53	23.69	0	1	1160	51	22.74	5/25	1	0	23	
		1971/72	1980/81	36	49	12	764	53	20.64	0	2	1964	68	28.88	5/25	1	0	30	
Barnard LJ	(T)	1976/77	1981/82	23	35	3	882	106	27.56	2	2	252	5	50.40	1/10	0	0	12	
	(TB)	1974/75	1981/82	16	28	1	783	138	29.00	1	4	355	16	22.18	3/17	0	0	19	
		1974/75	1991/92	117	207	8	5157	138	25.91	4	29	2273	61	37.26	3/17	0	0	105	
Barnes A	(TB)	1977/78		3	4	0	54	21	13.50	0	0	63	3	21.00	2/23	0	0	1	
		1975/76	1977/78	5	8	0	98	30	12.25	0	0	95	5	19.00	2/8	0	0	2	
Barraclough AD	(T)	1947/48		5	3	0	18	12	6.00	0	0							8	1
Barron RJ	(TB)	1968/69		1	2	0	39	37	19.50	0	0							2	1
Barrow A	(TB)	1982/83		6	12	0	365	91	30.41	0	2	29	2	14.50	2/29	0	0	11	
		1974/75	1982/83	60	113	4	2976	111*	27.30	2	18	186	9	20.66	2/17	0	0	46	
Bath BF	(T)	1967/68	1973/74	46	84	4	2532	108*	31.65	1	19	1241	46	26.97	6/94	2	0	28	
	(TB)	1966/67	1967/68	8	14	3	710	180	64.54	3	3	13	1	13.00	1/9	0	0	5	
		1966/67	1973/74	54	98	7	3242	180	35.62	4	22	1254	47	26.68	6/94	2	0	33	
Baumgartner HV	(T)	1911/12	1913/14	5	8	0	58	16	7.25	0	0	443	22	20.13	7/34	1	1	4	
		1903/04	1913/14	14	24	2	173	21*	7.86	0	0	1296	70	18.51	8/109	6	2	9	
Bayne SW	(TB)	1977/78		1	2	0	45	40	22.50	0	0							2	
Beaumont R	(T)	1911/12	1913/14	6	10	1	543	121	60.33	1	4	2	0			0	0	3	
		1908/09	1913/14	31	47	4	1086	121	25.25	1	5	2	0			0	0	11	
Becker DF	(T)	1971/72	1974/75	13	20	5	169	29	11.26	0	0	853	32	26.65	5/49	1	0	5	
	(TB)	1971/72	1974/75	12	16	2	316	57	22.57	0	1	1004	49	20.48	5/31	2	0	10	
		1968/69	1974/75	35	49	8	770	57	18.78	0	4	2588	112	23.10	6/23	4	0	18	
Beckett EE	(T)	1919/20	1922/23	3	4	0	35	23	8.75	0	0							1	
Begbie DW	(T)	1933/34	1949/50	35	51	8	1929	207*	44.86	5	6	1589	74	21.47	7/96	5	2	15	
		1933/34	1949/50	58	85	9	2727	207*	35.88	6	8	2085	88	23.69	7/96	5	2	27	
Begg Y	(T)	1991/92		1	2	1	15	11*	15.00	0	0							5	1
	(TB)	1991/92		1	1	0	13	13	13.00	0	0							4	
		1991/92		2	3	1	28	13	14.00	0	0							9	1
Bell TW	(T)	1906/07		2	3	0	23	21	7.66	0	0							1	
Bennet HJG	(T)	1912/13		2	4	1	28	16*	9.33	0	0							0	
Benning ID	(TB)	1986/87		3	3	3	37	27*		0	0	155	7	22.14	2/34	0	0	3	
Bense BD	(T)	1963/64		1	2	0	2	2	1.00	0	0	47	2	23.50	1/16	0	0	0	
	(TB)	1962/63	1963/64	7	10	3	10	6	1.42	0	0	398	20	19.90	4/49	0	0	1	
		1962/63	1963/64	8	12	3	12	6	1.33	0	0	445	22	20.22	4/49	0	0	1	
Berry AV	(T)	1912/13	1913/14	5	7	0	105	57	15.00	0	1							5	4
		1912/13	1923/24	6	8	0	106	57	13.25	0	1							5	4
Berry RW	(TB)	1975/76	1976/77	3	4	1	93	52*	31.00	0	1							12	2
Beves G	(T)	1894/95	1898/99	9	16	1	229	60	15.26	0	1	201	8	25.12	2/13	0	0	6	
		1888	1898/99	18	31	1	370	60	12.33	0	1	201	8	25.12	2/13	0	0	11	
Bissett GF	(T)	1929/30		1	1	1	8	8*		0	0	63	2	31.50	2/63	0	0	0	
		1922/23	1929/30	21	31	12	294	33	15.47	0	0	1816	67	27.10	7/29	5	0	8	

		First	Last	M	I	NO	Runs	HS	Avg	100	50	Runs	Wkts	Avg	Best	5i	10m	ct	st
Blewett JW	(T)	1957/58	1958/59	2	2	0	7	5	3.50	0	0	88	1	88.00	1/48	0	0	1	
	(TB)	1959/60		2	1	0	22	22	22.00	0	0	136	3	45.33	2/107	0	0	4	
		1950/51	1959/60	22	37	5	710	110*	22.18	1	2	1372	43	31.90	6/30	2	0	14	
Bloom ML	(T)	1946/47		1	1	0	0	0	0.00	0	0	39	0			0	0	1	
Boa PM	(T)	1993/94		1	2	0	12	8	6.00	0	0							1	
	(TB)	1993/94		6	9	2	368	69	52.57	0	4	14	0			0	0	3	
		1993/94		7	11	2	380	69	42.22	0	4	14	0			0	0	4	
Bock EG	(T)	1934/35		5	5	2	22	6*	7.33	0	0	256	20	12.80	5/8	1	0	7	
		1928/29	1939/40	19	28	8	281	78	14.05	0	1	889	32	27.78	5/8	1	0	12	
Bond KJ	(TB)	1965/66		3	5	1	124	61*	31.00	0	1							3	
		1965/66	1972/73	26	45	4	860	71*	20.97	0	5	4	0			0	0	49	1
Boonzaaier NR	(T)	1984/85		1	2	0	46	39	23.00	0	0							1	
	(TB)	1983/84	1984/85	7	12	1	192	52*	17.45	0	2	15	1	15.00	1/15	0	0	2	
		1983/84	1989/90	22	37	4	604	54	18.30	0	4	419	9	46.55	3/37	0	0	29	
Booyens WA	(TB)	1987/88		1	2	0	16	16	8.00	0	0	71	1	71.00	1/31	0	0	0	
Botha PC	(TB)	1985/86	1986/87	2	3	0	6	4	2.00	0	0	89	5	17.80	4/28	0	0	2	
		1984/85	1987/88	8	11	4	97	26*	13.85	0	0	430	17	25.29	4/28	0	0	4	
Botha PJ	(T)	1989/90	1991/92	17	30	3	579	78	21.44	0	3	588	13	45.23	3/54	0	0	7	
	(TB)	1987/88	1990/91	20	35	4	943	109	30.41	3	4	992	40	24.80	5/54	1	0	9	
		1987/88	1993/94	52	90	8	1997	124*	24.35	4	8	2314	73	31.69	5/54	1	0	23	
Bowden MP	(T)	1889/90		1	2	1	189	126*	189.00	1	1	7	2	3.50	2/7	0	0	0	2
		1883	1889/90	86	132	17	2316	189*	20.13	3	7	35	2	17.50	2/7	0	0	73	14
Brain DM	(T)	1910/11	1911/12	3	2	1	3	3	3.00	0	0	193	5	38.60	2/28	0	0	4	
Breakey C	(T)	1939/40		1	1	0	1	1	1.00	0	0	25	0			0	0	0	
Breakey JC	(T)	1973/74		2	4	0	59	39	14.75	0	0							4	1
	(TB)	1970/71	1973/74	13	24	0	720	123	30.00	2	3							44	3
		1970/71	1973/74	16	30	0	795	123	26.50	2	3							49	4
Briscoe AW	(T)	1931/32	1939/40	30	47	6	2022	191	49.31	5	10							14	
		1931/32	1939/40	35	56	8	2189	191	45.60	6	10	19	0			0	0	15	
Brissenden SW	(T)	1927/28	1932/33	10	10	2	27	14*	3.37	0	0	867	44	19.70	6/43	1	1	4	
Brockett WB	(T)	1960/61		1	2	0	0	0	0.00	0	0	62	0			0	0	0	
	(TB)	1960/61	1963/64	9	11	2	66	17	7.33	0	0	779	42	18.54	5/53	1	0	3	
		1960/61	1963/64	10	13	2	66	17	6.00	0	0	841	42	20.02	5/53	1	0	3	
Bromham CG	(T)	1941/42		1	1	0	18	18	18.00	0	0							3	
		1939/40	1946/47	8	15	3	205	39*	17.08	0	0							18	1
Brothers EM	(T)	1928/29		3	3	0	2	1	0.66	0	0	30	0			0	0	0	
Brown LS	(T)	1930/31	1945/46	11	13	4	118	26*	13.11	0	0	916	46	19.91	6/30	4	1	12	
		1930/31	1947/48	38	55	9	778	75	16.91	0	3	3642	147	24.77	6/30	10	2	27	
Bruorton DR	(T)	1951/52	1952/53	10	16	3	459	88	35.30	0	3	206	5	41.20	3/69	0	0	9	
Bull KE	(T)	1929/30		3	4	1	19	8	6.33	0	0	231	13	17.76	4/70	0	0	5	
Bunyard GS	(T)	1959/60	1960/61	11	13	1	128	35	10.66	0	0	787	32	24.59	5/35	1	0	4	
	(TB)	1959/60		1	2	1	38	26	38.00	0	0	103	7	14.71	4/36	0	0	1	
		1959/60	1962/63	14	17	3	192	35	13.71	0	0	1082	48	22.54	5/35	1	0	7	
Bussell EP	(T)	1952/53		1								88	6	14.66	4/37	0	0	0	
Butler BCH	(T)	1957/58		1	2	0	15	8	7.50	0	0							0	
		1957/58	1967/68	10	17	0	307	78	18.05	0	2	4	0			0	0	4	

		First	Last	M	I	NO	Runs	HS	Avg	100	50	Runs	Wkts	Avg	Best	5i	10m	ct	st
Byng JA	(T)	1906/07		1	1	0	2	2	2.00	0	2							0	
Cameron HB	(T)	1924/25	1934/35	26	33	1	1520	182	47.50	6	5							38	17
		1924/25	1935	107	161	17	5396	182	37.47	11	28	13	0			0	0	155	69
Campbell HH	(T)	1926/27	1928/29	5	5	1	101	42*	25.25	0	0	215	12	17.91	3/38	0	0	7	
Campbell T	(T)	1906/07	1909/10	5	7	2	58	28	11.60	0	0							9	2
		1906/07	1912	29	42	12	365	48	12.16	0	0							40	12
Carlisle AM	(TB)	1966/67	1967/68	5	8	0	53	17	6.62	0	0							4	
Carlstein PR	(T)	1958/59	1971/72	33	55	5	1867	229	37.34	3	6	48	0			0	0	14	
	(TB)	1960/61	1969/70	9	15	2	592	103	45.53	1	5	8	0			0	0	8	
		1954/55	1979/80	148	255	16	7554	229	31.60	9	46	480	9	53.33	3/37	0	0	82	
Carr RB	(T)	1964/65		1	2	1	28	28*	28.00	0	0	45	0			0	0	2	
		1960	1964/65	2	3	2	35	28*	35.00	0	0	107	0			0	0	2	
Carter CP	(T)	1910/11		7	6	0	84	26	14.00	0	0	434	34	12.76	6/39	2	0	9	
		1897/98	1924	107	142	28	1333	80*	11.69	0	3	6796	366	18.56	7/37	23	2	64	
Catterall RH	(T)	1920/21	1933/34	25	39	4	1110	128	31.71	1	6	624	19	32.84	4/22	0	0	11	
		1920/21	1933/34	124	203	8	5849	147	29.99	9	31	1629	53	30.73	4/22	0	0	52	
Cawood CH	(T)	1939/40		1	1	1	53	53*		0	1							1	2
		1939/40	1949/50	2	3	1	68	53*	34.00	0	1							2	3
Cawse CE	(T)	1928/29	1933/34	5	7	0	49	17	7.00	0	0	300	12	25.00	4/66	0	0	5	
Chapman PDM	(T)	1949/50		1	1	1	9	9*		0	0	54	1	54.00	1/21	0	0	0	
Chappell CS	(T)	1927/28		1	2	0	0	0	0.00	0	0							2	
Charnas M	(T)	1952/53	1960/61	21	27	5	218	32	9.90	0	0	965	33	29.24	6/36	2	0	12	
	(TB)	1959/60		4	5	0	58	41	11.60	0	0	289	12	24.08	4/16	0	0	0	
		1952/53	1960/61	26	34	5	277	41	9.55	0	0	1303	46	28.32	6/36	2	0	12	
Chatterton EV	(T)	1966/67	1970/71	19	19	7	108	17	9.00	0	0							59	6
	(TB)	1963/64	1970/71	17	24	2	295	44	13.40	0	0							51	12
		1963/64	1970/71	38	47	9	514	54	13.52	0	1							116	18
Cheetham JR	(TB)	1968/69	1969/70	6	10	0	347	77	34.70	0	1							8	
		1968/69	1972/73	10	16	0	581	124	36.31	1	2	0	0			0	0	9	
Cheetham RS	(TB)	1970/71		2	3	1	114	110*	57.00	1	0							2	
		1970/71	1975/76	13	24	2	398	110*	18.09	1	1	24	2	12.00	2/13	0	0	8	
Chothia S	(TB)	1976/77		4	3	1	40	28*	20.00	0	0	182	6	30.33	2/17	0	0	1	
Christy JAJ	(T)	1925/26	1929/30	15	20	2	1089	175	60.50	6	1	209	13	16.07	4/19	0	0	4	
		1925/26	1935/36	65	108	9	3670	175	37.07	11	15	894	32	27.93	4/19	0	0	33	
Chubb GWA	(T)	1936/37	1950/51	22	25	7	464	71*	25.77	0	3	1703	83	20.51	7/54	3	0	5	
		1931/32	1951	49	61	15	835	71*	18.15	0	5	3826	160	23.91	7/54	7	0	12	
Clack TG	(T)	1910/11		2	1	0	0	0	0.00	0	0	59	3	19.66	1/12	0	0	2	
		1906/07	1910/11	4	4	0	4	3	1.00	0	0	182	10	18.20	5/43	1	0	2	
Clark BJ	(T)	1965/66	1966/67	8	15	1	381	76	27.21	0	3							4	
	(TB)	1967/68		1	1	0	57	57	57.00	0	1	0	0			0	0	0	
		1965/66	1967/68	9	16	1	438	76	29.20	0	4	0	0			0	0	4	
Clark DA	(T)	1949/50	1953/54	12	17	8	213	79	23.66	0	1	1054	43	24.51	5/59	2	0	5	
Clarke ST	(T)	1983/84	1985/86	20	22	7	277	78*	18.46	0	1	1534	94	16.31	6/19	8	1	10	
		1977/78	1989/90	238	265	44	3269	100*	14.79	1	5	18397	942	19.52	8/62	59	10	146	
Clayton LH	(T)	1929/30	1932/33	6	11	2	240	86	26.66	0	1	332	16	20.75	5/51	1	0	3	
		1929/30	1932/33	7	13	2	240	86	21.81	0	1	487	19	25.63	5/51	1	0	5	

		First	Last	M	I	NO	Runs	HS	Avg	100	50	Runs	Wkts	Avg	Best	5i	10m	ct	st
Cochran JAK	(T)	1929/30	1931/32	3	3	0	18	13	6.00	0	0	222	12	18.50	3/34	0	0	1	
		1929/30	1931/32	6	7	1	25	13	4.16	0	0	361	15	24.06	3/34	0	0	2	
Coen SK	(T)	1932/33	1935/36	8	14	0	348	86	24.85	0	2	29	0			0	0	3	
		1921/22	1938/39	51	92	6	2808	173	32.65	6	14	1087	22	49.40	4/92	0	0	22	
Coetzee FJ	(T)	1964/65		1	1	0	9	9	9.00	0	0	75	2	37.50	1/32	0	0	1	
Connerty JW	(T)	1929/30		2	3	1	85	42*	42.50	0	0	91	0			0	0	1	
		1920/21	1929/30	3	5	1	108	42*	27.00	0	0	91	0			0	0	2	
Conte MC	(TB)	1972/73	1976/77	13	20	2	670	107	37.22	2	1							12	
Conyngham DP	(T)	1926/27	1927/28	4	6	2	145	63	36.25	0	1	279	7	39.85	2/10	0	0	4	
		1921/22	1930/31	22	33	10	348	63	15.13	0	2	1778	86	20.67	5/20	6	1	18	
Cook AE	(T)	1912/13	1913/14	4	7	1	63	28	10.50	0	0	2	0			0	0	2	
		1906/07	1913/14	13	22	1	506	101	24.09	1	3	278	10	27.80	3/35	0	0	6	
Cook SJ	(T)	1972/73	1993/94	153	269	30	10345	228	43.28	28	42	36	1	36.00	1/15	0	0	38	
	(TB)	1973/74	1978/79	14	25	2	1147	146	49.86	4	6	2	0			0	0	12	
		1972/73	1993/94	263	463	55	20676	313*	50.67	63	83	107	3	35.66	2/25	0	0	151	
Cook VN	(T)	1936/37		3	4	0	44	21	11.00	0	0	136	7	19.42	4/51	0	0	0	
Cooke GP	(T)	1993/94		1	1	0	2	2	2.00	0	0	40	1	40.00	1/26	0	0	0	
	(TB)	1993/94		4	4	0	21	11	5.25	0	0	244	15	16.26	4/68	0	0	1	
		1993/94		5	5	0	23	11	4.60	0	0	284	16	17.75	4/68	0	0	1	
Cooper AE	(T)	1896/97	1897/98	2	3	1	7	4	3.50	0	0	190	13	14.61	8/80	1	1	2	
		1890/91	1897/98	5	9	2	82	41	11.71	0	0	362	22	16.45	8/80	1	1	3	
Cooper AHC	(T)	1912/13	1928/29	34	54	4	1722	171*	34.44	4	8	531	15	35.40	3/9	0	0	26	
		1912/13	1928/29	37	60	4	1788	171*	31.92	4	8	556	15	37.06	3/9	0	0	27	
Cooper FW	(T)	1912/13	1913/14	4	6	2	82	52*	20.50	0	1	220	11	20.00	4/14	0	0	1	
Cope DG	(T)	1897/98		3	5	0	92	39	18.40	0	0							2	
Corbett PL	(T)	1966/67		4	7	0	164	69	23.42	0	1							3	
	(TB)	1966/67		2	2	0	113	79	56.50	0	1	87	1	87.00	1/34	0	0	4	
		1958/59	1968/69	40	69	1	2232	237	32.82	3	13	121	1	121.00	1/34	0	0	49	
Corin RHM	(TB)	1960/61		6	12	0	345	75	28.75	0	2							14	1
Cradock TT	(T)	1904/05		2	3	0	27	18	9.00	0	0							2	
		1904/05	1909/10	3	5	0	37	18	7.40	0	0	13	0			0	0	2	
Creese WH	(T)	1897/98		1	1	1	2	2*		0	0	28	1	28.00	1/28	0	0	1	
		1897/98	1913/14	2	2	1	4	2*	4.00	0	0	28	1	28.00	1/28	0	0	1	
Cresswell VG	(T)	1990/91		1														3	1
	(TB)	1988/89	1990/91	9	16	5	378	70	34.36	0	2							25	4
		1980/81	1990/91	46	78	10	1740	102	25.58	1	9							113	18
Crews B	(T)	1951/52		2	4	0	46	15	11.50	0	0	26	0			0	0	0	
		1945/46	1958/59	16	31	1	588	110	19.60	2	0	128	3	42.66	3/53	0	0	8	
Cullinan DJ	(T)	1991/92	1993/94	17	30	6	1273	337*	53.04	1	7	32	0			0	0	16	
		1983/84	1994	95	167	24	5568	337*	38.93	11	32	70	3	23.33	2/27	0	0	89	
Curnow SH	(T)	1928/29	1945/46	31	50	4	2257	192*	49.06	7	7							10	
		1928/29	1945/46	51	87	6	3409	224	42.08	9	11							18	
Dacey LS	(T)	1939/40	1941/42	2	3	0	75	58	25.00	0	1							2	

		First	Last	M	I	NO	Runs	HS	Avg	100	50	Runs	Wkts	Avg	Best	5i	10m	ct	st
Davies DD	(T)	1913/14		1	1	0	24	24	24.00	0	0							1	
		1902/03	1913/14	6	10	2	200	45	25.00	0	0							4	
Davies EQ	(T)	1938/39		1								82	6	13.66	6/82	1	0	0	
		1929/30	1945/46	16	24	6	64	17	3.55	0	0	1302	47	27.70	6/80	2	0	5	
Davies GR	(TB)	1959/60	1965/66	6	11	0	203	81	18.45	0	2	39	1	39.00	1/17	0	0	7	
Davies RE	(T)	1945/46		3	2	1	11	10	11.00	0	0	198	13	15.23	4/78	0	0	1	
		1930/31	1945/46	26	26	13	128	28*	9.84	0	0	2748	112	24.53	7/67	7	2	19	
Day NT	(T)	1975/76	1981/82	17	24	5	408	68*	21.47	0	2	9	0			0	0	42	2
	(TB)	1975/76	1981/82	25	44	8	1821	174*	50.58	6	8	5	0			0	0	75	8
		1975/76	1991/92	105	188	21	5081	174*	30.42	7	31	14	0			0	0	312	29
Deane HG	(T)	1923/24	1929/30	25	30	1	1180	165	40.68	5	5	15	0			0	0	24	
		1919/20	1930/31	100	138	12	3795	165	30.11	6	18	99	3	33.00	3/23	0	0	63	
De Vaal PD	(T)	1969/70	1978/79	59	92	20	2025	95	28.12	0	11	3850	112	34.37	7/76	3	0	35	
	(TB)	1967/68	1975/76	19	32	3	934	89	32.20	0	5	1219	48	25.39	6/94	1	0	14	
		1965/66	1992/93	109	175	34	4208	100*	29.84	1	23	7315	240	30.47	7/76	6	1	65	
Devitt VP	(T)	1929/30		1	1	1	29	29*		0	0	33	3	11.00	2/19	0	0	1	
Dickenson FO	(T)	1898/99		1	2	0	38	34	19.00	0	0	16	0			0	0	0	
Difford AN	(T)	1908/09	1911/12	4	6	0	278	91	46.33	0	3							1	
		1904/05	1911/12	16	28	0	824	103	29.42	1	6	32	2	16.00	1/13	0	0	8	
Difford ID	(T)	1893/94	1906/07	4	7	3	174	53*	43.50	0	1	9	3	3.00	3/9	0	0	2	
Dindar N	(T)	1991/92		1	2	0	6	6	3.00	0	0	67	3	22.33	2/45	0	0	1	
	(TB)	1991/92		2	3	0	37	14	12.33	0	0	81	2	40.50	1/25	0	0	2	
		1991/92		3	5	0	43	14	8.60	0	0	148	5	29.60	2/45	0	0	3	
Dinsdale SC	(T)	1974/75		2	3	0	19	11	6.33	0	0	51	2	25.50	2/29	0	0	1	
	(TB)	1974/75	1975/76	7	14	2	449	88	37.41	0	4	85	5	17.00	4/24	0	0	2	
		1969/70	1975/76	15	26	2	581	88	24.20	0	4	160	8	20.00	4/24	0	0	8	
Dixon CD	(T)	1912/13	1924/25	17	19	5	101	27	7.21	0	0	1403	67	20.94	7/16	5	0	13	
		1912/13	1924/25	33	39	8	184	27	5.93	0	0	2556	106	24.11	7/16	6	1	21	
Dixon TJ	(T)	1889/90		1	2	0	1	1	0.50	0	0							0	
Dodds PM	(T)	1955/56		1	1	0	2	2	2.00	0	0	66	2	33.00	2/24	0	0	0	
		1955/56	1963/64	39	51	13	333	27*	8.76	0	0	3489	120	29.07	7/51	7	2	10	
Doig JGE	(T)	1897/98		1	2	0	4	4	2.00	0	0							1	
Donaldson IC	(TB)	1974/75		1	1	0	7	7	7.00	0	0	15	0			0	0	0	
Douglas WH	(T)	1892/93		2	2	0	50	50	25.00	0	1	25	3	8.33	2/0	0	0	0	
Drake AH	(TB)	1979/80	1981/82	7	13	1	125	41*	10.41	0	0	6	2	3.00	1/1	0	0	5	
Drummer FTM	(T)	1968/69	1971/72	5	3	3	18	10*		0	0	365	5	73.00	2/69	0	0	2	
	(TB)	1971/72	1972/73	3	4	2	23	13	11.50	0	0	206	9	22.88	3/30	0	0	2	
		1958/59	1972/73	36	51	21	741	62	24.70	0	3	3209	127	25.26	8/28	2	1	13	
Duff WD	(T)	1919/20	1924/25	8	7	3	53	18*	13.25	0	0	610	21	29.04	4/37	0	0	6	
		1919/20	1924/25	10	11	3	72	18*	9.00	0	0	752	24	31.33	4/37	0	0	7	
Duffus LG	(T)	1923/24	1934/35	5	4	1	104	48	34.66	0	0							9	1
Dumbrill R	(T)	1965/66	1967/68	11	16	1	255	51	17.00	0	1	776	44	17.63	5/35	3	1	8	
		1960/61	1967/68	51	82	7	1761	94	23.48	0	13	2909	132	22.03	5/34	5	1	35	
Duminy JP	(T)	1927/28	1928/29	5	8	3	409	168*	81.80	1	3	271	11	24.63	6/40	1	0	3	
		1919/20	1929	13	23	4	557	168*	29.31	1	3	368	12	30.66	6/40	1	0	11	
Dunlop DW	(TB)	1973/74	1984/85	16	30	2	771	119	27.53	1	2	3	0			0	0	6	

		First	Last	M	I	NO	Runs	HS	Avg	100	50	Runs	Wkts	Avg	Best	5i	10m	ct	st
Du Plessis SJ	(TB)	1988/89		1	2	0	10	5	5.00	0	0							0	
Du Preez AL	(TB)	1975/76		1	2	1	24	18*	24.00	0	0							0	
Du Preez VF	(TB)	1979/80		3	6	0	92	29	15.33	0	0	27	0			0	0	0	
		1978/79	1993/94	110	211	16	5675	200*	29.10	10	27	1073	28	38.32	3/19	0	0	59	
During AA	(T)	1966/67	1979/80	13	22	1	501	75	23.85	0	4	189	7	27.00	4/77	0	0	20	
	(TB)	1963/64	1973/74	31	54	7	2061	155*	43.85	7	8	504	29	17.37	4/52	0	0	20	
		1963/64	1979/80	48	82	11	2719	155*	38.29	7	13	751	38	19.76	4/52	0	0	47	
During JP	(T)	1910/11		1	1	0	27	27	27.00	0	0							2	
		1907/08	1910/11	7	12	1	231	67	21.00	0	2	27	3	9.00	2/10	0	0	5	
Du Toit JD	(TB)	1990/91		4	7	2	48	25*	9.60	0	0	164	9	18.22	3/31	0	0	2	
		1975/76	1991/92	73	125	11	2570	148	22.54	3	8	3731	147	25.38	6/26	6	1	51	
Du Toit SD	(T)	1946/47		1	1	1	18	18*		0	0	44	0			0	0	0	
		1946/47	1955/56	26	42	6	804	116	22.33	1	2	1217	34	35.79	3/25	0	0	19	
Dyer DD	(T)	1975/76	1980/81	49	85	7	2798	164*	35.87	5	15	32	0			0	0	54	
	(TB)	1981/82		4	7	1	125	28*	20.83	0	0							4	
		1965/66	1981/82	109	191	18	5651	196*	32.66	8	29	46	0			0	0	149	8
Dyke-Poynter REJ	(T)	1925/26	1928/29	7	6	0	74	27	12.33	0	0	403	9	44.77	4/41	0	0	3	
Easterbrook JW	(T)	1920/21		1	1	0	12	12	12.00	0	0	34	1	34.00	1/21	0	0	2	
		1913/14	1930/31	8	10	3	195	64	27.85	0	1	422	16	26.37	5/63	1	0	5	
Eaton DP	(T)	1963/64		1	2	0	12	12	6.00	0	0	8	0			0	0	0	
Edwards DN	(TB)	1978/79		4	8	0	301	95	37.62	0	2							2	
		1975/76	1983/84	28	54	0	1158	95	21.44	0	6							27	
Ehret BW	(TB)	1989/90		1	2	0	2	2	1.00	0	0	56	1	56.00	1/28	0	0	0	
Eksteen CE	(T)	1988/89	1993/94	36	40	13	245	26*	9.07	0	0	3942	140	28.15	7/29	8	1	29	
	(TB)	1987/88	1990/91	5	5	2	63	31	21.00	0	0	306	7	43.71	2/49	0	0	4	
		1985/86	1993/94	56	70	20	537	44	10.74	0	0	5144	181	28.41	7/29	8	1	42	
Ellis AG	(TB)	1970/71		4	4	1	99	44*	33.00	0	0	219	15	14.60	4/47	0	0	5	
Ellis JR	(T)	1951/52		2	3	0	37	29	12.33	0	0							3	
		1938/39	1951/52	4	7	1	115	62	19.16	0	1	130	3	43.33	3/93	0	0	3	
Elworthy FW	(T)	1912/13	1929/30	12	17	6	149	44	13.54	0	0	930	38	24.47	6/60	2	0	3	
		1912/13	1929/30	14	21	7	171	44	12.21	0	0	1133	42	26.97	6/60	2	0	3	
Elworthy S	(TB)	1987/88		2	3	0	32	19	10.66	0	0	222	11	20.18	4/56	0	0	0	
		1987/88	1993/94	40	67	14	1117	56	21.07	0	2	4121	138	29.86	6/37	4	1	12	
Emslie OD	(TB)	1960/61		1	2	0	20	12	10.00	0	0							0	
		1958/59	1960/61	2	4	0	39	13	9.75	0	0							0	
Endean WR	(T)	1945/46	1960/61	53	91	12	3534	247	44.73	9	12	72	1	72.00	1/7	0	0	63	7
		1945/46	1964	134	230	25	7757	247	37.83	15	34	73	2	36.50	1/1	0	0	158	13
Engelbrecht H	(TB)	1990/91		2	4	1	85	38	28.33	0	0							0	
		1990/91	1991/92	3	6	1	87	38	17.40	0	0	26	0			0	0	0	
Esterhuizen D	(T)	1966/67	1968/69	6	5	3	6	3*	3.00	0	0	345	10	34.50	2/35	0	0	0	
	(TB)	1966/67	1968/69	10	13	6	42	9*	6.00	0	0	748	38	19.68	5/29	3	1	3	
		1966/67	1968/69	16	18	9	48	9*	5.33	0	0	1093	48	22.77	5/29	3	1	3	
Estwick RO	(T)	1987/88	1989/90	16	15	5	161	43*	16.10	0	0	1234	70	17.62	5/17	3	0	7	
		1982/83	1989/90	37	49	12	376	43*	10.16	0	0	3088	141	21.90	6/68	6	0	16	

		First	Last	M	I	NO	Runs	HS	Avg	100	50	Runs	Wkts	Avg	Best	5i	10m	ct	st
Eustice R	(T)	1951/52		1	1	1	17	17*		0	0							2	
Fairclough J	(T)	1981/82		4	1	1	9	9*		0	0	307	13	23.61	5/44	2	0	2	
	(TB)	1980/81	1981/82	8	7	6	35	11	35.00	0	0	437	30	14.56	6/31	1	1	1	
		1964/65	1981/82	16	14	12	69	11	34.50	0	0	1025	53	19.33	6/31	3	1	4	
Fairon GP	(T)	1960/61	1969/70	10	7	4	77	27	25.66	0	0	729	21	34.71	5/45	1	0	6	
	(TB)	1960/61	1969/70	12	18	2	189	36	11.81	0	0	917	29	31.62	5/45	1	0	7	
		1960/61	1969/70	22	25	6	266	36	14.00	0	0	1646	50	32.92	5/45	2	0	13	
Farquharson RA	(T)	1923/24	1927/28	3	4	0	148	61	37.00	0	1							2	
Faulkner GA	(T)	1902/03	1909/10	17	27	7	991	148*	49.55	2	4	1072	77	13.92	7/39	5	1	18	
		1902/03	1924	118	197	23	6366	204	36.58	13	32	7826	449	17.42	7/26	33	8	94	
Featherstone NG	(T)	1969/70	1977/78	43	71	6	1613	101	24.81	1	5	550	16	34.37	4/46	0	0	24	
	(TB)	1967/68	1976/77	17	26	3	1015	92	44.13	0	10	394	15	26.26	3/31	0	0	22	
		1967/68	1981/82	329	528	54	13922	147	29.37	12	88	4986	181	27.54	5/32	4	0	277	
Fellows-Smith JP	(T)	1958/59	1959/60	13	20	4	587	102*	36.68	2	2	750	37	20.27	5/57	1	0	10	
		1953	1964	94	157	21	3999	109*	29.40	5	21	4414	149	29.62	7/26	6	1	69	
Fernley DL	(TB)	1963/64		2	3	0	47	34	15.66	0	0							2	
		1954/55	1963/64	11	17	1	461	106	28.81	1	1	0	0			0	0	6	
Field GE	(TB)	1975/76		4	5	2	3	2	1.00	0	0	161	12	13.41	5/16	1	0	2	
Field S	(T)	1890/91		1	2	0	35	21	17.50	0	0							1	1
Finlason CE	(T)	1889/90		1	1	0	2	2	2.00	0	0	22	0			0	0	0	
		1888/89	1890/91	5	9	1	213	154*	26.62	1	0	287	14	20.50	4/37	0	0	2	
Finlay IW	(TB)	1967/68		1	2	0	5	3	2.50	0	0							1	
		1965	1975/76	43	69	5	1640	150	25.62	2	8	691	18	38.38	3/17	0	0	29	
Fitzgerald PH	(TB)	1978/79		3	4	4	11	9*		0	0	177	5	35.40	3/30	0	0	1	
Flanagan FF	(T)	1945/46		3	5	1	84	28*	21.00	0	0	103	6	17.16	4/49	0	0	0	
		1936/37	1945/46	14	24	4	416	101	20.80	1	0	519	16	32.43	4/49	0	0	5	
Flanagan JPD	(T)	1967/68	1974/75	27	43	9	597	52	17.55	0	1	1357	45	30.15	5/41	1	0	15	
	(TB)	1965/66	1977/78	25	39	5	1110	98	32.64	0	8	1555	60	25.91	8/113	2	1	28	
		1965/66	1977/78	57	91	15	1835	98	24.14	0	9	3191	116	27.50	8/113	3	1	48	
Fleischer F	(T)	1890/91		1	2	0	38	33	19.00	0	0							1	
Floquet BH	(T)	1902/03	1912/13	10	17	0	466	104	27.41	1	4	130	4	32.50	2/8	0	0	5	
		1902/03	1912/13	11	18	0	466	104	25.88	1	4	145	4	36.25	2/8	0	0	7	
Floquet CE	(T)	1904/05	1910/11	5	6	3	92	29	30.66	0	0	151	4	37.75	2/50	0	0	2	
		1904/05	1910/11	6	8	4	104	29	26.00	0	0	175	4	43.75	2/50	0	0	2	
Foley WBH	(T)	1925/26	1936/37	28	38	6	1613	153	50.40	1	12	75	0			0	0	8	
		1925/26	1947/48	35	51	7	1941	153	44.11	1	14	75	0			0	0	10	
Folster JH	(T)	1919/20	1922/23	3	3	1	15	10*	7.50	0	0	75	1	75.00	1/74	0	0	0	
Forbes A	(T)	1946/47		3	4	3	23	18	23.00	0	0	189	3	63.00	1/27	0	0	0	
Forrest JE	(T)	1952/53		1	1	0	6	6	6.00	0	0							0	
Foster NA	(T)	1991/92		1								82	3	27.33	3/60	0	0	0	
		1980	1993	230	269	59	4343	107*	20.68	2	11	22196	908	24.44	8/99	50	8	116	
Fotheringham HR	(T)	1978/79	1988/89	83	137	15	4760	184	39.01	13	21							77	
	(TB)	1981/82	1986/87	3	4	0	410	134	102.50	2	2	12	0			0	0	3	
		1971/72	1989/90	147	247	27	8814	184	40.06	21	48	490	7	70.00	3/48	0	0	135	

		First	Last	M	I	NO	Runs	HS	Avg	100	50	Runs	Wkts	Avg	Best	5i	10m	ct	st
Fox JS	(TB)	1963/64		1	2	0	22	17	11.00	0	0	8	1	8.00	1/8	0	0	0	
		1954/55	1963/64	18	34	2	773	75	24.15	0	3	246	6	41.00	3/17	0	0	7	
Frames AS	(T)	1921/22	1927/28	6	9	0	89	16	9.88	0	0	150	3	50.00	2/35	0	0	1	
Frank CN	(T)	1919/20	1925/26	13	21	1	444	108	22.20	1	1							3	
		1919/20	1925/26	17	29	1	683	152	24.39	2	1							3	
Fuller JHF	(T)	1939/40		1	1	0	22	22	22.00	0	0							0	
		1935/36	1947/48	15	27	2	582	107*	23.28	1	1	13	0			0	0	4	
Fullerton GM	(T)	1945/46	1950/51	16	22	0	756	123	34.36	2	4	24	1	24.00	1/7	0	0	25	9
		1942/43	1951	63	97	8	2768	167	31.10	3	20	107	3	35.66	2/41	0	0	64	18
Fullerton IR	(T)	1958/59	1965/66	22	40	1	1429	145	36.64	4	6							7	
	(TB)	1959/60	1965/66	3	6	1	192	56	38.40	0	2							0	
		1958/59	1965/66	31	56	2	1853	145	34.31	5	8	8	0			0	0	11	
Funston KJ	(T)	1954/55	1959/60	27	44	4	1134	136*	28.35	1	7							7	
	(TB)	1959/60		2	4	1	83	70	27.66	0	1							3	
		1946/47	1961/62	84	145	8	4164	160	30.39	5	23	43	2	21.50	2/32	0	0	36	
Furniss AD	(T)	1949/50		1	2	1	12	12*	12.00	0	0	93	4	23.25	3/20	0	0	1	
Fussell BJ	(T)	1957/58		1	2	0	0	0	0.00	0	0							1	
	(TB)	1963/64		2	3	0	198	115	66.00	1	0							1	
		1957/58	1963/64	3	5	0	198	115	39.60	1	0							2	
Gamble MA	(T)	1968/69	1972/73	2	1	0	3	3	3.00	0	0	153	5	30.60	2/17	0	0	2	
	(TB)	1968/69	1972/73	4	4	1	79	26	26.33	0	0	338	17	19.88	8/72	1	0	3	
		1968/69	1972/73	6	5	1	82	26	20.50	0	0	491	22	22.31	8/72	1	0	5	
Garda I	(TB)	1976/77		2	4	0	77	54	19.25	0	1							0	
Gardner WT	(T)	1912/13	1920/21	4	7	3	79	35*	19.75	0	0	26	1	26.00	1/9	0	0	1	
Gartly JDE	(T)	1931/32	1932/33	3	5	1	38	10	9.50	0	0							2	1
Gaydon CB	(T)	1932/33	1936/37	11	19	2	336	73	19.76	0	2	571	16	35.68	4/22	0	0	1	
		1930/31	1936/37	15	26	2	455	73	18.95	0	3	787	18	43.72	4/22	0	0	2	
Georgeu G	(T)	1941/42		1	2	1	88	68*	88.00	0	1							1	
		1931/32	1949/50	44	74	9	2033	154	31.27	3	12	809	9	89.88	1/7	0	0	21	
Gibb PJM	(T)	1952/53	1956/57	14	16	0	421	203	26.31	1	1							34	7
Gibbs KL	(T)	1956/57	1959/60	14	22	3	201	36	10.57	0	0	1083	32	33.84	4/33	0	0	4	
	(TB)	1959/60		4	5	1	98	80*	24.50	0	1	280	12	23.33	4/51	0	0	1	
		1951/52	1959/60	32	53	19	481	80*	14.14	0	1	2772	101	27.44	5/79	1	0	15	
Goldsmith MH	(TB)	1974/75		1	1	0	12	12	12.00	0	0	82	3	27.33	2/45	0	0	0	
Goldstein FS	(T)	1970/71		2	4	0	93	51	23.25	0	1							1	
	(TB)	1969/70	1970/71	6	9	0	231	51	25.66	0	1							8	
		1966	1977/78	89	163	4	4810	155	30.25	2	32	53	1	53.00	1/3	0	0	62	
Gordon N	(T)	1933/34	1948/49	22	23	8	90	20	6.00	0	0	1821	96	18.96	6/61	5	0	7	
		1933/34	1948/49	29	31	10	109	20	5.19	0	0	2803	126	22.24	6/61	8	0	8	
Gordon-Campbell RJ	(T)	1945/46		3	5	1	168	77	42.00	0	2	14	0			0	0	5	
Graham JM	(T)	1906/07		3	5	0	51	25	10.20	0	0	34	2	17.00	2/19	0	0	0	
Grainger C	(TB)	1991/92	1993/94	7	11	0	290	70	26.36	0	1							3	

		First	Last	M	I	NO	Runs	HS	Avg	100	50	Runs	Wkts	Avg	Best	5i	10m	ct	st
Greve VS	(T)	1967/68	1974/75	14	23	2	420	124	20.00	1	0	558	10	55.80	4/80	0	0	13	
	(TB)	1967/68	1977/78	34	60	4	1636	185*	29.21	1	10	2351	93	25.27	7/71	2	0	26	
		1967/68	1977/78	49	84	6	2056	185*	26.35	2	10	3034	108	28.09	7/71	2	0	41	
Griessel LW	(TB)	1985/86	1986/87	5	8	0	130	42	16.25	0	0							3	
		1978/79	1986/87	17	30	0	618	162	20.60	1	1							10	
Grieveson RE	(T)	1929/30	1939/40	26	37	7	970	107*	32.33	1	6	7	0			0	0	15	7
		1929/30	1939/40	30	42	8	1130	107*	33.23	1	7	7	0			0	0	25	11
Griffiths EA	(T)	1906/07		4	4	0	44	37	11.00	0	0							3	
Grinaker OW	(T)	1946/47	1949/50	5	9	0	177	48	19.66	0	0	17	0			0	0	4	
		1942/43	1949/50	7	13	0	285	73	21.92	0	1	17	0			0	0	4	
Gyngell AH	(T)	1932/33	1934/35	11	14	2	123	33	10.25	0	0	1012	32	31.62	5/110	1	0	5	
		1932/33	1945/46	21	32	6	643	152*	24.73	1	2	1492	42	35.52	5/110	1	0	8	
Hall AE	(T)	1920/21	1930/31	25	31	11	103	22	5.15	0	0	2483	143	17.36	8/80	14	5	9	
		1920/21	1930/31	46	57	21	134	22	3.72	0	0	4501	234	19.23	8/80	21	6	13	
Hall N	(T)	1935/36		1	2	1	3	3	3.00	0	0	74	1	74.00	1/74	0	0	0	
Halliwell EA	(T)	1892/93	1908/09	12	21	2	431	83	22.68	0	1	35	0			0	0	14	10
		1891/92	1908/09	60	96	8	1702	92	19.34	0	8	175	3	58.33	2/49	0	0	75	37
Hamilton EP	(T)	1936/37		1	1	0	33	33	33.00	0	0							0	
		1936/37		2	3	0	65	33	21.66	0	0							0	
Hammond HW	(T)	1921/22		1	1	0	35	35	35.00	0	0							0	
Hand CR	(T)	1912/13		2	4	0	75	31	18.75	0	0							0	
		1912/13	1919/20	3	6	0	91	31	15.16	0	0	9	0			0	0	1	
Handfield CR	(T)	1908/09		1	1	0	5	5	5.00	0	0							2	
Hankey SE	(TB)	1965/66	1969/70	7	8	5	71	34*	23.66	0	0	343	19	18.05	5/25	1	0	3	
Hanley RW	(T)	1976/77	1986/87	60	40	17	115	18	5.00	0	0	4356	218	19.98	7/31	11	1	15	
	(TB)	1976/77	1977/78	2	1	0	0	0	0.00	0	0	129	14	9.21	5/20	2	1	1	
		1970/71	1986/87	113	99	44	320	33*	5.81	0	0	8491	408	20.81	7/31	23	3	39	
Hansen ETE	(T)	1966/67		1	2	1	19	16	19.00	0	0	23	0			0	0	0	
	(TB)	1965/66		2	4	1	48	28*	16.00	0	0	128	2	64.00	1/30	0	0	1	
		1952/53	1966/67	16	31	4	642	88	23.77	0	2	859	16	53.68	3/54	0	0	7	
Harris LR	(T)	1952/53	1965/66	22	33	5	560	70	20.00	0	3	1	0			0	0	18	
	(TB)	1960/61	1966/67	13	21	1	683	116	34.15	1	5	19	0			0	0	13	
		1952/53	1966/67	35	54	6	1243	116	25.89	1	8	20	0			0	0	31	
Harris TA	(T)	1936/37	1948/49	30	41	2	1835	191*	47.05	4	8	20	0			0	0	27	
		1933/34	1948/49	55	80	7	3028	191*	41.47	6	16	33	0			0	0	52	
Harrison JS	(T)	1889/90		1	2	0	20	11	10.00	0	0							1	
Harrison RF	(T)	1946/47		2	4	2	102	73*	51.00	0	1	274	6	45.66	3/111	0	0	0	
Hathorn CMH	(T)	1897/98	1906/07	13	20	0	353	91	17.65	0	2	12	0			0	0	4	
		1897/98	1910/11	87	142	9	3541	239	26.62	9	12	52	1	52.00	1/16	0	0	27	
Haysman MD	(T)	1993/94		8	14	0	374	52	26.71	0	2	132	2	66.00	1/22	0	0	11	
		1982/83	1993/94	103	184	22	5977	180	36.89	13	24	676	5	135.20	2/19	0	0	140	
Hazelhurst WC	(T)	1904/05		4	5	0	88	51	17.60	0	1	159	5	31.80	2/28	0	0	0	
Heaney LJ	(T)	1934/35	1951/52	27	28	6	250	47	11.36	0	0	1963	93	21.10	6/45	5	0	2	
		1934/35	1951/52	29	31	6	277	47	11.08	0	0	2174	100	21.74	6/45	5	0	3	

		First	Last	M	I	NO	Runs	HS	Avg	100	50	Runs	Wkts	Avg	Best	5i	10m	ct	st
Heather PJ	(T)	1910/11	1912/13	11	17	3	608	109*	43.42	1	5	258	7	36.85	2/25	0	0	3	
		1904/05	1913/14	13	20	3	673	109*	39.58	1	6	297	10	29.70	3/39	0	0	3	
Hector AR	(T)	1968/69	1970/71	9	12	3	94	34	10.44	0	0	617	20	30.85	3/30	0	0	11	
	(TB)	1962/63	1969/70	7	9	0	129	38	14.33	0	0	515	20	25.75	4/35	0	0	9	
		1962/63	1970/71	34	50	6	595	49	13.52	0	0	2950	117	25.21	5/22	4	0	29	
Heeley HN	(T)	1910/11		5	6	2	72	27	18.00	0	0							5	
Heine PS	(T)	1955/56	1964/65	18	24	2	273	34	12.40	0	0	1496	93	16.08	7/61	7	2	7	
		1951/52	1964/65	61	97	14	1255	67	15.12	0	4	5924	277	21.38	8/92	20	4	34	
Helfrich DG	(T)	1936/37		2	4	0	173	77	43.25	0	2	42	2	21.00	2/29	0	0	1	
		1929/30	1939/40	28	52	0	1301	92	25.01	0	10	343	12	28.58	3/87	0	0	11	1
Henning M	(T)	1957/58	1964/65	9	15	3	311	61	25.91	0	1	127	8	15.87	4/23	0	0	3	
	(TB)	1959/60	1965/66	13	22	5	584	100*	34.35	1	3	449	19	23.63	3/103	0	0	9	
		1957/58	1965/66	22	37	8	895	100*	30.86	1	4	576	27	21.33	4/23	0	0	12	
Hepker VN	(T)	1929/30		1	1	0	0	0	0.00	0	0							0	
Herbert SR	(T)	1923/24	1926/27	12	15	1	366	87	26.14	0	2							1	
		1923/24	1927/28	13	17	1	385	87	24.06	0	2							2	
Hester HC	(TB)	1966/67		2	3	1	57	47	28.50	0	0							7	
		1963/64	1970/71	4	6	2	67	47	16.75	0	0							10	
Hewitt GM	(TB)	1993/94		2	3	0	37	22	12.33	0	0							0	
Hickson JAE	(T)	1889/90		1	2	0	11	11	5.50	0	0							0	
		1889/90	1896	4	5	1	11	11	2.75	0	0							8	1
Hings JT	(T)	1894/95	1896/97	3	6	0	59	38	9.83	0	0	246	12	20.50	4/73	0	0	0	
Hoar HRV	(T)	1931/32		1	2	1	12	7	12.00	0	0	118	3	39.33	2/39	0	0	1	
Hobson MR	(T)	1993/94		6	7	5	14	8*	7.00	0	0	620	22	28.18	7/61	1	0	3	
	(TB)	1993/94		2	3	1	21	20	10.50	0	0	160	4	40.00	2/40	0	0	1	
		1985/86	1993/94	37	45	12	250	26	7.57	0	0	3063	110	27.84	7/61	3	0	11	
Holmes NCM	(T)	1963/64	1964/65	3	6	0	86	49	14.33	0	0							4	3
	(TB)	1962/63	1963/64	10	16	1	626	165	41.73	2	2	6	1	6.00	1/6	0	0	24	2
		1962/63	1968/69	23	38	3	1089	165	31.11	2	4	33	1	33.00	1/6	0	0	33	5
Hooper JJ	(T)	1985/86	1989/90	9	8	5	71	38*	23.66	0	0	330	13	25.38	2/5	0	0	1	
	(TB)	1984/85	1988/89	18	16	8	58	17*	7.25	0	0	1493	72	20.73	7/29	2	0	5	
		1979/80	1989/90	29	28	15	158	38*	12.15	0	0	1849	85	21.75	7/29	2	0	6	
Horak DJ	(TB)	1965/66		3	6	1	212	111	42.40	1	1	14	1	14.00	1/14	0	0	2	
Howell DH	(T)	1986/87		1	2	0	55	51	27.50	0	1							0	
	(TB)	1986/87	1988/89	15	25	1	640	151	26.66	1	2	2	0			0	0	9	
		1976/77	1991/92	80	139	5	3491	151	26.05	5	17	8	0			0	0	118	12
Hubbard AN	(T)	1974/75	1976/77	3	1	0	0	0	0.00	0	0	248	6	41.33	3/76	0	0	1	
	(TB)	1973/74	1976/77	13	12	7	42	12	8.40	0	0	964	48	20.08	7/52	1	1	5	
		1973/74	1976/77	16	13	7	42	12	7.00	0	0	1212	54	22.44	7/52	1	1	6	
Huddy ME	(TB)	1960/61		1	2	0	20	20	10.00	0	0							2	
Hughes GP	(TB)	1978/79		1	2	0	59	47	29.50	0	0							1	
Hunter BL	(TB)	1962/63		2	3	1	27	14	13.50	0	0							2	
Hutton RA	(T)	1975/76		2	2	1	14	14*	14.00	0	0	142	0			0	0	0	
		1962	1975/76	281	410	58	7561	189	21.48	5	29	15008	625	24.01	8/50	21	3	216	

		First	Last	M	I	NO	Runs	HS	Avg	100	50	Runs	Wkts	Avg	Best	5i	10m	ct	st
Ince RG	(T)	1920/21	1923/24	9	14	3	151	27	13.72	0	0	529	27	19.59	6/44	2	0	9	
Inchbold SJ	(T)	1936/37	1945/46	10	10	4	36	13	6.00	0	0							20	13
		1936/37	1945/46	11	11	4	36	13	5.14	0	0							20	15
Innes GAS	(T)	1963/64	1964/65	8	15	4	372	140*	33.81	1	0	199	3	66.33	1/8	0	0	6	
		1950/51	1964/65	75	134	15	4001	140*	33.62	7	21	733	16	45.81	6/22	1	0	60	
Ironside DEJ	(T)	1947/48	1955/56	28	29	10	98	16*	5.15	0	0	2472	115	21.49	7/36	6	0	10	
		1947/48	1955/56	31	33	12	135	16*	6.42	0	0	2747	130	21.13	7/36	7	0	11	
Irvine BL	(T)	1969/70	1976/77	64	115	9	5068	193	47.81	16	21	72	0			0	0	171	5
		1962/63	1976/77	157	271	26	9919	193	40.48	21	46	142	1	142.00	1/39	0	0	240	7
Jack SD	(T)	1990/91	1993/94	28	32	9	384	42	16.69	0	0	2701	128	21.10	8/51	7	2	7	
	(TB)	1989/90		2	4	1	29	18*	9.66	0	0	207	6	34.50	3/50	0	0	0	
		1989/90	1993/94	31	38	11	434	42	16.07	0	0	2982	140	21.30	8/51	7	2	7	
Jackson DC	(T)	1912/13		2	3	1	105	47*	52.50	0	0	45	0			0	0	3	
		1908/09	1912/13	10	17	1	277	59	17.31	0	1	392	23	17.04	4/36	0	0	6	
Jackson IM	(TB)	1971/72	1974/75	5	9	2	118	36	16.85	0	0							7	
Jacobs S	(T)	1989/90	1993/94	30	48	8	750	101*	18.75	1	3	1872	70	26.74	6/35	2	0	17	
	(TB)	1987/88	1993/94	8	12	6	244	102*	40.66	1	0	481	24	20.04	3/21	0	0	8	
		1987/88	1993/94	39	62	15	1045	102*	22.23	2	3	2404	99	24.28	6/35	3	0	26	
James JW	(T)	1951/52		2	3	0	47	23	15.66	0	0							0	
James M	(T)	1987/88	1988/89	11	11	5	55	11*	9.16	0	0	887	21	42.23	5/55	1	0	1	
	(TB)	1987/88	1989/90	5	7	2	54	22	10.80	0	0	435	28	15.53	7/45	3	1	7	
		1987/88	1989/90	16	18	7	109	22	9.90	0	0	1322	49	26.97	7/45	4	1	8	
Jardine AJ	(T)	1927/28		1	2	1	10	10*	10.00	0	0							0	
Jennings RV	(T)	1975/76	1989/90	105	134	36	2360	120	24.08	1	9	1	0			0	0	385	34
	(TB)	1973/74	1980/81	16	27	3	886	168	36.91	1	4							42	10
		1973/74	1992/93	159	220	46	4160	168	23.90	3	15	1	0			0	0	567	54
Johnson CL	(T)	1893/94	1898/99	3	6	1	107	52	21.40	0	1	140	3	46.66	1/27	0	0	1	
		1893/94	1898/99	4	8	1	117	52	16.71	0	1	197	3	65.66	1/27	0	0	2	
Johnson GW	(T)	1981/82		1	1	0	9	9	9.00	0	0	70	0			0	0	1	
	(TB)	1984/85		5	7	1	136	50	22.66	0	1	42	1	42.00	1/37	0	0	5	
		1965	1985	390	605	78	12922	168	24.51	11	54	17601	567	31.04	7/76	23	3	315	
Johnston MO	(T)	1993/94		3	4	1	26	19*	8.66	0	0							13	1
	(TB)	1993/94		3	5	0	134	108	26.80	1	0							13	4
		1993/94		6	9	1	160	108	20.00	1	0							26	5
Jones CHK	(T)	1936/37	1946/47	12	19	1	722	105*	40.11	1	4	189	8	23.62	3/23	0	0	6	
Jordaan LCR	(T)	1991/92		1	2	2	11	9*		0	0	23	0			0	0	0	
	(TB)	1990/91	1991/92	7	4	0	24	9	6.00	0	0	477	19	25.10	4/28	0	0	1	
		1990/91	1993/94	22	23	7	86	12*	5.37	0	0	1658	64	25.90	5/72	1	0	3	
Joubert FE	(TB)	1975/76		5	5	0	45	37	9.00	0	0	254	13	19.53	3/22	0	0	1	
		1972/73	1982/83	22	34	11	243	37	10.56	0	0	1559	53	29.41	4/31	0	0	5	
Jurgensen N	(TB)	1976/77	1981/82	7	12	1	209	39	19.00	0	0							3	
Kahn HM	(T)	1931/32		1	2	0	48	35	24.00	0	0							0	

		First	Last	M	I	NO	Runs	HS	Avg	100	50	Runs	Wkts	Avg	Best	5i	10m	ct	st
Kallicharran AI	(T)	1981/82	1983/84	17	27	2	1236	151	49.44	4	4	311	11	28.27	5/45	1	0	8	
		1966/67	1990	505	834	86	32650	243*	43.64	87	160	4030	84	47.97	5/45	1	0	323	
Katz SJ	(T)	1966/67		3	4	2	24	13	12.00	0	0							6	1
	(TB)	1966/67	1967/68	4	4	0	46	41	11.50	0	0							14	
		1961/62	1967/68	9	12	3	105	41	11.66	0	0							24	1
Keightley-Smith AW	(T)	1931/32	1949/50	4	5	0	71	43	14.20	0	0	210	9	23.33	6/66	1	0	0	
		1931/32	1949/50	5	7	1	112	43	18.66	0	0	293	14	20.92	6/66	2	0	1	
Kempis GS	(T)	1892/93	1893/94	3	5	0	59	20	11.80	0	0	200	7	28.57	4/34	0	0	3	
Kennedy AB	(T)	1922/23	1927/28	4	5	1	80	32	20.00	0	0	121	7	17.28	3/36	0	0	4	
Kerby JC	(T)	1954/55	1956/57	5	6	2	33	14*	8.25	0	0	295	17	17.35	4/28	0	0	2	
	(TB)	1960/61		6	10	2	148	44	18.50	0	0	470	34	13.82	7/35	3	1	0	
		1954/55	1963/64	23	36	6	429	44	14.30	0	0	1665	83	20.06	7/35	4	1	2	
Kerr JFM	(T)	1921/22	1922/23	2	3	0	22	12	7.33	0	0	3	1	3.00	1/3	0	0	2	
Kerr KJ	(T)	1979/80	1989/90	19	15	6	126	49*	14.00	0	0	1592	42	37.90	4/59	0	0	16	
	(TB)	1978/79	1989/90	49	61	14	791	74	16.82	0	3	3045	145	21.00	6/37	7	1	42	
		1978/79	1989/90	83	89	25	1040	74	16.25	0	3	5674	211	26.89	6/37	8	1	64	
Kerr WR	(T)	1968/69	1974/75	33	47	12	883	147*	25.22	1	2	2075	71	29.22	6/58	1	0	10	
	(TB)	1967/68	1977/78	14	20	3	317	100*	18.64	1	0	558	23	24.26	7/41	1	0	11	
		1967/68	1977/78	47	67	15	1200	147*	23.07	2	2	2633	94	28.01	7/41	2	0	21	
Kidd WDB	(T)	1951/52		2	3	0	13	7	4.33	0	0							4	
Kimber SR	(T)	1949/50	1956/57	15	25	0	750	171	30.00	1	3							7	
Kinsley PH	(T)	1957/58	1960/61	8	16	0	419	69	26.18	0	3							3	
	(TB)	1959/60		4	6	0	260	87	43.33	0	3							1	
		1957/58	1960/61	12	22	0	679	87	30.86	0	6							4	
Kirsh W	(T)	1986/87		1	2	0	59	36	29.50	0	0							1	
	(TB)	1982/83	1987/88	19	35	3	798	109	24.93	1	3	75	2	37.50	2/66	0	0	14	
		1982/83	1987/88	31	58	5	1441	119	27.18	2	5	75	2	37.50	2/66	0	0	19	
Klette JE	(TB)	1976/77		3	6	1	276	154	55.20	1	1							4	
		1967/68	1976/77	5	10	2	329	154	41.12	1	1							6	
Klinck FG	(T)	1890/91	1892/93	3	5	0	41	33	8.20	0	0	55	2	27.50	1/19	0	0	2	
Knodell TE	(T)	1982/83		1	1	0	5	5	5.00	0	0							8	
	(TB)	1981/82		2	3	2	84	39	84.00	0	0							3	1
		1981/82	1982/83	3	4	2	89	39	44.50	0	0							11	1
Kotze JJ	(T)	1902/03		4	5	1	47	22*	11.75	0	0	248	34	7.29	8/18	3	1	1	
		1901	1910/11	72	105	25	688	60	8.60	0	1	6217	348	17.86	8/18	30	9	31	
Kourie AJ	(T)	1974/75	1986/87	89	118	31	2816	127*	32.36	2	12	7414	327	22.67	8/113	20	3	111	
	(TB)	1970/71	1988/89	22	35	9	1247	120	47.96	3	6	1178	56	21.03	7/68	1	0	18	
		1970/71	1988/89	127	175	45	4470	127*	34.38	5	21	9869	421	23.44	8/113	24	3	148	
Kuhn SA	(TB)	1986/87	1987/88	5	6	0	66	20	11.00	0	0							13	
		1979/80	1987/88	8	12	1	159	22	14.45	0	0							21	1
Lacey HS	(T)	1945/46		2	3	0	175	102	58.33	1	1	5	0			0	0	0	
		1945/46	1956/57	21	40	1	1155	102*	29.61	2	3	31	0			0	0	18	4

		First	Last	M	I	NO	Runs	HS	Avg	100	50	Runs	Wkts	Avg	Best	5i	10m	ct	st
Laing DR	(T)	1989/90	1993/94	23	35	5	757	101*	25.23	1	4	1281	38	33.71	3/18	0	0	13	
	(TB)	1989/90	1993/94	11	17	0	323	61	19.00	0	2	701	21	33.38	3/35	0	0	3	
		1989/90	1993/94	38	58	5	1146	101*	21.62	1	6	2130	62	34.35	3/18	0	0	20	
Lamb C	(T)	1913/14		1	1	0	21	21	21.00	0	0							0	
Lance HR	(T)	1961/62	1970/71	52	84	9	2990	169	39.86	8	13	2440	92	26.52	5/52	1	0	60	
		1958/59	1971/72	103	171	18	5336	169	34.87	11	25	4284	167	25.65	6/55	2	0	101	
Langebrink AC	(T)	1927/28	1932/33	16	25	1	788	122	32.83	1	4	498	21	23.71	5/45	1	0	4	
Langton ACB	(T)	1931/32	1941/42	15	23	2	460	58	21.90	0	3	1229	50	24.58	6/114	1	0	12	
		1931/32	1941/42	52	74	13	1218	73*	19.96	0	7	4969	193	25.74	6/53	9	2	41	
Lawrance J	(T)	1913/14		1	1	0	15	15	15.00	0	0							0	
Le Roux FL	(T)	1908/09	1928/29	27	37	7	1046	102	34.86	2	8	1515	68	22.27	6/28	4	0	11	
		1908/09	1928/29	34	51	7	1258	102	28.59	2	9	1837	93	19.75	6/28	6	0	15	
Levick FO	(T)	1933/34		1	1	0	40	40	40.00	0	0							1	
		1933/34	1948/49	5	7	2	53	40	10.60	0	0							3	1
Levick RPO	(T)	1931/32		4	4	2	31	24	15.50	0	0	329	9	36.55	4/100	0	0	3	
Levy C	(T)	1945/46	1946/47	5	5	0	39	20	7.80	0	0	252	11	22.90	5/45	1	0	8	
Lewin L	(T)	1932/33	1933/34	4	4	2	26	17	13.00	0	0	217	7	31.00	3/35	0	0	2	
		1925/26	1933/34	12	15	7	139	22	17.37	0	0	964	35	27.54	4/140	0	0	8	
Lewis DW	(T)	1972/73		1	2	1	0	0*	0.00	0	0	48	0			0	0	0	
	(TB)	1972/73		1	1	0	15	15	15.00	0	0	9	0			0	0	0	
		1960	1972/73	14	20	7	122	29*	9.38	0	0	958	21	45.61	4/42	0	0	3	
Ley T	(T)	1919/20		1	2	1	10	7	10.00	0	0	96	0			0	0	0	
Lilley AR	(T)	1978/79		4	3	2	19	18*	19.00	0	0	191	9	21.22	4/9	0	0	0	
		1970/71	1978/79	47	58	20	543	38	14.28	0	0	3189	132	24.15	5/24	4	0	22	
Lindsay DT	(T)	1964/65		1	2	1	67	55*	67.00	0	1							0	
		1958/59	1973/74	124	214	15	7074	216	35.54	12	36	14	0			0	0	292	41
Lindsay JD	(T)	1933/34	1936/37	2	3	0	1	1	0.33	0	0							0	
		1933/34	1948/49	29	45	14	346	51	11.16	0	1							39	16
Lindsay NV	(T)	1906/07	1926/27	34	48	3	1569	160*	34.86	3	10	379	19	19.94	4/27	0	0	10	
		1906/07	1926/27	42	64	3	2030	160*	33.27	5	11	668	24	27.83	4/27	0	0	16	
Lindsay-Smith D	(T)	1967/68	1974/75	18	27	2	787	108	31.48	1	4	18	0			0	0	14	
	(TB)	1966/67	1974/75	14	21	4	765	92*	45.00	0	7	35	0			0	0	10	
		1966/67	1974/75	32	48	6	1552	108	36.95	1	11	53	0			0	0	24	
Lister-James CM	(T)	1990/91		1	2	0	12	8	6.00	0	0	78	1	78.00	1/78	0	0	1	
	(TB)	1990/91		3	2	2	40	33*		0	0	130	4	32.50	2/32	0	0	4	
		1983/84	1990/91	35	54	13	1033	98	25.19	0	3	1719	56	30.69	4/38	0	0	21	
Lloyd EL	(T)	1923/24	1928/29	11	14	1	275	48	21.15	0	0							3	
Lodwick JR	(T)	1960/61	1963/64	5	5	1	28	11*	7.00	0	0	279	13	21.46	4/19	0	0	1	
	(TB)	1959/60	1963/64	8	12	2	146	53*	14.60	0	1	460	16	28.75	5/35	1	0	0	
		1959/60	1963/64	13	17	3	174	53*	12.42	0	1	739	29	25.48	5/35	1	0	1	
Loeser PS	(T)	1933/34	1948/49	6	6	1	117	45	23.40	0	0							8	4
Lohmann GA	(T)	1897/98		1	1	0	9	9	9.00	0	0	105	6	17.50	3/33	0	0	0	
		1884	1897/98	293	427	39	7247	115	18.67	3	29	25295	1841	13.73	9/28	176	57	337	
Lomas GE	(T)	1890/91		1	2	0	54	47	27.00	0	0	14	0			0	0	1	
Losper H	(TB)	1978/79	1981/82	4	6	2	21	9	5.25	0	0	279	14	19.92	7/86	1	1	1	
Luckin MW	(T)	1910/11		2	3	0	25	25	8.33	0	0							1	

		First	Last	M	I	NO	Runs	HS	Avg	100	50	Runs	Wkts	Avg	Best	5i	10m	ct	st
Lundie EB	(T)	1913/14		2	2	0	32	29	16.00	0	0	166	4	41.50	4/73	0	0	4	
		1908/09	1913/14	9	16	1	126	29	8.40	0	0	659	26	25.34	6/52	1	0	7	
Lundie PG	(TB)	1963/64		1	2	2	7	7*		0	0	92	4	23.00	3/31	0	0	0	
Lurie SA	(TB)	1990/91		2	2	1	5	5*	5.00	0	0	114	4	28.50	3/52	0	0	0	
McAdam SJ	(T)	1970/71		2	1	0	9	9	9.00	0	0	85	4	21.25	3/49	0	0	1	
	(TB)	1970/71		2	3	0	7	6	2.33	0	0	170	7	24.28	4/65	0	0	1	
		1967/68	1973/74	31	36	11	228	31	9.12	0	0	2383	82	29.06	4/39	0	0	13	
McAlpine NM	(T)	1932/33	1936/37	4	5	0	60	27	12.00	0	0	185	10	18.50	4/13	0	0	0	
Macaulay MJ	(T)	1957/58	1965/66	18	23	5	155	25	8.61	0	0	1177	49	24.02	6/69	2	0	8	
	(TB)	1959/60	1965/66	5	8	0	62	46	7.75	0	0	336	22	15.27	5/40	2	0	4	
		1957/58	1978/79	69	91	23	888	59	13.05	0	2	5357	234	22.89	7/49	16	4	45	
McBride B	(T)	1983/84	1992/93	21	29	8	328	84	15.61	0	1							80	7
	(TB)	1982/83	1989/90	40	59	14	1181	101	26.24	1	7	9	0			0	0	131	11
		1980/81	1992/93	81	127	29	2042	101	20.83	1	10	9	0			0	0	258	25
McCarthy J	(T)	1897/98		4	7	4	49	30	16.33	0	0	152	7	21.71	3/41	0	0	2	
McCubbin GR	(T)	1922/23		2	2	1	102	97	102.00	0	1	1	0			0	0	0	
McDonald EG	(T)	1904/05	1910/11	5	6	2	37	21*	9.25	0	0							1	
McKay CD	(T)	1927/28	1928/29	3	4	2	201	102*	100.50	1	0							3	
		1920/21	1931/32	32	58	8	1669	111*	33.38	3	7							26	5
Mackay JRM	(T)	1906/07		4	7	0	247	90	35.28	0	2							2	
		1902/03	1906/07	20	33	2	1556	203	50.19	6	7							5	
Mackay-Coghill D	(T)	1963/64	1973/74	65	87	21	1157	87	17.53	0	4	5672	245	23.15	7/40	12	1	63	
	(TB)	1962/63		2	3	0	88	47	29.33	0	0	94	8	11.75	3/20	0	0	2	
		1962/63	1973/74	73	101	22	1400	87	17.72	0	5	6057	264	22.94	7/40	12	1	68	
McKenzie KA	(T)	1971/72	1986/87	105	157	20	5105	188	37.26	9	27	114	1	114.00	1/19	0	0	108	
	(TB)	1968/69	1975/76	17	29	1	1125	127*	40.17	3	5	19	0			0	0	21	
		1966/67	1986/87	133	208	23	6756	188	36.51	13	34	133	1	133.00	1/19	0	0	141	
McKeown AC	(T)	1945/46		1	1	0	1	1	1.00	0	0	54	2	27.00	2/28	0	0	1	
McKinnon AH	(T)	1963/64	1967/68	21	28	12	213	23*	13.31	0	0	2064	95	21.72	6/25	12	2	7	
	(TB)	1968/69		1	2	0	11	10	5.50	0	0	121	6	20.16	3/54	0	0	0	
		1952/53	1968/69	111	152	39	1687	62	14.92	0	4	9937	470	21.14	7/37	38	9	32	
MacLaren N	(T)	1945/46	1949/50	4	7	1	80	26	13.33	0	0							2	3
McMillan BM	(T)	1985/86	1988/89	19	29	7	824	85	37.45	0	7	1102	53	20.79	5/39	1	0	18	
	(TB)	1984/85	1985/86	8	13	0	261	129	20.07	1	1	601	24	25.04	2/40	0	0	10	
		1984/85	1994	94	150	25	4743	136	37.94	7	28	6229	230	27.12	5/35	4	0	94	
McMillan GE	(T)	1978/79	1987/88	30	34	9	463	60	18.52	0	1	1323	59	22.42	4/43	0	0	19	
	(TB)	1977/78	1989/90	34	51	14	1474	156*	39.83	3	7	1583	88	17.98	6/33	2	0	27	
		1977/78	1989/90	78	109	32	2441	156*	31.70	3	10	3845	185	20.78	6/33	4	0	53	
McMillan Q	(T)	1928/29	1929/30	4	5	1	358	185*	89.50	1	2	360	17	21.17	6/48	1	0	1	
		1928/29	1931/32	50	76	16	1607	185*	26.78	1	6	5033	189	26.62	9/53	12	2	30	
MacNab GN	(T)	1986/87		1	1	1	12	12*		0	0	92	6	15.33	3/41	0	0	0	
	(TB)	1982/83	1986/87	13	13	4	54	30	6.00	0	0	867	30	28.90	4/29	0	0	3	
		1980/81	1986/87	15	16	6	67	30	6.70	0	0	1028	36	28.55	4/29	0	0	3	

		First	Last	M	I	NO	Runs	HS	Avg	100	50	Runs	Wkts	Avg	Best	5i	10m	ct	st
Maile JBR	(T)	1951/52	1953/54	12	16	5	309	64*	28.09	0	1	334	8	41.75	2/36	0	0	12	
		1951/52	1960/61	35	58	8	1134	108	22.68	1	3	1853	75	24.70	7/27	3	0	35	
Malraison WH de R	(T)	1904/05		2	2	0	41	28	20.50	0	0							1	
Manack A	(T)	1991/92	1992/93	2	2	0	9	7	4.50	0	0	168	0			0	0	0	
	(TB)	1991/92		4	6	3	36	22*	12.00	0	0	346	11	31.45	3/59	0	0	0	
		1991/92	1992/93	6	8	3	45	22*	9.00	0	0	514	11	46.72	3/59	0	0	0	
Manack HA	(T)	1991/92		2	3	0	58	33	19.33	0	0	22	0			0	0	3	
	(TB)	1991/92		5	9	0	251	66	27.88	0	1	40	1	40.00	1/17	0	0	3	
		1991/92		7	12	0	309	66	25.75	0	1	62	1	62.00	1/17	0	0	6	
Mare BL	(TB)	1981/82		2	3	0	9	8	3.00	0	0	168	4	42.00	3/49	0	0	2	
Maritz C	(T)	1919/20	1922/23	2	4	0	87	36	21.75	0	0	56	1	56.00	1/49	0	0	0	
		1910/11	1933/34	16	29	4	771	169	30.84	1	4	893	37	24.13	5/55	3	0	13	
Marshall E	(T)	1902/03		2	2	0	12	12	6.00	0	0							1	
Martin GJ	(T)	1971/72	1975/76	7	9	6	16	6*	5.33	0	0	519	12	43.25	4/26	0	0	0	
	(TB)	1972/73	1975/76	2	2	0	5	4	2.50	0	0	130	2	65.00	2/39	0	0	1	
		1971/72	1975/76	9	11	6	21	6*	4.20	0	0	649	14	46.35	4/26	0	0	1	
Martin H	(TB)	1970/71		5	6	0	190	53	31.66	0	1							5	
		1970/71	1971/72	10	13	0	392	64	30.15	0	2	81	0			0	0	14	
Marvin EW	(T)	1908/09		2	3	0	47	29	15.66	0	0							0	
Marx IB	(T)	1949/50	1950/51	3	5	0	88	49	17.60	0	0	126	5	25.20	2/9	0	0	0	
Marx WFE	(T)	1920/21	1921/22	6	10	0	531	240	53.10	2	1	257	9	28.55	2/58	0	0	2	
		1920/21	1921/22	9	16	0	656	240	41.00	2	1	401	13	30.84	3/85	0	0	2	
Matthews BA	(T)	1989/90		1								45	1	45.00	1/45	0	0	0	
	(TB)	1989/90		2	1	1	28	28*		0	0	195	10	19.50	4/43	0	0	0	
		1984/85	1989/90	37	35	18	157	28*	9.23	0	0	2742	116	23.63	5/32	1	0	6	
Matthews JP	(T)	1973/74		2	2	1	10	8	10.00	0	0	119	2	59.50	2/52	0	0	0	
	(TB)	1973/74	1977/78	4	2	1	8	8*	8.00	0	0	189	8	23.62	3/48	0	0	2	
		1971/72	1977/78	10	6	3	19	8*	6.33	0	0	660	20	33.00	3/48	0	0	3	
Meintjes DJ	(T)	1911/12	1925/26	30	46	4	780	87	18.57	0	1	1276	52	24.53	8/63	1	1	16	
		1910/11	1925/26	52	78	7	1146	87	16.14	0	2	2698	91	29.64	8/63	1	1	25	
Melle BG von B	(T)	1923/24		6	5	0	161	59	32.20	0	1	164	8	20.50	5/47	1	0	3	
		1908/09	1923/24	62	101	9	2535	145	27.55	3	13	2931	114	25.71	7/48	9	1	33	
Melle MG	(T)	1948/49	1951/52	14	20	4	193	50	12.06	0	1	929	43	21.60	8/8	1	1	4	
		1948/49	1953/54	52	68	20	544	59	11.33	0	2	3990	160	24.93	9/22	6	2	22	
Melville A	(T)	1936/37	1948/49	22	29	2	1091	153	40.40	1	7	4	0			0	0	13	
		1928/29	1948/49	190	295	15	10598	189	37.85	25	53	3959	132	29.99	5/17	7	0	156	
Meyer JR	(TB)	1993/94		1								73	2	36.50	1/25	0	0	0	
		1990/91	1993/94	12	16	1	152	32	10.13	0	0	830	30	27.66	3/33	0	0	2	
Milton JG	(T)	1913/14		1	1	0	6	6	6.00	0	0	43	1	43.00	1/43	0	0	0	
		1913/14		2	3	0	23	13	7.66	0	0	121	1	121.00	1/43	0	0	0	
Minnaar N	(T)	1979/80		2	1	0	8	8	8.00	0	0	142	5	28.40	4/71	0	0	0	
	(TB)	1979/80		4	8	1	127	78	18.14	0	1	246	13	18.92	5/61	1	0	6	
		1972/73	1979/80	16	27	3	273	78	11.37	0	1	973	44	22.11	5/61	1	0	9	
Mitchell B	(T)	1925/26	1949/50	56	82	15	3282	179	48.98	8	16	3277	154	21.27	6/33	12	2	81	
		1925/26	1949/50	173	281	30	11395	195	45.39	30	55	6382	249	25.63	6/33	15	2	228	

		First	Last	M	I	NO	Runs	HS	Avg	100	50	Runs	Wkts	Avg	Best	5i	10m	ct	st
Mitchell DH	(T)	1954/55		2	3	0	16	10	5.33	0	0	161	4	40.25	3/58	0	0	2	
		1954/55	1957/58	3	4	1	21	10	7.00	0	0	202	5	40.40	3/58	0	0	3	
Mitchell F	(T)	1902/03	1903/04	7	10	1	414	102	46.00	1	3							5	
		1894	1914	199	306	19	9176	194	31.97	17	40	834	36	23.16	5/57	1	0	148	2
Mitchell JC	(TB)	1975/76		1	2	0	5	4	2.50	0	0	109	9	12.11	6/64	1	0	0	
		1969/70	1978/79	49	93	5	2184	77	24.81	0	13	1754	56	31.32	6/54	3	0	28	
Mitchley CD	(T)	1982/83	1984/85	8	6	1	95	25*	19.00	0	0	651	34	19.14	6/53	1	0	2	
	(TB)	1982/83	1988/89	26	40	5	450	44	12.85	0	0	2184	95	22.98	5/39	4	0	13	
		1982/83	1991/92	52	71	11	801	58	13.35	0	1	4305	192	22.42	6/53	9	0	25	
Mitchley CJ	(TB)	1967/68	1968/69	8	11	0	224	66	20.36	0	2							20	9
Mitchley MJ	(T)	1990/91	1991/92	2	4	0	53	23	13.25	0	0							1	
	(TB)	1986/87	1991/92	27	45	5	1147	156	28.67	2	5	139	2	69.50	1/5	0	0	30	
		1986/87	1992/93	32	55	5	1302	156	26.04	2	5	139	2	69.50	1/5	0	0	31	
Moore BP	(TB)	1973/74	1976/77	3	3	1	6	4	3.00	0	0	137	4	34.25	1/18	0	0	1	
		1973/74	1976/77	5	7	3	23	11*	5.75	0	0	272	5	54.40	1/18	0	0	2	
Morkel JWH	(T)	1912/13	1913/14	6	10	0	175	84	17.50	0	1	39	0			0	0	4	
Morrison I	(T)	1956/57		1	1	0	0	0	0.00	0	0							1	
		1956/57		2	3	0	23	14	7.66	0	0							1	
Morton H	(T)	1897/98		1	1	1	13	13*		0	0							1	1
Mosenthal HF	(T)	1889/90		1	1	0	5	5	5.00	0	0							0	
Moses EC (later changed name to Murray EC)																			
	(T)	1912/13	1922/23	8	12	1	109	31	9.90	0	0	251	16	15.68	4/32	0	0	7	
		1911	1922/23	11	18	1	125	31	7.35	0	0	291	17	17.11	4/32	0	0	10	
Mossop DN	(TB)	1974/75	1975/76	4	5	3	27	14	13.50	0	0	270	7	38.57	3/46	0	0	0	
Motley AW	(T)	1964/65		1	1	0	22	22	22.00	0	0	23	1	23.00	1/23	0	0	0	
	(TB)	1959/60	1965/66	10	15	3	211	49	17.58	0	0	572	26	22.00	5/75	1	0	2	
		1959/60	1965/66	11	16	3	233	49	17.92	0	0	595	27	22.03	5/75	1	0	2	
Motley KG	(T)	1982/83		1	1	0	11	11	11.00	0	0							0	
	(TB)	1982/83		1	2	0	23	23	11.50	0	0	56	0			0	0	0	
		1978/79	1982/83	24	45	7	856	97	22.52	0	2	102	3	34.00	1/9	0	0	15	
Moulder JH	(T)	1909/10	1912/13	10	16	2	195	34	13.92	0	0	210	6	35.00	3/33	0	0	4	
		1902	1912/13	36	52	6	757	70	16.45	0	1	413	14	29.50	3/33	0	0	13	
Muller GAB	(T)	1964/65		2	3	1	1	1	0.50	0	0	102	0			0	0	3	
Muller HSJ	(T)	1951/52		3	4	2	14	6*	7.00	0	0	287	5	57.40	1/45	0	0	0	
Murray EC - see Moses EC																			
Muzzell RK	(T)	1968/69	1976/77	32	60	4	1906	168	34.03	3	6	138	2	69.00	2/12	0	0	14	
	(TB)	1969/70	1977/78	11	14	1	494	238*	38.00	1	1	500	25	20.00	6/69	1	0	11	
		1964/65	1977/78	75	128	12	4052	238*	34.93	7	18	2028	61	33.24	6/69	1	0	49	
Needham PG	(T)	1950/51	1960/61	6	7	4	6	4	2.00	0	0	506	13	38.92	4/43	0	0	1	
Neilson DR	(T)	1972/73	1980/81	75	90	27	1146	67	18.19	0	1	6140	242	25.37	6/38	10	1	29	
	(TB)	1968/69	1975/76	12	17	6	450	78	40.90	0	4	515	15	34.33	3/33	0	0	6	
		1968/69	1980/81	87	107	33	1596	78	21.56	0	5	6655	257	25.89	6/38	10	1	35	
Nel JG	(T)	1945/46	1948/49	5	6	1	6	5	1.20	0	0	210	8	26.25	4/52	0	0	1	
Nelson TD	(T)	1923/24		1	2	0	7	7	3.50	0	0							1	

		First	Last	M	I	NO	Runs	HS	Avg	100	50	Runs	Wkts	Avg	Best	5i	10m	ct	st
Neser VH	(T)	1921/22	1924/25	6	11	0	286	90	26.00	0	3							12	6
		1919	1924/25	18	29	2	743	90	27.51	0	7							28	15
Neustetel CM	(T)	1906/07		2	3	0	14	9	4.66	0	0							2	
Newberry C	(T)	1910/11	1913/14	12	16	3	189	42	14.53	0	0	945	38	24.86	6/28	1	0	18	
		1910/11	1913/14	16	24	3	251	42	11.95	0	0	1213	49	24.75	6/28	1	0	21	
Newby WC	(T)	1889/90		1	1	0	2	2	2.00	0	0	8	0			0	0	2	
Newnham LCA	(T)	1920/21		1	1	0	9	9	9.00	0	0	26	3	8.66	3/14	0	0	0	
		1903/04	1920/21	2	3	0	12	9	4.00	0	0	64	5	12.80	3/14	0	0	0	
Newson ES	(T)	1929/30	1939/40	10	11	1	121	30	12.10	0	0	553	26	21.26	4/51	0	0	8	
		1929/30	1949/50	24	34	3	553	114	17.83	1	2	1562	60	26.03	5/54	1	0	13	
Nickel A	(T)	1951/52	1953/54	6	8	1	35	14	5.00	0	0	374	18	20.77	7/43	1	1	3	
Niemeyer WE	(T)	1903/04	1906/07	4	5	1	7	5	1.75	0	0	83	4	20.75	3/17	0	0	5	
Nimr-Springer MC	(TB)	1976/77		1	1	1	14	14*		0	0	41	1	41.00	1/21	0	0	0	
		1976/77	1978/79	6	4	1	34	15	11.33	0	0	469	12	39.08	3/21	0	0	4	
Norden RW	(T)	1903/04	1906/07	8	13	5	128	45*	16.00	0	0	290	20	14.50	8/12	1	1	7	
Norris CR	(T)	1984/85		6	11	0	141	55	12.81	0	1	198	10	19.80	3/27	0	0	6	
	(TB)	1982/83	1985/86	20	35	8	1020	126*	37.77	3	2	1072	48	22.33	7/31	2	0	13	
		1982/83	1993/94	56	96	12	2479	126*	29.51	3	12	1844	74	24.91	7/31	2	0	40	
Nourse AW	(T)	1925/26	1926/27	9	9	0	634	204	70.44	3	2	209	11	19.00	3/14	0	0	9	
		1896/97	1935/36	228	371	39	14216	304*	42.81	38	60	7125	305	23.36	6/33	13	1	171	
Nupen EP	(T)	1920/21	1936/37	38	47	2	832	89	18.48	0	5	3165	219	14.45	9/48	23	9	13	
		1920/21	1936/37	74	105	14	1635	89	17.96	0	8	6077	334	18.19	9/48	33	12	34	
Nupen NRP	(T)	1945/46		1	1	0	2	2	2.00	0	0							0	
Ochse AE	(T)	1890/91	1894/95	3	6	0	215	99	35.83	0	1	75	2	37.50	2/27	0	0	1	
		1888/89	1894/95	5	10	0	231	99	23.10	0	1	75	2	37.50	2/27	0	0	1	
O'Linn S	(T)	1957/58	1965/66	32	52	7	1673	102	37.17	1	11	90	2	45.00	2/14	0	0	45	3
	(TB)	1959/60	1962/63	5	7	2	400	120*	80.00	1	3	17	0			0	0	8	
		1945/46	1965/66	92	156	29	4525	120*	35.62	4	29	119	2	59.50	2/14	0	0	97	6
Ontong RC	(T)	1976/77	1977/78	13	16	3	183	54	14.07	0	1	937	34	27.55	4/30	0	0	4	
	(TB)	1977/78		1	2	0	28	16	14.00	0	0	140	4	35.00	4/111	0	0	1	
		1972/73	1989/90	362	596	86	15071	204*	29.55	20	77	25972	836	31.06	8/67	33	4	178	
Oxenham HA	(T)	1906/07		1	1	0	5	5	5.00	0	0	28	1	28.00	1/21	0	0	0	
Page HA	(T)	1981/82	1993/94	44	53	12	758	58	18.48	0	2	3301	144	22.92	7/38	3	0	10	
	(TB)	1981/82	1988/89	17	27	8	554	57	29.15	0	2	1120	55	20.36	5/44	1	0	4	
		1981/82	1993/94	84	111	28	1695	60	20.42	0	5	6427	258	24.91	7/38	5	0	22	
Park M	(TB)	1981/82	1983/84	3	2	2	3	2*		0	0	207	9	23.00	3/47	0	0	0	
Parker GC	(T)	1929/30		1	1	0	35	35	35.00	0	0	19	1	19.00	1/19	0	0	0	
		1929/30	1937/38	2	3	1	71	35	35.50	0	0	19	1	19.00	1/19	0	0	1	
Parkin DC	(T)	1898/99		1	2	1	25	14	25.00	0	0	108	1	108.00	1/108	0	0	3	
		1889/90	1902/03	12	24	2	334	63*	15.18	0	1	974	48	20.29	6/25	3	1	8	
Parkin DHC	(T)	1945/46		1	2	1	32	31	32.00	0	0	3	0			0	0	0	
Parkyns SC	(T)	1936/37	1937/38	4	5	3	34	21*	17.00	0	0	310	19	16.31	5/21	1	0	2	
		1936/37	1937/38	5	6	3	35	21*	11.66	0	0	407	22	18.50	5/21	1	0	3	

		First	Last	M	I	NO	Runs	HS	Avg	100	50	Runs	Wkts	Avg	Best	5i	10m	ct	st
Parrymore TH	(T)	1982/83		3	2	2	18	14*		0	0	188	12	15.66	4/8	0	0	0	
	(TB)	1982/83	1986/87	5	7	3	37	13*	9.25	0	0	401	20	20.05	4/49	0	0	1	
		1982/83	1986/87	8	9	5	55	14*	13.75	0	0	589	32	18.40	4/8	0	0	1	
Patel MF	(TB)	1977/78		2	2	1	28	15*	28.00	0	0	93	1	93.00	1/27	0	0	1	
Patrick WE	(T)	1955/56	1961/62	13	23	1	422	60	19.18	0	2							5	
	(TB)	1959/60		1	2	0	34	21	17.00	0	0							2	
		1955/56	1961/62	15	26	1	481	60	19.24	0	2							9	
Peens A	(TB)	1983/84		3	6	0	80	39	13.33	0	0							3	
Pegler SJ	(T)	1908/09	1912/13	6	8	0	83	36	10.37	0	0	198	7	28.28	4/22	0	0	1	
		1908/09	1930	103	150	18	1677	79	12.70	0	5	8324	425	19.58	8/54	32	5	56	
Perring JB	(T)	1913/14	1922/23	12	17	0	440	70	25.88	0	3	139	4	34.75	2/28	0	0	2	
Petersen RNE	(T)	1939/40	1941/42	6	5	2	85	43*	28.33	0	0	257	12	21.41	3/26	0	0	5	
		1939/40	1942/43	7	6	2	90	43*	22.50	0	0	312	15	20.80	3/26	0	0	5	
Phillips JG	(T)	1937/38		1	2	0	2	2	1.00	0	0	36	3	12.00	2/33	0	0	1	
		1931/32	1937/38	16	31	2	667	100	23.00	1	3	487	22	22.13	7/51	2	0	5	
Pickerill JHM	(T)	1936/37	1949/50	16	21	3	321	72*	17.83	0	2	272	10	27.20	3/5	0	0	15	
		1936/37	1951/52	24	36	5	1027	143*	33.12	3	4	352	13	27.07	3/5	0	0	23	
Pickerill VJ	(T)	1919/20	1923/24	8	10	2	119	34	14.87	0	0	486	23	21.13	5/26	1	0	4	
Pienaar RF	(T)	1979/80	1992/93	42	76	9	2623	152*	39.14	6	13	385	9	42.77	2/34	0	0	18	
	(TB)	1977/78	1980/81	14	24	2	619	71	28.13	0	6	558	25	22.32	4/35	0	0	8	
		1977/78	1993/94	171	295	26	9538	153	35.45	17	53	5079	153	33.19	5/24	3	0	71	
Pinkerton AD	(T)	1950/51	1954/55	13	20	2	508	82	28.22	0	3	370	6	61.66	2/6	0	0	8	
Pistorius DI	(T)	1956/57	1961/62	3	4	0	36	19	9.00	0	0	163	4	40.75	3/39	0	0	3	
	(TB)	1960/61		1	2	0	34	20	17.00	0	0	42	2	21.00	1/17	0	0	2	
		1956/57	1961/62	4	6	0	70	20	11.66	0	0	205	6	34.16	3/39	0	0	5	
Pithey DB	(T)	1967/68		6	7	0	120	51	17.14	0	1	518	16	32.37	5/130	1	0	1	
		1956/57	1967/68	99	160	13	3420	166	23.26	3	14	7388	240	30.78	7/47	13	1	55	
Piton JHD	(T)	1889/90	1890/91	2	3	1	77	37	38.50	0	0	204	13	15.69	7/82	2	1	4	
		1889/90	1893/94	5	8	1	138	37	19.71	0	0	222	13	17.07	7/82	2	1	6	
Plint AJ	(TB)	1979/80	1981/82	7	12	2	228	39*	22.80	0	0	353	11	32.09	3/60	0	0	5	
		1979/80	1989/90	8	14	3	233	39*	21.18	0	0	529	17	31.11	4/82	0	0	6	
Pollock AG	(T)	1991/92		1	1	1	2	2*		0	0	72	0			0	0	0	
	(TB)	1991/92	1993/94	8	7	5	27	11	13.50	0	0	591	29	20.37	4/57	0	0	1	
		1991/92	1993/94	9	8	6	29	11	14.50	0	0	663	29	22.86	4/57	0	0	1	
Pollock GA	(T)	1991/92		1	2	1	66	49	66.00	0	0							0	
	(TB)	1991/92	1993/94	5	10	0	304	115	30.40	1	1							2	
		1991/92	1993/94	6	12	1	370	115	33.63	1	1							2	
Pollock RG	(T)	1978/79	1986/87	67	101	14	4804	233	55.21	14	24	21	0			0	0	57	
		1960/61	1986/87	262	437	54	20940	274	54.67	64	99	2062	43	47.95	3/46	0	0	248	
Porter FW	(T)	1911/12		1	1	0	32	32	32.00	0	0							0	
		1908/09	1926/27	11	19	0	307	62	16.15	0	1	203	10	20.30	4/70	0	0	5	
Pothas N	(T)	1993/94		5	8	0	122	45	15.25	0	0							17	2
	(TB)	1993/94		3	3	1	27	13	13.50	0	0							8	
		1993/94		8	11	1	149	45	14.90	0	0							25	2

		First	Last	M	I	NO	Runs	HS	Avg	100	50	Runs	Wkts	Avg	Best	5i	10m	ct	st
Quinn NA	(T)	1933/34		2	3	1	35	24*	17.50	0	0	251	4	62.75	2/73	0	0	1	
		1927/28	1933/34	51	63	15	438	32	9.12	0	0	3866	186	20.78	8/37	12	3	10	
Radford NV	(T)	1979/80	1988/89	59	56	13	424	45	9.86	0	0	5193	233	22.28	9/102	10	1	29	
	(TB)	1978/79	1980/81	15	21	5	394	45	24.62	0	0	1390	61	22.78	6/41	3	1	9	
		1978/79	1994	286	287	71	3407	76*	15.77	0	7	25927	972	26.67	9/70	46	7	130	
Rael LC	(TB)	1965/66		4	7	0	76	35	10.85	0	0	174	7	24.85	6/105	1	0	3	
Ralph WW	(T)	1946/47		4	5	2	6	3	2.00	0	0	179	4	44.75	2/19	0	0	1	
Ralphs H	(T)	1945/46		1	1	0	26	26	26.00	0	0							0	
		1945/46	1951/52	10	18	1	608	157	35.76	2	1							12	9
Rankin GK	(T)	1933/34		1	1	0	1	1	1.00	0	0	34	0			0	0	0	
Redick AW	(T)	1912/13	1921/22	7	11	4	82	29	11.71	0	0	312	12	26.00	4/69	0	0	6	
		1912/13	1921/22	8	13	4	86	29	9.55	0	0	395	14	28.21	4/69	0	0	9	
Reich W	(TB)	1963/64		1	2	1	7	4*	7.00	0	0	48	4	12.00	3/21	0	0	0	
Reid RB	(TB)	1981/82		1	2	0	19	13	9.50	0	0	5	2	2.50	2/5	0	0	0	
		1979/80	1991/92	43	78	6	1789	107	24.84	1	11	14	2	7.00	2/5	0	0	27	
Reid WO	(T)	1892/93	1894/95	4	7	1	103	49*	17.16	0	0	19	4	4.75	4/19	0	0	1	
Reilly NMD	(T)	1966/67	1967/68	7	8	4	90	37	22.50	0	0	280	12	23.33	3/20	0	0	1	
	(TB)	1965/66	1966/67	5	8	0	140	41	17.50	0	0	566	8	70.75	2/45	0	0	1	
		1957/58	1967/68	42	69	5	1256	136	19.62	1	3	2499	72	34.70	6/37	2	0	28	
Rex AC	(T)	1962/63	1964/65	11	20	0	557	102	27.85	1	1	5	0			0	0	7	
	(TB)	1962/63	1965/66	6	11	0	411	81	37.36	0	4	19	0			0	0	3	
		1962/63	1965/66	17	31	0	968	102	31.22	1	5	24	0			0	0	10	
Rhodes NR	(TB)	1993/94		3	3	0	122	67	40.66	0	1							3	
Rice CEB	(T)	1970/71	1991/92	160	255	46	7632	150*	36.51	11	39	7644	366	20.88	7/62	9	1	109	
	(TB)	1969/70	1972/73	6	8	2	296	81	49.33	0	3	475	30	15.83	5/65	1	0	2	
		1969/70	1993/94	482	766	123	26331	246	40.95	48	137	20922	930	22.49	7/62	23	1	401	
Richards BA	(T)	1970/71		1	2	0	207	140	103.50	1	1							0	
		1964/65	1982/83	339	576	58	28358	356	54.74	80	152	2886	77	37.48	7/63	1	0	367	
Richardson JH	(TB)	1959/60	1960/61	6	12	2	247	64	24.70	0	2							15	4
		1952/53	1960/61	22	42	3	785	72	20.12	0	4							41	7
Ridgway RK	(TB)	1962/63		1	2	1	9	8	9.00	0	0	69	1	69.00	1/42	0	0	0	
		1956/57	1962/63	4	5	2	44	16*	14.66	0	0	241	9	26.77	4/34	0	0	1	
Riley JR	(TB)	1986/87		6	2	1	6	6	6.00	0	0	534	9	59.33	2/50	0	0	2	
Rindel MJR	(TB)	1983/84		3	6	1	141	81	28.20	0	1	49	2	24.50	1/17	0	0	2	
		1983/84	1993/94	71	133	15	4358	157*	36.93	9	21	973	22	44.22	2/13	0	0	43	
Rippon WV	(TB)	1991/92	1993/94	5	8	0	266	92	33.25	0	3	18	0			0	0	3	
		1985/86	1993/94	9	15	0	335	92	22.33	0	3	18	0			0	0	5	
Ritchie GG	(T)	1954/55	1965/66	28	51	3	758	59	15.79	0	1	579	14	41.35	3/29	0	0	26	
	(TB)	1959/60	1968/69	23	35	0	999	107	28.54	1	7	826	24	34.41	4/38	0	0	23	
		1954/55	1968/69	51	86	3	1757	107	21.16	1	8	1405	38	36.97	4/38	0	0	49	
Rivett CW	(T)	1949/50		1	2	1	12	12*	12.00	0	0	80	2	40.00	2/65	0	0	0	
Roberts B	(T)	1982/83	1988/89	18	27	3	799	174	33.29	2	1	34	1	34.00	1/4	0	0	13	
	(TB)	1982/83	1988/89	31	54	2	1638	130	31.50	1	11	1110	44	25.22	5/68	1	0	27	
		1982/83	1991	205	333	34	9182	184	30.70	13	40	2948	89	33.12	5/68	1	0	166	1

		First	Last	M	I	NO	Runs	HS	Avg	100	50	Runs	Wkts	Avg	Best	5i	10m	ct	st
Rogers S	(TB)	1963/64		1	2	0	7	6	3.50	0	0							0	
Roothman JB	(T)	1947/48	1949/50	8	12	0	310	76	25.83	0	2							4	
		1947/48	1952/53	18	31	1	857	99	28.56	0	4	0	0			0	0	10	
Rose A	(T)	1904/05		2	2	1	52	42*	52.00	0	0	60	4	15.00	3/43	0	0	1	
Rose RSK	(T)	1934/35	1946/47	7	8	3	9	4	1.80	0	0	461	21	21.95	6/46	1	0	4	
		1933/34	1946/47	10	13	4	17	5*	1.88	0	0	847	29	29.20	6/46	1	0	5	
Rose-Innes A	(T)	1893/94		2	4	2	21	10	10.50	0	0	46	4	11.50	2/9	0	0	0	
		1888/89	1893/94	7	13	4	70	20	7.77	0	0	311	18	17.27	5/43	1	0	5	
Rosholt AM	(T)	1945/46		1	1	0	31	31	31.00	0	0							0	
Routledge TW	(T)	1892/93	1896/97	7	14	1	387	77	29.76	0	2	69	3	23.00	2/26	0	0	3	
		1889/90	1896/97	12	24	1	492	77	21.39	0	2	69	3	23.00	2/26	0	0	5	
Rowan AMB	(T)	1939/40	1949/50	15	20	5	374	71*	24.93	0	2	1589	94	16.90	9/19	8	3	7	
		1939/40	1951	58	82	20	1492	100*	24.06	1	4	6408	273	23.47	9/19	20	7	25	
Rowan DA	(T)	1947/48		4	1	0	1	1	1.00	0	0	479	19	25.21	7/91	1	0	1	
Rowan EAB	(T)	1929/30	1953/54	77	125	7	5902	306*	50.01	15	27	29	0			0	0	42	
		1929/30	1953/54	157	258	17	11710	306*	48.58	30	54	168	4	42.00	3/11	0	0	83	
Rubidge Y	(TB)	1980/81		6	8	1	71	21	10.14	0	0							9	
Rule KJ	(T)	1984/85	1989/90	5	8	0	35	9	4.37	0	0							3	
	(TB)	1983/84	1989/90	24	42	2	1195	112*	29.87	2	6	6	0			0	0	27	1
		1983/84	1993/94	38	68	6	1793	122	28.91	4	9	6	0			0	0	51	3
Rush WRG	(T)	1925/26	1928/29	4	5	0	81	38	16.20	0	0	188	4	47.00	1/19	0	0	1	
		1923/24	1928/29	9	15	0	273	79	18.20	0	1	629	21	29.95	5/53	2	0	2	
Rushmere MW	(T)	1993/94		8	13	2	358	82*	32.54	0	3	8	0			0	0	3	
	(TB)	1993/94		1	1	0	188	188	188.00	1	0							1	
		1983/84	1993/94	91	162	28	5770	188	43.05	16	25	41	2	20.50	1/0	0	0	52	
Rutherfoord JHH	(T)	1912/13		2	4	0	8	6	2.00	0	0							2	
Sacco D	(TB)	1962/63		5	8	0	217	80	27.12	0	1							4	
Sadler LA	(T)	1945/46	1952/53	9	15	1	416	85	29.71	0	3							3	
Sansbury DJ	(TB)	1975/76		1	1	1	3	3*		0	0	51	3	17.00	3/51	0	0	0	
Saunders RO	(T)	1912/13	1913/14	4	8	1	78	20	11.14	0	0	198	6	33.00	4/109	0	0	2	
Schuurman DJ	(T)	1890/91	1894/95	2	4	2	88	50	44.00	0	1	27	0			0	0	2	
Schwarz RO	(T)	1902/03	1909/10	20	28	2	742	78	28.53	0	6	779	60	12.98	7/25	3	0	28	
		1901	1914	125	192	24	3798	102	22.60	1	20	7000	398	17.58	8/55	25	3	108	
Scott M	(TB)	1959/60		2	2	2	3	2*		0	0	107	8	13.37	4/20	0	0	2	
Scott MWL	(T)	1971/72		1	1	1	0	0*		0	0	97	3	32.33	3/73	0	0	1	
		1965/66	1971/72	15	22	8	79	38	5.64	0	0	1279	46	27.80	5/47	1	0	8	
Seccombe DT	(TB)	1972/73	1976/77	17	31	0	787	120	25.38	1	2	10	0			0	0	7	
Seccombe JT	(T)	1939/40	1945/46	5	8	0	176	58	22.00	0	1							2	
		1939/40	1948/49	14	26	1	775	114	31.00	1	4							6	
Seccull AW	(T)	1894/95	1896/97	2	4	1	82	64	27.33	0	1	108	4	27.00	3/46	0	0	1	
		1889/90	1896/97	7	12	2	229	64	22.90	0	2	253	15	16.86	6/48	1	0	4	
Seeff L	(T)	1991/92	1992/93	8	14	2	465	87	38.75	0	4							6	
		1977/78	1992/93	113	210	20	6558	188	34.51	11	36	148	5	29.60	1/6	0	0	90	

		First	Last	M	I	NO	Runs	HS	Avg	100	50	Runs	Wkts	Avg	Best	5i	10m	ct	st
Selsick PL	(TB)	1983/84	1990/91	11	21	2	581	183	30.57	1	2							6	
		1983/84	1990/91	16	31	2	686	183	23.65	1	2	12	0			0	0	9	
Serrurier LR	(T)	1931/32		1	1	0	56	56	56.00	0	1	30	1	30.00	1/11	0	0	2	
		1925	1931/32	30	46	8	1281	171	33.71	3	7	1127	42	26.83	5/103	1	0	17	
Shalders WA	(T)	1902/03	1906/07	13	21	1	447	93	22.35	0	2	27	0			0	0	4	
		1897/98	1908/09	88	152	8	3351	105	23.27	2	14	139	6	23.16	3/30	0	0	38	
Shaw BP	(T)	1945/46	1947/48	7	11	1	218	60	21.80	0	2	369	11	33.54	3/16	0	0	5	
Shepstone GH	(T)	1897/98	1904/05	13	19	1	432	104	24.00	1	0	563	35	16.08	5/17	3	1	5	
		1895/96	1904/05	22	34	1	693	104	21.00	1	1	682	42	16.23	5/17	3	1	11	
Sherwell PW	(T)	1902/03	1906/07	9	13	0	274	71	21.07	0	2							13	8
		1902/03	1913/14	58	91	16	1808	144	24.10	3	6							67	53
Siebert KH	(T)	1957/58		1	2	1	12	6*	12.00	0	0	51	2	25.50	1/4	0	0	0	
Simon A	(TB)	1965/66		2	4	1	125	52*	41.66	0	1							3	
Sinclair DM	(T)	1903/04	1904/05	2	2	0	26	26	13.00	0	0	57	5	11.40	3/22	0	0	2	
Sinclair JH	(T)	1892/93	1911/12	36	58	1	1117	136	19.59	1	6	3088	193	16.00	8/40	19	5	25	
		1892/93	1911/12	129	214	6	4483	136	21.55	6	21	10527	491	21.43	8/32	33	10	65	
Skjoldhammer KP	(T)	1982/83		1	1	0	0	0	0.00	0	0	129	2	64.50	1/3	0	0	0	
	(TB)	1979/80	1981/82	6	10	3	72	16*	10.28	0	0	372	14	26.57	4/56	0	0	3	
		1979/80	1982/83	7	11	3	72	16*	9.00	0	0	501	16	31.31	4/56	0	0	3	
Skottowe AB	(T)	1920/21	1922/23	6	8	0	14	6	1.75	0	0	424	16	26.50	4/43	0	0	3	
Slatem JJ	(T)	1893/94	1905/06	17	27	1	728	154	28.00	1	3	69	4	17.25	3/6	0	0	7	1
Smith CA	(T)	1889/90		1	2	0	18	18	9.00	0	0	97	7	13.85	4/36	0	0	1	
		1882	1896	143	247	28	2986	85	13.63	0	10	7730	346	22.34	7/16	19	1	97	
Smith CA	(T)	1923/24		1	2	0	17	12	8.50	0	0	16	0			0	0	1	
Smith CJE	(T)	1893/94	1904/05	7	12	0	303	70	25.25	0	2	102	2	51.00	2/28	0	0	6	
		1893/94	1904/05	10	18	1	409	70	24.05	0	2	102	2	51.00	2/28	0	0	8	
Smith FE	(T)	1906/07		1	2	0	31	28	15.50	0	0	43	0			0	0	0	
		1893	1908	68	87	28	578	45	9.79	0	0	3951	194	20.36	6/12	9	3	31	
Smith FW	(T)	1890/91	1893/94	2	4	0	95	43	23.75	0	0	133	3	44.33	2/73	0	0	0	
		1888/89	1895/96	5	10	1	140	43	15.55	0	0	133	3	44.33	2/73	0	0	2	
Smith FW	(T)	1941/42		1	2	0	14	9	7.00	0	0							0	
Smith HE	(T)	1905/06	1906/07	4	6	0	138	53	23.00	0	1							1	
		1905/06	1908/09	15	23	2	395	53	18.80	0	1							2	
Smith PE	(T)	1989/90	1991/92	3	4	2	17	9*	8.50	0	0	169	6	28.16	3/36	0	0	0	
	(TB)	1987/88	1993/94	17	17	6	97	37	8.81	0	0	1391	55	25.29	5/50	1	0	3	
		1984/85	1993/94	33	43	18	261	37	10.44	0	0	2421	82	29.52	5/50	1	0	7	
Smith SB	(T)	1989/90	1990/91	18	32	2	849	115	28.30	1	4	40	1	40.00	1/35	0	0	18	
		1981/82	1990/91	90	155	9	5248	263	35.94	12	26	77	1	77.00	1/35	0	0	66	
Snell RP	(T)	1988/89	1993/94	27	34	4	361	44	12.03	0	0	2543	107	23.76	6/33	6	1	6	
	(TB)	1988/89		1	2	1	5	3*	5.00	0	0	71	2	35.50	2/56	0	0	0	
		1987/88	1994	62	78	14	1104	94	17.25	0	4	5351	191	28.01	6/33	6	1	16	
Snooke S de la C	(T)	1920/21		1	1	0	50	50	50.00	0	1							3	
		1904/05	1920/21	32	53	5	798	74	16.62	0	4	224	19	11.78	7/29	1	1	31	
Snooke SJ	(T)	1909/10	1923/24	5	7	0	176	64	25.14	0	2	180	3	60.00	1/9	0	0	1	
		1897/98	1923/24	124	202	16	4821	187	25.91	7	24	3017	120	25.14	8/70	3	1	82	

		First	Last	M	I	NO	Runs	HS	Avg	100	50	Runs	Wkts	Avg	Best	5i	10m	ct	st
Snyman OJA	(TB)	1977/78		3	6	0	72	24	12.00	0	0	3	0			0	0	2	
		1972/73	1977/78	13	23	1	546	133*	24.81	1	2	123	4	30.75	2/35	0	0	7	
Solomon WRT	(T)	1892/93	1898/99	3	5	1	61	52	15.25	0	1							3	
		1892/93	1905/06	5	9	1	73	52	9.12	0	1	6	1	6.00	1/6	0	0	5	
Somers Vine RE	(T)	1931/32	1945/46	7	13	1	449	119	37.41	1	2	103	0			0	0	2	
		1931/32	1945/46	10	19	2	508	119	29.88	1	2	115	0			0	0	5	
Spencer-Young R	(TB)	1967/68		1	1	0	62	62	62.00	0	1							0	
		1962/63	1967/68	10	19	0	502	94	26.42	0	5	0	0			0	0	13	
Sprenger AH	(T)	1923/24		1	2	0	10	10	5.00	0	0							0	
		1908/09	1923/24	11	21	4	223	56	13.11	0	1	218	11	19.81	4/38	0	0	7	
Stanley S	(T)	1959/60	1960/61	5	6	1	11	6	2.20	0	0	634	20	31.70	5/60	2	1	0	
	(TB)	1959/60		1	2	2	6	5*		0	0	89	2	44.50	2/89	0	0	0	
		1959/60	1963/64	14	24	7	70	16	4.11	0	0	1540	49	31.42	5/60	2	1	2	
Stein GH	(T)	1952/53		3	6	2	110	38*	27.50	0	0							2	
	(TB)	1960/61		6	12	0	385	88	32.08	0	3							1	
		1952/53	1960/61	9	18	2	495	88	30.93	0	3							3	
Stephens CG	(T)	1972/73	1974/75	4	8	1	210	49	30.00	0	0							5	
	(TB)	1973/74	1977/78	12	21	4	736	150*	43.29	3	1							14	
		1968/69	1977/78	38	63	11	2273	165	43.71	7	7	2	0			0	0	41	
Stevenson GD	(T)	1992/93	1993/94	2	1	0	16	16	16.00	0	0	225	2	112.50	1/83	0	0	0	
	(TB)	1990/91	1993/94	12	10	4	110	40*	18.33	0	0	956	25	38.24	5/76	1	0	6	
		1990/91	1993/94	14	11	4	126	40*	18.00	0	0	1181	27	43.74	5/76	1	0	6	
Stewart DAC	(T)	1948/49	1960/61	7	10	2	71	32	8.87	0	0	376	9	41.77	4/33	0	0	5	
	(TB)	1960/61		2	4	1	100	54	33.33	0	1	63	2	31.50	2/36	0	0	3	
		1948/49	1960/61	9	14	3	171	54	15.54	0	1	439	11	39.90	4/33	0	0	8	
Steyn GE	(T)	1958/59	1962/63	4	7	3	95	23	23.75	0	0	271	11	24.63	5/96	1	0	0	
	(TB)	1962/63	1963/64	9	14	3	353	57	32.09	0	1	749	35	21.40	7/46	2	0	11	
		1957/58	1963/64	24	38	9	529	57	18.24	0	1	1814	92	19.71	7/32	6	0	15	
Steyn SSL	(T)	1930/31		2	3	1	71	40*	35.50	0	0							2	
		1924/25	1937/38	36	61	5	1514	261*	27.03	3	2	102	1	102.00	1/12	0	0	16	
Stoll WA	(T)	1910/11		3	3	0	19	11	6.33	0	0							0	
Stranger T	(T)	1912/13		2	4	1	0	0*	0.00	0	0	107	1	107.00	1/49	0	0	2	
Stricker HB	(T)	1912/13	1913/14	3	4	1	70	66*	23.33	0	1	161	2	80.50	1/23	0	0	3	
Stricker LA	(T)	1906/07	1911/12	7	10	0	374	101	37.40	1	1	21	1	21.00	1/12	0	0	1	
		1906/07	1912	60	96	4	2105	146	22.88	2	9	303	8	37.87	3/13	0	0	29	2
Strydom JJ	(T)	1990/91	1991/92	5	10	1	123	30	13.66	0	0	12	0			0	0	6	
	(TB)	1990/91	1991/92	8	15	3	544	97	45.33	0	6	57	1	57.00	1/42	0	0	6	
		1980/81	1993/94	97	179	17	4404	119*	27.18	8	28	330	11	30.00	3/23	0	0	85	
Sturgeon EH	(T)	1924/25		1	2	1	24	14*	24.00	0	0	17	0			0	0	0	
Susskind MJ	(T)	1912/13	1936/37	48	67	2	2838	171	43.66	9	13	23	0			0	0	52	
		1909	1936/37	97	149	11	4775	171	34.60	11	23	81	1	81.00	1/13	0	0	85	3
Sutherland HJ	(T)	1924/25	1925/26	2	4	0	52	31	13.00	0	0							0	
Sweet NL	(TB)	1969/70		1	2	0	29	25	14.50	0	0							0	
Sylvester MW	(TB)	1967/68		1	1	0	7	7	7.00	0	0							1	
		1967/68	1971/72	3	2	0	70	63	35.00	0	1							1	

		First	Last	M	I	NO	Runs	HS	Avg	100	50	Runs	Wkts	Avg	Best	5i	10m	ct	st
Tagg V	(TB)	1962/63	1963/64	5	9	0	228	71	25.33	0	3	102	0			0	0	9	
Taliadoros GD	(TB)	1979/80		3	6	1	88	41	17.60	0	0							1	
Taliadoros Z	(TB)	1960/61		4	5	3	18	11*	9.00	0	0	364	10	36.40	5/112	1	0	0	
Tancred AB	(T)	1896/97	1898/99	2	4	0	68	39	17.00	0	0	39	1	39.00	1/22	0	0	0	
		1888/89	1898/99	11	21	1	708	106	35.40	1	5	220	8	27.50	3/22	0	0	6	
Tancred LJ	(T)	1896/97	1919/20	31	49	2	1532	160	32.59	4	7	39	2	19.50	1/17	0	0	25	
		1896/97	1919/20	130	219	12	5695	160	27.51	11	27	190	8	23.75	4/43	0	0	73	
Tancred VM	(T)	1897/98	1898/99	6	11	1	267	65	26.70	0	2							4	
		1897/98	1898/99	7	13	1	292	65	24.33	0	2							4	
Tandy JH	(T)	1908/09	1913/14	4	5	2	15	14*	5.00	0	0	73	3	24.33	2/15	0	0	3	
		1908/09	1913/14	5	7	2	26	14*	5.20	0	0	200	9	22.22	4/30	0	0	5	
Tayfield A	(T)	1950/51	1962/63	40	62	5	1263	205	22.15	2	2	1747	59	29.61	6/75	1	1	40	
	(TB)	1959/60		2	2	0	71	36	35.50	0	0	46	5	9.20	5/26	1	0	0	
		1948/49	1962/63	50	74	7	1483	205	22.13	2	4	2537	85	29.84	6/75	3	1	42	
Tayfield C	(T)	1951/52	1957/58	21	35	4	827	102	26.67	1	6	809	35	23.11	4/27	0	0	4	
		1951/52	1963/64	37	65	4	1457	112	23.88	2	8	1490	56	26.60	4/27	0	0	12	
Tayfield HJ	(T)	1956/57	1962/63	27	39	8	747	77	24.09	0	1	2825	109	25.91	6/57	6	1	28	
		1945/46	1962/63	187	259	47	3668	77	17.30	0	10	18890	864	21.86	9/113	67	16	149	
Taylor AI	(T)	1949/50	1960/61	50	85	3	2663	180	32.47	6	11	986	32	30.81	4/52	0	0	32	
		1949/50	1960/61	52	89	3	2717	180	31.59	6	11	986	32	30.81	4/52	0	0	32	
Taylor HW	(T)	1925/26	1930/31	17	23	1	1498	169	68.09	6	7	43	0			0	0	10	
		1909/10	1935/36	206	339	26	13105	250*	41.86	30	64	560	22	25.45	4/36	0	0	75	
Taylor JG	(T)	1939/40		2	2	0	4	4	2.00	0	0	159	4	39.75	2/48	0	0	0	
Teeger JA	(T)	1992/93		3	3	0	13	6	4.33	0	0							10	2
	(TB)	1991/92		4	8	4	75	19	18.75	0	0							12	
		1991/92	1992/93	7	11	4	88	19	12.57	0	0							22	2
Thompson DS	(TB)	1979/80		1	1	0	21	21	21.00	0	0	38	1	38.00	1/22	0	0	0	
Thompson RA	(T)	1908/09	1912/13	10	12	2	79	22	7.90	0	0	517	37	13.97	7/46	1	0	5	
		1908/09	1912/13	11	13	3	99	22	9.90	0	0	541	37	14.62	7/46	1	0	5	
Thorp BD	(T)	1958/59	1964/65	5	7	3	63	45	15.75	0	0	427	16	26.68	4/17	0	0	0	
	(TB)	1959/60	1960/61	9	11	5	91	32	15.16	0	0	638	29	22.00	5/51	1	0	1	
		1958/59	1964/65	15	19	8	156	45	14.18	0	0	1151	51	22.56	5/51	2	0	1	
Tillim AF	(T)	1961/62	1966/67	22	33	4	530	57*	18.27	0	1	1490	58	25.68	7/34	4	0	6	
	(TB)	1962/63	1963/64	5	7	1	72	21	12.00	0	0	500	22	22.72	5/68	1	0	3	
		1958/59	1968/69	36	53	6	729	57*	15.51	0	1	2242	92	24.36	7/34	5	0	11	
Tomlinson OW	(T)	1906/07	1913/14	6	7	4	51	17*	17.00	0	0	250	16	15.62	5/90	1	0	3	
		1906/07	1913/14	8	10	6	87	35	21.75	0	0	288	16	18.00	5/90	1	0	3	
Townsend FN	(T)	1898/99		1	2	0	22	15	11.00	0	0							0	
		1896	1900	12	20	4	230	56	14.37	0	1							13	3
Tross SD	(T)	1913/14		1	1	0	14	14	14.00	0	0							0	
		1913/14		2	3	0	54	40	18.00	0	0							0	
Tucker GB	(TB)	1985/86		2	4	0	52	31	13.00	0	0							1	
Tudhope H	(T)	1890/91	1892/93	3	6	3	43	17	14.33	0	0	410	12	34.16	3/22	0	0	5	
Turner FG	(T)	1941/42		1	2	1	3	2*	3.00	0	0							0	
		1931/32	1941/42	4	7	2	52	19	10.40	0	0	30	1	30.00	1/30	0	0	0	

		First	Last	M	I	NO	Runs	HS	Avg	100	50	Runs	Wkts	Avg	Best	5i	10m	ct	st
Turner GJ	(T)	1992/93		2	3	1	50	27	25.00	0	0							0	
		1984/85	1992/93	44	70	6	1791	101*	27.98	1	10	1539	27	57.00	4/94	0	0	26	
Ulyate CA	(T)	1955/56		1	2	0	26	25	13.00	0	0	61	1	61.00	1/57	0	0	1	
		1955/56	1965/66	4	8	1	110	55	15.71	0	1	178	5	35.60	3/58	0	0	2	
Upton AH	(TB)	1970/71	1971/72	2	4	1	60	44	20.00	0	0							1	
Van Beuge TW	(TB)	1974/75		5	7	0	107	33	15.28	0	0							16	
Van Boeckel PH	(TB)	1983/84		2	4	0	50	16	12.50	0	0							0	
Van der Bijl VAP	(T)	1982/83		8	6	1	63	30	12.60	0	0	715	41	17.43	7/46	1	0	0	
		1967/68	1982/83	156	188	48	2269	87	16.20	0	9	12692	767	16.54	8/35	46	12	51	
Van der Knaap DS	(T)	1971/72	1977/78	21	21	9	193	44	16.08	0	0	1792	57	31.43	6/61	4	0	14	
	(TB)	1967/68	1978/79	21	22	7	96	14*	6.40	0	0	1528	62	24.64	5/37	3	0	25	
		1967	1978/79	43	43	16	289	44	10.70	0	0	3389	121	28.00	6/61	7	0	39	
Van der Linden WJ	(T)	1974/75	1977/78	13	23	1	701	98	31.86	0	4	47	0			0	0	6	
	(TB)	1974/75	1983/84	32	58	6	1316	135*	25.30	2	4	795	30	26.50	4/37	0	0	27	
		1974/75	1983/84	45	81	7	2017	135*	27.25	2	8	842	30	28.06	4/37	0	0	33	
Van der Merwe D	(TB)	1985/86		3	6	0	50	23	8.33	0	0							2	
		1985/86		5	9	0	85	23	9.44	0	0							2	
Van der Merwe EA	(T)	1928/29	1937/38	8	11	2	70	19	7.77	0	0							11	12
		1927/28	1937/38	27	36	9	287	35*	10.62	0	0							35	29
Van der Westhuizen JP	(TB)	1991/92	1993/94	6	9	4	213	46*	42.60	0	0	460	9	51.11	2/8	0	0	3	
Vandrau BM	(TB)	1963/64		2	4	0	46	29	11.50	0	0							0	
Vandrau MJ	(T)	1993/94		1	2	0	29	24	14.50	0	0	114	9	12.66	5/42	1	0	1	
	(TB)	1990/91	1993/94	4	6	1	75	36	15.00	0	0	385	17	22.64	5/85	1	0	1	
		1990/91	1994	33	54	8	943	66	20.50	0	3	2401	68	35.30	5/42	2	0	18	
Van Duyker JC	(TB)	1987/88		1	1	0	3	3	3.00	0	0	70	3	23.33	2/16	0	0	1	
		1982/83	1987/88	19	29	10	98	42	5.15	0	0	1523	72	21.15	6/70	1	1	7	
Van Velden AD	(T)	1946/47		1								31	0			0	0	2	
Van Wezel AW	(T)	1931/32		2	3	1	44	24	22.00	0	0							1	
Van Wyk M	(T)	1972/73	1978/79	3	3	0	8	3	2.66	0	0	149	4	37.25	2/42	0	0	1	
	(TB)	1968/69	1980/81	31	42	8	744	84	21.88	0	3	1466	47	31.19	5/46	2	0	17	
		1968/69	1980/81	34	45	8	752	84	20.32	0	3	1615	51	31.66	5/46	2	0	18	
Van Wyk WH	(TB)	1985/86		4	2	1	0	0*	0.00	0	0	311	15	20.73	7/55	1	0	1	
Varnals GD	(T)	1958/59	1960/61	12	24	0	590	95	24.58	0	5							1	
	(TB)	1959/60		6	10	0	315	65	31.50	0	2							1	
		1955/56	1964/65	49	91	4	2628	151*	30.20	4	15	2	0			0	0	15	
Varty JB	(TB)	1971/72	1972/73	5	7	0	115	49	16.42	0	0							5	
Venn H	(T)	1931/32		1	1	0	8	8	8.00	0	0							1	
Venter JF	(TB)	1990/91		2	3	0	33	22	11.00	0	0							0	
		1989/90	1993/94	28	45	3	1292	193	30.76	1	8	1316	36	36.55	5/14	2	0	11	
Venter MS	(T)	1979/80	1989/90	22	38	5	882	132*	26.72	1	5							18	
	(TB)	1979/80	1989/90	50	96	6	2918	225*	32.42	5	12	21	0			0	0	27	
		1979/80	1989/90	81	151	11	4136	225*	29.54	6	19	21	0			0	0	50	
Vermeulen VBN	(TB)	1991/92		2	4	0	106	78	26.50	0	1							0	

		First	Last	M	I	NO	Runs	HS	Avg	100	50	Runs	Wkts	Avg	Best	5i	10m	ct	st
Videgauz A	(TB)	1981/82		2	3	1	62	57	31.00	0	1							1	
Viljoen A	(TB)	1979/80	1981/82	5	5	0	1	1	0.20	0	0	263	13	20.23	3/54	0	0	1	
Viljoen KG	(T)	1936/37	1948/49	27	39	8	1952	124	62.96	7	8	102	3	34.00	1/11	0	0	7	
		1926/27	1948/49	133	209	25	7964	215	43.28	23	30	722	29	24.89	4/23	0	0	50	
Viljoen SF	(T)	1934/35		4	4	3	81	35*	81.00	0	0	156	3	52.00	2/11	0	0	6	
		1931/32	1946/47	20	29	8	478	72	22.76	0	1	1143	47	24.31	6/91	1	0	16	
Vincent CL	(T)	1920/21	1930/31	11	13	5	241	75*	30.12	0	1	812	51	15.92	6/50	5	1	5	
		1920/21	1942/43	85	117	29	1582	83	17.97	0	5	7006	293	23.91	7/36	16	2	68	
Vintcent CH	(T)	1889/90		1	2	1	62	60*	62.00	0	1	119	6	19.83	4/70	0	0	0	
		1888/89	1904/05	6	12	2	119	60*	11.90	0	1	364	10	36.40	4/70	0	0	2	
Vogler AEE	(T)	1904/05	1909/10	11	17	2	339	57	22.60	0	1	640	51	12.54	6/12	3	0	11	
		1903/04	1912	83	136	19	2375	103	20.29	1	8	7182	393	18.27	10/26	31	7	81	
Von Mengershausen HM																			
	(T)	1919/20	1920/21	2	3	1	16	15*	8.00	0	0							0	
		1919/20	1924/25	4	5	1	22	15*	5.50	0	0							4	
Vorster LP	(T)	1986/87	1989/90	21	34	4	874	174	29.13	1	3	10	1	10.00	1/10	0	0	17	
	(TB)	1985/86	1989/90	15	25	2	835	117	36.30	1	7	31	0			0	0	14	
		1985/86	1993/94	66	114	15	3283	188	33.16	6	17	41	1	41.00	1/10	0	0	46	
Vorster LW	(T)	1963/64	1964/65	2	4	0	69	48	17.25	0	0	36	0			0	0	0	
	(TB)	1963/64	1968/69	10	14	4	654	111	65.40	1	5	117	4	29.25	2/12	0	0	5	
		1963/64	1968/69	13	20	4	730	111	45.62	1	5	153	4	38.25	2/12	0	0	5	
Waite JHB	(T)	1953/54	1965/66	56	93	11	2849	159*	34.74	8	12	2	0			0	0	146	22
		1948/49	1965/66	199	314	34	9812	219	35.04	23	45	8	0			0	0	427	84
Walker PM	(T)	1956/57	1957/58	4	8	0	85	27	10.62	0	0	188	6	31.33	5/72	1	0	8	
		1956	1972	469	788	110	17650	152*	26.03	13	92	23881	834	28.63	7/58	25	2	697	
Wallach B	(T)	1897/98	1904/05	8	9	5	32	13	8.00	0	0							7	5
		1897/98	1904/05	15	18	7	100	30	9.09	0	0							16	11
Wallers WD	(T)	1957/58	1959/60	2	4	0	33	25	8.25	0	0	10	0			0	0	2	
Walsh FA	(T)	1925/26	1934/35	20	19	6	314	44	24.15	0	0	1344	71	18.92	6/35	2	0	11	
Walshe AWP	(T)	1897/98	1904/05	5	8	0	29	16	3.62	0	0	3	0			0	0	5	
		1890/91	1904/05	12	21	0	285	88	13.57	0	1	115	7	16.42	5/18	1	0	14	
Walter KA	(T)	1957/58	1963/64	40	55	24	464	38	14.96	0	0	3446	173	19.91	6/45	8	1	24	
	(TB)	1959/60	1965/66	6	10	1	99	55	11.00	0	1	727	34	21.38	5/19	1	0	5	
		1957/58	1965/66	50	69	25	594	55	13.50	0	1	4605	217	21.22	6/45	9	1	34	
Ward JH	(T)	1946/47	1952/53	19	29	4	705	95	28.20	0	3	73	2	36.50	1/14	0	0	10	
		1946/47	1957/58	21	33	5	861	95	30.75	0	4	73	2	36.50	1/14	0	0	10	
Ward TA	(T)	1909/10	1925/26	27	36	8	520	75	18.57	0	2							32	21
		1909/10	1925/26	92	137	31	1635	75	15.42	0	6	11	0			0	0	107	68
Warne FB	(T)	1941/42		1	1	0	66	66	66.00	0	1	113	4	28.25	2/48	0	0	0	
		1926/27	1942/43	95	168	15	3275	115	21.40	3	13	4801	138	34.78	6/51	4	1	31	
Washington WAI	(T)	1906/07		2	3	0	8	8	2.66	0	0	32	0			0	0	0	
		1900	1906/07	48	69	6	1384	100*	21.96	1	7	32	0			0	0	18	
Watcham DG	(T)	1931/32	1936/37	2	3	1	7	5	3.50	0	0	49	2	24.50	2/49	0	0	0	

		First	Last	M	I	NO	Runs	HS	Avg	100	50	Runs	Wkts	Avg	Best	5i	10m	ct	st
Watson GLG	(T)	1964/65	1975/76	28	36	7	505	83	17.41	0	1	1817	70	25.95	5/41	1	0	19	
	(TB)	1965/66	1975/76	9	12	2	324	53	32.40	0	3	832	30	27.73	5/36	1	0	9	
		1964/65	1975/76	37	48	9	829	83	21.25	0	4	2649	100	26.49	5/36	2	0	28	
Webster TC	(TB)	1990/91	1991/92	5	7	4	144	42*	48.00	0	0	342	14	24.42	6/65	1	0	2	
Weideman IFN	(T)	1980/81	1982/83	5	4	2	34	30*	17.00	0	0	277	16	17.31	4/29	0	0	3	
	(TB)	1980/81	1982/83	11	13	2	199	47*	18.09	0	0	855	49	17.44	4/39	0	0	9	
		1980/81	1986/87	40	55	12	662	47*	15.39	0	0	3017	135	22.34	6/43	2	0	18	
Weightman NR	(T)	1971/72	1972/73	4	6	3	36	19	12.00	0	0	206	10	20.60	5/37	1	0	2	
	(TB)	1971/72	1972/73	4	7	2	111	24	22.20	0	0	198	11	18.00	4/48	0	0	1	
		1971/72	1972/73	8	13	5	147	24	18.37	0	0	404	21	19.23	5/37	1	0	3	
Weinstein LJ	(T)	1966/67		3	5	0	130	60	26.00	0	1							5	
	(TB)	1966/67		1	2	0	157	89	78.50	0	2							0	
		1959/60	1967/68	25	47	1	1176	120	25.56	1	6							16	
Weir RS	(TB)	1990/91		1								63	0			0	0	0	
Welthagen AJ	(T)	1972/73		1	2	1	7	6	7.00	0	0	82	2	41.00	2/70	0	0	0	
	(TB)	1971/72	1972/73	6	8	4	41	12	10.25	0	0	395	19	20.78	5/54	1	0	0	
		1971/72	1972/73	7	10	5	48	12	9.60	0	0	477	21	22.71	5/54	1	0	0	
White BM	(T)	1990/91	1993/94	14	27	0	587	108	21.74	1	2	173	7	24.71	2/3	0	0	10	
	(TB)	1988/89	1993/94	10	19	0	588	109	30.94	1	2	42	1	42.00	1/2	0	0	11	
		1988/89	1993/94	24	46	0	1175	109	25.54	2	4	215	8	26.87	2/3	0	0	21	
White GC	(T)	1902/03	1911/12	14	22	2	667	83	33.35	0	6	563	40	14.07	6/48	3	1	3	
		1902/03	1912	97	152	17	3740	162*	27.70	4	17	3109	155	20.05	7/33	8	2	46	
White RC	(T)	1965/66	1972/73	36	57	1	1600	117	28.57	3	6	22	0			0	0	8	
	(TB)	1965/66	1971/72	10	15	0	896	205	59.73	3	3							5	
		1960/61	1972/73	141	248	4	6824	205	27.96	10	35	589	17	34.64	3/17	0	0	67	
Whytock LJ	(T)	1920/21	1923/24	5	6	1	55	23	11.00	0	0							4	1
Wickham FJ	(T)	1937/38	1939/40	2								95	15	6.33	5/13	2	1	0	
		1932/33	1939/40	12	14	3	140	55	12.72	0	1	846	33	25.63	5/13	2	1	7	
Wienand GV	(T)	1936/37		1	2	0	45	32	22.50	0	0	13	0			0	0	2	
		1934/35	1953/54	18	31	2	739	102	25.48	1	3	728	46	15.82	8/38	1	1	5	
Williams MG	(T)	1893/94		2	4	0	32	29	8.00	0	0							0	
		1890/91	1893/94	3	6	0	78	30	13.00	0	0							0	
Wilson AS	(T)	1961/62	1965/66	4	6	0	174	94	29.00	0	1							0	
	(TB)	1965/66		1	2	0	32	30	16.00	0	0							2	
		1961/62	1965/66	5	8	0	206	94	25.75	0	1							2	
Wilson JC	(T)	1905/06		1	2	0	1	1	0.50	0	0	16	1	16.00	1/16	0	0	2	
		1891/92	1905/06	2	4	1	18	15*	6.00	0	0	37	1	37.00	1/16	0	0	4	
Wimble BS	(T)	1889/90		1	1	0	4	4	4.00	0	0	53	5	10.60	4/8	0	0	0	
		1889/90	1890/91	3	5	0	105	37	21.00	0	0	239	15	15.93	5/77	1	0	1	
Wimble CS	(T)	1890/91		1	2	0	108	62	54.00	0	1							0	
		1890/91	1891/92	2	4	0	108	62	27.00	0	1							0	
Wimble PS	(T)	1892/93		2	4	0	47	45	11.75	0	0	31	1	31.00	1/13	0	0	2	
Winslow PL	(T)	1949/50	1955/56	28	45	1	1046	94	23.77	0	6	38	1	38.00	1/12	0	0	36	
		1949	1961/62	75	124	6	2755	139	23.34	2	13	61	1	61.00	1/12	0	0	85	
Witte EV	(T)	1945/46		3	3	1	22	12	11.00	0	0	206	12	17.16	4/49	0	0	3	
		1942/43	1954/55	28	37	11	311	51	11.96	0	1	2323	93	24.97	6/53	4	0	10	

		First	Last	M	I	NO	Runs	HS	Avg	100	50	Runs	Wkts	Avg	Best	5i	10m	ct	st
Witte RC	(T)	1936/37	1951/52	3	6	0	138	89	23.00	0	1							4	
		1933/34	1951/52	5	10	1	168	89	18.66	0	1	50	1	50.00	1/25	0	0	5	
Wooler RC	(T)	1945/46	1946/47	6	9	2	153	51*	21.85	0	1							5	5
Wright NE	(T)	1989/90	1991/92	19	37	2	1117	107	31.91	1	8	134	5	26.80	2/7	0	0	14	
	(TB)	1978/79	1990/91	32	62	8	1900	128*	35.18	3	9	231	6	38.50	3/58	0	0	29	
		1978/79	1993/94	76	143	10	4302	128*	32.34	5	27	775	21	36.90	3/13	0	0	60	
Wright VMF	(T)	1936/37		1	1	0	0	0	0.00	0	0							0	
		1936/37	1946/47	2	3	0	3	2	1.00	0	0							0	
Wynne OE	(T)	1937/38	1946/47	15	23	3	736	200*	36.80	2	2	28	0			0	0	4	
		1937/38	1958/59	37	64	3	2268	200*	37.18	7	8	47	0			0	0	20	
Yachad M	(T)	1981/82	1993/94	36	63	6	1871	200	32.82	3	9	11	1	11.00	1/11	0	0	26	
	(TB)	1978/79	1985/86	13	25	1	773	154	32.20	1	4	13	0			0	0	14	
		1978/79	1993/94	103	193	10	6365	200	34.78	14	32	26	1	26.00	1/11	0	0	76	
Yates GC	(T)	1991/92		1	1	0	25	25	25.00	0	0	125	7	17.85	5/46	1	0	0	
	(TB)	1991/92		2	2	0	10	9	5.00	0	0	116	1	116.00	1/29	0	0	0	
		1991/92		3	3	0	35	25	11.66	0	0	241	8	30.12	5/46	1	0	0	
Zulch JW	(T)	1908/09	1923/24	21	33	3	1641	185	54.70	5	8							8	
		1908/09	1923/24	53	91	6	3558	185	41.85	9	17	122	5	24.40	3/28	0	0	19	

The only, or final, line states a player's career record in all first-class cricket. The career record stated is that as at the end of the 1993/94 South African season, the 1994 English season, or the 1993/94 season of any other country where applicable. (T) Denotes a player's career record in first-class cricket for Transvaal matches, excluding matches for Transvaal B, which appear separately denoted by (TB).

The figues for Transvaal matches include Sir Abe Bailey's Transvaal XI v Natal in 1897/98 and Transvaal v Rest of South Africa (actually Transvaal Invitation XI with B.A.Richards as a guest player) in 1970/71.

SOUTH AUSTRALIAN CRICKETERS 1877-1984

Compiled and Published by
The Association of Cricket Statisticians
Haughton Mill, Retford, Notts.

Price: £2.50 (issued free to members of the Association in 1984)

Printed by Peartree Printers, Chandos Pole Street, Derby.

Previous Books in this series:

Warwickshire Cricketers 1843-1973
Worcestershire Cricketers 1899-1974
Somersetshire Cricketers 1875-1974
Middlesex Cricketers 1850-1976
Leicestershire Cricketers 1879-1977
Nottinghamshire Cricketers 1835-1978
Gloucestershire Cricketers 1870-1979
Irish Cricketers 1855-1980
Scottish Cricketers 1905-1980
Surrey Cricketers 1839-1980
Derbyshire Cricketers 1871-1981
Kent Cricketers 1834-1983
Northants Cricketers 1899-1984

Victorian Cricketers 1850-1978
Queensland Cricketers 1892-1979
New South Wales Cricketers 1855-1981
Tasmanian Cricketers 1850-1982
Western Australian Cricketers 1892-1983

Companion Books are:

A Guide to First Class Matches in the British Isles since 1864
A Guide to Important Matches in the British Isles 1709-1863
A Guide to First Class Matches in Australia (revised edition)
A Guide to First Class Matches in New Zealand
A Guide to First Class Matches in South Africa
A Guide to First Class Matches in the West Indies.

Also being published by the Association is a series of books containing the full scores of all first-class matches. Each book contains 100 to 150 matches and the series so far covers 1860 to 1892 inclusive.

For Details of publications in stock and membership please write to:
Roger Page, 55 Tarcoola Drive, Yallambie, Victoria 3085 or
The Administration Officer, 36 Campion Street, Derby.

INTRODUCTION

This booklet, the sixth and last in the Australian State series, contains a biographical register and career figures of all cricketers who played in first-class matches for South Australia between 1877-78 and 1983-84. It lists also those players who appeared in first-class cricket within Australia or for Australian teams overseas without ever representing a state.

Though cricket was played in South Australia within a few years of its founding as a colony in 1836, little or no contact was made with neighbouring colonies until the South Australian Cricket Association was formed in 1871 and its ground, the Adelaide Oval was ready for important matches two years later. W.G.Grace's English XI was the first team to oppose a representative South Australian side in March 1874, while Tasmania became the colony's initial first-class opponents in November 1877.

South Australia's population has always been concentrated around the capital city, more so than in the other Australian states. Not surprisingly, therefore, members of South Australian teams have been drawn almost exclusively from the metropolitan clubs affiliated with the South Australian Cricket Association. In 1871 nine clubs were represented on the Committee of Management, the most notable being Hindmarsh, North Adelaide and Norwood.

Electoral cricket was introduced to Adelaide in 1897-98 with seven clubs competing, including East Torrens, Port Adelaide, Sturt and West Torrens which still participate today. The other clubs in the 1983-84 competition were Adelaide (formed 1905-06), Glenelg (1908-09), University (1908-09), Kensington (1923-24), Prospect (1928-29), Woodville (1946-47), Salisbury (1965-66) and Tea Tree Gully (1983-84).

With regard to the entries in the biographical section, please note:

a. Places of birth, death or present address are located in South Australia unless otherwise indicated.

b. Unusual abbreviations of christian names or nicknames of players have been shown, but not commonly used abbreviations such as Bill or Bob.

c. An asterisk beside a player's name indicates that doubt exists as to whether the person was the South Australian cricketer.

d. The date in brackets after each surname is the season of the player's first appearance for the state.

e. The club(s) or country town listed is that for which the cricketer played during his first-class career; or in the case of some last-century players, the club(s) with which they were prominently associated.

Many people made substantial contributions to the register. Special thanks are due to Ian Everett, in Adelaide, for strenuous efforts over several years. Graham Pellen succeeded in locating the whereabouts of most surviving players while Norm Sowden, Alf James, Geoff Sando, Ray Webster, Mervyn Shaw and Bob Sizer rendered valuable assistance. Additional help came from Philip Thorn in England.

Ken Williams prepared the two maps, showing the majority of places listed in the text. He also compiled the career records. Charlie Wat and Philip Bailey helped to check the statistics.

Roger Page,
October, 1984

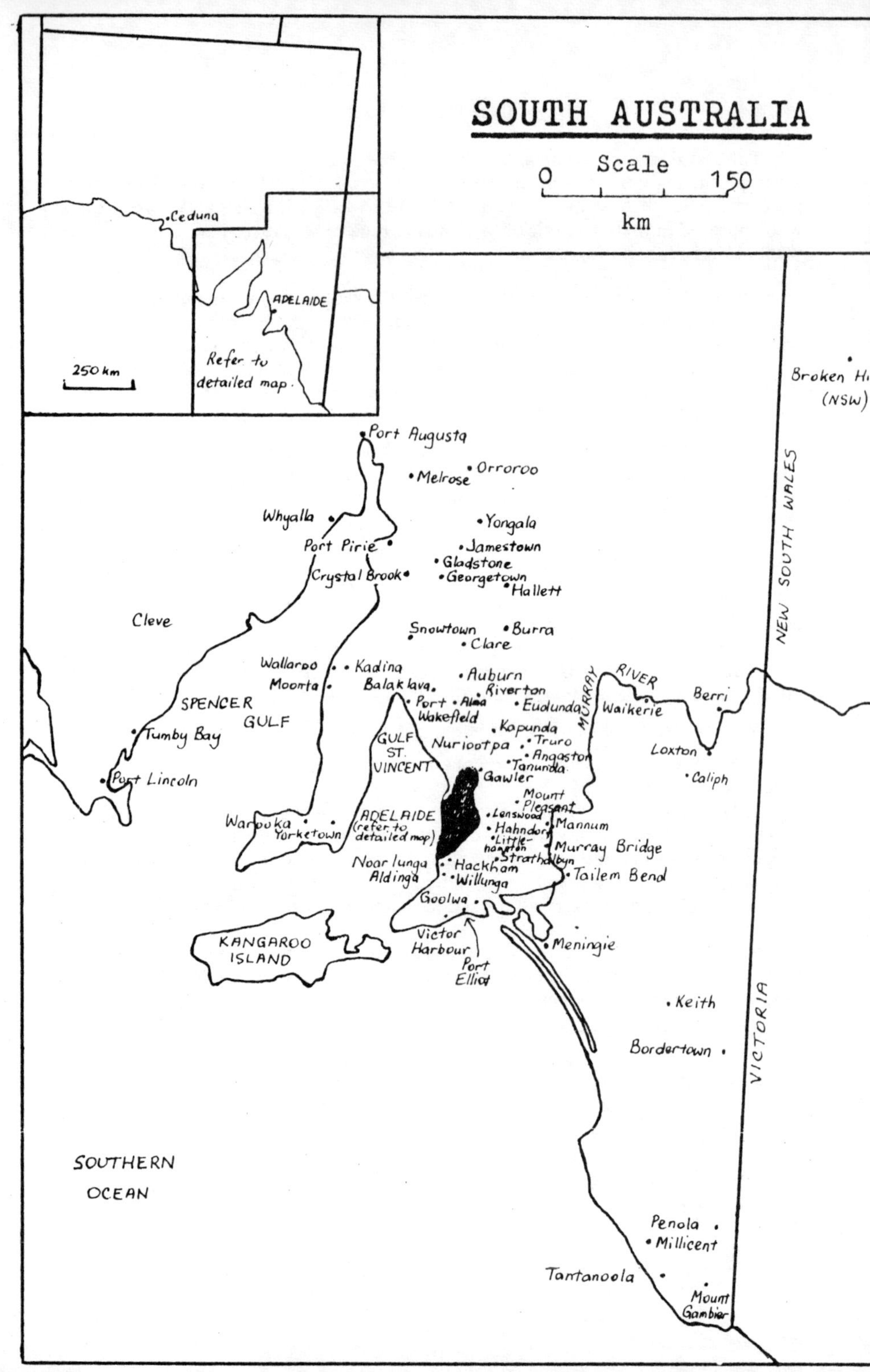

SOUTH AUSTRALIA
Scale
0
150
km
Ceduna
ADELAIDE
Refer to detailed map.
250 km
Broken Hill (NSW)
NEW SOUTH WALES
VICTORIA
Port Augusta
Melrose
Orroroo
Whyalla
Yongala
Port Pirie
Jamestown
Gladstone
Crystal Brook
Georgetown
Hallett
Cleve
Snowtown
Burra
Clare
Wallaroo
Kadina
Auburn
Moonta
Balaklava
Riverton
MURRAY RIVER
Waikerie
Berri
Port Wakefield
Alma
Eudunda
SPENCER GULF
Kapunda
Tumby Bay
GULF ST. VINCENT
Nuriootpa
Truro
Angaston
Loxton
Tanunda
Port Lincoln
Gawler
Caliph
Mount Pleasant
Lenswood
Warooka
Yorketown
ADELAIDE (refer to detailed map)
Hahndorf
Mannum
Littlehampton
Murray Bridge
Strathalbyn
Noarlunga
Hackham
Aldinga
Willunga
Tailem Bend
Goolwa
Victor Harbour
Port Elliot
Meningie
KANGAROO ISLAND
Keith
Bordertown
SOUTHERN OCEAN
Penola
Millicent
Tantanoola
Mount Gambier

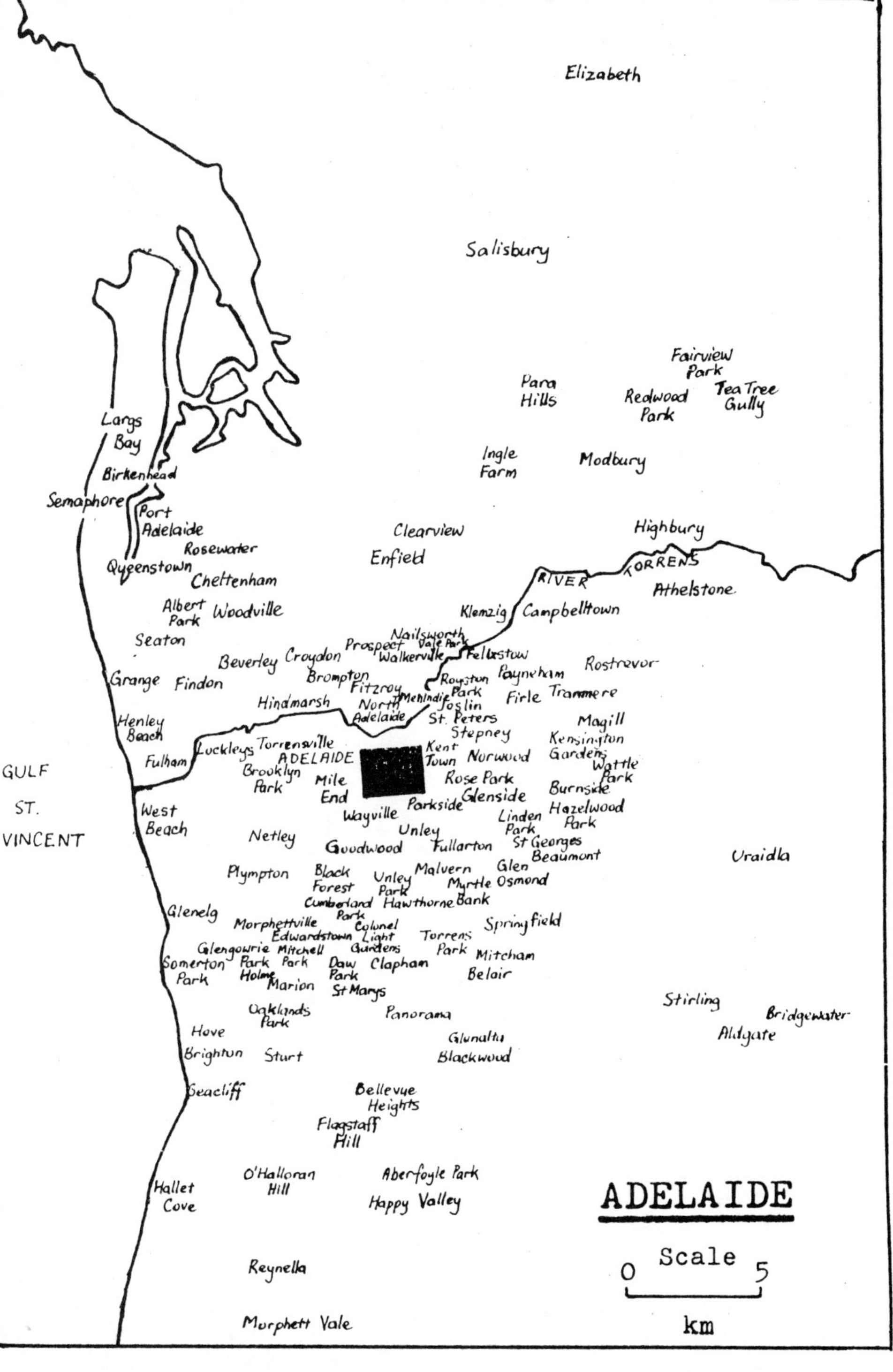
Elizabeth
Salisbury
Fairview Park
Para Hills
Redwood Park
Tea Tree Gully
Largs Bay
Ingle Farm
Modbury
Birkenhead
Semaphore
Port Adelaide
Clearview
Highbury
Rosewater
Enfield
Queenstown
RIVER TORRENS
Cheltenham
Athelstone
Albert Park
Woodville
Klemzig
Campbelltown
Seaton
Nailsworth
Vale Park
Prospect
Walkerville
Felixstow
Beverley
Croydon
Rostrevor
Grange
Findon
Brompton
Fitzroy
Royston Park
Payneham
Menindie
Firle
Tranmere
Hindmarsh
North Adelaide
Joslin
St. Peters
Magill
Henley Beach
Stepney
Torrensville
Kent Town
Kensington Gardens
ADELAIDE
Norwood
Wattle Park
Fulham
Lockleys
Brooklyn Park
GULF ST. VINCENT
Mile End
Rose Park
Burnside
Glenside
Parkside
Hazelwood Park
West Beach
Wayville
Linden Park
Unley
Netley
St Georges
Goodwood
Fullarton
Beaumont
Uraidla
Glen Osmond
Plympton
Black Forest
Unley Park
Malvern
Myrtle Bank
Cumberland Park
Hawthorne
Glenelg
Springfield
Morphettville
Colonel Light Gardens
Edwardstown
Torrens Park
Glengowrie
Mitchell Park
Mitcham
Somerton Park
Park Holme
Daw Park
Clapham
Belair
Marion
St Marys
Stirling
Oaklands Park
Panorama
Bridgewater
Aldgate
Hove
Glenalta
Brighton
Sturt
Blackwood
Seacliff
Bellevue Heights
Flagstaff Hill
O'Halloran Hill
Aberfoyle Park
Hallet Cove
Happy Valley
ADELAIDE
Scale
0
5
km
Reynella
Morphett Vale

CRICKETERS WHO HAVE REPRESENTED SOUTH AUSTRALIA IN A FIRST-CLASS MATCH 1877-78 TO 1983-84

William **Colin** ALEXANDER (1925-26) b. Gawler, Sept. 14, 1907. Add: 3 Howson Court, Mont Albert, Vic. Tour: New Zealand 1927-28.	RHB/OB	University
Albert Mark AMBLER (1920-21) b. Murray Bridge, Sept. 27 1892. d. Prospect, Nov. 27, 1970.	RHB/WK	North Adelaide
William AMOS (1890-91) b. May 9, 1861. d. Adelaide, May 14, 1935.		North Adelaide
Geoffrey Robert ATTENBOROUGH (1972-73) b. Adelaide, Jan. 17, 1951. Add: 3 Iona Road, Aberfoyle Park.		Adelaide
Victor **Cecil** AUSTEN (1945-46) b. Kew, Vic., Nov. 30, 1918. Add: 72 Erskine Road, Macleod.	RHB/RFM	Prospect
Charles James BACKMAN (1911-12) b. Adelaide, 1890. d. in action on the first day of the landing at Gallipolli, April 25, 1915.	RHB/RM	Adelaide
Clayvel Lindsay ("Jack") BADCOCK (1934-35) b. Exton, Tas., April 10, 1914. d. Exton, Tas., Dec. 13, 1982. Tests: 7 Tour: England 1938 Tasmania 1929-30 to 1933-34	RHB	Adelaide
Kenneth James BAGSHAW (1946-47) b. Kadina, Oct. 23, 1920. Add: 6 Rooth Place, Watson, A.C.T.	RHB/RFM	East Torrens
Alfred John Thomas BAILEY (1953-54) b. Adelaide, March 3, 1932. Add: 2 Trigalana Place, Frenchs Forest, N.S.W.	RHB/RFM	Glenelg
Bertram Theodore ("Dick") BAILEY (1896-97) b. Dec 4, 1874 d. Payneham, Oct. 3, 1964.	RHB/LB	West Adelaide/ Norwood/Sturt
Ernest Albert BAILEY (1906-07) b. Nov. 15, 1881. Brother of B.T.Bailey.		Adelaide
David Murray BALLANS (1889-90) b. at sea, June 30, 1868. d. Goodwood, June 26, 1957	RHB	South Adelaide
Jeffrey Robert BARNES (1972-73) b. Glenelg, Jan 9, 1948. Add: 35 North St., Henley Beach.	LHB/LFM	West Torrens
Albert James ("Alby") BARTLETT (1925-26) b. Unley, April 23, 1900. d. Woodville, Oct. 6, 1968.	RHB	Sturt

John William BEAGLEY (1956-57) b. Adelaide, March 23, 1933. Add: 3 Morice Court, Darwin, N.T.	RHB/RFM	Woodville
Albert Austen ("Bert") BEDFORD (1956-57) b. Adelaide, Sept. 12, 1932. Add: 8 Kathrina St., O'Halloran Hill.	LHB/SLA	Adelaide
Philip Malcolm BEDNALL (1948-49) b. Burra, Jan 27. 1931. Add: 63 Quinlan Ave., St. Marys.	RHB	Prospect
Floyd Chester BENNETT (1945-46) b. North Perth, W.A., April 12, 1919. Add: 11 Beadnell Crescent, Bridgewater. Western Australia 1950-51, 1951-52.	RHB/RM	University
Rex Leland BENNETT (1922-23) b. Snowtown, June 25, 1896. d. Collaroy, N.S.W., Dec. 14, 1963. Tasmania 1924-25, 1925-26.	RHB/WK	North Adelaide
*Thomas BENNETT (1894-95) b. Littlehampton, Oct. 11, 1866. d. Dec. 12, 1942.		South Adelaide
Jeffrey John BENTON (1972-73) b. Mildure, Vic., Oct. 9, 1953. Add: 229 Findon Road, Findon.	RHB/RM	Woodville
John Lawrence BEVAN (1877-78) b. near Swansea, Wales, May 10, 1857.	LHB/LFM	Hindmarsh
Glenn Andrew BISHOP (1982-83) b. North Adelaide, Feb. 25, 1960. Add: 104 Harvey Road, Elizabeth North.	RHB	Salisbury
Graham Ash BLACK (1949-50) b. Adelaide, May 14, 1924. Add: 6 Herbert St, Medindie.	RHB	Sturt
Robert Kevin BLEWETT (1975-76) b. Prospect, March 30, 1943. Add: 26 Wicks Road, Highbury.	RHB/SLA	East Torrens
Harry BLINMAN (1880-81) b. Adelaide, Dec. 30, 1861. d. Adelaide, July 23, 1950.	RHB	Norwood
George Thomas BLOOMFIELD (1908-09) b. Feb. 5, 1882. d. North Adelaide, Dec. 1, 1958.	LHB	North Adelaide
Rex Pole BLUNDELL (1964-65) b. Adelaide, May 8, 1942. Add: 52 Ingerson St., West Beach.	RHB/WK	West Torrens
Robert Dyas BOTTEN (1877-78) b. Lewisham, Kent, 1853. d. Medindie, April 26, 1935.	RHB	North Adelaide

Bruce Leonard BOWLEY (1947-48) RHB/RFM Kensington/East Torrens
b near Clare, Jan. 1, 1922.
Add: 25 Tennyson Ave., Tranmere.
Son of E.L.Bowley.

Edwin **Leonard** BOWLEY (1922-23) RHB/RFM Kensington
b. Sevenhill, near Clare, Feb. 27, 1888.
d. Woodville, April 22, 1963.

Craig Edwin BRADLEY (1983-84) RHB Port Adelaide
b. Ashford, Oct. 23, 1964.
Add: 6 Chester Cres., Pooraka.

Sir Donald George Bradman (1935-36) RHB Kensingston
b. Cootamundra, N.S.W., Aug. 27, 1908.
Add: 2 Holden St., Kensington Gardens.
Tests: 52 Tours: England 1930, 1934, 1938, 1948
New South Wales, 1927-28 to 1933-34
Author of 5 books on cricket.

Clive BRAYBROOK (1921-22) RHB/LB Sturt
b. Goodwood, Sept. 27, 1901.
Add: 20 Milloo St., Swan Hill, Vic.

John Holmes BRIDESON (1883-84) RHB Hindmarsh
b. Rushworth, Vic., July 9, 1856.
d. of typhoid at Hawthorn, Vic., Feb. 20, 1887.

Hugh Hossick Mackay BRIDGMAN (1912-13) LHB/RM West Torrens
b. Feb. 1, 1890.
d. Torrensville, Dec. 3, 1953.

Gordon Victor BROOKS (1961-62) RHB/RFM Woodville
b. Ceduna, May 30, 1938.
Add: 50 Knight St., Rochedale, Qld.

Walter BULLOUGH (1880-81) LHB/LAB Hindmarsh
b. Leeds, Eng., Oct. 21, 1855.
d. Hindmarsh "after one day's severe illness", Sept. 17, 1888.

Garth ("Gath") BURTON (1939-40) RHB/RFM Kensington
b. Forestville, Jan. 26, 1913.
Add: 9 Yarmouth St., Brighton.

Jack Richard BURTON (1951-52) RHB/RFM Prospect
b. Cleve, Nov. 3, 1923.
Add: 13 Knighton Road, Elizabeth North.

Robert Alastair CAMERON (1957-58) RHB/RM University
b. North Adelaide, Sept. 6, 1938.
Add: Barlee Place, Aspley, Qld.

Gordon Cathcart CAMPBELL (1909-10) /WK Adelaide/Sturt
b. Myrtle Bank, June 4, 1885.
d. North Adelaide, Aug 13, 1961.
Tour: North America 1913.

Thomas Andrew CARLTON (1928-29) LHB/LM Adelaide/Prospect
b. Footscray, Vic., Dec. 8, 1890.
d. Moreland, Vic., Dec. 17, 1973.
Tour: New Zealand to Australia 1913-14.
Canterbury 1909-10 to 1914-15; Victoria 1919-20 to 1922-23; Otago 1920-21; 1921-22.

Ian Robert CARMICHAEL (1983-84) RHB/LFM Adelaide
b. Hull, Eng., Dec. 17, 1960.
Add: 6 Tilbrook Cres., South Brighton.

Arthur James CARRACHER (1896-97) /LM North Adelaide
b. Minxmay? July 7, 1867.
d. North Adelaide, Oct. 15, 1935.

Edward John CARRAGHER (1922-23) RHB/LBG West Torrens
b. Broken Hill, N.S.W., May 24, 1891.
d. Sydney, Nov. 28, 1977.

Walter Evered CATCHLOVE (1931-32) RHB Glenelg
b. North Adelaide, Feb. 24, 1907.
Add: 32 The Circle, Avalon Beach, N.S.W.

Thomas **Ainslie** CATERER (1884-85) LHB/LFM Adelaide
b. Woodville, May 16, 1858.
d. Walkerville, Aug. 25, 1924.

Barry Leon CAUSBY (1973-74) RHB/OB Adelaide/Salisbury
b. Adelaide, Sept. 9, 1948.
Add: 4 Foord Ave., Gawler East.
Cousin of J.P.Causby.

John Phillip CAUSBY (1960-61) RHB Colts/Woodville
b. Hindmarsh, Oct. 27, 1942.
Add: 24 Brentwood Road, Flinders Park.

Cornelius Thomas ("Con") CHAMBERLAIN (1905-06) RHB East Torrens
b.
d. Rose Park, Nov. 14, 1943.

William **Leonard** CHAMBERLAIN (1907-08) RHB/RM East Torrens
b. Port Adelaide, Jan. 15, 1889.
dead.
Brother of C.T. & J.Chamberlain (W.A.)

Gregory Stephen CHAPPELL (1966-67) RHB/RM,LB Glenelg
b. Unley, Aug. 7, 1948.
Tests: 87 Tours: New Zealand 1969-70; England 1972; West Indies 1972-73; New Zealand 1973-74; England 1975; International Wanderers to South Africa 1975-76; New Zealand 1976-77; England 1977; Pakistan 1979-80; England 1980; New Zealand 1981-82; Sri Lanka 1982-83.
Queensland 1973-74 to 1983-84. Somerset 1968, 1969.

Ian Michael CHAPPELL (1961-62) RHB/LB Glenelg/West Torrens
b. Unley, Sept. 26, 1943.
Tests: 75 Tours: South Africa 1966-67; England 1968; Ceylon, India & South Africa 1969-70; England 1972; New Zealand 1973-74; International Wanderers to South Africa 1974-75 & 1975-76; England 1975.
Lancashire (v. Cambridge Univ.) 1963; Gov.-Gen's XI v West Indies (Auckland) 1968-69.
Cricket author and television commentator.

Trevor Martin CHAPPELL (1972-73) RHB/RM Glenelg
b. Glenelg, Oct. 21, 1952.
Add: 35 Fonteney Road, North Ryde, N.S.W.
Tests: 3 Tours: D.H.Robins to South Africa 1975-76; England 1981.
Western Australia 1976-77; New South Wales 1979-80 to 1983-84.

Hubert George Williams CHINNER (1898-99) RHB Sturt
b. Brighton Aug. 30, 1870
d. Unley Park, June 12, 1953.

Henry Carew CHITTLEBOROUGH (1883-84) RHB/Lobs Sturt
b. Wallaroo Mines, April 14, 1861.
d. Malvern, June 25, 1925.

Robert Thomas CHRISTENSEN (1982-83) RHB/LFM Woodville
b. Hindmarsh, Oct. 31, 1959.
Add: 9 Tunbridge St., Woodville South.

Graham Cornelius ("Clacka") CLARKE (1965-66) LHB/LM Salisbury/Prospect
b. Laura, July 10, 1939.
Add: 13 Milton Ave., Clearview.

Norman ("Norrie") CLAXTON (1898-99) RHB/RFM North Adelaide
b. North Adelaide, Nov. 2, 1877.
d. North Adelaide, Dec. 5, 1951.
Noted all-round sportsman; donated the Claxton Shield in 1934, the trophy of the Australian Baseball championship.

William Griffiths Hambridge CLAXTON (1883-84) LHB North Adelaide
b. Adelaide, March 19, 1855.

Peter John CLEMENTS (1972-73) RHB/LBG University
b. Glenelg, Jan. 23, 1953.
Add: 14 Sanders St., Rainbow, Vic.

Michael Thomas ("Mick") CLINGLY (1957-58) RHB/LM Woodville
b. Prospect, April 18, 1932.
Add: 48 Swan St., Grange.

Stanley Herwin CLUTTERBUCK (1913-14) /SLA North Adelaide
b. Kapunda, May 27, 1888.
d. Adelaide, Jan. 24, 1972.

Timothy Peter Michael COLLEY (1955-56) LHB Colts
b. Sydney, July 10, 1935.
Add: 105 Cliff St., Glengowrie.

Frank Henry Kenneth COLLINS (1933-34) RHB/RFM Port Adelaide
b. Dec. 16, 1911.
Add: Dergholm (Vic.)

Ephraim Henry COOMBE (1887-88) South Adelaide
b. Gawler, Aug. 26, 1858.
d. Semaphore, April 5, 1917.

Percy Howard COOMBE (1903-04) RHB/RM,LB West Torrens
b. Brompton, Jan. 7, 1880.
d. Prospect, July 28, 1947.

William Osborne COOPER (1914-15) /RFM Glenelg
b. North Adelaide, Feb. 13, 1891.
d. Glenelg, June 28, 1930.

Gary John COSIER (1974-75) RHB/RM Prospect
b. Richmond, Vic., April 25, 1953.
Tests: 18 Tours: New Zealand 1976-77; England 1977; West Indies 1977-78.
Victoria 1971-72 & 1980-81. Queensland 1977-78 to 1979-80.

Harold Norman Jack COTTON (1935-36) RHB/RF Prospect
b. Prospect, Dec. 3, 1914.
d. Malvern, April 6, 1966.

Robert Francis COWAN (1904-05) RHB/RMF West Adelaide
b. Angaston, May 3, 1880.
d. Neutral Bay, N.S.W., Nov 11, 1962

Reginald Jack CRAIG (1945-46) RHB/LBG Prospect
b. Adelaide, Aug. 8, 1916.
Add: 11 Burton Ave., Park Holme.

John Edwin CRAIGIE (1887-88) RHB South Adelaide
b. Adelaide, Aug. 25, 1866.
d. circa 1922.

John Neville CRAWFORD (1909-10) RHB/RFM East Torrens/Glenelg
b. Cane Hill, Eng., Dec. 1, 1886.
d. Epsom, Eng., May 2, 1963.
Tests: England 12 Tours: M.C.C. to South Africa 1905-06; M.C.C. to Australia 1907-08; North America 1913; New Zealand 1913-14.
Surrey 1904-1921; Otago 1914-15; Wellington 1917-18.
Author of *Trip to Kangaroo Land* (1909).

Jeffrey John Crowe (1977-78) RHB/RM West Torrens
b. Auckland, Sept. 14, 1958.
Tests: New Zealand 10. Tours: New Zealand to England 1983; New Zealand to Sri Lanka 1983-84.
Auckland 1982-83, 1983-84.
Brother of M.D.Crowe (Somerset & New Zealand).

Kenneth George CUNNINGHAM (1960-61) LHB/RM Adelaide
b. Adelaide, July 26, 1939.
Add: 2 Jordan Court, Panorama.
Tour: New Zealand 1966-67.

Barry George CURTIN (1972-73) RHB Port Adelaide
b. Rose Park, June 30, 1951.
Add: 281 Henley Beach Road, Brooklyn Park.

Paul CURTIN (1974-75) LHB/LB Port Adelaide
b. Rose Park, May 10, 1954.
Add: 12 Brougham Place, Alberton.
Northern Districts (N.Z.) 1980-81.
Brother of B.G. & P.D.Curtin.

Peter Donald CURTIN (1971-72) RHB/LBG Port Adelaide
b. Rose Park, Sept. 22, 1949.
Add: 10 Lammington St., Ingle Farm.

Louis David CURTIS (1950-51) RHB/RFM Caliph
b. Loxton, Aug. 5, 1928.
Add: Caliph.

Hampton Neil DANSIE (1949-50) RHB/LB Kensington
b. Nuriootpa, July 2, 1928.
Add: 3 Barons St., Tranmere.

Joseph DARLING (1893-94) LHB North Adelaide/Sturt/Adelaide
b. Glen Osmond, Nov. 21, 1870.
d. Hobart, Jan. 2, 1946.
Tests: 34 Tours: England and North America 1896; England 1899; England and South Africa 1902; England 1905.

Warrick Maxwell ("Rick") DARLING (1975-76) b. Waikerie, May 1, 1957. Add: 12/34 Addison Road, Black Forest. Tests: 14 Tours: West Indies 1977-78; India 1979-80.	RHB	Salisbury/ West Torrens
John Richard DAVEY (1981-82) b. Bournemouth, Eng., Aug. 26, 1957. Add: 4 Wake St., Redwood Park.	RHB/WK	Salisbury
John Ryan DAVEY (1933-34) b. Broken Hill, N.S.W., Sept. 20, 1913. Add: 10/103 King William Road, Unley.	RHB/RFM	University
Herbert John DAY (1898-99) b. April 1, 1868. d. Hindmarsh, Oct. 14, 1947.		West Torrens
William DELANEY (1888-89) b. circa 1868.	/RFM	Adelaide
Pitre Cesar DESMAZEURES (1909-10) b. Collingwood, Vic., Aug. 17, 1880. d. New Norfolk, Tas., Oct. 7, 1942. Victoria 1906-07.	LHB/LAB	North Adelaide
Charles Sydney DEVERSON (1930-31) b. Alberton, Nov. 2, 1907. d. Port Adelaide, Feb. 2, 1945.	RHB/RFM	Port Adelaide
Charles Edward DOLLING (1905-06) b. Wokuna, Sept. 4, 1886. d. Adelaide, June 11, 1936. Tour: New Zealand 1913-14.	RHB	East Torrens/University/West Torrens
Malcolm Charles DOLMAN (1981-82) b. North Adelaide, June 14, 1960. Add: 10 Boothby St., Clapham.	LHB/SLC	Sturt
John Stuart DONALDSON (1972-73) b. Adelaide, April 14, 1950. Add: 24 Orleana St., Flagstaff Hill.	RHB/WK	Teachers Colleges
Bruce DOOLAND (1945-46) b. Adelaide, Nov 1, 1923. d. Adelaide, Sept. 8, 1980. Tests: 3 Tours: New Zealand 1945-46; Commonwealth to India & Ceylon 1950-51; C.G.Howard's XI to India 1956-57. Commonwealth XI v England XI (Hastings) 1951. Nottinghamshire 1953 to 1957.	RHB/LBG	West Torrens
Granville Stuart ("Jimmy") DOWN (1911-12) b. Bathurst, N.S.W., May 24, 1883 d. N.S.W. 1969-70 Tour: North America 1913.	RHB	Adelaide
Donnell Raymond DOWNEY (1925-26) b. Parkside, April 3, 1907. d. Adelaide, Jan. 23, 1966.	RHB/WK	Sturt
John DRENNAN (1953-54) b. Adelaide, Nov. 13, 1932. Add: 27 Mayfair Drive, West Beach. Tours: New Zealand 1956-57; South Africa 1957-58.	RHB/RFM	Woodville

Charles Francis DREW (1911-12) — RHB — University
b. Koorunga, April 24, 1888.
d. Adelaide, Feb. 19, 1960.
Brother of T.M.Drew.

Thomas Mitchell ("Tiny") DREW (1897-98) — LHB — Adelaide
b. Sept. 9, 1875.
d. Toowoomba, Qld., Jan. 9, 1928.
London County (v. Leics.) 1903.

Richard Harris ("Rick") DREWER (1974-75) — LHB — Adelaide
b. Parkside, June 12, 1946.
Add: 7 Brook St., Torrens Park.

John Robert DUCKER (1952-53) — RHB/WK — Prospect
b. Prospect, June 12, 1934.
Add: 20 Kantilla Drive, Athelstone.

Robert Wayne DUGAN (1978-79) — LHB/SLA — West Torrens
b. Broken Hill, N.S.W., Aug. 10, 1959.
Add: 10 Huntington Ave., Fulham

Lance Desmond DULDIG (1940-41) — RHB — Port Adelaide
b. Eudunda, Feb. 21, 1922.
Add: 14 Sturt Place, Beaumont.
Tour: New Zealand 1949-50.

Robert Henry ("Harry") DYER (1893-94) — LHB — South Adelaide
b. Alma, circa 1864.
d. circa 1947.

Anthony **Mark** EATON (1976-77) — LHB — Prospect
b. Prospect, June 11, 1953.
Add: 1 Chase Grove, Vale Park.

Alfred Charles EDWARDS (1892-93) — Hindmarsh
b. Dec. 9, 1869.
dead

Frederick Raymond EDWARDS (1934-35) — RHB/WK — East Torrens
b. circa 1909

Reginald Sidney ELLIS (1945-46) — LHB/SLC — Sturt
b. Angaston, Nov. 26, 1917
Add: 1 Geoffrey Ave., Port Noarlunga
Tours: Services in England 1945; Services to India
Tours: Services in England 1945; Services to India & Ceylon 1945-46.
Dominions v. England (Lord's) 1945.

Alfred ENEBERG (1951-52) — RHB/LB — Port Adelaide
b. Port Adelaide, Nov. 30, 1928.
Add: 16 Daytone Ave., Killara, N.S.W.

Ernest James ENGLAND (1950-51) — RHB — University
b. Bunbury, W.A., May 26, 1927.
Add: 60 Broome St., Perth, W.A.
Western Australia 1945-46, 1952-53, 1953-54.

William ENGLEFIELD (1946-47) — RHB/WK — Port Adeaide
b. Leichhardt, N.S.W., Oct. 6, 1947.
Add: 46 Pennant Ave., Ryde, N.S.W.

L.W.EVAN (1885-86) RHB Adelaide
b.

Arthur Ernest Herbert EVANS (1895-96) LHB//B Norwood/E.Torrens
b. East Adelaide, July 12, 1871.
d, Bordertown, March 26, 1950.

Richard EVANS (1892-93) Hindmarsh

Graeme Stanley FARRELL (1966-67) LHB Prospect
b. Norwood, Feb. 4, 1943.

Alan Leslie FAVELL (1983-84) RHB East Torrens
b. North Adelaide, June 6, 1960.
Add: 24 Leonard St., Magill.
Son of L.E.Favell.

Leslie Ernest FAVELL (1951-52) RHB/RM East Torrens
b. Arncliffe, N.S.W., Oct. 6, 1929.
Add: 24 Leonard St., Magill.
Tests: 19 Tours: West Indies 1954-55; New Zealand 1956-57; South Africa 1957-58; Pakistan & India 1959-60; New Zealand 1966-67.
Radio cricket commentator. Author of *By hook Or by Cut.*

John James FERRIS (1895-96) LHB/LM Norwood
b. Sydney, May 21, 1867.
d. Durban, Nov. 21, 1900.
Tests: Australia 8, England 1. Tours: England 1888, 1890; England to South Africa 1891-92. New South Wales 1887-88 to 1890-91, 1897-98. M.C.C. etc. 1891. Gloucestershire 1892 to 1895.

Harry Medcalf FISHER (1920-21) RHB/RFM University/North Adelaide
b. North Adelaide, May 28, 1899.
d. Launceston South, Tasmania, Oct. 14, 1982.

Robert Alexander FRASER (1974-75) LHB Sturt
b. Parkside, Feb. 13, 1954.
Add: 73 Grange Road, Colonel Light Gardens.

Eric Walter FREEMAN (1964-65) RHB/RFM Port Adelaide
b. Largs Bay, July 13, 1944.
Add: 29 Wallace St., Balaklava.
Tests: 11 Tours: New Zealand 1966-67; England 1968; India & South Africa 1969-70.

John FRICK (1976-77) LHB/SLA Prospect
b. Medindie, March 24, 1957.
Add: 2 Brennan St., Millicent.

Allan Russell FROST (1965-66) RHB/RF Kensington
b. Adelaide, Feb. 12, 1942.
Add: 26 Highfield Drive, Tea Tree Gully.
Tour: New Zealand 1966-67.

Paul William GALLOWAY (1968-69) RHB Port Adelaide
b. North Sydney, Sept. 14, 1943.
Add: 2 Gurner Terrace, Grange.

Joel GARNER (1982-83) RHB/RF Glenelg
b. Christchurch, Barbados, Dec. 16, 1952.
Tests: West Indies 42 Tours: (for West Indies) Australia & New Zealand 1979-80; England 1980; Pakistan 1980-81; Australia 1981-82; England 1984.
Somerset 1977 to 1983.

Rodney Arthur Howard GEHAN (1962-63) RHB/RF Woodville
b. Werribee, Vic., Nov 12, 1942.
Add: 30 Cahill Crescent, Nakara, Darwin.

Donald Raeburn Algernon ("Algy") GEHRS (1902-03) RHB/LB/WK North Adelaide/Port Adelaide
b. Victor Harbour, Nov. 29, 1880.
d. Kings Park, June 25, 1953.
Tests: 6 Tours: New Zealand 1904-05; England 1905.

Steven Robert GENTLE (1978-79) RHB/WK Adelaide
b. Rose Park, May
b. Rose Park, May 30, 1955.
Add: 37 William St., South Plympton.

C.H.GIBBS (1877-78) RHB/Long stop Kensington

Lancelot Richard GIBBS (1969-70) RHB/OB Glenelg
b. Georgetown, Guyana, Sept. 29, 1934.
Tests: West Indies 79 Tours: (for West Indies) India & Pakistan 1958-59; Australia 1960-61; England 1963; England 1966; India & Ceylon 1966-67; Australia & New Zealand 1968-69; England 1969; England 1973; India & Pakistan 1974-75; Australia 1975-76.
British Guiana (Guyana) 1953-54 to 1974-75. Warwickshire 1967 to 1973.
Rest of World v. England 1970.

Vincent Roy ("Dick") GIBSON (1939-40) LHB/LM East Torrens
b. Rose Park, May 14, 1916.
d. Sydney, Nov. 28, 1983.

George GIFFEN (1877-78) RHB/RM/OB Norwood/North Adelaide/W.Adelaide
b. Adelaide, March 27, 1859.
d. Adelaide, Nov. 29, 1927.
Tests: 31 Tours: England 1882, 1884, 1886; England & North America 1893; England & North America 1896.
Smokers v. Non-Smokers (Lord's) 1884.
Author of *With Bat & Ball.*

Walter Frank GIFFEN (1882-83) RHB Norwood/W.Adelaide
b. Adelaide, Sept. 20, 1861.
d. North Unley, June 28, 1949.
Tests: 3 Tour: England & North America 1893.
Brother of G.Giffen.

Robert James GILBOURNE (1967-68) LHB Prospect
b. Adelaide, July 16, 1943.
Add: 18 Douglas St., Marion.

Leonard George ("Jack") GILES (1950-51) RHB Sturt
b. Yorketown, June 17, 1921.
Add: 8/42 Cambridge St., Epping, N.S.W.

Charles George GODFREY (1885-86) RHB South Adelaide
b. Adelaide, Nov. 17, 1860.
d. Rose Park, March 27, 1940.

Keith Geoffrey GOGLER (1946-47) RHB/OB East Torrens
b. Port Adelaide, May 1, 1923.
d. Glenelg North, Aug. 24, 1983.

Benjamin Ryall GOODE (1945-46) RHB Sturt/Adelaide
b. Port Lincoln, Jan. 23, 1924.
Add: 93 Cross Road, Hawthorn.

Henry Alfred GOODEN (1877-78) RHB Norwood
b. Adelaide, Jan. 12, 1858.
d. North Fitzroy, March 30, 1904.
Brother of J.E.Gooden.

James Edward GOODEN (1880-81) Norwood
b. Brentford, Eng., Dec 23, 1845.
d. Norwood, July 17, 1913.

Norman Leslie GOODEN (1912-13) RHB West Torrens
b. Norwood, Dec. 27, 1889.
d. Unley Park, July 5, 1966.
Nephew of J.E.Gooden.

James Edward GOODFELLOW (1880-81) /LM,SLA Kensington
b. Surrey, Eng., Aug. 21, 1850.
d. Malvern, July 22, 1924.

Gary Weech GOODMAN (1980-81) RHB/OB Woodville
b. Sydney, Dec. 6, 1953.
Add: Port Sorell, Tasmania.
Tasmania 1978-79, 1979-80 & 1983-84.

Fred Keen GOULD (1922-23) RHB Sturt
b. Hindmarsh, Sept. 18, 1891.
d. Kingswood, Feb. 15, 1954.

Colin Spicer GRANT (1956-57) LHB Port Adelaide
b. Alberton, June 22, 1927.
Add: 46 Henley Beach Road, Lockleys.

Cecil Douglas GRAY (1921-22) RHB/LM West Torrens
b. April 28, 1902.
Dead.

Albert ("Alby") GREEN (1894-95) RHB/RAB Norwood
b. Medindie, N.S.W., Jan. 28, 1874.
d. circa 1924.
Noted Australian Rules footballer.

Donald Malcolm GREGG (1954-55) LHB/RMF Port Adelaide
b. Tumby Bay, Sept. 17, 1924.
Add: 7 Yamba Grove, West Lakes Shore.

George Edward GRIFFITHS (1965-66) RHB/OB Adelaide
b. Glebe, N.S.W., April 9, 1938.
Add: 7 Manning Parade, Dundas, N.S.W.
New South Wales 1962-63, 1964-65, 1967-68.

Clarence Victor GRIMMETT (1924-25) RHB/LBG Kensington/Adelaide Colts
b. Caversham, near Dunedin, Dec.25, 1891.
d. Kensington Gardens, May 2, 1980.
Tests: 37 Tours: England 1926; New Zealand 1927-28; England 1930; England 1934; South Africa 1935-36.
Wellington 1911-12 to 1913-14. Victoria 1918-19 to 1923-24.
Author of *Getting Wickets* (1930); *Tricking The Batsman* (1934); & *Grimmett On Cricket* (1948).

Brian Percival GROVE (1952-53) RHB/RFM Sturt
b. Adelaide, Feb. 23, 1921.
Add: 6 Meadowvale Road, Springfield.

Lancelot Townsend GUN (1924-25) b. Adelaide, April 13, 1903. d. Adelaide, May 25, 1958.	LHB/RFM	University/ N.Adelaide
Gordon GURR (1905-06) b. Adelaide, March 7, 1878.		
Alfred Thomas HACK (1927-28) b. Glenelg, June 12, 1905. d. South Terrace, of complications following an appendicitis operation, Feb. 4, 1933.	RHB/WK	Glenelg
Frederick Theodore HACK (1898-99) b. Aldinga, Aug. 24, 1877. d. Sydney, circa 1949.	RHB	Sturt
Reginald Norman HACK (1933-34) b. Glenelg, Feb. 25, 1907. d. Keith, Oct. 13, 1971. Son of F.T.Hack; brother of A.T.Hack.	LHB/RFM	Glenelg
John Arno HALBERT (1961-62) b. Hyde Park, Sept. 5, 1937. Add: 2 Ingrid St., Clapham.	RHB	Sturt
Ronald Andrewes HALCOMBE (1926-27) b. Petersburg, March 19, 1906. Add: 8 Sutcliffe Court, Highton, Vic. Western Australia 1928-29 to 1939-40. Cricket broadcaster.	RHB/RF	Colts
Harry Le HALDANE (1886-87) b. July 13, 1865	RHB/Lobs	Adelaide
Ronald Arthur HAMENCE (1935-36) b. Hindmarsh, Nov. 25, 1915. Add: 10 Koonga Ave., Rostrevor. Tests: 3 Tours: New Zealand 1945-46; England 1948.	RHB/RM	Colts/W.Torrens
Jeffrey Roy HAMMOND (1969-70) b. North Adelaide, April 19, 1950. Add: 21 Lovelock St., Highbury. Tests: 5 Tours: England 1972; West Indies 1972-73.	RHB/RFM	East Torrens/Prospect/Kensington
Anthony John HANDRICKAN (1976-77) b. Largs Bay, Jan. 6, 1959. Add: 29 Warrigal St., Para Hills.	RHB	Port Adelaide
Leopole Harry HANSON (1905-06) b. Woodville, Sept. 27, 1883.		West Torrens
Christopher Louis HARMS (1982-83) b. Albury, N.S.W., April 21, 1956. Add: 1 Sheila Court, Rostrevor.	LHB/OB	East Torrens
David HARRIS (1953-54) b. Alberton, Dec 19, 1930. Add: 11 Nareeda Way, West Lakes. Nephew of G.W.Harris.	RHB	Port Adelaide
Gordon William HARRIS (1920-21) b. Alberton, Dec. 11, 1897. d. Kensington Park, June 30, 1974.	RHB	Port Adelaide

Kim Phillip HARRIS (1981-82) RHB Adelaide
b. North Adelaide, Jan. 24, 1952.
Add: 2 Flinders Ave., Colonel Light Gardens.

Colin William HARRISON (1966-67) RHB/LBG Woodville
b. West Croydon, May 10, 1928.
Add: 12 Walkom Ave., Woodville South.

Neil James Napier HAWKE (1960-61) RHB/RMF Port Adelaide
b. Cheltenham, June 27, 1939.
Add: 15 Crompton Drive, Wattle Park.
Tests: 27 Tours: England, India & Pakistan 1964; West Indies 1964-65; South Africa 1966-67; England 1968; Commonwealth to Pakistan 1970-71.
Western Australia 1959-60. Tasmania 1968-69. Rest of World v. Barbados (Bridgetown) 1966-67. International Cavaliers v. Barbados (Scarborough) 1969.

Henry HAY (1902-03) RHB/RFM Sturt
b. Adelaide, March 30, 1874.
d. Adelaide, May 16, 1960.

Michael Donald HAYSMAN (1982-83) RHB/OB Glenelg
b. North Adelaide, April 22, 1961.
Add: 2 Harberton Road, South Brighton.
Tour: Zimbabwe 1982-83. Leicestershire 1984.

Charles Waterfield HAYWARD (1891-92) Norwood
b. Stepney, June 6, 1967.
d. North Adelaide, Feb. 2, 1934.

Lindsay Hudson HEAD (1957-58) RHB/LB West Torrens
b. North Adelaide, Sept. 16, 1935.
Add: 12 Glenburnie Ave., Torrens Park.
Noted Australian Rules footballer.

Herbert Venters HEAIRFIELD (1940-41) RHB/WK West Torrens
b. Adelaide, Feb. 28, 1907.
Add: 1/57 High St., Grange.
Noted lawn bowler.

Henry Francis Trafford ("Harry") HEATH (1923-24) RHB/LM East Torrens
b. Kadina, Dec. 19, 1885.
d. Edinburgh, July 9, 1967.
A.I.F. (v. Oxford Univ.) 1919.

Michael HENDRICKS (1970-71) RHB/WK Adelaide
b. Corrimal, N.S.W., Dec. 12, 1942.
Add: 46 The Strand, Reynella.
New South Wales 1969-70.

Donald A.HENRY (1920-21) RHB Sturt

Peter Jeffrey HERBERT (1971-72) RHB East Torrens
b. Adelaide, Jan. 8, 1947.
Add: 34 Lambert Road, Royston Park.

William Albert HEWER (1898-99) RHB/LB Sturt
b. May 7, 1877.
d. Wayville, June 2, 1948.

Jesse Bollard HIDE (1880-81) RHB/RMF South Adelaide
b. Eastbourne, Eng., March 12, 1857.
d. Edinburgh, March 19, 1924.
Sussex 1876 to 1893.

Barry Neil HIERN (1972-73) RHB/RFM Glenelg
b. North Adelaide, Aug. 8, 1951.
Add: Woodley Cres., Aberfoyle Park.
Son of R.N.Hiern.

Ross Noel HIERN (1949-50) RHB/RFM Kensington/Adelaide
b. Adelaide, Aug. 2, 1922
Add: 34 Austral Terrace, Morphettville.

Andrew Mark Jefferson HILDITCH (1982-83) RHB Glenelg
b. North Adelaide, May 20, 1956.
Add: 20 King George Ave., Hove.
Tests: 9 Tour: India 1979-80.
New South Wales 1976-77 to 1980-81.
Son-in-law of R.B.Simpson (N.S.W.)

Arthur ("Farmer") HILL (1889-90) RHB North Adelaide
b. Adelaide, May 28, 1871.
d. Glenelg, June 22, 1936.

Clement HILL (1892-93) LHB/occ.WK East Torrens/Sturt/North Adelaide/ East Adelaide
b. Adelaide, March 18, 1877.
d. Melbourne, Sept. 5, 1945.
Tests: 49 Tours: England & North America 1896; England 1899; England & South Africa 1902; New Zealand 1904-05; England 1905.

Henry John HILL (1903-04) RHB/LAB East Torrens
b. Adelaide, July 7, 1878.
d. Kensington Park, Oct. 30, 1906.

Leslie Roy HILL (1905-06) RHB/RFM East Torrens
b. Adelaide, April 27, 1884.
d. North Adelaide, Dec. 15, 1952.

Leon Trevor HILL (1958-59) RHB/OB Adelaide
b. West Croydon, Feb. 28, 1936.
Add: 69 Greythorn Road, North Balwyn, Victoria.
Queensland 1962-63.

Percival ("Peter") HILL (1892-93) RHB North Adelaide
b. Kent Town, July 4, 1868.
d. Adelaide, July 24, 1950.

Peter Distin HILL (1949-50) RHB West Torrens
b. Adelaide, Jan. 28, 1923.
Add: 14 Vansittart Place, Beaumont.

Rowland James HILL (1893-94) RHB/WK Adelaide
b. Parkside, Oct. 18, 1868.
d. Glenelg, Jan. 10, 1929.

Stanley ("Solly") HILL (1909-10) RHB East Torrens
b. Adelaide, Aug. 22, 1885.
d. Englefield Green, Eng., May 10, 1970.
New South Wales 1912-13.
Brother of A., C., H.J., L.R., & P.Hill.

Ernest John HISCOCK (1890-91) RHB Adelaide
b. Angaston, April 8, 1868.
d. Alberton, of inflammation of the bowl, Dec. 9, 1895.

Robert **Alan** HITCHCOCK (1958-59) RHB/RFM West Torrens
b. North Adelaide, May 14, 1938.
Add: 4 Holt St., Netley.

Malcolm Gordon Ferguson HODGE (1960-61) LHB/SLA Glenelg
b. Adelaide, Aug. 28, 1934.
Add: Tischer Road, Hahndorf.

Rodney Malcolm HOGG (1975-76) RHB/RF Prospect/Woodville
b. Richmond, Vic., March 5, 1951.
Tests: 34 Tours: India 1979-80; Sri Lanka & England 1981; Sri Lanka 1982-83; West Indies 1983-84.

Graeme Blake HOLE (1950-51) RHB/OB East Torrens/Glenelg
b. Concord West, N.S.W., Jan. 6, 1931.
Add: 55 Brigalow Ave., Kensington Gardens.
Tests: 18 Tour: England 1953.
New South Wales 1949-50. Commonwealth XI v M.C.C. (Colombo) 1951-52.

Raymond Sidney HOLMAN (1940-41) RHB/LBG Port Adelaide
b. Port Adelaide, Sept., 17, 1919.
Add: 97 Addison Road, Rosewater.

Leslie George ("Jack") HOLTON (1929-30) /RFM West Torrens
b. circa 1900.
d. circa 1949.

Robert Otto HOMBURG (1896-97) RHB/RFM Port Austral
b. Orroroo, Jan. 31, 1876.
d. Medindie, Oct. 21, 1948.

Brian William HONE (1928-29) RHB University
b. Semaphore, July 1, 1907.
d. Paris, May 28, 1978.
Oxford University 1931 to 1933. Brother of G.M.Hone.
Author of *Cricket Practice & Tactics* (1937). Distinguished educationalist.

Garton Maxwell ("Gar") HONE RHB/LBG University
b. Morphett Vale, Feb. 21, 1901.
Add: 4 Wahroonga Ave., Wattle Park.

David William HOOKES (1975-76) LHB/LM,SLC West Torrens
b. Mile End, May 3, 1955.
Add: 33B Waterfall Gully Road, Beaumont.
Tests: 19 Tours: England 1977; Pakistan 1979-80; Sri Lanka 1982-83; West Indies 1983-84.

John Rasell HORLEY (1960-61) LHB Prospect
b. Medindie, Jan. 23, 1936.
Add: 59A Collins St., Enfield.

Jack Aymat James HORSELL (1937-38) RHB/WK Sturt
b. Stepney, July 12, 1914.
Add: 1/46 Davenport Terrace, Seacliff Park.

Kenneth George HORSNELL (1953-54) LHB/LFM East Torrens/Kensington
b. Adelaide, Sept. 3, 1933
Add: 14 Morcomb St., Stepney.

Graham Warwick Charles HOUSE (1974-75) RHB/LB East Torrens
b. Busselton, W.A., Sept. 4, 1950.
Add: 37 Glenleigh Road, Busselton, W.A.
Western Australia 1972-73, 1973-74.

Leonard Easther HOWARD (1908-09) /RF Port Adelaide
b. Adelaide, April 18, 1886.

Victor HUGO (1897-98) /RM West Adelaide
b. Adelaide, Nov. 25, 1877.

Brian Morgan HURN (1957-58) LHB/RFM Colts/Kensington
b. Angaston, March 4, 1939.
Add: Angaston.

*Gilbert Ernest HUTTON (1905-06) /RFM Sturt
b. Feb. 15, 1884.

Mervyn Douglas HUTTON (1930-31) RHB/LB Sturt
b. Port Augusta, Aug. 24, 1911.
Add: 1 Regent St., Glenelg North.
Cousin of M.P.Hutton; nephew of W.F.P.Hutton.

Maurice Percy ("Moggy") HUTTON (1928-29) LHB Sturt
b. Parkside, March 21, 1903.
d. Mitcham, Feb 20, 1940.
Son of W.F.P.Hutton.

Norman Harvey HUTTON (1934-35) LHB/RFM Sturt
b. Adelaide, Aug. 10, 1911.
d. Fullarton, Aug. 27, 1965.
Son of W.F.P.Hutton; brother of M.P.Hutton; cousin of N.D.Hutton.

William Frederick Percival HUTTON (1905-06) /WK Sturt
b. Melrose, Oct. 2, 1876.
d. Millswood, Oct. 1, 1951.

Brian Keith ILLMAN (1960-61) RHB/RFM Colts
b. Unley, Oct. 23, 1937.
Add: 3 Bligh St., Panorama.

Gordon Bradford INKSTER (1926-27) RHB/WK Port Adelaide
b. Adelaide, June 30, 1893.
d. Bondi, N.S.W., March 22, 1957.

Robert John INVERARITY (1979-80) RHB/SLA Kensington
b. Subiaco, W.A., Jan. 31, 1944.
Add: 6 Holden St., Kensington Park.
Tests: 6 Tours: England 1968; New Zealand 1969-70; England 1972.
Western Australia 1962-63 to 1978-79.

Arthur Paul JAMES (1914-15) /RFM East Torrens
b. Fullarton, May 31, 1883.

Ronald Victor JAMES (1946-47) RHB/LM Adelaide
b. Paddington, N.S.W., May 23, 1920.
d. Auburn, N.S.W., April 28, 1983.
New South Wales 1938-39 to 1945-46; 1948-49 to 1950-51.

Dudley Garfield ("Doug") JAMIESON (1931-32) RHB/RM Kensington
b. Redruth, July 4, 1912.
d. Burnside, Jan. 14, 1979.

Barrington Noel ("Barry") JARMAN (1955-56) RHB/WK Woodville
b. Hindmarsh, Feb. 17, 1936.
Add: 28 High St., Burnside.
Tests: 19 Tours: New Zealand 1956-57; South Africa 1957-58; Pakistan & India 1959-60; England 1961; England & India 1964; West Indies 1964-65; New Zealand 1966-67; England 1968.

Alfred ("Fred") JARVIS (1889-90) RHB/RFM Hindmarsh/ West Torrens
b. Hindmarsh, Feb. 15, 1868.
d. Semaphore, Aug. 12, 1938.
Brother of A.H.Jarvis.

Arthur Harwood ("Affie") JARVIS (1877-78) RHB/WK Hindmarsh
b. Hindmarsh, Oct. 19, 1860.
d. Hindmarsh, Nov. 15, 1933.
Tests: 11 Tours: England 1880, 1886, 1888, 1893.

Harwood Samuel Coombe JARVIS (1905-06) RHB/WK West Torrens
b. Brompton, Aug. 30, 1884.
d. Port Pirie, Oct. 10, 1936.
Son of A.H.Jarvis.

Terrence James JENNER (1967-68) RHB/LBG Mt. Gambier/Prospect/Kensington
b. Mt. Lawley, W.A., Sept. 8, 1944.
Add: 37 Mannara Road, Salisbury North.
Tests: 9 Tours: New Zealand 1969-70; West Indies 1972-73; D.H.Robins to South Africa 1974-75.
Western Australia 1963-64 to 1966-67.

Claude Burrows JENNINGS (1902-03) RHB/occ.WK East Adelaide/ North Adelaide
b. East St.Kilda, Vic., June 5, 1884
d. Adelaide, June 20, 1950.
Tests: 6 Tour: England 1912.
Queensland 1910-11, 1911-12.

Eric Alfred JOHNSON (1926-27) RHB Kensington
b. July 11, 1902.
d. Adelaide, Jan. 10, 1976.

David Allan JOHNSTON (1978-79) RHB/RFM Glenelg
b. Melbourne, Dec. 4, 1954.
Add: 5/47 Park St., Hyde Park.
Son of W.A.Johnston (Vic.)

Ernest ("Jonah") JONES (1892-93) RHB/RF South Adelaide/ Port Adelaide
b. Auburn, Sept. 30, 1869.
d. Adelaide, Nov 23, 1943.
Tests: 19 Tours: England & North America 1896; England 1899; England & South Africa 1902-03.
Western Australia 1906-07, 1907-08.

W.JONES (1881-82) /LFM Hindmarsh
b. circa 1861.

Anthony Douglas JOSE (1947-48) RHB/RFM University
b. Adelaide, Feb. 17, 1929.
d. Los Angeles, Feb. 3, 1972.
Oxford University 1950, 1951. Kent 1951, 1952. Free Foresters 1953.
Son of G.E.Jose.

Gilbert Edgar JOSE (1918-19) RHB University
b. China, Nov 1, 1899.
d. at Changi prisoner-of-war camp, Singapore, March 27, 1942.

Edwin **Huntley** KEKWICK (1899-1900) RHB North Adelaide
b. Grange, March 5, 1875.
d. Adelaide, Aug. 29, 1950.

Benjamin **Charles** Ernest KEMP (1884-85) b. Plymouth, Eng., 1864. d. Albert Park, Vic., Dec. 3, 1940. Victoria 1891-92, 1897-98.	LHB/SLA	South Adelaide
Cornelius James ("Con") KENNEALLY (1949-50) b. Adelaide, July 28, 1926. Add: 166 Brighton Road, Somerton Park.	RHB	Glenelg
John Michael KIERSE (1939-40) b. Nhill, Vic., Jan. 11, 1918. Add: 60 Pulsford Road, Prospect.	RHB/RFM	Colts
James **Francis** KING (1877-78) b. Hindmarsh, May 23, 1851. d. Hindmarsh, June 28, 1921.	RHB/RF(r)	Hindmarsh
Norman Reginald KING (1949-50) b. Mile End, April 9, 1915. d. Linden Park, May 25, 1973.	RHB/LBG	West Torrens
Harold Peter KIRKWOOD (1901-02) b. Sept. 15, 1882 d. Unley, May 19, 1943.	RHB/LB	East Torrens/ Adelaide
Eugene Henry KITSON (1912-13) b. Nov. 28, 1889. Dead.	RHB	Adelaide
Thomas Elliott KLOSE (1939-40) b. Adelaide, Jan. 22, 1918. Add: 63 Balfour St., Nailsworth.	RHB/LM	Prospect
William KNILL (1880-81) b. Vic., Jan. 28, 1859. d. North Adelaide, July 8, 1940.	RHB/occ.WK	North Adelaide
Jeffrey Peter KOWALICK (1966-67) b. Maylands, July 22, 1946. Add: 14 Oxford St., Hyde Park.	LHB/RFM	Sturt
Daryl John LAMBERT (1976-77) b. Prospect, Oct. 8, 1946. Add: 13 Toolaby Ave., Beaumont.	LHB/SLA	East Torrens
Gilbert Roche Andrews LANGLEY (1945-46) b. North Adelaide, Sept. 14, 1919. Add: 10 Cambridge Terrace, Unley. Tests: 26 Tours: South Africa 1949-50; England 1953; West Indies 1954-55; England, Pakistan & India 1956.	RHB/WK	Sturt
Jeffrey Noel LANGLEY (1969-70) b. Adelaide, Oct. 28, 1948. Add: 49 Lewis St., Camp Hill, Qld. Queensland 1974-75 to 1977-78, 1979-80. Nephew of G.R.A.Langley.	RHB	Adelaide/Sturt
Henry ("Harry") LAYCOCK (1931-32) b. Edwardstown, Oct. 31, 1901. Add: McMahon's Road, Morphett Vale.	RHB/LB	Sturt

Brian Hedley ("Bill") LEAK (1935-36) RHB Colts/Sturt
b. Adelaide, May 5, 1917.
Add: 3 Centre Way, Belair.

Ernest Howard LEAK (1895-96) RHB Austral/E.Adelaide/Adelaide/Pt Adelaide
b. Oct. 28, 1872.
d. Adelaide, Aug. 22, 1945.

Stanley Garfield LEAK (1912-13) RHB Sturt
b. Goodwood, March 12, 1886.
d. Millswood, Jan. 10, 1963.

Phillip Keith ("Perka") LEE (1925-26) RHB/RM,OB East Torrens
b. Gladstone, Sept. 15, 1904.
d. Adelaide, Aug. 9, 1980.
Tests: 2

Robert William LEE (1956-57) RHB Adelaide
b. Adelaide, Jan. 31, 1927.
Add: 44 Fawnbrake Cres., West Beach.

Graham Bruce LEVY (1961-62) LHB University
b. North Adelaide, Feb. 10, 1938.
Add: 344 Shepherds Hill Road, Blackwood.

Keith LEWIS (1948-49) RHB Prospect
b. Prospect, Feb. 4, 1923.
Add: 14 Beryl St., Broadview.

Kevin John LEWIS (1981-82) LHB/LB West Torrens
b. Hindmarsh, Nov. 27, 1947.
Add: 89 East Terrace, Henley Beach.

Lance R.LEWIS (1926-27) RHB North Adelaide

John Charles LILL (1955-56) RHB/RM University/Sturt
b. Adelaide, Dec. 7, 1933.
Add: 288 Williams Road, Toorak, Vic.
Tour: New Zealand 1959-60.

George Grieve LISTON (1887-88) Norwood
b. April 29, 1860
d. Kent Town, Dec. 6, 1929.

Robert Grantley LLOYD (1960-61) RHB/LB Kensington
b. Gladstone, Oct. 24, 1940.
Add: 38 Delmore Cres., Mt. Waverley, Vic.

Albert Roy LONERGAN (1929-30) RHB Colts/Adelaide
b. Maylands, W.A., Dec. 6, 1909.
d. Adelaide, Oct. 22, 1956.
New South Wales 1935-36.

David Cameron LOVELL (1980-81) RHB Kensington
b. North Adelaide, Feb. 17, 1955.
Add: 14 St Margaret's Drive, Stirling.

Eustice Alfred ("Bunny") LOVERIDGE (1920-21) RHB/RM,LB East Torrens
b. Yongala, April 14, 1891.
d. Adelaide, July 29, 1959.

Frank Russell LUCAS (1919-20) RHB/RFM Sturt
b. Port Pirie, Nov. 11, 1888.

Thomas Turland LUCAS (1877-78) Norwood
b. Feb. 18, 1852.
d. Norwood, March 13, 1945.

John James LYONS (1884-85) RHB/RM Norwood
b. Gawler, May 21, 1863.
d. Adelaide, July 21, 1927.
Tests: 14 Tours: England 1888, 1890; England & North America 1893.

Donald Ernest McALLISTER (1964-65) RHB Port Adelaide
b. Hindmarsh, Nov. 19, 1936.
Add: 24 Ferdinand Crescent, Coolbellup, W.A.

Andrew McBETH (1906-07) /LFM West Torrens
b. June 17, 1876.
d. March 17, 1945.
New South Wales 1899-1900 to 1903-04.

Kevin Joseph McCARTHY (1964-65) RHB/RFM Prospect/Glenelg
b. Rose Park, Oct. 11, 1945.
Add: 83 Brighton Road, Glenelg North.

Raymond Vincent McCORMICK (1959-60) RHB/OB West Torrens
b. Mile End, Jan. 30, 1931.
Add: 33 Lorraine Ave, Lockleys.

Douglas Gordon McKAY (1925-26) RHB/RFM University/Adelaide
b. North Adelaide, July 2, 1904
Add: 118 Buxton St., North Adelaide.
Nephew of H.J.McKay.

Henry James McKAY (1912-13) LHB/SLA Sturt
b. Goodwood, Jan 1, 1883.
d. Hawthorn, Feb. 12, 1926.

John McKENZIE (1884-85) LHB/RF/WK South Adelaide/ Port Adelaide/Norwood
b. Oct. 11, 1862.
d. Hazelwood Park, July 1944.

Ian Murray McLACHLAN (1960-61) RHB/LB Sturt
b. Adelaide, Oct. 2, 1936.
Add: 5 Fuller Court, Walkerville.
Tour: E.W.Swanton's XI to West Indies 1960-61.
Cambridge University 1956 to 1958.
Brother of A.A.McLachlan (Cambridge University)

Donald McRAE (1906-07) RHB Adelaide
b. Aldinga, June 13, 1873.
d. Prospect, Oct. 22, 1940.

William Ashley MAGAREY (1890-91) RHB Adelaide
b. North Adelaide, Jan. 30, 1868.
North Adelaide, Oct. 18, 1929.

Ashley Alexander MALLETT (1967-68) RHB/OB Sturt/Prospect/Glenelg
b. Chatswood, N.S.W., July 13, 1945.
Tests: 38 Tours: England 1968; Ceylon, India & South Africa 1969-70; England 1972; New Zealand 1973-74; England 1975; International Wanderers to South Africa 1975-76; England 1980.
Cricket journalist & author.

John Lewis MANN (1945-46) RHB/SLA Sturt
b. Strathalbyn, April 26, 1919.
d. Lockleys, Sept. 24, 1969.

John Stephen MANNING (1951-52) LHB/SLA Glenelg
b. Adelaide, June 11, 1924.
Add: Hallett.
Northamptonshire 1954 to 1960.

Lynn Alexander MARKS (1965-66) LHB Glenelg
b. Randwick, N.S.W., Aug. 15, 1942.
Add: 10 Siobhan Place, Mona Vale, N.S.W.
New South Wales 1962-63 to 1964-65; 1966-67 to 1968-69.
Son of A.E.Marks (N.S.W.); brother of N.G.Marks (N.S.W.)

Charles MARTIN (1895-96) South Adelaide

John Wesley MARTIN (1958-59) LHB/SLC East Torrens
b. Wingham, N.S.W., July 28, 1931.
Add: Burrell Creek, N.S.W.
Tests: 8 Tours: New Zealand 1956-57 & 1959-60; Cavaliers to India & South Africa 1962-63; England & India 1964; South Africa 1966-67.
New South Wales 1956-57, 1957-58; 1959-60 to 1967-68.

John George Facey MATTHEWS (1900-01) RHB North Adelaide
b. Sept. 27, 1876.
d. Prospect, Oct. 8, 1963.

Richard Edgar MAYNE (1906-07) RHB East Torrens
b. Jamestown, July 2, 1882.
d. Carrum, Vic., Oct. 26, 1961.
Tests: 4 Tours: New Zealand 1909-10; England & North America 1912; North America 1913; England & South Africa 1921-22; Victoria to New Zealand 1924-25.
Victoria 1918-19 to 1925-26.

Leonard MICHAEL (1939-40) RHB/WK Prospect
b. Adelaide, June 3, 1921.
Add: 68 Archer St., North Adelaide.

Roy Foster MIDDLETON (1912-13) RHB East Torrens
b. Adelaide, Sept. 18, 1889.
d. Adelaide, March 19, 1975.
Member of South Australian Cricket Association Committee 1914-15, 1915-16, and 1924-25 to 1964-65.

Brian Gordon MITCHELL (1978-79) RHB Glenelg
b. Glenelg North, March 15, 1959.
Add: 8 Vienna Ave., Aberfoyle Park.

*William D.MOFFAT (1877-78) RHB Kensington
b. Aug. 31, 1858.

H.MOORE (1891-92) North Adelaide

Robert MORONEY (1920-21) LHB/RFM Port Adelaide
b. Jan. 23, 1885.

Francis Lonsdale MORTON (1921-22) RHB/RF East Torrens
b. Rose Park, Dec. 21, 1901.
d. Caulfield, Vic., Oct. 14, 1971.
Tour: New Zealand 1927-28.
Victoria 1926-27 to 1931-32.

Alban George ("Johnnie") MOYES (1912-13) RHB/LB University
b. Gladstone, Jan. 2, 1893.
d. Chatswood, N.S.W., Jan. 18, 1963.
Victoria 1919-20, 1920-21.
Famous cricket author, journalist and radio commentator.

Charles Rule MOYLE (1910-11) /WK Adelaide
b. April 16, 1884.

Edward James **Ross** MOYLE (1933-34) RHB/WK Kensington
b. Moonta, Oct. 15, 1913.
d. Egypt, as a result of wounds received in action in the Middle East, Oct. 24, 1942.

Mervyn Edgar MUELLER (1937-38) RHB Prospect
b. Adelaide, Oct. 3, 1914.
Add: 94 Raglan Ave., South Plympton.

David Lloyd MUNDY (1969-70) RHB/RM Teachers Colleges
b. Enfield, June 30, 1947.
Add: 13 Granville St., Semaphore Park.

John Tinline MURRAY (1911-12) RHB/RM East Torrens
b. Dec. 1, 1892.
d. Stirling, Sept. 19, 1974.
Tour: A.I.F. to England 1919 & South Africa 1919-20.

John MUSGROVE (1887-88) /LF South Adelaide

Howard James Charles MUTTON (1959-60) RHB/OB Kensington
b. Angaston, Oct. 21, 1924.
Add: 9 Wahroonga Ave., Wattle Park.

John Eric NASH (1970-71) RHB Teachers Colleges/Sturt/East Torrens
b. North Adelaide, April 16, 1950
Add: 12 Kneebone St., Goodwood.

Philip Mesmer NEWLAND (1899-1900) RHB/WK East Torrens
b. Feb. 2, 1875.
d. Westbury, Aug. 11, 1916.
Tours: New Zealand 1904-05; England 1905.

Richard Dudley NIEHUUS (1946-47) LHB Glenelg
b. St Peters, July 6, 1917.
Add: 68 College Road, Somerton Park.

Holmesdale Carl ("Jack") NITSCHKE (1929-30) LHB East Torrens
b. Adelaide, April 14, 1905.
d. Adelaide, Sept. 29, 1982.
Tests: 2
Noted race horse owner and breeder.

Geffery NOBLET (1945-46) RHB/RFM Glenelg
b. Adelaide, Sept. 14, 1916.
Add: 22 Korana St., South Plympton.
Tests: 3 Tour: South Africa 1949-50. Commonwealth XI v. England XI (Hastings) 1956.

John NOEL (1880-81) RHB/RAB Hindmarsh
b. Hindmarsh, March 28, 1856.
d. Largs Bay, Jan. 9, 1938.

Thomas Reginald O'CONNELL (1935-36) b. Adelaide, March 10, 1916. Add: Hawker Road, Aldinga.	LHB/LFM	Colts
Donald Frederick Gregory O'CONNOR (1983-84) b. Gilgandra, N.S.W., July 20, 1958. Add: 5 Philip Court, Rostrevor.	LHB	East Torrens
John Dennis Alphonsus O'CONNOR (1906-07) b. Sydney, Sept. 9, 1875. d. Lewisham, N.S.W., Aug. 23, 1941. Tests: 4 Tour: England 1909. New South Wales 1904-05, 1905-06.	LHB/RM	North Adelaide/ West Torrens
Patrick Andreas OHLSTROM (1923-24) b. Warooka, Dec. 16, 1890. d. Adelaide, June 10, 1940.	LHB/OB	University
Kevin Ignatius O'NEILL (1946-47) b. Adelaide, Aug. 16, 1919. Add: 8 Cadna Ave., Felixstow.	RHB/RFM	Kensington
Francis **James** OSBORN (1953-54) b. Albert Park, Feb. 13, 1935. Add: 30 Frogmore Cres., Park Orchards, Vic.	LHB/LBG	Colts
Robert Martin O'SHANNASSY (1976-77) b. Hindmarsh, March 7, 1949. Add: 3 Hoylake Cres., Fairview Park.	RHB/RM	Prospect
Norman Hamilton OSWALD (1936-37) b. Prospect, Oct. 31, 1916. d. Adelaide, June 22, 1970.	RHB/LBG	Colts/Sturt
George Hamilton PALMER (1924-25) b. Eastwood, Aug. 2, 1903. Add: 8/219 Findon Road, Findon.	LHB/LFM	East Torrens
Jack Stirling ("Jock") PALMER (1932-33) b. East Adelaide, Oct. 20, 1903. d. Glenelg, Dec. 11, 1979.	RHB	East Torrens
Ronald Arthur PARKER (1933-34) b. Goodwood, Feb. 23, 1916. Add: 255 Jackson St., San Francisco.	RHB	Glenelg/Sturt
Russell John PARKER (1974-75) b. Sudbury, Middlesex, Eng., Aug. 3, 1952. Add: 32 Glencoe Road, Reynella.	RHB/LB	Glenelg
George Thomas PARKIN (1889-90) b. Oct. 11, 1864.	RHB/RM,OB	South Adelaide
Samuel David Haslam PARKINSON (1981-82) b. Adelaide, July 8, 1960. Add: 31 Giles St., Magill.	LHB/LFM	Kensington
Cyril Norman PARRY (1925-26) b. Queenstown, Oct. 14, 1900. d. Kew, Vic., July 6, 1984. Tasmania 1931-32 to 1933-34.	RHB/WK	West Torrens

Trevor John PEARSON (1969-70) RHB/RFM Woodville
b. Goodwood, Oct. 13, 1943.
Add: 66 Smith Road, Salisbury East.

Arthur Howard PELLEW (1900-01) West Torrens
b. Riverton, Jan. 20, 1878.

Clarence Everard ("Nip") PELLEW (1913-14) RHB/RM University/Prospect North Adelaide
b. Port Pirie, Sept. 21, 1893.
d. Adelaide, May 9, 1981
Tests: 10 Tours: A.I.F. to England 1919 & South Africa 1919-20; England 1921 and South Africa 1921-22.

John Harold ("Nip") PELLEW (1903-04) RHB/LB North Adelaide
b. Truro, July 17, 1882.
Brother of A.H.Pellew.

Lancelot Vivian PELLEW (1919-20) RHB University
b. Port Elliott, Dec. 15, 1899.
d. Adelaide, Dec. 8, 1970.
Tour: New Zealand 1920-21.
Brother of C.E.Pellew; cousin of A.H. & J.H.Pellew.

Arthur Ernest PETERS (1898-99) RHB East Torrens
b. March 8, 1872.
d. Henley Beach, Sept. 24, 1903.

Aldam Murr PETTINGER (1880-81) RHB North Adelaide
b. Kent Town, July 30, 1859.
d. Lower Mitcham, Aug. 18, 1950.

Edward George PHILLIPS (1877-78) RHB North Adelaide
b. March 1, 1851.
d. North Adelaide, Feb. 8, 1933.

Edward Lauriston ("Lawrence") PHILLIPS (1919-20) /RFM North Adelaide
b. Adelaide, Sept. 2, 1892.
d. circa 1970.

Wayne Bentley PHILLIPS (1977-78) LHB/occ.WK Sturt
b. Adelaide, March 1, 1958.
Add: 3/25 Mathias Ave., Cumberland Park.
Tests: 10 Tours: Pakistan 1982-83; Zimbabwe 1982-83; West Indies 1983-84

Colin John PINCH (1950-51) RHB/SLA Adelaide
b. Brownsville, N.S.W., June 23, 1921.
Add: 23 Marine Ave., Hallett Cove.
New South Wales 1949-50.

Brian Harold PITTMAN (1959-60) LHB Kensington
b. Adelaide, June 17, 1930.
Add: 401 The Parade, Kensington Gardens.

Louis Bertrand POWER (1926-27) RHB/LBG University
b. Prospect, Oct. 10, 1905.
Add: 34 Moore St., Somerton Park.
Brother of L.J.Power.

Laurence James POWER (1920-21) RHB North Adelaide
b. North Adelaide, July 31, 1898.
d. Glenelg, March 20, 1963.
Noted operatic tenor.

Alfred Henry PRETTY (1908-09) b. Willunga, Jan. 29, 1874. d. Mile End, June 21, 1929.	/LB	West Torrens
Walter Davies PRICE (1913-14) b. March 24, 1886. d. Adelaide, July 29, 1944.	/RM	Sturt
Wayne PRIOR (1974-75) b. Salisbury, Sept. 30, 1952. Add: Griggs Road, Mt. Pleasant.	RHB/RF	Salisbury
David Edward PRITCHARD (1918-19) b. Queenstown, Jan. 5, 1893. d. Myrtle Bank, July 4, 1983.	LHB	Port Adelaide
Maxwell Charles PUCKETT (1964-65) b. Unley, June 3, 1935. Add: 14 Kenton St., Lockleys. Son of C.W.Puckett (W.A.)	RHB/RMF	West Torrens
Ernest Ivan PYNOR (1948-49) b. Essendon, Vic., April 23, 1920. Add: 14 Dempster Court, Donvale, Vic.	RHB/OB	Sturt
Brian Maxwell QUIGLEY (1958-59) b. Henley Beach, Dec. 27, 1935. Add: 850 Upper Brookfield Road, Upper Brookfield, Qld.	RHB/RFM	University
John QUILTY (1881-82) b. Adelaide, 1860. d. Adelaide, May 9, 1942.	LHB/LAB	Norwood
Karl Hugo QUIST (1908-09) b. Milsons Point, N.S.W., Aug. 18, 1875. d. Plympton, March 31, 1957. New South Wales 1899-1900; Western Australia 1905-06.	RHB	Adelaide
Phillip Douglas REBBECK (1971-72) b. North Adelaide, July 31, 1948 Add: 6 Clinton Ave., Myrtle Bank.	RHB	Adelaide
Jone Cole ("Dinny") REEDMAN (1877-78) b. Adelaide, Oct. 9, 1865 d. Gilberton, March 23, 1924. Test: 1	RHB/RM	South Adelaide/North Adelaide
John Newman Stace REES (1905-06) b. Adelaide, Sept. 2, 1880. d. St.Peters, Jan 17, 1959.	RHB/occ.WK	North Adelaide
Robert Blackie C.REES (1903-04) b. Hindmarsh, April 15, 1882. d. Bowmans Green, Eng., Sept. 20, 1966. Brother of J.N.S.Rees.	RHB/LBG	North Adelaide
W.REID (1892-93)		North Adelaide
Barry Anderson RICHARDS (1970-71) b. Durban, South Africa, July 21, 1945. Tests: South Africa 4. Natal 1964-65 to 1982-83. Gloucestershire 1965. Hampshire 1968 to 1978.	RHB/OB	Prospect

Thomas Oliver RICHARDS (1880-81) RHB/RAB Norwood
b. July 5, 1855.

Arthur John RICHARDSON (1918-19) RHB/OB East Torrens/Colts
b. Sevenhill, near Clare, July 24, 1888.
d. Adelaide, Dec. 23, 1973.
Tests: 9 Tour: England 1926.
Western Australia 1927-28 to 1929-30. Sir L.Parkinson's XI v West Indies (Blackpool) 1933.
Test umpire in West Indies 1934-35. Brother-in-law of E.L.Bowley.
Author of Cricket Coaching Manual (S.A.C.A. 1947).

Joseph ("Jock") RICHARDSON (1905-06) /WK Adelaide
b. Feb. 28, 1878.
d. Glenelg, June 13, 1951.

Victor York RICHARDSON (1918-19) RHB/RM Sturt
b. Unley, Sept. 7, 1894.
d. Fullarton, Oct. 29, 1969.
Tests: 19 Tours: New Zealand 1920-21, 1927-28; England 1930; South Africa 1935-36.
Distinguished all-round sportsman; noted radio commentator; author of *The Vic. Richardson Story.*

Arthur Frederick RICHTER (1935-36) RHB/LBG East Torrens
b. Port Pirie, Sept. 1, 1908.
d. Adelaide, Aug. 16, 1936.
Nephew of E.Jones.

Kenneth Lovett RIDINGS (1938-39) RHB/LBG West Torrens
b. Unley, Feb. 7, 1920.
d. on active service, Bay of Biscay, May 17, 1943.
Brother of P.L.Ridings.

Philip Lovett RIDINGS (1937-38) RHB/RMF West Torrens
b. Adelaide, Oct. 2, 1917.
Add: 4 Rockingham St., West Beach.
Tour: New Zealand 1949-50.

Stephen RIGAUD (1877-78) /RF Kensington
b. Nov 25, 1856.

William **Norman** RILEY (1925-26) RHB/LFM East Torrens
b. Hyde Park, April 9, 1894.
d. North Adelaide, Oct. 2, 1960.

William **Maurice** ROBERTS (1937-38) RHB/OB Port Adelaide
b. Wallaroo Mines, Aug. 26, 1916.
Add: 100 Trimmer Parade, Seaton.

Trevor John ROBERTSON (1977-78) RHB/WK Port Adelaide
b. Rose Park, Nov. 20, 1947.
Add: 54 Riverside Drive, Fulham.

Donnell ("Don") ROBINS (1964-65) RHB/RM Sturt
b. Adelaide, March 2, 1934.
Add: 14 Old Belair Road, Belair.

Rayford Harold ROBINSON (1937-38) RHB/LBG Prospect
b. Stockton, N.S.W., March 26, 1914.
d. Stockton, N.S.W., Aug. 10, 1965.
Test: 1

New South Wales 1934-35 to 1936-37; 1939-40.
Otago 1946-47 to 1948-49.

Barrie Charles ROBRAN (1971-72) RHB Prospect
b. Whyalla, Sept. 25, 1947.
Add: 14 Cambridge Terrace, Vale Park.

Douglas John Rolfe (1979-80) RHB Kensington
b. Wheelers Hill, Vic., Feb. 26, 1953
Add: 8 Arnold Ave., Firle.
Victoria 1975-76.

Arthur Victor Hugo ROSMAN (1898-99) RHB East Adelaide
b. Barossa Valley, Nov. 26, 1870.
d. Adelaide, Feb. 10, 1948.

Robert Charles ROXBY (1954-55) RHB/LBG Sturt
b. Newcastle, N.S.W., March 16, 1926.
Add: 64 Opey Ave., Hyde Park.
New South Wales 1953-54.

Joshua Upcott ("Joe") RUNDELL (1883-84) RHB/RF North Adelaide
b. Bendigo, Vic., May 6, 1861.
d. Alberton, Jan. 7, 1922.

Percy Davies RUNDELL (1912-13) RHB/RM,LB Port Adelaide/Glenelg
b. Adelaide, Nov. 20, 1890
d. North Adelaide, March 24, 1979.
Son of J.U.Rundell.

Albert James ("Bulla") RYAN (1925-26) RHB/RM Adelaide/Sturt
b. Adelaide, April 27, 1904.
Add: 7 Craigie St., Birkenhead.

Jack Westall RYMILL (1921-22) LHB Kensingston/East Torrens
b. Winninnie Station, near Broken Hill, N.S.W., March 20, 1901.
d. Adelaide, Feb. 11, 1976.

Christopher Bagot SANGSTER (1927-28) RHB/RMF University
b. Burra, May 1, 1908.
Add: 16 George St., Unley Park.

John Fraser SANGSTER (1961-62) RHB/LM University
b. Adelaide, Jan. 21, 1942.
Add: 4 Abbotshall Road, Hawthorn.
Son of C.B.Sangster.

Murray Alfred James SARGENT (1960-61) RHB/LB Glenelg
b. Adelaide, Aug. 23, 1928.
Add: 31 Esplanade, Somerton Park.
Leicestershire 1951, 1952.

Dean Keith SAYERS (1981-82) RHB/RMF Woodville
b. Hindmarsh, June 11, 1954.
Add: 25/45 Barry Road, Oaklands Park.

Karl Joseph SCHNEIDER (1926-27) LHB/LBG East Torrens
b. Hawthorn, Vic., Aug. 15, 1905.
d. of leukaemia at Kensington Park, Sept. 25, 1928.
Tour: New Zealand 1927-28.
Victoria 1922-23, 1924-25.

Bruce SCHULTZ (1936-37) RHB/RFM East Torrens
b. Joslin, March 13, 1913.
d. Modbury, Jan. 11, 1980.
Son of J.W.E.Schultz.

Julian William Eugene ("Ernie") SCHUTZ (1919-20) RHB/WK East Torrens
b. Somerton, Sept. 25, 1888.
d. Berri, Aug. 8, 1966.

Darryl Bryan SCOTT (1983-84) RHB Sturt
b. Glenelg South, March 9, 1961.
Add: 46 Hendale St., Morphetville.

Jack SCOTT (1937-38) RHB/LM West Torrens
b. N.S.W. circa 1916.

John Drake SCOTT (1925-26) RHB/RF Sturt
b. Sydney, Jan. 31, 1888.
d. Springbank, April 7, 1974.
New South Wales 1908-09 to 1924-25.
Test Umpire (10 matches)

Bernard Vincent SCRYMGOUR (1890-91) Adelaide
b. Adelaide, July 31, 1864.
d. Medindie, April 16, 1943.

Reginald Hugh Durning ("Rex") SELLERS (1959-60) RHB/LBG Kensington
b. Bulsar, India, Aug. 20, 1940.
Add: 15 Clearview Terrace, Flagstaff Hill.
Test: 1 Tour: England & India 1964.

Victor Poole SELTH (1918-19) RHB/WK Sturt
b. Parkside, June 1, 1895.
d. Daw Park, Sept. 2, 1967.

Duncan A.SHARPE (1961-62) RHB/OB Woodville
b. Rawalpindi, India (now Pakistan), Aug. 3, 1937.
Tests: Pakistan 3.
Pakistan (domestic) 1955-56 to 1960-61.

Alan Gordon SHEPHERD (1931-32) RHB West Torrens
b. Adelaide, Dec. 29, 1912.
Add: 13 Keys Road, Lower Mitcham.

Hartley **Robert** SHEPHERDSON (1935-36) LHB/RFM Glenelg
b. Mt. Gambier, Sept. 4, 1913.
Add: 170 Eglinton St., Kew, Vic.

Herbert **Neil** SHEPLEY (1925-26) RHB/RMF Kensington
b. Adelaide, Oct. 7, 1899.
d. Tranmere, Nov 14, 1953.

Alan Bruce SHIELL (1964-65) RHB East Torrens
b. St. Peters, April 25, 1945.
Add: 29 Myer Road, Sturt.

Henry William C? SHORT (1904-05) East Adelaide
b. March 31, 1884.

Robert Frank SIMUNSEN (1972-73) LHB Woodville
b. Adelaide, June 7, 1941.
Add: 2 Pine Lodge Crescent, Seaton.

Andrew Thomas SINCOCK (1974-75) RHB/RFM East Torrens/Adelaide
b. Adelaide, June 7, 1951
Add: 22 Braeside Ave., Reynella.
Second cousin of D.J. & P.D.Sincock.

David John SINCOCK (1960-61) RHB/SLC University/Glenelg
b. North Adelaide, Feb. 1, 1942.
Add: 44 Wesley St., Elanora Heights, N.S.W.
Tests: 3 Tours: Cavaliers to India & South Africa 1962-63; West Indies 1964-65.

Harrold Keith SINCOCK (1929-30) RHB/LB Colts
b. Parkside, Dec. 10, 1907.
d. Plympton, Feb. 2, 1982.
Second cousin of R.J.Sincock (Vic.)

Peter Damien SINCOCK (1974-75) RHB Glenelg
b. North Adelaide, July 8, 1948.
Add: 37 Lutana Crescent, Mitchell Park.
Brother of D.J.Sincock; son of H.K.Sincock.

Peter Raymond SLEEP (1976-77) RHB/LBG Kensington/
b. Penola, May 4, 1957.
Add: 59 Harris Road, Salisbury East.
Tests: 4 Tours: India 1979-80; Pakistan 1982-83.

Alexander Frank ("Alick") SLIGHT (1886-87) LHB North Adelaide
b. Emerald Hill, Vic., April 13, 1861.
Brother of J.Slight (Vic.) & W.Slight (Vic. & S.Aust.)

William SLIGHT (1880-81) RHB/RAB North Adelaide
b. Emerald Hill, Vic., Sept. 19, 1858.
d. Adelaide, Dec. 23, 1941.
Victoria 1877-78.

Laurence Maxwell SMART (1950-51) RHB/RM Glenelg
b. Crystal Brook, Feb. 16, 1928.
Add: 24 Oxford Road, Aldgate.

Andrew Edwin SMITH (1913-14) RHB/LBG East Torrens/West Torrens
b. Port Adelaide, Sept. 1, 1889.
d. Adelaide, May 18, 1983.

Lavington Albert ("Lavvy") SMITH (1933-34) RHB Prospect
b. Medindie, Oct. 9, 1904.
d. Adelaide, May 9, 1953.

Garfield St.Aubrun SOBERS (1961-62) LHB/LFM,SL C Prospect
b. Bridgetown, Barbados, July 28, 1936.
Add: 22 Entally Drive, Glen Waverley, Vic.
Tests: West Indies 93 Tours: (with West Indies teams unless otherwise stated) New Zealand 1955-56; England 1957; India & Pakistan 1958-59; Australia 1960-61; England 1963 England 1966; India & Ceylon 1966-67; Australia & New Zealand 1968-69; England 1969; Rest of the World to Australia 1971-72; England 1973.
Barbados 1952-53 to 1973-74. Nottinghamshire 1968 to 1974.
Author (or co-author) of 6 books on cricket.

Philip Horley SQUIRES (1962-63) LHB/LBG Kensington
b. Uraidla, June 18, 1939.
Add: 2 Solero Ave., Reynella.

Graham Edwin STANFORD (1968-69) LHB/RFM West Torrens
b. Adelaide, April 25, 1948.
Add: 593 Grange Road, Grange.
Third Cousin of R.M.Stanford.

Ross Milton STANFORD (1935-36) RHB West Torrens
b. Fulham, Sept. 25, 1917.
Add: 14 Debney St., Fulham Gardens.
Tour: Services in England 1945 and India & Ceylon 1945-46.

Cecil Leonard Berry STARR (1926-27) RHB/OB Colts/Adelaide
b. Quorn, July 20, 1907.
Add: 380 Anzac Highway, Plympton.

Donald Macdonald STEELE (1911-12) RHB University
b. East Adelaide, Aug. 17, 1892.
d. Adelaide, July 13, 1962.
Brother of K.N.Steele.

Kenneth Nugent STEELE (1913-14) RHB/RFM University
b. St Peters, Dec. 17, 1889.
d. North Adelaide, Dec. 19, 1956.

Gavin Byron STEVENS (1952-53) RHB Glenelg/Adelaide
b. Adelaide, Feb. 29, 1932.
Add: 36 Lewis St., Brighton.
Tests: 4 Tour: Pakistan & India 1959-60.

William Leslie STILLMAN (1977-78) RHB Adelaide
b. Alexandria, Vic., Oct. 5, 1949.
Add: 30 Huntingdon Drive, Glenalta.
Victoria 1970-71 to 1975-76.

William Stuart STIRLING (1908-09) RHB/LM Adelaide/East Torrens
b. Jamestown, March 19, 1891.
d. Adelaide, July 18, 1971.
Tour: A.I.F. to England 1919 & South Africa 1919-20.

Donald John SUTHERLAND (1969-70) LHB/OB Teachers Colleges
b. Adelaide, Nov. 28, 1949.
Add: 14 Hinton St., Underdale.

Crawford SYMONDS (1945-46) LHB/WK Prospect
b. North Adelaide, Feb. 15, 1915.
Add: 7 Durant St., Plympton.

John Henry TARDIF (1889-90) LHB Adelaide
b. Gawler, May 17, 1860.
d. Prospect, June 14, 1920.

Reginald Crump TEAGLE (1930-31) RHB/RFM Colts
b. Parkside, Feb. 27, 1909.
Add: 17 Campbell Road, Parkside.

Francis Lawrence TEISSEIRE (1939-40) RHB Adelaide
b. Adelaide, July 8, 1917.
Add: 12 Farrell St., Glenelg South.

Wilheim THAMM (1902-03) /WK West Torrens
b. July 2, 1871.

Arthur Churchill THOMAS (1898-99) | RHB | Sturt
b. Unley, May 4, 1869.
d. Unley, April 28, 1934.

Raymon Cedric THOMAS (1952-53) | RHB/RFM | Colts
b. Adelaide, Nov. 18, 1932.
Add: 67 Booth Ave., Morphet Vale.

Horace **Malcolm** THOMPSON (1935-36) | RHB/RFM | Sturt
b. Malvern, Oct. 29, 1913.
d. in a road accident at Kalgoorlie, W.A., March 19, 1936.

Wilfred John ("Bill") THURGALAND (1920-21) | LHB/LFM | Port Adelaide
b. Queenstown, March 11, 1892.
d. Campbelltown, July 12, 1974.

Bertram Joseph TOBIN (1930-31) | RHB/RFM | Colts/Adelaide
b. North Adelaide, Nov. 11, 1910.
d. Adelaide, Oct. 19, 1969.

Richard James **Bruce** TOWNSEND (1907-08) | LHB/RM | East Torrens/Sturt
b. Aug. 12, 1886.
d. Waikerie, Jan. 17, 1960.

Joseph Patrick Francis ("Ike") TRAVERS (1895-96) | LHB/SLA | Austral/Port Adelaide East Adelaide
b. Adelaide, Jan. 10, 1871
d. Adelaide, Sept. 15, 1942.
Test: 1

Jack TREGONING (1939-40) | RHB/RFM | University
b. Adelaide, June 13, 1919.
Add: 72 Buxton St., North Adelaide.

Peter Grant TRETHEWEY (1957-58) | RHB/RFM | Colts/West Torrens
b. Adelaide, May 12, 1935.
Add: 7 Keston Ave., Mosman, N.S.W.
Queensland 1962-63.

Dean Frederick TROWSE (1951-52) | RHB | Colts/Kensington
b. Adelaide, Oct. 18, 1931.
Add: 29 Marney St., Chapel Hill.

Thomas TURNER (1885-86) | /LM | South Adelaide
b. circa 1865.
Victoria 1887-88.

Roland William ("Rolly") VAUGHTON (1946-47) | RHB/WK | Adelaide
b. Angaston, May 4, 1914.
d. Adelaide, Jan. 5, 1979.

Brian Alfred VINCENT (1980-81) | LHB/RFM | Glenelg
b. Unley, Feb. 16, 1960.
Add: 529 States Road, Hackham.
Brother of R.G.Vincent.

Russell George VINCENT (1976-77) | RHB/WK | Sturt
b. Jamestown, March 23, 1954.
Add: 64 Collins Parade, Hackham.

Edmund George Chalwin ("Baby") WAINWRIGHT (1922-23) LHB/LB Adelaide
b. North Adelaide, May 18, 1903.
Add: 3 Patten Court, Herne Hill, Vic.

Mervyn George WAITE (1930-31) RHB/RM,OB West Torrens/Glenelg
b. Kent Town, Jan. 7, 1911.
Add: Fisher St., Georgetown.
Tests: 2 Tour: England 1938.

Alfred Edward ("Topsy") WALDRON (1881-82) LHB Norwood
b. Mornington, Vic., Feb. 26, 1857.
d. Adelaide, June 7, 1929.

Charles William WALKER (1928-29) RHB/WK Colts/West Torrens/Prospect
b. Brompton, Feb. 19, 1909.
d. on active service at Soltau, Russia, Dec. 18, 1942.
Tours: England 1930, 1938.

Edgar Allen WALKLEY (1900-01) RHB/RAB West Torrens
b. Dec. 12, 1878.

Thomas Welbourne ("Tim") WALL (1924-25) RHB/RF Colts/Prospect
b. Semaphore, May 13, 1904.
d. Adelaide, March 26, 1981.
Tests: 18 Tours: England 1930, 1934.

Laurence Stanley WALSH (1930-31) RHB Sturt
b. North Adelaide, Feb. 8, 1902.
d. St.Georges, Jan. 12, 1976.

Norman Arthur WALSH (1923-24) RHB Colts
b. North Adelaide, Feb. 8, 1902.
d. Adelaide, Dec. 7, 1969.
Twin brother of L.S.Walsh.

Francis Anthony WARD (1935-36) RHB/LBG Adelaide/Sturt
b. Sydney, Feb. 23, 1909.
d. Sydney, May 25, 1974.
Tests: 4 Tour: England 1938.

Robert William WATERS (1901-02) /RM Port Adelaide
b. Gravesend, Kent, 1874.
d. of pneumonia at Woodville, Feb. 20, 1912.

Colin Ralph WEBB (1945-46) RHB Sturt
b. Adelaide, Jan. 20, 1926.
Add: 25 Wooltana Ave, Myrtle Bank.
Brother of K.N.Webb.

Kenneth Norman WEBB (1946-47) RHB/RF Sturt
b. Adelaide, Feb. 27, 1921.
Add: 8 Mersey St., Cumberland Park.

Harold Wynne ("Darkie") WEBSTER (1910-11) /WK North Adelaide/South Adelaide
b. Sydney, Feb. 17, 1889.
d. Randwick, N.S.W., Oct. 7, 1949.
Tour: England & North America 1912.

Leonard Rex WEEKLEY (1950-51) RHB/LB Woodville
b. Port Wakefield, July 21, 1922.
Add: 8 St.Peters St., Glenelg East.

Albert Edmund WEEKS (1887-88) South Adelaide
b. July 23, 1864.

Alexander John ("Alec") WEIR (1949-50) RHB/RFM Port Adelaide
b. Largs Bay, March 15, 1921.
Add: 22 Kybunga Terrace, Largs North.

Henry Edward Patrick ("Harry") WHITFIELD (1926-27) RHB/RFM East Torrens
b. 1904.
d. of blood poisoning at Royston Park, Jan. 14, 1937.

Richard Smallpeice ("Dick") WHITINGTON (1932-33) RHB University/Sturt
b. Unley Park, June 30, 1912.
d. Sydney, March 13, 1984.
Tour: Services in England 1945 & India 1945-46.
Cricket author and journalist.

William James WHITTY (1908-09) RHB/LFM East Torrens/Glenelg
b. Sydney, Aug. 15, 1886.
d. Tantanoola, Jan. 30, 1974.
Tests: 14 Tours: England 1909; New Zealand 1909-10; England & North America 1912.
New South Wales 1907-08.
H.D.G.Leveson-Gower's XI v. Camb. Univ. 1912.

Robert Stangways WIGLEY (1888-89) RHB Adelaide
b. Windsor, Vic., March 15, 1864.
d. Glenelg, April 20, 1926.

John Winstanley Symons WILKIN (1949-50) RHB/WK University
b. Adelaide, April 28, 1924.
Add: 4 South Terrace, Kensington Gardens.

Alfred WILKINSON (1885-86) /RAB North Adelaide
b. circa 1864.

Norman Leonard WILLIAMS (1919-20) RHB/LBG Port Adelaide
b. Semaphore, Sept. 23, 1899.
d. Semaphore, May 31, 1947.

Robert **Graham** WILLIAMS (1932-33) RHB/RFM Colts/East Torrens
b. April 4, 1911.
d. Adelaide, Aug. 21, 1978.
Tour: Services in England 1945.
Dominions v. England (Lord's) 1945.

Hurtle Binks WILLSMORE (1913-14) RHB/LB University/Sturt
b. Beverley, Dec. 26, 1889.
Add: 13 Paisley Ave., Torrens Park.

John William WILSON (1950-51) RHB/SLA Adelaide
b. Albert Park, Vic., Aug. 20, 1921. East Torrens
Add: 9 Millswood Cres., Millswood.
Test: 1 Tour: England & India 1956.
Victoria 1949-50.

Stanley Vincent WILSON (1975-76) RHB/RFM Adelaide
b. Midland, W.A., Sept. 23, 1948.
Add: 79 Glyndbourne Ave., Thornlie, W.A.
Western Australia 1968-69, 1972-73.

Cyril Legh WINSER (1913-14) RHB/WK Sturt/Adelaide
b. High Legh,Staffordshire, Eng., Nov. 27, 1884.
d. Geelong, Vic.,, Dec. 20, 1983.
The oldest-lived Australian first-class cricketer.

Graham John WINTER (1981-82) RHB/RM University
b. Medindie, Nov. 6, 1955.
Add: 2A Buckingham St., Gilberton.

Hartley Lionel WOOD (1959-60) RHB West Torrens
b. Flinders Park, April 5, 1930.
Add: 30 Dauntsey Road, Elizabeth North.

Ashley James WOODCOCK (1967-68) RHB University/Kensington
b. Adelaide, Feb. 27, 1947
Add: 18 William St., Norwood.
Test: 1 Tour: New Zealand 1973-74.

John Robert Herbert ("Bert") WOODFORD (1908-09)LHB/WK Sturt
b. Camberwell, Vic., June 23, 1881.
d. Fitzroy, Vic., May 1, 1949.
Victoria 1901-02 to 1907-08; 1911-12, 1912-13.

Arthur Henry WOOLCOCK (1909-10) Sturt
b. June 10, 1887.
d. Adelaide, June 29, 1975.

Albert William WRIGHT (1905-06) RHB/LB Adelaide
b. Mildura, Vic., Sept. 24, 1875.
d. North Adelaide, Dec. 23, 1938.

Kevin John WRIGHT (1980-81) RHB/WK Kensington
b. North Fremantle, W.A., Dec. 27, 1953.
Add: 25 Adelaide St., Maylands.
Tests: 10 Tour: India 1979-80
Western Australia 1974-75 to 1979-80.

Raymond Robert WRIGHT (1933-34) LHB/SLA Kensington
b. Kensington, Nov. 11, 1914.
d. Springfield, Jan. 20, 1965.

Dennis Brian YAGMICH (1974-75) RHB/WK Kensington
b. Victoria Park, W.A., Aug. 23, 1948.
Add: 11 Regent St., Mt. Lawley, W.A.
Western Australia 1972-73, 1973-74.

YOUNIS Ahmed Mohammad (1972-73) LHB/SLA Prospect
b. Jullundur, Pakistan, Oct. 20, 1947.
Tests: Pakistan 2 Tours: Cavaliers to Jamaica 1969-70; Commonwealth to Pakistan 1970-71; D.H.Robins to South Africa 1973-74 & 1974-75; International Wanderers to South Africa 1974-75 & 1975-76.
Pakistan (domestic) 1961-62 to 1969-70. Surrey 1965 to 1978. Worcestershire 1979 to 1983. Glamorgan 1984.

Robert John ZADOW (1979-80) RHB Salisbury
b. Mannum, Jan. 17, 1955.
Add: 6 Kareda Ave., Campbelltown.

Paul William ZSCHORN (1910-11) Sturt
b. circa 1887.

MISCELLANEOUS AUSTRALIAN FIRST-CLASS PLAYERS

Charles William BEAL
b. Sydney, June 24, 1855.
d. Randwick, N.S.W., Feb. 5, 1921.
Australians v Somerset 1882.
Manager: Australian teams to England 1882, 1888.
Nephew of J.C.Beal (N.S.W.)

C.O? BLANCHARD — RHB — East Melbourne/
b. circa 1842
"Surrey" v "The World" (Melbourne) 1861-62.

Colin David BREMNER — RHB/WK — Hawthorn-East Melbourne
b. Hawthorn, Vic., Jan. 29, 1920
Add: 12 Cornish Place, Holder, A.C.T.
Services in India & Australia 1945-46
Dominions v England (Lord's) 1945.

Frederick Collier CHRISTY
b. Sept. 9, 1822.
"Surrey" v "The World" (Melbourne) 1861-62.
Surrey Club 1846 to 1848.

Hartley Samuel CRAIG — LHB/WK — Colts(Adelaide)
b. Prospect, S.Aust., Sept. 19, 1917.
Add: 5 Jennifer Ave., Ridgehaven, S.Aust.
Dominions v England (Lord's) 1945.

Joseph H.DAVIS — RHB
b. circa 1916
Australians v Central India(Ajmer) and All India (Madras) 1935-36.

Norman G.DUCKER
b. in New South Wales 1886.
Australians v Philadelphia (Haverford) 1912.

J.HARDIE
Australians v England XI (Harrogate) 1886.

Thomas HOGG — RHB/RFM(r) — Tasmania
b. Hobart, March 12, 1845.
d. Trevallyn, Tas., July 13, 1890.
Combined N.S.W., Tas., S.Aust. XIII v Victoria (Melbourne) 1872-73.
Great-uncle of G.C.H.Hogg (N.S.W.) and J.E.P.Hogg (N.S.W. & Qld).

Hector Henry ("Harry") HYSLOP — RHB/WK?
b. Southampton, Dec. 13, 1840.
d. Cosham, Sept. 11, 1920.
Australians v England XI (Harrogate) 1886.
Hampshire 1876, 1877.

Wilfred Charles IVORY — /WK — St.Kilda
b. South Yarra, Vic., Sept. 12, 1888.
d. North Brighton, Vic., Oct. 13, 1975.
Rest of Australia v Australian XI (Melbourne) 1910-11

William MACGREGOR — RHB/WK — University (Melbourne
b. St. Kilda, Feb. 23, 1888.
d. Benalla, Oct. 5, 1980.
Australians to New Zealand 1913-14.

Samuel MORCOM /WK Norwood(S.Aust)
b. 1847.
d. after being "run over by a heavily-laden wagon in Rundle St.", Adelaide, Jan. 15, 1888.
Combined N.S.W., Tas., S.Aust. XIII v Victoria (Melbourne) 1872-73.

M.E.O'BRIEN Melbourne
G.Anderson's XI v. G.Parr's XI (Melbourne) 1863-64.

Maharaja of PATIALA (Bhupinder Dingh)
b. Patiala, India, Oct. 12, 1891.
d. Patiala, India, March 23, 1938.
Captained 1935-36 Australians v Patiala XI (led by his son) at Patiala.
India (domestic) 1915-16 to 1937-38.
Father of Yuvraj of Patiala (India).

E.PENFOLD
Australians v Philadelphia (Manheim) 1912.

Charles Frederick Thomas PRICE LHB/SLA Marrickville
b. Sydney, Feb. 17, 1917.
Services in England 1945, India & Australia 1945-46.

W.SIMMONDS Richmond (Vic.)
G.Anderson's XI v G.Parr's XI (Melbourne) 1863-64.

Sir Arthur SIMS RHB
b. Spridlington, Lincolnshire, July 27, 1877.
d. East Hoathly, Sussex, April 27, 1969.
Captained Australian team in New Zealand 1913-14.
New Zealand to Australia 1898-99.
Canterbury 1896-97 to 1912-13
New Zealand v. Australia 1904-05 and 1909-10.

Struan McKinley SMITH RHB/LM North Sydney
b. Sydney, June 4, 1906.
Rest of Australia v. 1926 Australians (Sydney) 1926-27.

George TAIT East Melbourne
b. Parramatta, N.S.W., April 12, 1844.
d. East Malvern, Vic., Dec. 21, 1934.
G.Parr's XI v G.Anderson's XI (Melbourne) 1863-64.
Notable figure in the Presbyterian Church in Australia.

Leslie B.TARRANT
Australians v. Patiala XI (Patiala) 1935-36.
Son of F.A.Tarrant (Vic. & Middlesex)

Richard C.TEECE RHB University (Sydney)
b. Bay of Islands, Oct. 27, 1847.
d. Point Piper, N.S.W., Dec. 13, 1928.
Combined N.S.W., Tas., S.Aust. XIII v. Victoria (Melbourne) 1872-73.
Prominent N.S.W. cricket administrator; secretary of the Association from 1868 to 1870.

Hector Norman TENNENT RHB
b. Hobart, April 6, 1843.
d. Westminster, Eng., April 16, 1904.
Australians v Orleans Club (Twickenham) 1878.
M.C.C. 1865 to 1876. Lancashire 1865, 1870.
Brother of J.P.Tennent (Vic.) and W.Tennent (Lancashire 1867)

Harry THORPE /LAB Parramatta
Combined Australia v. Vernon's English team (Melbourne) 1887-88.

Charles Samuel WINNING LHB/SLA Paddington
b. Paddington, July 17, 1889.
d. Newport, N.S.W., April 20, 1967.
A.I.F. in England 1919, South Africa & Australia 1919-20.

Samuel Moses James WOODS RHB/RFM
b. Ashfield, N.S.W., April 14, 1867.
d. Taunton, Eng., April 30, 1931.
Tests: Australia 3, England 3.
Assisted 1888 Australians in England (6 matches)
Tours: Hawke to North America 1891-92; England to South Africa 1895-96; Priestley to West Indies 1896-97; Ranjitsinhji to North America 1899-1900.
Wyatt's XI v. Australians (Portsmouth) 1886.
Cambridge University 1888 to 1891. Somerset 1891 to 1910.

James Allen WORKMAN RHB Port Adelaide
b. Peterhead, S.Aust., March 17, 1917.
d. Westminster, Eng., Dec. 23, 1970.
Services in England 1945, India, Ceylon & Australia 1945-46.

CAREER RECORDS

In the details set out below, the first line against each player's name shows his career record in first-class matches for South Australia; players who appeared in first-class matches other than for South Australia have two lines of figures, the second of which shows the player's career record in all first-class matches.

Career records are complete to the end of the 1984 English season.

Name	*From*	*To*	*M*	*I*	*NO*	*R*	*HS*	*Avge*	*100s*	*R*	*W*	*Avge*	*BB*	*5wi*	*10wm*	*ct*	*st*
Alexander, W.C.	1925-26	1928-29	21	36	2	1217	133	35.79	3	120	3	40.00	1/10	-	-	9	
	1925-26	1928-29	26	43	2	1414	133	34.48	3	120	3	40.00	1/10	-	-	11	
Ambler, A.M.	1920-21	1925-26	22	40	13	283	41	10.48	-	did	not	bowl				28	29
Amos, W.	1890-91	1892-93	2	4	0	18	9	4.50	-	129	1	129.00	1/87	-	-	-	
Attenborough, G.R.	1972-73	1980-81	57	85	14	738	54	10.39	-	6170	193	31.96	7/90	8	2	21	
Austen, V.C.	1945-46		1	2	0	4	2	2.00	-	77	0					1	
Backman, C.J.	1911-12		1	2	0	16	16	8.00	-	53	3	17.66	3/53	-	-	1	
Badcock, C.L.	1934-35	1940-41	40	65	7	3282	325	56.58	12	did	not	bowl				13	
	1929-30	1940-41	97	159	16	7371	325	51.54	26	44	0					41	
Bagshaw, K.J.	1946-47	1947-48	4	7	0	58	27	8.28	-	11	1	11.00	1/11	-	-	-	
Bailey, A.J.T.	1953-54	1955-56	3	4	2	14	10*	7.00	-	208	3	69.33	2/84	-	-	1	
Bailey, B.T.	1896-97	1901-02	8	15	0	247	57	16.46	-	45	1	45.00	1/23	-	-	5	
Bailey, E.A.	1906-07		1	2	1	23	23*	23.00	-	did	not	bowl				-	
Ballans, D.M.	1889-90	1892-93	2	3	0	16	15	5.33	-	15	0					-	
Barnes, J.R.	1972-73	1974-75	11	17	1	272	88	17.00	-	1180	26	45.38	6/90	1	-	2	
Bartlett, A.J.	1925-26		1	2	1	11	7	11.00	-	did	not	bowl				-	
Beagley, J.W.	1956-57	1959-60	18	27	5	129	19	5.86	-	1889	51	37.03	6/121	1	-	5	
Bedford, A.A.	1956-57	1958-59	15	22	5	277	32*	16.29	-	1373	33	41.60	4/80	-	-	10	
Bednall, P.M.	1948-49		2	4	0	32	19	8.00	-	did	not	bowl				-	
Bennett, F.C.	1945-46		6	12	1	175	56*	15.90	-	137	4	34.25	1/20	-	-	4	
	1945-46	1951-52	8	16	2	248	56*	17.71	-	137	4	34.25	1/20	-	-	5	
Bennett, R.L.	1922-23		5	9	2	78	28*	11.14	-	did	not	bowl				6	6
	1922-23	1925-26	8	15	2	163	38	12.53	-	did	not	bowl				9	7
Bennett, T.	1894-95		1	2	0	5	5	2.50	-	did	not	bowl				-	
Benton, J.J.	1977-78		2	4	0	82	42	20.50	-	21	0					2	
Bevan, J.L.	1877-78		1	1	0	0	0	0.00	-	59	14	4.21	8/36	2	1	1	
Bishop, G.A.	1982-83	1983-84	12	20	1	595	90	31.31	-	32	0					5	
Black, G.A.	1949-50	1950-51	6	11	1	115	33	11.50	-	8	0					1	
Blewett, R.K.	1975-76	1978-79	25	43	0	1070	112	24.88	2	1207	30	40.23	4/88	-	-	24	
Blinman, H.	1880-81	1895-96	23	40	7	663	73*	20.09	-	did	not	bowl				16	
Bloomfield, G.T.	1908-09		3	5	0	132	65	26.40	-	did	not	bowl				2	
Blundell, R.P.	1964-65	1970-71	24	38	2	552	66	15.33	-	did	not	bowl				64	13
Botten, R.D.	1877-78		1	1	0	17	17	17.00	-	did	not	bowl				1	
Bowley, B.L.	1947-48	1951-52	30	54	3	1092	169	21.41	2	1914	54	35.44	4/70	-	-	19	
Bowley, E.L.	1922-23	1924-25	7	13	0	450	192	34.61	1	104	1	104.00	1/52	-	-	6	
Bradley, C.E.	1983-84		2	3	0	25	15	8.33	-	did	not	bowl				2	

Name	From	To	M	I	NO	R	HS	Avge	100s	R	W	Avge	BB	5wi	10wm	ct	st
Bradman, D.G.	1935-36	1948-49	44	63	8	5753	369	104.60	25	0	0					36	1
	1927-28	1948-49	234	338	43	28067	452*	95.14	117	1367	36	37.97	3/35	-	-	131	1
Braybrook, C.	1921-22		1	2	1	27	26	27.00	-	103	3	34.33	3/52	-	-	-	
Brideson, J.	1883-84		1	2	0	52	52	26.00	-	75	0					-	
Bridgman, H.H.M.	1912-13	1922-23	10	18	2	252	65	15.75	-	533	9	59.22	2/25	-	-	6	
Brooks, G.V.	1961-62	1963-64	26	31	15	41	6	2.56	-	2029	61	33.26	4/11	-	-	13	
Bullough, W.	1880-81		2	4	1	43	26*	14.33	-	176	8	22.00	3/54	-	-	1	
Burton, G.	1939-40		3	5	3	32	11*	16.00	-	301	9	33.44	5/99	1	-	1	
Burton, J.R.	1951-52		1	2	0	8	8	4.00	-	118	1	118.00	1/118	-	-	-	
Cameron, R.A.	1957-58	1958-59	4	6	1	118	88*	23.60	-	356	4	89.00	1/26	-	-	1	
Campbell, G.C.	1909-10	1914-15	17	28	2	421	43	16.19	-	did	not	bowl				21	14
	1909-10	1914-15	23	35	2	497	43	15.06	-	did	not	bowl				28	20
Carlton, T.A.	1928-29	1931-32	27	48	18	384	34	12.80	-	2173	77	28.22	5/64	1	-	24	
	1909-10	1931-32	60	103	28	1153	63	15.37	-	4554	185	24.61	6/42	7	2	48	
Carmichael, I.R.	1983-84		11	11	3	11	4	1.37	-	1446	41	35.26	6/112	3	-	2	
	1983-84	1984	18	17	6	17	4*	1.54	-	2107	58	36.32	6/112	4	-	5	
Carracher, A.J.	1896-97		2	3	1	30	14	15.00	-	102	7	14.57	5/24	1	-	1	
Carragher, E.J.	1922-23		2	3	2	32	17*	32.00	-	316	5	63.20	2/102	-	-	-	
Catchlove, W.E.	1931-32	1933-34	9	16	1	355	103*	23.66	1	did	not	bowl				-	
Caterer, T.A.	1884-85		1	2	1	0	0*	0.00	-	42	1	42.00	1/42	-	-	-	
Causby, B.L.	1973-74	1980-81	32	59	2	1722	174*	30.21	4	80	1	80.00	1/34	-	-	19	
Causby, J.P.	1960-61	1973-74	63	113	7	3067	137	28.93	3	0	0					25	
Chamberlain, C.T.	1905-06	1910-11	3	5	0	31	18	6.20	-	74	1	74.00	1/59	-	-	-	
Chamberlain, W.L.	1907-08	1913-14	19	36	1	775	103	22.14	1	751	18	41.72	3/36	-	-	18	
Chappell, G.S.	1966-67	1972-73	57	100	10	4133	156*	45.92	11	1662	54	30.77	3/19	-	-	63	
	1966-67	1983-84	321	542	72	24535	247*	52.20	74	8717	291	29.95	7/40	5	-	376	
Chappell, I.M.	1961-62	1979-80	109	188	18	8873	205*	52.19	26	3304	80	41.30	5/29	1	-	133	1
	1961-62	1979-80	262	448	41	19680	209	48.35	59	6614	176	37.57	5/29	2	-	312	1
Chappell, T.M.	1972-73	1975-76	17	33	3	603	70	20.10	-	60	1	60.00	1/35	-	-	7	
	1972-73	1983-84	85	145	13	3934	150	29.80	5	1391	56	24.83	4/12	-	-	46	
Chinner, H.G.W.	1898-99	1899-00	3	6	1	114	37*	22.80	-	did	not	bowl				1	
Chittleborough, H.C.	1883-84	1884-85	2	4	0	19	9	4.75	-	8	0					3	
Christensen, R.T.	1982-83	1983-84	4	5	1	42	27	10.50	-	265	3	88.33	1/37	-	-	2	
Clarke, G.C.	1965-66	1970-71	6	9	2	89	19*	12.71	-	402	10	40.20	3/117	-	-	1	
Claxton, N.	1898-99	1909-10	39	73	2	2090	199*	29.43	1	2272	66	34.42	5/56	3	-	26	
Claxton, W.G.H.	1883-84	1895-96	2	4	0	154	73	38.50	-	192	6	32.00	5/116	1	-	-	
Clements, P.J.	1972-73	1974-75	5	8	2	113	48*	18.83	-	154	7	22.00	4/64	-	-	4	
Clingly, M.T.	1957-58	1959-60	5	9	0	79	20	8.77	-	489	9	54.33	3/15	-	-	5	
Clutterbuck, S.H.	1913-14		1	2	0	2	2	1.00	-	78	0					-	
Colley, T.P.M.	1955-56		3	4	0	63	57	15.75	-	did	not	bowl				-	
Collins, F.H.K.	1933-34	1935-36	15	23	4	311	37*	16.36	-	1100	24	45.83	5/78	1	-	9	
Coombe, E.H.	1887-88		1	1	0	10	10	10.00	-	did	not	bowl				-	
Coombe, P.H.	1903-04	1914-15	8	14	2	19	6	1.58	-	607	17	35.70	6/59	1	-	1	
Cooper, W.O.	1914-15		1	2	1	41	25	41.00	-	93	4	23.25	2/33	-	-	-	
Cosier, G.J.	1974-75	1976-77	24	43	1	1504	130	35.80	2	888	39	22.76	3/20	-	-	22	
	1971-72	1980-81	91	161	9	5005	168	32.92	7	2301	75	30.68	3/20	-	-	75	

Name	From	M	I	NO	R	HS	Avge	100s	R	W	Avge	BB	5wi	10wm	ct	st	
Cotton, H.N.J.	1935-36	1940-41	25	29	15	165	37*	11.78	-	2074	76	27.28	5/49	1	-	21	
Cowan, R.F.	1904-05	1905-06	4	8	1	69	25	9.85	-	199	6	33.16	4/104	-	-	2	
Craig, R.J.	1945-46	1950-51	31	56	1	1677	141	30.49	4	500	9	55.55	3/37	-	-	16	1
Craigie, J.E.	1887-88		2	4	1	56	36	18.66	-	did	not	bowl				-	
Crawford, J.N.	1909-10	1913-14	22	41	4	1512	163	40.86	2	2864	120	23.86	8/66	11	3	26	
	1904	1921	210	325	34	9488	232	32.60	15	16842	815	20.66	8/24	57	12	162	
Crowe, J.J.	1977-78	1981-82	34	65	7	1964	157	33.86	5	19	1	19.00	1/10	-	-	35	
	1977-78	1983-84	62	109	10	3353	157	33.86	7	19	1	19.00	1/10	-	-	64	
Cunningham, K.G.	1960-61	1973-74	89	153	14	5144	203	37.00	9	1507	45	33.48	3/16	-	-	62	
	1960-61	1973-74	97	164	16	5497	203	37.14	9	1700	50	34.00	3/16	-	-	66	
Curtin, B.G.	1972-73	1977-78	20	36	0	915	106	25.41	2	did	not	bowl				22	
Curtin, Paul	1974-75		1	2	1	10	8	10.00	-	55	1	55.00	1/55	-	-	1	
	1974-75	1980-81	5	10	4	76	17	12.66	-	306	6	51.00	2/36	-	-	4	
Curtin, P.D.	1971-72		1	1	0	0	0	0.00	-	29	1	29.00	1/26	-	-	1	
Curtis, L.D.	1950-51		1	2	0	18	17	9.00	-	46	0					1	
Dansie, H.N.	1949-50	1966-67	124	228	9	7543	185	34.44	18	2998	90	33.31	5/61	1	-	48	
Darling, J.	1893-94	1907-08	42	77	3	2571	210	34.74	3	7	0					32	
	1893-94	1907-08	202	333	25	10635	210	34.52	19	55	1	55.00	1/5	-	-	148	
Darling, W.M.	1975-76	1983-84	63	116	16	3783	134	37.83	6	16	0					21	
	1975-76	1983-84	87	158	17	5091	134	36.10	8	23	0					30	
Davey, J.R.	1933-34	1934-35	5	9	5	26	15	6.50	-	429	9	47.66	2/28	-	-	2	
Davey, J.R.	1981-82		1		did	not	bat			did	not	bowl				4	2
Day, H.J.	1898-99		1	2	0	28	14	14.00	-	did	not	bowl				1	
Delaney, W.	1888-89	1892-93	6	11	2	63	20	7.00	-	184	8	23.00	4/29	-	-	3	
Deamazures, P.C.	1909-10		1	1	0	0	0	0.00	-	4	0					1	
	1906-07	1909-10	2	3	0	23	18	7.66	-	13	0					1	
Deverson, C.S.	1930-31		3	5	3	29	18	14.50	-	255	10	25.50	4/60	-	-	4	
Dolling, C.E.	1905-06	1922-23	20	39	1	1428	140	37.57	3	71	1	71.00	1/15	-	-	10	
	1905-06	1922-23	29	51	1	1744	140	34.88	4	71	1	71.00	1/15	-	-	10	
Dolman, M.C.	1981-82	1982-83	6	3	1	6	6	3.00	-	564	14	40.28	4/114	-	-	-	
Donaldson, J.S.	1972-73	1973-74	7	14	1	192	81	14.76	-	did	not	bowl				6	0
Dooland, B.	1945-46	1957-58	29	45	4	870	74	21.21	-	4108	118	34.81	6/97	5	-	30	
	1945-46	1957-58	214	326	33	7141	115*	24.37	4	22332	1016	21.98	8/20	84	23	186	
Down, G.S.	1911-12		4	8	1	79	23	11.28	-	11	0					-	
	1911-12	1912-13	7	11	1	156	47	15.60	-	11	0					1	
Downey, D.R.	1925-26		1	1	0	12	12	12.00	-	did	not	bowl				1	1
Drennan, J.	1953-54	1958-59	27	46	5	434	63*	10.58	-	2493	84	29.67	6/69	4	-	6	
	1953-54	1958-59	46	60	12	569	63*	11.85	-	3490	136	25.66	6/69	6	-	12	
Drew, C.F.	1911-12		1	2	0	27	18	13.50	-	did	not	bowl				1	
Drew, T.M.	1897-98		3	5	2	58	33*	19.33	-	12	0					2	
	1897-98	1903	4	7	2	65	33*	13.00	-	33	0					4	
Drewer, R.H.	1974-75	1975-76	14	25	0	659	90	26.36	-	did	not	bowl				12	
Ducker, J.R.	1952-53	1962-63	30	50	8	1094	76	26.04	-	16	0					48	12
Dugan, R.W.	1978-79	1981-82	5	6	5	38	21*	38.00	-	278	2	139.00	1/20	-	-	1	
Duldig, L.D.	1940-41	1952-53	36	68	5	2027	121*	32.17	1	3	0					14	
	1940-41	1952-53	40	72	5	2107	121*	31.44	1	3	0					16	

Name	From	To	M	I	NO	R	HS	Avge	100s	R	W	Avge	BB	5wi	10wm	ct	st
Dyer, R.H.	1893-94	1895-96	8	14	1	345	102	26.53	1	did	not	bowl				4	
Eaton, A.M.	1976-77		3	6	1	96	42*	19.20	-	did	not	bowl				-	
Edwards, A.C.	1892-93		1	1	0	60	60	60.00	-	did	not	bowl				2	
Edwards, F.R.	1934-35		5	9	4	78	22*	15.60	-	did	not	bowl				7	2
Ellis, R.S.	1945-46		1	2	0	1	1	0.50	-	210	5	42.00	5/210	1	-	-	
	1945	1945-46	21	28	12	47	10*	2.93	-	2070	78	26.53	6/144	6	1	6	
Eneberg, A.	1951-52		1	2	0	22	22	11.00	-	30	0					-	
England, E.J.	1950-51	1951-52	5	9	0	319	102	35.44	1	did	not	bowl				1	
	1945-46	1953-54	10	17	1	532	102	33.25	1	11	0					5	
Englefield, W.	1946-47		4	5	3	27	13*	13.50	-	did	not	bowl				8	4
Evan, L.W.	1885-86	1890-91	2	3	0	5	3	1.66	-	did	not	bowl				1	
Evans, A.E.H.	1895-96	1903-04	18	33	2	366	39	11.80	-	1213	32	37.90	5/33	1	-	14	
Evans, R.	1892-93		1	1	0	32	32	32.00	-	did	not	bowl				-	
Farrell, G.S.	1966-67		7	14	0	313	66	22.35	-	3	0					4	
Favell, A.L.	1983-84		1	2	1	40	40*	40.00	-	did	not	bowl				-	
Favell, L.E.	1951-52	1969-70	143	258	5	9656	164	38.16	23	171	1	171.00	1/0	-	-	75	
	1951-52	1969-70	202	347	9	12379	190	36.62	27	345	5	69.00	1/0	-	-	110	
Ferris, J.J.	1895-96		1	1	0	0	0	0.00	-	3	0					1	
	1886-87	1897-98	198	328	56	4264	106	15.67	1	14260	813	17.53	8/41	63	11	90	
Fisher, H.M.	1920-21	1923-24	8	14	4	71	22	7.10	-	1010	17	59.41	5/96	1	-	7	
Fraser, R.A.	1974-75	1978-79	7	13	0	166	33	12.76	-	10	0					5	
Freeman, E.W.	1964-65	1973-74	44	70	4	1208	69	18.30	-	3932	150	26.21	8/47	5	2	37	
	1964-65	1973-74	83	123	6	2244	116	19.17	1	6690	241	27.75	8/47	7	2	60	
Frick, J.	1976-77		4	8	0	58	18	7.25	-	240	5	48.00	2/52	-	-	-	
Frost, A.R.	1965-66	1967-68	19	28	11	69	12	4.05	-	1788	59	30.30	5/51	2	-	4	
	1965-66	1967-68	24	35	12	114	27	4.95	-	2091	72	29.04	5/28	3	-	6	
Galloway, P.W.	1968-69	1969-70	11	20	1	477	78	25.10	-	16	0					4	
Garner, J.	1982-83		8	13	1	138	22	11.50	-	976	55	17.74	7/78	4	2	3	
	1975-76	1984	147	164	39	2176	104	17.40	1	11799	665	17.74	8/31	41	7	98	
Gehan, R.A.H.	1962-63		1	2	1	4	2*	4.00	-	88	2	44.00	2/51	-	-	-	
Gehrs, D.R.A.	1902-03	1920-21	49	92	6	3387	170	39.38	13	346	7	49.42	2/9	-	-	35	4
	1902-03	1920-21	83	142	12	4377	170	33.66	13	416	8	52.00	2/9	-	-	71	4
Gentle, S.R.	1978-79	1983-84	2	3	1	35	21*	17.50	-	did	not	bowl				9	2
Gibbs, C.H.	1877-78		1	1	0	47	47	47.00	-	did	not	bowl				1	
Gibbs, L.R.	1969-70		8	14	6	88	21*	11.00	-	632	18	35.11	4/84	-	-	6	
	1953-54	1975-76	330	352	150	1729	43	8.55	-	27878	1024	27.22	8/37	50	10	203	
Gibson, V.R.	1939-40	1946-47	8	10	1	166	50	18.44	-	606	13	46.61	3/80	-	-	5	
Giffen, G.	1877-78	1903-04	64	114	7	4667	271	43.61	11	9597	412	23.29	9/91	47	17	67	
	1877-78	1903-04	251	421	23	11758	271	29.54	18	21782	1023	21.29	10/66	95	30	195	
Giffen, W.F.	1882-83	1901-02	31	55	4	943	89	18.49	-	15	0					17	
	1882-83	1901-02	47	80	6	1178	89	15.91	-	15	0					23	
Gilbourne, R.J.	1967-68	1971-72	11	20	3	279	79	16.41	-	18	0					3	
Giles, L.G.	1950-51	1951-52	5	8	0	164	54	20.50	-	did	not	bowl				4	

Name	From	To	M	I	NO	R	HS	Avge	100s	R	W	Avge	BB	5wi	10wm	ct	st
Godfrey, C.G.	1885-86	1888-89	5	9	0	356	119	39.55	1	did	not	bowl				5	
Gogler, K.G.	1946-47	1948-49	9	15	0	335	75	22.33	-	282	7	40.28	3/16	-	-	3	
Goode, B.R.	1945-46	1949-50	3	6	1	131	72*	26.20	-	did	not	bowl				2	
Gooden, H.A.	1877-78	1880-81	3	5	1	66	49	16.50	-	24	1	24.00	1/24	-	-	-	
Gooden, J.E.	1880-81	1892-93	9	16	1	172	39	11.46	-	36	1	36.00	1/11	-	-	4	
	1872-73	1892-93	10	17	1	175	39	10.93	-	36	1	36.00	1/11	-	-	5	
Gooden, N.L.	1912-13	1913-14	2	4	1	196	102	65.33	1	did	not	bowl				1	
Goodfellow, J.E.	1880-81		1	2	0	7	6	3.50	-	51	1	51.00	1/14	-	-	1	
Goodman, G.W.	1980-81		4	8	0	109	43	13.62	-	10	0					5	
	1978-79	1983-84	19	35	2	703	94	21.30	-	439	3	146.33	1/29	-	-	11	
Gould, F.K.	1922-23	1924-25	7	14	1	255	55*	19.61	-	did	not	bowl				1	
Grant, C.S.	1956-57		2	4	0	73	42	18.25	-	did	not	bowl				1	
Gray, C.D.	1921-22	1922-23	3	5	1	85	30*	21.25	-	175	2	87.50	1/3	-	-	1	
Green, A.	1894-95	1898-99	7	12	4	141	35*	17.62	-	41	1	41.00	1/32	-	-	1	
Gregg, D.M.	1954-55	1956-57	15	22	3	129	27*	6.78	-	1313	44	29.84	5/9	3	-	3	
Griffiths, G.E.	1965-66	1966-67	10	18	2	370	67	23.12	-	659	14	47.07	2/28	-	-	5	
	1962-63	1967-68	19	31	2	649	67	22.37	-	1203	24	50.12	2/28	-	-	14	
Grimmett, C.V.	1924-25	1940-41	105	163	27	2723	71*	20.02	-	16566	668	24.79	9/180	62	16	58	
	1911-12	1940-41	248	321	54	4720	71*	17.67	-	31740	1424	22.28	10/37	127	33	139	
Grove, B.P.	1952-53		3	6	0	93	43	15.50	-	140	3	46.66	2/10	-	-	2	
Gun, L.T.	1924-25	1926-27	8	14	2	552	136*	46.00	2	38	2	19.00	2/38	-	-	2	
Gurr, G.	1905-06		1	1	0	0	0	0.00	-	did	not	bowl				-	
Hack, A.T.	1927-28	1931-32	22	40	3	1081	100	29.21	1	38	0					20	12
Hack, F.T.	1898-99	1908-09	38	73	2	2138	158*	30.11	3	295	5	59.00	2/39	-	-	18	
	1898-99	1908-09	39	75	2	2147	158*	29.41	3	295	5	59.00	2/39	-	-	20	
Hack, R.N.	1933-34		1	1	0	5	5	5.00	-	49	1	49.00	1/33	-	-	1	
Haddrick, R.N.	1951-52	1952-53	3	6	1	69	27	13.80	-	did	not	bowl				1	
Halbert, J.A.	1961-62		2	3	0	8	5	2.66	-	4	0					-	
Halcombe, R.A.	1926-27	1927-28	5	6	4	6	3*	3.00	-	480	13	36.92	4/61	-	-	2	
	1926-27	1939-40	25	33	13	100	14*	5.00	-	2052	54	38.00	5/40	1	-	7	
Haldane, H.L.	1886-87	1893-94	11	18	1	250	70	14.70	-	94	6	15.66	3/26	-	-	5	2
Hamence, R.A.	1935-36	1950-51	69	116	7	4244	173	38.93	11	35	1	35.00	1/7	-	-	21	
	1935-36	1950-51	99	155	15	5285	173	37.75	11	239	8	29.87	2/13	-	-	34	
Hammond, J.R.	1969-70	1980-81	46	70	25	749	53	16.64	-	3550	124	28.62	6/54	5	-	27	
	1969-70	1980-81	69	87	31	922	53	16.46	-	5315	184	28.88	6/15	8	-	36	
Handrickan, A.J.	1976-77	1977-78	8	15	0	448	113	29.86	1	did	not	bowl				6	
Hanson, L.H.	1905-06		3	5	1	32	12	8.00	-	226	4	56.50	2/102	-	-	-	
Harms, C.L.	1982-83	1983-84	8	15	2	273	46*	21.00	-	492	11	44.72	3/96	-	-	9	
Harris, D.	1953-54	1959-60	25	49	0	1103	77	22.51	-	61	0					11	
Harris, G.W.	1920-21	1930-31	34	64	3	2054	183	33.67	3	30	2	15.00	2/8	-	-	14	
	1920-21	1930-31	37	69	3	2294	183	34.75	4	30	2	15.00	2/8	-	-	14	
Harris, K.P.	1981-82	1983-84	11	20	1	471	97	24.78	-	did	not	bowl				9	
Harrison, C.W.	1966-67		4	7	3	34	19*	8.50	-	335	9	37.22	4/82	-	-	2	
Hawke, N.J.N.	1960-61	1967-68	60	95	26	2067	141*	29.95	1	5803	211	27.50	8/61	12	4	36	
	1959-60	1970-71	145	198	57	3383	141*	23.99	1	12088	458	26.39	8/61	23	5	85	

Name	From	To	M	I	NO	R	HS	Avge	100s	R	W	Avge	BB	5wi	10wm	ct	st
Hay, H.	1902-03	1903-04	5	9	4	54	18*	10.80	-	437	16	27.31	9/67	1	-	2	
Haysman, M.D.	1982-83	1983-84	18	32	3	1278	153	44.06	3	219	0					21	
	1982-83	1984	24	44	7	1520	153	41.08	4	219	0					33	
Hayward, C.W.	1891-92		3	4	0	30	27	7.50	-	did	not	bowl				2	
Head, L.H.	1957-58	1958-59	9	17	2	425	78	28.33	-	145	2	72.50	1/0	-	-	6	
Heairfield, H.V.	1940-41		1	2	1	4	4*	4.00	-	did	not	bowl				1	0
Heath, H.F.T.	1923-24		2	4	1	35	21	11.66	-	214	7	30.57	5/43	1	-	3	
	1919	1923-24	3	4	1	35	21	11.66	-	225	7	32.14	5/43	1	-	3	
Hendricks, M.	1970-71	1974-75	32	52	15	656	66	17.72	-	did	not	bowl				68	11
	1969-70	1974-75	41	66	19	799	66	17.00	-	did	not	bowl				99	20
Henry, D.A.	1920-21		3	5	1	63	24	15.75	-	did	not	bowl				2	
Herbert, P.J.	1971-72		4	8	0	152	37	19.00	-	did	not	bowl				2	
Hewer, W.A.	1898-99	1910-11	7	12	3	222	83*	24.66	-	384	11	34.90	5/149	1	-	3	
Hide, J.B.	1880-81	1882-83	4	8	0	83	48	10.37	-	153	6	25.50	3/37	-	-	5	
	1876	1893	176	323	20	4824	173	15.92	4	9673	441	21.70	8/47	19	4	112	
Hiern, B.N.	1972-73	1973-74	13	20	14	125	24*	20.83	-	1231	33	37.30	3/36	-	-	8	
Hiern, R.N.	1949-50	1953-54	12	18	4	121	25	8.64	-	1033	28	36.89	5/49	1	-	5	
Hilditch, A.M.J.	1982-83	1983-84	19	34	2	1483	230	46.34	4	17	0					14	
	1976-77	1983-84	53	96	3	3481	230	37.43	5	21	0					43	
Hill, A.	1889-90	1893-94	5	10	1	121	60	13.44	-	did	not	bowl				-	
Hill, C.	1892-93	1922-23	87	160	9	8027	365*	53.15	24	220	7	31.42	2/6	-	-	61	
	1892-93	1924-25	252	416	21	17213	365*	43.57	45	323	10	32.30	2/6	-	-	168	1
Hill, H.J.	1903-04		1	2	0	10	10	5.00	-	45	3	15.00	3/27	-	-	1	
Hill, L.R.	1905-06	1910-11	18	33	1	583	123	18.21	1	1320	28	47.14	5/82	1	-	8	
Hill, L.T.	1958-59	1960-61	15	27	0	524	100	19.40	1	284	6	47.33	2/47	-	-	5	
	1958-59	1962-63	17	31	0	584	100	18.83	1	412	8	51.50	2/47	-	-	9	
Hill, P.	1892-93		1	1	0	2	2	2.00	-	did	not	bowl				-	
Hill, P.D.	1949-50		1	2	0	11	11	5.50	-	did	not	bowl				1	
Hill, R.J.	1893-94		1	2	1	3	3*	3.00	-	did	not	bowl				0	0
Hill, S.	1909-10	1911-12	11	20	0	343	62	17.15	-	did	not	bowl				3	
	1909-10	1912-13	12	22	0	372	62	16.90	-	did	not	bowl				3	
Hiscock, E.J.	1890-91	1893-94	4	7	0	58	39	8.28	-	did	not	bowl				2	
Hitchcox, R.A.	1958-59	1959-60	11	17	4	148	63	11.38	-	1089	37	29.43	6/71	2	-	7	
Hodge, M.G.F.	1960-61		6	8	1	47	15	6.71	-	559	10	55.90	2/24	-	-	3	
Hogg, R.M.	1975-76	1983-84	39	58	10	590	43	12.29	-	3601	165	21.82	7/53	10	2	9	
	1975-76	1983-84	89	121	22	1037	52	10.47	-	7600	320	23.75	7/73	18	4	21	
Hole, G.B.	1950-51	1957-58	51	94	10	3401	226	40.48	9	1907	37	51.54	4/6	-	-	36	
	1949, 50	1957, 58	98	166	12	5647	226	36.66	11	2686	61	44.03	5/109	1	-	82	
Holman, R.S.	1940-41		1	2	0	4	3	2.00	-	did	not	bowl				-	
Holton, L.G.	1929-30	1932-33	2	3	1	11	7*	5.50	-	145	2	72.50	1/23	-	-	1	
Homburg, R.O.	1896-97	1898-99	2	4	1	21	10	7.00	-	49	3	16.33	3/18	-	-	-	
Hone, B.W.	1928-29	1929-30	11	20	3	860	137	50.58	3	1	0					8	
	1928-29	1933	44	75	6	2768	170	40.11	9	7	0					25	
Hone, G.M.	1919-20		1	2	0	20	18	10.00	-	21	0					-	
Hookes, D.W.	1975-76	1983-84	52	88	4	4179	193	49.75	12	804	14	57.42	2/19	-	-	47	
	1975-76	1983-84	90	152	9	6276	193	43.88	15	1072	19	56.42	3/114	-	-	68	

Name	From	To	M	I	NO	R	HS	Avge	100s	R	W	Avge	BB	5wi	10wm	ct	st
Horley, J.R.	1960-61		1	2	0	6	6	3.00	-	0	0					-	
Horsell, J.A.J.	1937-38	1938-39	2	3	0	39	39	13.00	-	did	not	bowl				5	3
Horsnell, K.G.	1953-54	1960-61	16	27	4	166	29	7.21	-	1396	44	31.72	6/80	2	1	7	
House, G.W.C.	1974-75		2	4	0	13	9	3.25	-	70	1	70.00	1/26	-	-	1	
	1972-73	1974-75	6	8	1	100	70*	14.28	-	286	7	40.85	2/5	-	-	3	
Howard, L.E.	1908-09	1913-14	6	8	5	16	5*	5.33	-	589	22	26.77	3/36	-	-	6	
Hugo, V.	1897-98	1899-00	9	14	1	81	25	6.23	-	579	23	25.17	4/69	-	-	8	
Hurn, B.M.	1957-58	1966-67	31	51	11	842	79*	21.05	-	2123	56	37.91	5/62	2	-	22	
Hutton, G.E.	1905-06		1	2	1	2	2*	2.00	-	40	1	40.00	1/20	-	-	-	
Hutton, M.D.	1930-31		1	2	1	20	20*	20.00	-	24	0					-	
Hutton, M.P.	1928-29		2	4	0	20	7	5.00	-	did	not	bowl				-	
Hutton, N.H.	1934-35		2	3	0	16	8	5.33	-	138	1	138.00	1/56	-	-	1	
Hutton, W.F.P.	1905-06		1	2	1	30	22*	30.00	-	did	not	bowl				0	0
Illman, B.K.	1960-61		6	9	3	32	14*	5.33	-	528	11	48.00	3/5	-	-	3	
Inkster, G.B.	1926-27	1927-28	6	10	3	86	18	12.28	-	did	not	bowl				13	14
Inverarity, R.J.	1979-80	1983-84	43	74	13	2151	126	35.26	3	2588	75	34.50	6/96	3	-	45	
	1962-63	1983-84	213	361	47	11414	187	36.35	26	5764	178	32.38	6/96	5	-	246	
James, A.P.	1914-15		4	8	1	93	23	13.28	-	467	13	35.92	3/56	-	-	6	
James, R.V.	1946-47	1947-48	16	27	1	1167	210	44.88	1	73	0					3	
	1938-39	1950-51	45	70	6	2582	210	40.34	4	199	1	199.00	1/65	-	-	23	
Jamieson, D.G.	1931-32	1932-33	8	16	3	114	34	8.76	-	561	11	51.00	4/83	-	-	5	
Jarman, B.N.	1955-56	1968-69	94	158	16	3447	196	24.27	3	5	0					234	65
	1955-56	1968-69	191	284	37	5615	196	22.73	5	98	3	32.66	1/17	-	-	431	129
Jarvis, Alfred	1889-90	1905-06	54	97	8	1767	154	19.85	1	4031	106	38.02	6/114	2	-	37	
	1889-90	1905-06	56	101	10	1867	154	20.51	1	4087	109	37.49	6/114	2	-	40	
Jarvis, A.H.	1877-78	1900-01	42	73	6	1188	98*	17.73	-	17	0					47	31
	1877-78	1900-01	141	226	23	3161	98*	15.57	-	63	1	63.00	1/9	-	-	114	82
Jarvis, H.S.C.	1905-06		2	3	0	5	3	1.66	-	did	not	bowl				2	0
Jenner, T.J.	1967-68	1976-77	77	117	19	2169	86	22.13	-	7733	259	29.85	7/127	12	1	59	
	1963-64	1976-77	131	199	38	3580	86	22.23	-	12520	389	32.18	7/84	14	1	87	
Jennings, C.B.	1902-03	1907-08	21	40	3	896	79	24.21	-	17	0					12	3
	1902-03	1912	60	103	7	2453	123	25.55	1	17	0					38	3
Johnson, E.A.	1926-27	1929-30	6	11	1	141	28	14.10	-	4	0					2	
Johnston, D.A.	1978-79	1982-83	10	13	6	170	59*	24.28	-	779	23	33.86	4/46	-	-	4	
Jones, E.	1892-93	1902-03	47	84	13	872	82	12.28	-	6498	248	26.20	8/157	23	4	31	
	1892-93	1907-08	144	209	27	2390	82	13.13	-	14638	641	22.83	8/39	47	9	107	
Jones, W.	1881-82	1883-84	2	4	2	31	26*	15.50	-	248	5	49.60	2/48	-	-	-	
Jose, A.D.	1947-48		3	4	1	19	8	6.33	-	271	6	45.16	2/33	-	-	1	
	1947-48	1953	29	44	8	269	39	7.47	-	2293	75	30.57	6/45	1	-	11	
Jose, G.E.	1918-19	1920-21	2	4	0	18	16	4.50	-	15	0					-	
Kekwick, E.H.	1899-00		2	3	0	2	2	0.66	-	did	not	bowl				-	
Kemp, B.C.E.	1884-85	1887-88	4	8	2	96	38	16.00	-	90	1	90.00	1/44	-	-	3	
	1884-85	1897-98	6	12	2	140	38	14.00	-	250	7	35.71	5/53	1	-	4	

Name	From	To	M	I	NO	R	HS	Avge	100s	R	W	Avge	BB	5wi	10wm	ct	st
Kenneally, C.J.	1949-50		2	4	0	20	9	5.00	-	8	0					-	
Kierse, J.M.	1939-40		1	1	0	23	23	23.00	-	25	1	25.00	1/19	-	-	-	
King, J.F.	1877-78	1884-85	7	13	2	145	34	13.18	-	169	6	28.16	2/40	-	-	4	
	1872-73	1884-85	8	14	2	146	34	12.16	-	173	6	28.83	2/40	-	-	4	
King, N.R.	1949-50	1950-51	5	9	3	147	40*	24.50	-	484	7	69.14	3/90	-	-	2	
Kirkwood, H.P.	1901-02	1913-14	13	26	2	477	67	19.87	-	745	25	29.80	6/76	1	-	15	
Kitson, E.H.	1912-13		1	2	0	56	34	28.00	-	did	not	bowl				-	
Klose, T.E.	1939-40	1949-50	25	43	4	895	80	22.94	-	1201	32	37.53	4/23	-	-	16	
Knill, W.	1880-81	1887-88	6	12	1	106	26	9.63	-	did	not	bowl				5	
Kowalick, J.P.	1966-67		1	1	1	0	0*	-	-	88	1	88.00	1/58	-	-	-	
Lambert, D.J.	1976-77	1977-78	6	11	3	156	41	19.50	-	493	8	61.62	3/115	-	-	1	
Langley, G.R.A.	1945-46	1956-57	55	92	15	2369	160*	30.76	4	did	not	bowl				130	30
	1945-46	1956-57	122	165	39	3236	160*	25.68	4	2	0					292	77
Langley, J.N.	1969-70	1978-79	6	8	0	56	13	7.00	-	did	not	bowl				4	
	1969-70	1979-80	28	47	3	934	117	21.22	2	did	not	bowl				26	
Laycock, H.	1931-32		1	2	0	28	21	14.00	-	94	3	31.33	3/92	-	-	3	
Leak, B.H.	1935-36	1940-41	8	14	1	216	79	16.61	-	did	not	bowl				5	
Leak, E.H.	1895-96	1909-10	12	22	2	341	68	17.05	-	21	0					7	
Leak, S.G.	1912-13		1	2	0	30	23	15.00	-	did	not	bowl				3	
Lee. P.K.	1925-26	1934-35	50	88	5	1498	106	18.04	2	4186	146	28.67	5/23	6	-	22	
	1925-26	1934-35	55	95	5	1669	106	18.54	2	4583	152	30.15	5/23	6	-	23	
Lee, R.W.	1956-57	1959-60	3	6	2	142	86	35.50	-	did	not	bowl				3	
Levy, G.B.	1961-62		1	1	0	41	41	41.00	-	did	not	bowl				1	
Lewis, K.	1948-49	1949-50	8	15	0	424	73	28.26	-	did	not	bowl				-	
Lewis, K.J.	1981-82		3	2	2	2	2*	-	-	343	2	171.50	1/54	-	-	1	
Lewis, L.R.	1926-27		2	4	1	106	61	35.33	-	57	3	19.00	2/27	-	-	-	
Lill, J.C.	1955-56	1965-66	60	112	4	4087	176	37.84	8	47	1	47.00	1/3	-	-	54	
	1955-56	1965-66	64	117	4	4109	176	36.86	8	47	1	47.00	1/3	-	-	56	
Liston, G.G.	1887-88		1	2	1	14	8*	14.00	-	did	not	bowl				-	
Lloyd, R.G.	1960-61	1966-67	16	30	1	840	138	28.96	2	38	1	38.00	1/18	-	-	13	
Lonergan, A.R.	1929-30	1934-35	39	72	3	3002	159	43.50	9	12	0					12	
	1929-30	1935-36	43	80	4	3137	159	41.27	9	12	0					14	
Lovell, D.C.	1980-81		3	6	0	124	74	20.66	-	did	not	bowl				2	
Loveridge, E.A.	1920-21	1922-23	5	9	0	195	94	21.66	-	428	8	53.40	4/102	-	-	4	
Lucas, F.R.	1919-20		3	6	0	16	10	2.66	-	320	10	32.00	5/152	1	-	1	
Lucas, T.T.	1877-78		1	1	0	43	43	43.00	-	did	not	bowl				-	
Lyons, J.J.	1884-85	1899-00	47	88	2	2980	145	34.65	8	1434	43	33.34	5/75	1	-	24	
	1884-85	1899-00	153	275	11	6752	149	25.57	11	3225	107	30.14	6/38	5	-	60	
McAllister, D.E.	1964-65		3	6	0	76	43	12.66	-	did	not	bowl				1	
McBeth, A.	1906-07	1907-08	5	10	3	90	36	12.85	-	538	14	38.42	4/41	-	-	3	
	1899-00	1907-08	28	46	16	215	36	7.16	-	2768	111	24.93	6/36	4	1	13	
McCarthy, K.J.	1964-65	1972-73	37	53	12	630	127	15.36	1	2875	95	30.26	6/112	1	-	15	
McCormick, R.V.	1959-60		6	11	4	138	49*	19.71	-	496	5	99.20	2/37	-	-	3	
McKay, D.G.	1925-26	1928-29	10	16	2	485	87	34.64	-	417	10	41.70	4/32	-	-	10	

Name	From	To	M	I	NO	R	HS	Avge	100s	R	W	Avge	BB	5wi	10wm	ct	st
McKay, H.J.	1912-13		3	5	2	44	17	14.66	-	243	7	34.71	4/76	-	-	2	
McKenzie, J.	1884-85	1901-02	22	38	9	402	37*	13.86	-	20	1	20.00	1/8	-	-	32	16
McLachlan, I.M.	1960-61	1963-64	31	55	3	2120	188*	40.76	8	112	0					19	
	1956	1963-64	72	128	10	3743	188*	31.72	9	382	6	63.66	2/33	-	-	41	
McLean, A.R.C.	1945-46	1950-51	20	35	4	897	213	28.93	2	2494	65	38.36	5/68	2	-	15	
McLean, I.R.	1976-77	1982-83	23	43	3	1042	111	26.05	2	did	not	bowl				9	
McLellan, R.M.	1979-80	1981-82	3	4	1	21	14*	7.00	-	272	7	38.85	4/18	-	-	-	
McRae, D.	1906-07		3	6	0	134	70	22.33	-	did	not	bowl				2	
Magarey, W.A.	1890-91		1	2	0	7	7	3.50	-	did	not	bowl				-	
Mallett, A.A.	1967-68	1980-81	91	131	29	1485	92	14.55	-	9534	390	24.44	7/57	20	2	49	
	1967-68	1980-81	183	230	59	2326	92	13.60	-	18208	693	26.27	8/59	33	5	105	
Mann, J.L.	1945-46	1946-47	7	12	5	199	62*	28.42	-	483	13	37.15	3/27	-	-	2	
Manning, J.S.	1951-52	1953-54	19	31	5	556	53*	21.38	-	1977	66	29.95	4/39	-	-	14	
	1951-52	1960	146	207	31	2766	132	15.71	1	11662	513	22.73	8/43	25	4	77	
Marks, L.A.	1965-66		9	18	0	555	127	30.83	1	did	not	bowl				3	
	1962-63	1968-69	33	62	1	1873	185	30.70	2	0	0					22	
Martin, C.	1895-96		3	5	0	40	13	8.00	-	did	not	bowl				2	
Martin, J.W.	1958-59		9	15	4	274	60	24.90	-	991	21	47.19	7/110	1	-	6	
	1956-57	1967-68	135	193	26	3970	101	23.77	1	13872	445	31.17	8/97	17	1	114	
Massey, R.E.C.	1983-84		2	1	0	17	17	17.00	-	155	4	38.75	2/53	-	-	-	
Matthews, J.G.F.	1900-01	1901-02	7	13	2	179	79	16.27	-	544	14	38.85	5/95	1	-	6	
Mayne, R.E.	1906-07	1914-15	37	70	1	2336	142	33.85	3	351	13	27.00	3/6	-	-	29	
	1906-07	1925-26	141	243	10	7624	209	32.72	14	440	13	33.84	3/6	-	-	80	
Michael, L.	1939-40	1951-52	21	35	3	571	85	17.84	-	did	not	bowl				27	5
Middleton, R.F.	1912-13	1914-15	5	10	1	151	34	16.77	-	did	not	bowl				1	
Mitchell, B.G.	1978-79		4	6	1	92	23	18.40	-	did	not	bowl				5	
Moffat, W.D.	1877-78		1	1	0	3	3	3.00	-	did	not	bowl				2	
Moore, H.	1891-92		1	1	0	0	0	0.00	-	24	1	24.00	1/11	-	-	-	
Moroney, R.	1920-21		1	2	0	10	9	5.00	-	68	0					-	
Morton, F.L.	1921-22	1922-23	5	9	3	74	23*	12.33	-	536	12	44.66	3/52	-	-	2	
	1921-22	1931-32	28	36	10	204	23*	7.84	-	3079	94	32.75	5/40	3	-	14	
Moyes, A.G.	1912-13	1914-15	13	25	0	708	104	28.32	1	247	5	49.40	2/22	-	-	14	
	1912-13	1920-21	16	30	0	883	104	29.43	1	268	5	53.60	2/22	-	-	16	
Moyle, C.R.	1910-11		2	4	0	49	24	12.25	-	did	not	bowl				7	1
Moyle, E.J.R.	1933-34	1939-40	15	19	0	496	98	26.10	-	did	not	bowl				15	1
Mueller, M.E.	1937-38		2	3	0	94	56	31.33	-	did	not	bowl				-	
Mundy, D.L.	1969-70		2	4	1	52	35*	17.33	-	166	1	166.00	1/56	-	-	1	
Murray, J.T.	1911-12	1925-26	17	32	2	1004	152	33.46	3	582	10	58.20	2/63	-	-	14	
	1911-12	1925-26	48	79	5	1964	152	26.54	4	694	12	57.88	2/63	-	-	38	
Musgrove, J.	1887-88		3	5	1	82	35	20.50	-	180	5	36.00	3/50	-	-	3	
Mutton, H.J.C.	1959-60		5	9	0	179	62	19.88	-	61	1	61.00	1/11	-	-	2	
Nash, J.E.	1970-71	1980-81	51	97	5	2624	134	28.52	3	12	0					30	
Newland, P.M.	1899-00	1905-06	16	31	7	461	77	19.20	-	did	not	bowl				20	12
	1899-00	1905-06	28	46	13	599	77	18.15	-	did	not	bowl				30	18
Niehuus, R.D.	1946-47	1947-48	10	18	1	603	137	35.47	1	did	not	bowl				-	

Name	From	To	M	I	NO	R	HS	Avge	100s	R	W	Avge	BB	5wi	10wm	ct	st
Nitschke, H.C.	1929-30	1934-35	41	77	3	3159	172	42.68	9	27	0					19	
	1929-30	1934-35	45	82	3	3320	172	42.02	9	27	0					22	
Noblet, G.	1945-46	1952-53	49	78	20	782	50*	13.48	-	4457	236	18.88	7/29	13	2	34	
	1945-46	1956	71	99	29	975	55*	13.92	-	5432	282	19.26	7/29	13	2	44	
Noel, J.	1880-81	1894-95	15	26	1	324	61	12.96	-	498	14	35.57	3/43	-	-	10	1
	1880-81	1894-95	16	27	1	326	61	12.53	-	559	14	39.92	3/43	-	-	10	1
O'Connell, T.R.	1935-36		6	6	0	189	53	31.50	-	287	8	35.87	3/42	-	-	6	
O'Connor, D.F.G.	1983-84		4	6	1	180	72	36.00	-	2	0					-	
O'Connor, J.D.A.	1906-07	1909-10	15	27	5	217	40*	9.86	-	2189	70	31.27	7/36	5	1	12	
	1904-05	1909-10	50	77	18	695	54	11.77	-	5255	224	23.45	7/36	18	5	32	
Ohlstrom, P.A.	1923-24		1	2	1	4	3	4.00	-	25	1	25.00	1/25	-	-	-	
O'Neill, K.I.	1946-47	1949-50	18	29	5	228	31	9.50	-	1559	48	32.47	5/28	2	-	3	
Osborn, F.J.	1953-54	1954-55	2	4	0	31	28	7.75	-	229	2	114.50	2/115	-	-	-	
O'Shannassy, R.M.	1976-77		4	8	2	125	48	20.83	-	284	5	56.80	2/54	-	-	3	
Oswald, N.H.	1936-37	1949-50	12	18	7	123	19*	11.18	-	1214	28	43.35	3/89	-	-	8	
Palmer, G.H.	1924-25	1929-30	9	14	8	55	17	9.16	-	869	12	72.41	4/50	-	-	7	
Palmer, J.S.	1932-33		1	2	0	37	22	18.50	-	did	not	bowl				-	
Parker, R.A.	1933-34	1936-37	13	19	1	484	88	26.88	-	did	not	bowl				2	
Parker, R.J.	1974-75	1978-79	9	18	1	269	62	15.82	-	19	1	19.00	1/8	-	-	5	
Parkin, G.T.	1889-90	1893-94	7	14	4	61	18	6.10	-	140	3	46.66	1/13	-	-	2	
Parkinson, S.D.H.	1981-82	1983-84	20	20	3	170	49	10.00	-	1775	55	32.27	7/98	2	-	9	
Parry, C.N.	1925-26	1930-31	10	18	4	208	69	14.85	-	did	not	bowl				14	13
	1925-26	1933-34	25	42	8	457	69	13.44	-	did	not	bowl				31	28
Pearson, T.J.	1969-70		3	4	3	10	5*	10.00	-	268	9	29.77	5/80	1	-	3	
Pellew, A.H.	1900-01		2	4	0	32	14	8.00	-	did	not	bowl				2	
Pellew, C.E.	1913-14	1928-29	23	43	2	1616	271	39.41	1	705	10	70.50	3/119	-	-	19	
	1913-14	1928-29	91	147	12	4536	271	33.60	9	849	12	70.75	3/119	-	-	45	
Pellew, J.H.	1903-04	1908-09	21	40	1	893	87	22.89	-	439	3	146.33	1/19	-	-	8	
Pellew, L.V.	1919-20	1922-23	10	19	0	604	81	31.78	-	90	0					-	
	1919-20	1922-23	15	24	0	656	81	27.33	-	119	1	119.00	1/23	-	-	2	
Peters, A.E.	1898-99		3	5	1	61	18	15.25	-	47	1	47.00	1/20	-	-	1	
Pettinger, A.M.	1880-81		1	2	0	12	12	6.00	-	did	not	bowl				1	
Phillips, E.G.	1877-78	1889-90	6	10	3	82	18	11.71	-	118	2	59.00	1/5	-	-	6	
Phillips, E.L.	1919-20	1920-21	3	6	1	43	19	8.60	-	275	5	55.00	4/87	-	-	2	
Phillips, W.B.	1977-78	1983-84	28	53	2	2204	260	43.21	6	3	0					25	0
	1977-78	1983-84	46	84	6	3241	260	41.55	8	3	0					53	1
Pinch, C.J.	1950-51	1959-60	61	110	7	4090	146*	39.70	12	242	8	30.25	2/1	-	-	23	
	1949-50	1959-60	63	113	7	4206	146*	39.67	12	242	8	30.25	2/1	-	-	26	
Pittman, B.H.	1959-60		1	2	0	20	16	10.00	-	did	not	bowl				-	
Power, L.B.	1926-27		2	4	0	77	33	19.25	-	76	4	19.00	3/41	-	-	1	
Power, L.J.	1920-21		1	2	0	51	44	25.50	-	did	not	bowl				-	
Pretty, A.H.	1908-09		1	2	0	1	1	0.50	-	113	3	37.66	3/113	-	-	1	
Price, W.D.	1913-14		1	2	1	12	7	12.00	-	72	2	36.00	2/36	-	-	-	
Prior, W.	1974-75	1981-82	46	59	29	185	27	6.16	-	4433	136	32.59	6/41	6	1	29	

Name	From	To	M	I	NO	R	HS	Avge	100s	R	W	Avge	BB	5wi	10wm	ct	st
Pritchard, D.E.	1918-19	1931-32	49	89	2	2963	167	34.05	6	104	3	34.66	1/4	-	-	51	
Puckett, M.C.	1964-65		1	1	1	1	1*	-	-	121	2	60.50	1/59	-	-	2	
Pynor, E.I.	1948-49	1949-50	3	4	1	52	37*	17.33	-	323	4	80.75	2/31	-	-	4	
Quigley, B.M.	1958-59	1960-61	11	20	4	158	30	9.87	-	1142	32	35.68	7/39	1	-	5	
Quilty, J.	1881-82	1882-83	2	4	1	2	2	0.66	-	130	11	11.81	9/55	1	1	1	
Quist, K.H.	1908-09	1911-12	7	12	1	157	44*	14.27	-	260	12	21.66	4/33	-	-	5	
	1899-00	1911-12	10	18	2	296	56	18.50	-	300	12	25.00	4/33	-	-	7	
Rebbeck, P.D.	1971-72		5	9	0	161	55	17.88	-	did	not	bowl				3	
Reedman, J.C.	1887-88	1908-09	76	141	8	3068	113	23.06	1	3657	114	32.07	7/54	6	1	65	
	1887-88	1908-09	81	151	8	3338	113	23.34	2	3787	118	32.09	7/54	6	1	68	
Rees, J.N.S.	1905-06		1	2	1	21	21*	21.00	-	did	not	bowl				0	1
Rees, R.B.C.	1903-04	1912-13	13	24	2	354	45	16.09	-	1592	57	27.92	6/80	5	2	6	
Reid, W.	1892-93		1	1	0	50	50	50.00	-	did	not	bowl					
Richards, B.A.	1970-71		10	16	2	1538	356	109.85	6	145	5	29.00	3/29	-	-	10	
	1964-65	1982-83	339	576	58	28358	356	54.74	80	2886	77	37.48	7/63	1	-	367	
Richards, T.O.	1880-81	1883-84	4	8	0	40	24	5.00	-	83	1	83.00	1/28	-	-	4	
Richardson, A.J.	1918-19	1926-27	45	85	4	3745	280	46.23	11	4583	117	39.17	5/52	2	-	22	
	1918-19	1933	86	139	13	5238	280	41.57	13	6555	209	31.36	6/28	7	1	34	
Richardson, J.	1905-06		2	3	0	54	29	18.00	-	did	not	bowl				0	1
Richardson, V.Y.	1918-19	1937-38	104	188	7	7698	231	42.53	21	399	3	133.00	1/5	-	-	128	
	1918-19	1937-38	184	297	12	10727	231	37.63	27	545	8	68.12	3/22	-	-	213	4
Richter, A.F.	1935-36		1	1	0	7	7	7.00	-	73	0					-	
Ridings, K.L.	1938-39	1940-41	18	29	3	864	151	33.23	2	182	7	26.00	4/26	-	-	6	
	1938-39	1940-41	19	31	3	919	151	32.82	2	182	7	26.00	4/26	-	-	6	
Ridings, P.L.	1937-38	1956-57	98	168	17	5622	186*	37.23	9	2769	58	47.74	4/66	-	-	54	
	1937-38	1956-57	102	173	17	5653	186*	36.23	9	2864	61	46.95	4/66	-	-	55	
Rigaud, S.	1877-78		1	1	1	8	8*	-	-	21	0					2	
Riley, W.N.	1925-26		1	1	0	45	45	45.00	-	35	0					1	
Roberts, W.M.	1937-38	1946-47	3	4	0	3	2	0.75	-	233	9	25.88	4/35	-	-	2	
Robertson, T.J.	1977-78	1979-80	32	50	7	873	96	20.30	-	did	not	bowl				82	12
Robins, D.	1964-65	1966-67	20	31	2	340	44	11.72	-	1747	52	33.59	6/58	3	-	12	
Robinson, R.H.	1937-38		7	12	0	259	62	21.58	-	10	0					4	
	1934-35	1948-49	46	81	4	2441	163	31.70	4	1654	44	37.59	4/45	-	-	24	
Robran, B.C.	1971-72		2	4	0	28	18	7.00	-	did	not	bowl				1	
Rolfe, D.J.	1979-80	1980-81	4	7	0	158	83	22.57	-	did	not	bowl				8	
	1975-76	1980-81	5	9	0	171	83	19.00	-	did	not	bowl				8	
Rosman, A.V.H.	1898-99		1	2	1	66	63	66.00	-	13	0					-	
Roxby, R.C.	1954-55	1958-59	12	20	4	250	41	15.62	-	853	11	77.54	3/82	-	-	8	
	1953-54	1958-59	16	25	4	322	41	15.33	-	1315	26	50.57	5/84	1	-	10	
Rundell, J.U.	1883-84	1884-85	2	4	0	27	15	6.75	-	120	8	15.00	5/31	1	-	-	
Rundell, P.D.	1912-13	1925-26	30	57	3	1722	122*	31.88	4	1696	25	67.84	3/34	-	-	10	
Ryan, A.J.	1925-26	1936-37	32	52	3	1453	144	29.65	2	824	19	43.36	4/13	-	-	31	
	1925-26	1936-37	33	53	4	1493	144	30.46	2	866	20	43.30	4/13	-	-	32	
Rymill, J.W.	1921-22	1926-27	21	37	3	1242	146	36.52	4	did	not	bowl				3	
	1921-22	1926-27	22	39	3	1260	146	35.00	4	did	not	bowl				3	

Name	From	To	M	I	NO	R	HS	Avge	100s	R	W	Avge	BB	5wi	10wm	ct	st
Sangster, C.B.	1927-28		2	2	0	116	62	58.00	-	48	1	48.00	1/14	-	-	1	
Sangster, J.F.	1961-62	1962-63	2	3	1	44	19	22.00	-	131	2	65.50	1/16	-	-	-	
Sargent, M.A.J.	1960-61		9	17	0	564	164	33.17	1	204	3	68.00	2/18	-	-	3	
	1951	1960-61	22	38	4	804	164	23.64	1	204	3	68.00	2/18	-	-	5	
Sayers, D.K.	1981-82		3	4	2	7	5*	3.50	-	172	3	57.33	2/43	-	-	-	
Schneider, K.J.	1926-27	1927-28	13	23	1	1125	146	51.13	5	247	8	30.87	2/10	-	-	2	
	1922-23	1927-28	20	33	2	1509	146	48.67	6	355	10	35.50	2/10	-	-	5	
Schultz, B.	1936-37		2	4	0	132	41	33.00	-	59	2	29.50	2/29	-	-	-	
Schultz, J.W.E.	1919-20	1921-22	4	8	3	44	19*	8.80	-	did	not	bowl				6	1
Scott, D.B.	1983-84		2	3	0	95	64	31.66	-	9	0					3	
Scott, J.	1937-38	1938-39	5	4	3	10	5*	10.00	-	363	7	51.85	2/19	-	-	2	
Scott, J.D.	1925-26	1928-29	20	34	7	461	86*	17.07	-	2653	70	37.90	6/58	3	-	13	
	1908-09	1928-29	59	91	15	1113	100	14.64	1	6427	227	28.31	6/48	12	1	35	
Scrymgour, B.V.	1890-91	1896-97	5	9	1	65	37	8.12	-	did	not	bowl				4	
Sellers, R.H.D.	1959-60	1966-67	39	60	12	856	87	17.83	-	3508	91	38.54	5/49	3	1	30	
	1959-60	1966-67	53	80	20	1089	87	18.15	-	4653	121	38.45	5/36	4	1	41	
Selth, V.P.	1918-19	1919-20	2	4	1	48	25	16.00	-	did	not	bowl				1	0
Sharpe, D.A.	1961-62	1965-66	14	25	2	515	72	22.39	-	43	1	43.00	1/35	-	-	9	
	1955-56	1965-66	37	60	4	1531	118	27.33	2	100	1	100.00	1/35	-	-	41	12
Shepherd, A.G.	1931-32	1934-35	12	21	0	383	80	18.23	-	did	not	bowl				4	
Shepherdson, H.R.	1935-36		1	1	1	28	28*	-	-	61	2	30.50	2/26	-	-	1	
Shepley, H.N.	1925-26		1	1	1	6	6*	-	-	70	2	35.00	2/43	-	-	-	
Shiell, A.B.	1964-65	1966-67	23	42	4	1276	202*	33.57	2	24	0					15	
Short, H.W.	1904-05		1	2	1	1	1*	1.00	-	57	1	57.00	1/57	-	-	-	
Simunsen, R.F.	1972-73		4	7	2	103	58	20.60	-	15	0					3	
Sincock, A.T.	1974-75	1983-84	39	61	31	625	47	20.83	-	3817	98	38.94	7/40	4	-	17	
Sincock, D.J.	1960-61	1965-66	35	53	14	679	61*	17.41	-	4775	134	35.63	7/48	10	1	21	
	1960-61	1965-66	46	65	17	838	61*	17.45	-	5863	159	36.87	7/48	10	1	27	
Sincock, H.K.	1929-30		2	4	0	66	31	16.50	-	126	4	31.50	2/34	-	-	1	
Sincock, P.D.	1974-75		5	10	0	174	48	17.40	-	11	0					-	
Sleep, P.R.	1976-77	1983-84	69	118	20	3447	144	35.17	6	5989	175	34.22	8/133	6	-	48	
	1976-77	1983-84	80	137	22	3695	144	32.13	6	6817	195	34.95	8/133	7	-	50	
Slight, A.F.	1886-87		1	2	1	17	16*	17.00	-	did	not	bowl				-	
Slight, W.	1880-81	1881-82	3	6	0	134	70	22.33	-	52	2	26.00	1/0	-	-	2	
	1877-78	1881-82	4	8	0	145	70	18.12	-	58	2	29.00	1/0	-	-	2	
Smart, L.M.	1950-51	1957-58	5	9	1	156	61	19.50	-	134	3	44.66	2/58	-	-	2	
Smith, A.E.	1913-14	1921-22	12	24	1	774	122	33.65	2	829	17	48.76	5/120	1	-	5	
Smith, L.A.	1933-34		1	1	0	9	9	9.00	-	did	not	bowl				-	
Sobers, G.St A.	1961-62	1963-64	26	45	2	2707	251	62.95	10	3565	137	26.02	7/110	8	-	26	
	1952-53	1974	383	609	93	28315	365*	54.87	86	28941	1043	27.74	9/49	36	1	407	
Squires, P.H.	1962-63		1	1	0	0	0	0.00	-	52	0					-	
Stanford, G.E.	1968-69		1	2	1	6	4*	6.00	-	87	0					-	
Stanford, R.M.	1935-36	1947-48	10	15	0	311	76	20.73	-	did	not	bowl				2	
	1935-36	1947-48	23	35	3	832	153	26.00	1	25	0					4	
Starr, C.L.B.	1926-27	1945-46	7	11	1	236	72	23.60	-	60	2	30.00	2/3	-	-	5	
Steele, D.M.	1911-12	1920-21	19	35	3	1142	113*	35.68	3	did	not	bowl				11	

Name	*From*	*To*	*M*	*I*	*NO*	*R*	*HS*	*Avge*	*100s*	*R*	*W*	*Avge*	*BB*	*5wi*	*10wm*	*ct*	*st*
Steele, K.N.	1913-14		2	4	0	18	11	4.50	-	99	0					-	
Stevens, G.B.	1952-53	1958-59	38	71	6	2720	259*	41.84	7	69	0					29	
	1952-53	1959-60	47	86	6	3061	259*	38.26	7	123	3	41.00	2/16	-	-	34	
Stillman, W.L.	1977-78		10	20	2	407	88*	22.61	-	27	0					9	
	1970-71	1977-78	28	54	2	1299	88*	24.98	-	27	0					20	
Stirling, W.S.	1908-09	1920-21	14	27	2	307	54	12.28	-	776	11	70.54	3/52	-	-	9	
	1908-09	1920-21	47	72	7	931	62	14.32	-	1891	61	31.00	5/26	3	-	32	
Strudwick, D.C.	1957-58		1	2	0	1	1	0.50	-	did	not	bowl				-	
Stuart, W.P.	1899-00	1908-09	8	15	3	158	38	13.16	-	did	not	bowl				6	
Sutherland, D.J.	1969-70	1971-72	11	19	0	428	64	22.52	-	98	6	16.33	4/45	-	-	4	
Symonds, C.	1945-46		4	7	1	57	13	9.50	-	did	not	bowl				8	0
Tardif, J.H.	1889-90	1892-93	4	8	0	102	41	12.75	-	did	not	bowl				3	
Teagle, R.C.	1930-31		2	4	0	32	20	8.00	-	12	0					4	
Teisseire, F.L.	1939-40		1	1	0	56	56	56.00	-	did	not	bowl				2	
Thamm, W.	1902-03		1	2	1	17	9	17.00	-	did	not	bowl				0	0
Thomas, A.C.	1898-99		1	1	0	0	0	0.00	-	did	not	bowl				-	
Thomas, R.C.	1952-53		6	8	1	64	31	9.14	-	547	9	60.77	2/71	-	-	1	
Thompson, H.M.	1935-36		1	2	0	19	12	9.50	-	104	1	104.00	1/34	-	-	-	
Thurgarland, W.J.	1920-21		1	2	0	37	26	18.50	-	43	0					-	
Tobin, B.J.	1930-31	1934-35	26	46	1	722	61	16.04	-	1991	51	39.03	4/31	-	-	17	
Townsend, R.J.B.	1907-08	1923-24	17	34	2	584	117	18.25	1	1499	37	40.51	5/27	2	-	14	
Travers, J.P.F.	1895-96	1906-07	36	67	23	750	77	17.04	-	3659	116	31.54	9/30	5	1	24	
	1895-96	1906-07	37	69	23	760	77	16.52	-	3673	117	31.39	9/30	5	1	25	
Tregoning, J.	1939-40	1947-48	2	3	0	18	17	6.00	-	9	1	9.00	1/9	-	-	4	
Trethewey, P.G.	1957-58	1961-62	27	40	18	77	13*	3.50	-	2546	88	28.93	7/69	6	1	10	
	1957-58	1962-63	28	42	19	79	13*	3.43	-	2621	92	28.48	7/69	6	1	10	
Trowse, D.F.	1951-52	1955-56	22	39	1	911	102	23.97	1	did	not	bowl				15	
Turner, T.	1885-86	1888-89	3	5	4	31	12	31.00	-	108	0					1	
	1885-86	1888-89	5	9	5	37	12	9.25	-	242	2	121.00	1/62	-	-	1	
Vaughton, R.W.	1946-47	1947-48	6	9	3	82	20	13.66	-	did	not	bowl				9	3
Vincent, B.A.	1980-81	1981-82	6	6	2	125	47	31.25	-	351	12	29.25	4/64	-	-	2	
Vincent, R.G.	1976-77		3	6	0	143	59	23.83	-	did	not	bowl				4	0
Wainwright, E.G.C.	1923-24	1925-26	9	15	0	237	56	15.80	-	347	5	69.40	3/52	-	-	6	
Waite, M.G.	1930-31	1945-46	72	114	10	3011	137	28.95	1	4238	120	35.31	5/42	1	-	51	
	1930-31	1945-46	103	155	15	3888	137	27.77	1	6071	192	31.61	7/101	5	-	66	
Waldron, A.E.	1881-82	1887-88	2	3	0	8	6	2.66	-	18	3	6.00	3/18	-	-	2	
Walker, C.W.	1928-29	1940-41	78	123	24	1456	71	14.70	-	did	not	bowl				139	113
	1928-29	1940-41	109	152	35	1754	71	14.99	-	did	not	bowl				171	149
Walkley, E.A.	1900-01	1901-02	4	7	0	107	53	15.28	-	123	1	123.00	1/35	-	-	2	
Wall, T.W.	1924-25	1935-36	53	81	17	749	53*	11.70	-	5209	178	29.26	10/36	3	1	26	
	1924-25	1935-36	108	135	33	1071	53*	10.50	-	9877	330	29.93	10/36	10	2	54	
Walsh, L.S.	1930-31		2	4	0	41	23	10.25	-	did	not	bowl				2	
Walsh, N.A.	1923-24	1925-26	9	17	1	242	34*	15.12	-	39	1	39.00	1/25	-	-	5	

Name	From	To	M	I	NO	R	HS	Avge	100s	R	W	Avge	BB	5wi	10wm	ct	st
Ward, F.A.	1935-36	1940-41	38	50	9	603	62	14.70	-	5044	187	26.97	7/62	12	2	26	
	1935-36	1940-41	66	80	17	871	62	13.82	-	7900	320	24.68	7/51	24	5	42	
Waters, R.W.	1901-02	1902-03	4	8	1	86	39*	12.28	-	174	3	58.00	3/53	-	-	4	
Watling, W.H.	1883-84	1888-89	5	8	0	160	58	20.00	-	did	not	bowl				2	
Watsford, G.	1882-83		1	2	0	2	2	1.00	-	did	not	bowl				-	
	1882-83	1885-86	2	4	0	22	10	5.50	-	23	0					-	
Watts	1947-48	1953-54	9	16	4	317	76	26.41	-	735	12	61.25	3/89	-	-	6	
Waye, L.S.	1912-13		1	2	0	2	2	1.00	-	6	0					1	
Webb, C.R.	1945-46		6	11	1	202	63	20.20	-	did	not	bowl				3	
Webb, K.N.	1946-47		2	2	1	16	10	16.00	-	154	1	154.00	1/0	-	-	-	
Webster, H.W.	1910-11	1911-12	6	12	0	136	39	11.33	-	did	not	bowl				5	2
	1910-11	1912	19	29	5	346	54	14.41	-	did	not	bowl				21	4
Weekley, L.R.	1950-51	1956-57	6	9	1	63	40	7.87	-	670	10	67.00	4/61	-	-	3	
Weeks, A.E.	1887-88		1	2	0	26	21	13.00	-	did	not	bowl				-	
Weir, A.J.	1949-50		1	2	0	2	2	1.00	-	74	2	37.00	1/34	-	-	-	
Whitfield, H.E.P.	1926-27	1931-32	24	44	4	977	91	24.42	-	2073	57	36.36	6/47	2	-	24	
	1926-27	1931-32	25	46	4	1065	91	25.35	-	2190	58	37.75	6/47	2	-	24	
Whitington, R.S.	1932-33	1939-40	36	58	2	1728	125	30.85	3	24	0					18	
	1932-33	1945-46	54	90	4	2782	155	32.34	4	91	1	91.00	1/4	-	-	32	
Whitty, W.J.	1908-09	1925-26	43	78	19	791	81	13.40	-	5678	178	31.89	7/66	8	1	14	
	1907-08	1925-26	119	171	44	1465	81	11.53	-	11489	491	23.39	8/27	26	4	35	
Wigley, R.S.	1888-89	1889-90	3	5	0	66	44	13.20	-	did	not	bowl					2
Wilkin, J.W.S.	1949-50		1	2	0	54	29	27.00	-	did	not	bowl				5	0
Wilkinson, A.	1885-86	1892-93	4	6	0	59	21	9.83	-	23	0					1	
Williams, N.L.	1919-20	1928-29	33	59	6	832	56	15.69	-	4593	116	39.59	6/40	8	3	12	
	1919-20	1928-29	34	61	6	850	56	15.45	-	4778	122	39.16	6/40	9	3	12	
Williams, R.G.	1932-33	1937-38	18	29	7	405	75*	18.40	-	1384	53	26.11	6/21	3	-	10	
	1932-33	1945-46	26	41	8	531	75*	16.09	-	1957	67	29.20	6/21	3	-	12	
Willsmore, H.B.	1913-14	1920-21	8	16	0	271	57	16.93	-	526	16	32.87	4/65	-	-	7	
Wilson, J.W.	1950-51	1957-58	55	82	42	247	19*	6.17	-	5746	182	31.57	6/55	6	-	13	
	1949-50	1957-58	78	97	47	287	19*	5.74	-	7019	230	30.51	7/11	9	1	17	
Wilson, S.V.	1975-76		1	2	2	0	0*	-	-	83	1	83.00	1/67	-	-	1	
	1968-69	1975-76	6	8	6	20	14*	10.00	-	554	14	39.57	4/29	-	-	1	
Winser, C.L.	1913-14	1920-21	5	9	1	64	23	8.00	-	did	not	bowl				8	6
Winter, G.J.	1981-82	1983-84	14	15	3	173	64	14.41	-	1317	43	30.62	7/65	3	-	5	
Wood, H.L.	1959-60		2	4	1	51	19	17.00	-	did	not	bowl				2	
Woodcock, A.J.	1967-68	1978-79	80	143	4	4403	141	31.67	5	did	not	bowl				67	
	1967-68	1978-79	85	151	4	4550	141	30.95	5	did	not	bowl				72	
Woodford, J.R.H.	1908-09		7	12	1	159	35	14.45	-	did	not	bowl				10	7
	1901-02	1912-13	15	24	4	249	35	12.45	-	51	1	51.00	1/51	-	-	18	12
Woolcock, A.H.	1909-10		3	5	1	74	37	18.50	-	37	1	37.00	1/20	-	-	1	
Wright, A.W.	1905-06	1920-21	29	52	21	235	53	7.58	-	3266	106	30.81	7/66	7	1	7	
	1905-06	1920-21	30	53	21	242	53	7.56	-	3390	110	30.81	7/66	7	1	8	
Wright, K.J.	1980-81	1983-84	40	62	13	1410	105	28.77	2	did	not	bowl				110	12
	1974-75	1983-84	85	128	33	2551	105	26.85	2	did	not	bowl				268	26
Wright, R.R.	1933-34		2	3	0	126	77	42.00	-	12	0					-	

Name	*From*	*To*	*M*	*I*	*NO*	*R*	*HS*	*Avge*	*100s*	*R*	*W*	*Avge*	*BB*	*5wi*	*10wm*	*ct*	*st*
Yagmich, D.B.	1974-75	1976-77	20	30	6	305	45	12.70	-	did	not	bowl				49	12
	1972-73	1976-77	24	33	9	319	45	13.29	-	did	not	bowl				73	13
Younis Ahmed	1972-73		6	11	0	289	69	26.27	-	122	2	61.00	2/26	-	-	4	
	2	1984	413	693	104	23122	221*	39.25	38	1639	39	42.02	4/10	-	-	232	
Zadow, R.J.	1979-80	1982-83	13	25	2	579	87	25.17	-	1	0					14	
Zschorn, P.W.	1910-11		2	3	0	13	12	4.33	-	did	not	bowl				3	

NOTES ON CAREER RECORDS

1. The career records are compiled from the currently published or forthcoming ACS Guides to first-class matches - Australia, British Isles, South Africa, New Zealand, West Indies, India.
2. The second line of figures for M.D.Haysman and W.B.Phillips include two first-class matches played by Young Australians in Zimbabwe 1982-83 (the Australian Cricket Board having reversed its earlier decision).
3. F.C.Christy (miscellaneous players' list): positive identification has not been made. The player concerned (Surrey v The World 1861-62) may be his brother, J.Christy, in which case the second line of figures should be deleted.

MISCELLANEOUS AUSTRALIAN FIRST-CLASS PLAYERS

The players listed below appeared in first-class matches for various Australian teams in Australia and/or overseas, without ever representing an Australian colony or state in a first-class match. The first line against each player's name shows his career record in first-class matches for Australian sides; players who appeared in first-class matches other than for Australian sides have two lines of figures, the second of which shows the player's career record in all first-class matches.

The line of figures for C.D.Bremner and H.S.Craig include their performances for Dominions v England at Lord's in 1945.

Name	*From*	*To*	*M*	*I*	*NO*	*R*	*HS*	*Avge*	*100s*	*R*	*W*	*Avge*	*BB*	*5wi*	*10wm*	*ct*	*st*
Beal, C.W.	1882		1	1	0	5	5	5.00	-	did	not	bowl				-	
Blanchard, C.	1861-62		1	2	0	11	11	5.50	-	did	not	bowl				-	
Bremner, C.D.	1945	1945-46	7	9	6	8	4*	2.66	-	did	not	bowl				4	6
Christy, F.C.	1861-62		1	2	0	0	0	0.00	-	did	not	bowl				-	
	1846	1861-62	3	6	0	5	5	0.83	-	did	not	bowl				-	
Craig, H.S.	1945		1	2	0	88	56	44.00	-	did	not	bowl				-	
Davis, J.H.	1935-36		2	4	1	5	4*	1.66	-	did	not	bowl				-	
Ducker, N.G.	1912		1	2	0	15	9	7.50	-	did	not	bowl				-	
Hardie, J.	1886		1	1	0	0	0	0.00	-	did	not	bowl				-	
Hogg, T.	1872-73		1	1	0	0	0	0.00	-	40	3	13.33	2/27	-	-	-	
Hyslop, H.H.	1886		1	1	0	1	1	1.00	-	did	not	bowl				1	
	1876	1886	9	16	1	121	34	8.06	-	31	2	15.50	2/12	-	-	7	11
Ivory, W.C.	1910-11		1	1	0	0	0	0.00	-	did	not	bowl				0	2
MacGregor, W.	1913-14		4	5	2	50	35	16.66	-	did	not	bowl				5	4
Morcom, S.	1872-73		1	2	0	4	4	2.00	-	did	not	bowl				-	
O'Brien, M.E.	1863-64		1	2	0	6	6	3.00	-	did	not	bowl				-	
Patiala, Maharaja of	1935-36		1	1	0	15	15	15.00	-	40	2	20.00	2/40	-	-	-	
	1915-16	1937-38	24	34	3	536	83	16.96	-	60	2	30.00	2/40	-	-	4	
Penfold, E.G.	1912		1	2	1	0	0*	0.00	-	did	not	bowl				-	
Price, C.F.T.	1945	1945-46	14	20	3	327	55	19.23	-	643	24	26.79	4/33	-	-	11	
Simmonds, W.	1863-64		1	1	0	3	3	3.00	-	did	not	bowl				1	
Sims, A.	1913-14		7	6	2	204	184*	51.00	1	did	not	bowl				5	
	1896-97	1913-14	53	93	10	2182	184*	26.28	2	409	19	21.52	5/36	1	-	51	
Smith, S.M.	1926-27		1	2	1	38	25	38.00	-	62	1	62.00	1/62	-	-	-	
Tait, G.	1863-64		1	2	0	7	4	3.50	-	did	not	bowl				1	
Tarrant, L.B.	1935-36		1	1	1	16	16*	-	-	did	not	bowl				2	
Teece, R.C.	1872-73		1	1	0	0	0	0.00	-	did	not	bowl				1	
Tennent, H.N.	1878		1	2	0	3	2	1.50	-	did	not	bowl				-	
	1865	1878	19	31	3	344	45*	12.28	-	20	0					8	
Thorpe, H.	1887-88		1	2	1	8	8	8.00	-	36	0					-	
Winning, S.C.	1919	1919-20	28	35	17	253	30	14.05	-	1605	67	23.95	6/30	3	-	22	
Woods, S.M.J.	1888		6	10	0	54	18	5.40	-	298	11	27.09	4/44	-	-	2	
	1886	1910	401	690	35	15345	215	23.42	19	21653	1040	20.82	10/69	77	21	279	
Workman, J.A.	1945	1945-46	16	29	2	549	76	20.33	-	6	1	6.00	1/6	-	-	5	

ERRATA, CORRIGENDA AND ADDENDA TO VICTORIAN CRICKETERS

Page 5	E.T.Austen: d. Melbourne, June 21, 1983
	A.J.Aylett: LB
	R.H.Bailey: b. October 5, 1876 (not 1976)
	W.H.Bailey: d. Geelong, Feb 27, 1983.
Page 7	H.H.G.Bracher: also LAB
Page 8	Richard Sinclair Brodie: d. circa 1854.
Page 13	J.L.Drew: LM (not RAB)
Page 15	F.E.Fontaine: d. Greensborough, Oct. 24, 1982.
Page 16	T.Grant: RHB
Page 17	A.P.Haddrick: b. July 14, 1868.
	H.W.Hart: b. Bulwarra, near Ballarat (not Fitzroy)
Page 20	E.H.Hutton: RHB.
Page 22	J.D.Kinnear: d. Moreland, Dec. 14, 1981.
	W.G.Kinnear: d. West Brunswick, Dec. 7, 1982.
Page 23	A.W.Lampard: d. Armadale, Jan. 11, 1984.
	W.M.Lawry: LM
Page 24	A.E.Liddicut: d. Parkdale, April 8, 1983.
Page 28	N.F.Mitchell: LHB (not RHB)
Page 29	H.L.Numa: d. Heidelberg, April 17, 1984.
Page 32	W.W.Reddrop: d. Parkville, March 31, 1983.
Page 34	H.C.A.Sandford: b. 1891 (not 1892)
	R.B.Scott: d. April 6, 1984.
Page 36	J.G.Stanes: d. Ferntree Gully, Feb. 7, 1983.
Page 38	E.K.Tolhurst: d. East Prahan, May 24, 1982.
Page 41	E.H.Whitlow: RM
Page 42	W.J.G.Woodbury: d.Moe, Aug. 31, 1983.

ERRATA, CORRIGENDA & ADDENDA TO QUEENSLAND CRICKETERS

Page 3	William Abell: b. circa 1875.
	C.W.Andrews: b. 1908, not 1901; d. June 9, 1962 on board S.S.Orion at Bombay
	J.W.Anderson: RFM
Page 5	F.M.Brew: b. Petrie Terrace; d. Sandgate.
Page 6	T.K.Caban: Timothy (not Timmothy); b. Jan. 15, 1952
Page 7	G.G.Cook: b. Chelmer; d. Chelmer, Sept. 12, 1982. at Cessnock, N.S.W.
Page 8	D.E.Cox: d. Dakabin, Jan. 9, 1982.
	G.S.Crouch: d. Indooroopilly.
Page 9	D.L.Ellis: b. Herston.
	F.W.Fett: first christian name probably Frederich.
	J.W.Fletcher: The player listed appeared in 3 matches in 1909-10 and was RHB.
	Jack Fletcher, South Brisbane, played in one match in 1919-20 and was RHB/LB
Page 10	J.E.Freeman: correct surname is Childe-Freeman.
	E.Gilbert: first name Edward; b. in 1905 or 1906.
	A.E.A.Goldman: delete d. in South Africa.
Page 11	C.S.Griffiths: d. Rockhampton, May 12, 1928.
Page 12	O.C.Hitchcock: RHB
	W.Hoare: RHB.
	P.M.Hornibrook: d. Spring Hill.
	A.Hurwood: d. Coffs Harbour, N.S.W., Sept. 26, 1982.
Page 13	H.Ironmonger: b. 1882 (not 1883 or 1881 as previously indicated)
	K.M.Jack: d. Buderim, Nov. 22, 1982.
	I.H.King: b. Herston.
Page 15	M.F.McCaffrey: b. Feb. 7, 1878.
Page 16	K.D.Mackay: d. Point Lookout, Stradbroke Island, June 13, 1982.
	Charles Costley Martin.
	A.D.A.Mayes: d. Spring Hill, Feb. 8, 1983.
Page 17	D.L.Miller: b. Holytown, Lanarkshire, Scotland; d. Clayfield, April 12, 1943.
	H.G.S.Morton: d. Herston.
	Kenneth Leonard Mario Mossop.
	W.Munro: RHB/RM.
	H.D.Noyes: b. Warwick.
Page 18	L.E.Oxenham: b. Nundah.
	R.K.Oxenham: b. Nundah.
	G.A.Poeppel: b. Nov. 6, 1893.
Page 19	R.C.Raymond: d. Murgon, Oct. 11, 1982.
	N.T.Rogers: b. Spring Hill; d. Annerley, May 27, 1982.
	W.D.Rowe: b. Brisbane; d. South Brisbane.
Page 20	James Francis Anthony Sheppard: b. Brisbane 1888.
Page 21	W.Sullivan: RHB/RM.
	D.Tallon: d. Bundaberg, Sept., 7, 1984.
Page 22	B.L.Webb: d. Greenslopes, Feb. 7, 1983.
Page 27	Fletcher, J. 1919 1-2-0-29-29-14.50 120-3-40.00-3/65-0-0 0
	Fletcher, J.W. 1909 3-6-0-47-97-16.16-0 49-0 2

ADDENDA TO NEW SOUTH WALES CRICKETERS

Page 6	R.Bardsley: d. Sydney, June 25, 1983.
Page 10	S.J.Carroll: d. Willoughby, Oct. 12, 1984.
Page 21	W.A.Hunt: d. Balmain, Dec. 30, 1983.
Page 26	A.E.Marks: d. Sydney, July 28, 1983.
Page 37	E.Trenerry: d. Woollahra, July 8, 1983.

CORRIGENDA AND ADDENDA TO TASMANIAN CRICKETERS

Page 7	L.J.Alexander: debut 1947-48
	G.H.Allan: debut 1922-23.
Page 8	Richard Thomas Bygrove Barnes: b. Hobart, Sept. 5, 1852.
Page 9	R.A.Broomby: d. Southport, Qld., May 5, 1984.
	A.O.Burrows: d. Sandy Bay, Jan. 4, 1984.
Page 10	F.B.Campbell: Francis, not Frank.
	N.G.Clayton: d. Auckland, circa 1867.
Page 12	A.H.Davis: d. Camberwell, Vic., March 5, 1943 (not 1947 or 1953).
Page 13	C.P.Hammond: d. Hollywood, United States, 1955.
	C.C.Hargrave: b. Kiveton.
Page 16	John Sidney Howe: b. Kotree, Sind, India, Dec. 27, 1868. d. Neutral Bay, N.S.W., July 29, 1939.
	K.Ibadulla played domestic cricket in Patistan 1953-54 & 1965-66.
Page 18	A.M.Lochner: Augustus, not August.
	J.C.Mace: d. Yateley, Hampshire, England.
Page 19	A.J.Marriott: b. England
Page 23	D.R.Smith: d.Port Fairy, Vic., 1933.
Page 25	John Maitland Ware.

ADDENDA & CORRIGENDA TO WESTERN AUSTRALIAN CRICKETERS

Page 5	L.H.Bandy: d. Scarborough, July 18, 1984
	A.J.Banks: b. Maryborough, Vic., Dec. 10, 1883; d. Toodyay, July 5, 1930.
Page 6	F.J.Bryant: b. 1909 (not 1907)
	F.J.Bryant: d. Glendalough, March 11, 1984.
Page 7	T.M.Coombe: b. 1877 (not 1887)
Page 8	T.H.Coyne: b. 1873 (not 1893)
	A.D.Drew: d. Shenton Park, Feb. 20, 1984.
Page 9	W.A.Evans: Allan should be in bold type.
Page 10	A.H.J.C.Heindrichs is the correct spelling.
	T.H.Hogue: d. 1956 (not 1955)
Page 15	R.W.Marsh also played for the Scarborough Club.
Page 18	H.W.H.Rigg made his debut in the 1946-47 season.
Page 19	W.T.Rowlands: d. Subiaco, May 18, 1984.
Page 20	G.D.Watson: second name should read Donald.
Page 34	Rowlands: initials are W.T.

NEW SOUTH WALES CRICKETERS 1855-1981

Compiled and Published by
The Association of Cricket Statisticians
Reg Offices: Haughton Mill, Retford, Notts.

Price: £2.50 (issued free to members of the Association).

A Companion volume on Queensland Cricketers 1892-1979, is still available from the publishers or from Roger Page, 55, Tarcoola Dr, Yallambie, Victoria 3085. Enquiries regarding membership of the Association may be sent to either address.

Printed by Tranter Printing Services, Bridge Works, London Road, Derby, England.

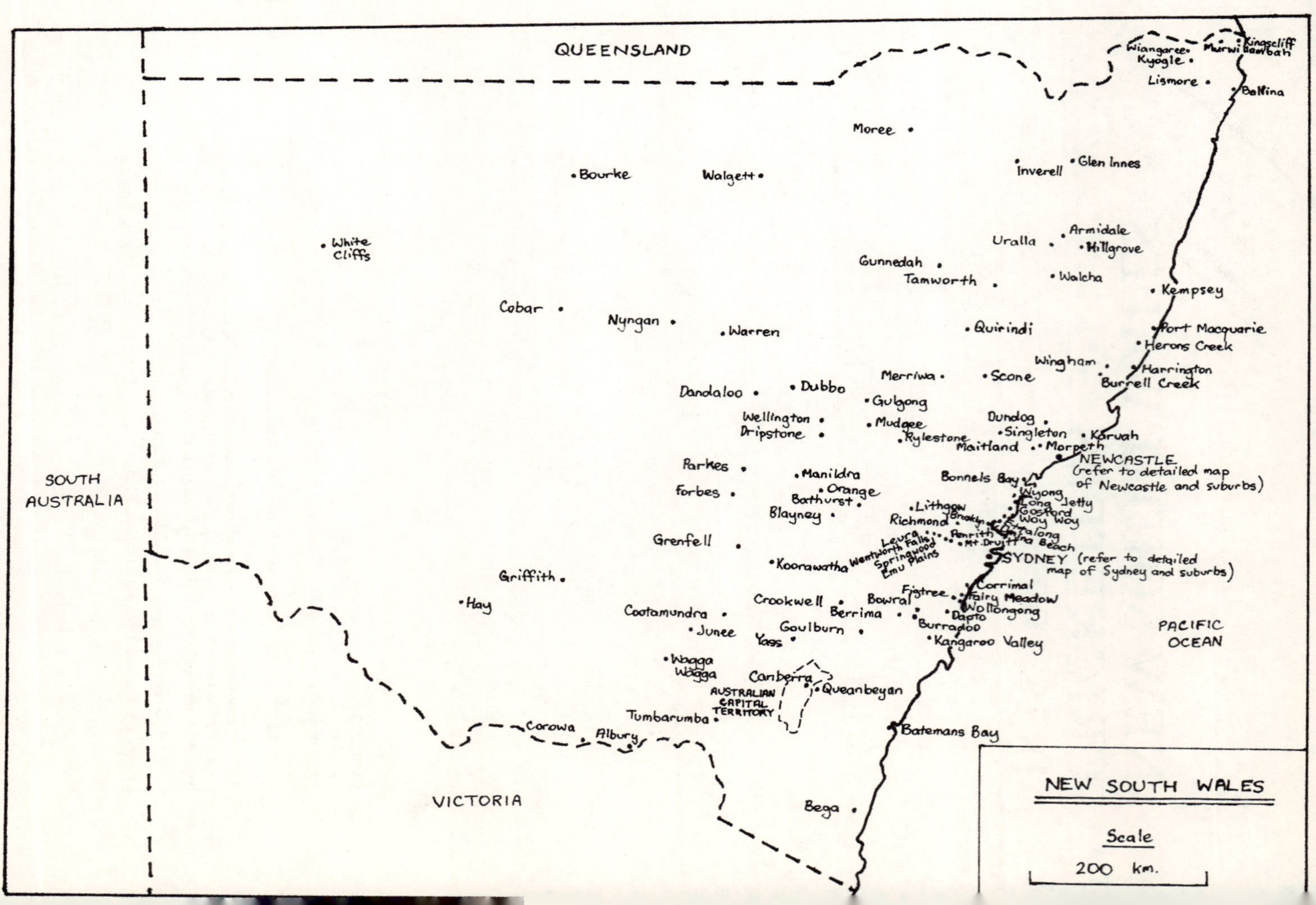

NEW SOUTH WALES
Scale
200 km.
QUEENSLAND
SOUTH AUSTRALIA
VICTORIA
PACIFIC OCEAN
AUSTRALIAN CAPITAL TERRITORY
Wiangaree
Kyogle
Murwillumbah
Kingscliff
Lismore
Ballina
Moree
Inverell
Glen Innes
Bourke
Walgett
White Cliffs
Armidale
Uralla
Hillgrove
Gunnedah
Tamworth
Walcha
Kempsey
Cobar
Nyngan
Warren
Quirindi
Port Macquarie
Herons Creek
Wingham
Harrington
Burrell Creek
Merriwa
Scone
Dandaloo
Dubbo
Gulgong
Wellington
Dripstone
Mudgee
Rylestone
Dundog
Singleton
Karuah
Maitland
Morpeth
NEWCASTLE
(refer to detailed map of Newcastle and suburbs)
Parkes
Manildra
Forbes
Orange
Bathurst
Blayney
Bonnels Bay
Wyong
Long Jetty
Gosford
Woy Woy
Ettalong
Lithgow
Brooklyn
Richmond
Penrith
Mt. Druitt
Leura
Wentworth Falls
Springwood
Emu Plains
Grenfell
Koorawatha
SYDNEY (refer to detailed map of Sydney and suburbs)
Griffith
Hay
Corrimal
Figtree
Fairy Meadow
Wollongong
Crookwell
Bowral
Berrima
Dapto
Burradoo
Cootamundra
Junee
Goulburn
Yass
Kangaroo Valley
Wagga Wagga
Canberra
Queanbeyan
Tumbarumba
Corowa
Albury
Batemans Bay
Bega

INTRODUCTION

This booklet, the third in the Australian State series, contains a biographical register and career figures of all cricketers who appeared in first-class cricket for New South Wales between 1855-56 and 1980-81.

Many people contributed to the register. In Sydney the main burden fell on Tony Dobbs, Alf James and Ronald Cardwell. Warwick Torrens (Brisbane), W.P.Reynolds (Perth), Ian Everett (Adelaide), Ray Heaps (Lismore) and Mike Perry (Canberra) rendered invaluable assistance along with Max Solling, sporting historian and authority on Glebe C.C., Clifford Winning, author of *Cricket Balmainia*, Ray Robinson, the famous cricket writer, and Norm Sowden of Melbourne. Former state players Alex Marks and Ken Gulliver co-operated generously. Thanks are due also to many Australian members of the Association of Cricket Statisticians, including Greg Manning, D.G.Moyes, Irving Rosenwater, Mervyn Shaw and Ray Webster, and to overseas members Philip Thorn, Robert Brooke, Maurice Alexander and C.J.Bartlett.

Ken Williams compiled the career records, assisted by Philip Bailey and Mervyn Shaw. He also prepared the three maps, showing the majority of places listed in the text.

With regard to entries in the biographical section, please note:

a. Places of birth, death or present address are located in New South Wales unless otherwise indicated (except for obvious places like London or Adelaide).

b. Unusual abbreviations of christian names or nicknames of players have been shown, but not commonly used abbreviations, like Bill or Bob.

c. A double asterisk beside a player's name indicates that a doubt exists as to whether the person was the New South Wales cricketer.

d. The date in brackets after each surname is the season of the player's first appearance for the State.

e. The club(s) or country town listed is that for which the cricketer played during his first-class career; in the case of some last-century players, the club(s) with which they were most prominently associated.

f. The following special symbols have been used:

(r)	round-arm bowler
(u)	under-arm bowler
RAB	right-arm bowler
LAB	left-arm bowler

Some explanation is needed on Sydney club cricket. Up to the 1890s the organisation was very fluid, with no fixed programme of matches, the leading clubs simply playing each other two or three times a season. During the late 1880s an *Electorate* competition arose, based on geographical districts, but few *name* players participated, as they preferred to play for the traditional club sides. However, in 1893-94, the *Electorate* cricket displaced club matches as a centre of interest and attracted the top players. The present system of Sydney *Grade* cricket developed from the *Electorate* system.

Any additions or alterations to the present work will be welcomed and published in future booklets.

Roger Page
October 1981

CRICKETERS WHO HAVE REPRESENTED NEW SOUTH WALES IN A FIRST-CLASS MATCH 1855-56 to 1980-81

Claude Septimus ACHURCH (1921-22) RHB Randwick
b. Dubbo, Aug. 16, 1896. d.Nambour, Qld., Aug. 15, 1979.

Edward William ADAMS (1919-20) RHB/RMF Petersham
b. Bathurst, July 10, 1896. d.Bexley, May 25, 1977.

Francis ADAMS (1858-59) Albert
b. County Fermanagh, Ireland, 1835. d. North Sydney, Feb. 10, 1911.

Henry D. ALLEN (1871-72) Albert

Reginald Charles ALLEN (1878-79) RHB/RFM University
b. Glebe, July 2, 1858. d.Sydney, May 2, 1952.
Test : 1. Uncle of G.O.B.Allen (Cambr U, Middlesex and England).

William Edward ALLEY (1945-46) LHB/RM Petersham
b. Brooklyn, March 2, 1919. Add: Downunder, Adsborough Lane, Adsborough, near Taunton, England.

Tours: Commonwealth to India, Pakistan and Ceylon 1949-50; Commonwealth to Rhodesia 1962-63; Cavaliers to South Africa 1962-63; Commonwealth to Pakistan 1963-64. Commonwealth XI v Essex 1953. Somerset 1957 to 1968. Test Umpire (England).

John Placid ALLEYNE (1927-28) RHB Glebe
b. Glebe, Aug. 1, 1908. d.Glebe, June 24, 1980.

Arthur Henry ALLSOPP (1929-30) RHB/WK Leeton
b. Lithgow, March 1, 1908. Add: 25 Midlothian St., Chadstone, Vic.
Tour: Australia to India 1935-36 (Tarrant). Victoria 1933-34 and 1934-35.

Gordon Stanley AMOS (1926-27) RHB/RFM Marrickville
b. Newtown, April 4, 1905. Add: Lot 172, McMillan St., Labrador, Qld.
Queensland 1927-28 to 1930-31; 1936-37.

Allan David ANDERSON (1971-72) RHB North Sydney
b. Greenwich, April 22, 1949. Add: 78, Woodland St., Balgowlah.

Peter Gordon ANDERSON (1966-67) LHB/WK Petersham
b. Camberwell, Vic., Oct. 4, 1933. Add: 32 Milton St., Canterbury, Vic.

Charles William ('Cassie') ANDREWS (1928-29) RHB Mosman
b. West Maitland, July 14, 1901. d. at sea near Bombay, 1962.
Queensland 1931-32 to 1936-37.

Thomas James Edwin ANDREWS (1912-13) RHB/LBG Petersham
b. Newtown, Aug. 26, 1890. d. Sydney, Jan. 28, 1970.
Tests: 16 Tours: England 1921, 1926; South Africa 1921-22; New South Wales to New Zealand 1923-24.

Percival Sinclair ARNOTT (1911-12) RHB/LBG Balmain
b. Newcastle, July 9, 1889. d. Strathfield, Dec. 23, 1950.
Tour: North America 1913.

Oswald Philip ASHER (1919-20) RHB/LBG Sydney/Paddington
b. Paddington, May 21, 1891. d. Waverton, July 16, 1970.
Tour: New Zealand 1920-21.

A.A. ('Rocco') ATKINS (1896-97) Redfern
Queensland 1895-96; 1899-1900 to 1905-06.

Sydney Walter ('Mof') AUSTIN (1892-93) RHB/RM,LB Waverley
b. *circa* 1867. d. Randwick, Sept 9, 1932.
Tour: New South Wales to New Zealand 1893-94. Queensland 1894-95.

Charles Ronald BAKER (1968-69) RHB Newcastle
b. Newcastle, March 24, 1939. Add:

Alexander Chalmers ('Alick') BANNERMAN (1876-7) RHB/RM(r) Warwick/Carlton
b. Paddington, March 21, 1854? d. Paddington, Sept. 19, 1924.
Tests: 28. Tours: England 1878, 1880, 1882, 1884, 1888, 1893; North America 1878, 1893. Non-Smokers (Lord's) 1884.
Brother of C.Bannerman.

Charles BANNERMAN (1870-71) RHB Warwick/Carlton
b. Woolwich, Kent, July 23, 1851. d. Surry Hills, Aug 20, 1930.
Tests: 3 Tour: England and North America 1878.
Test Umpire (12 matches)

Eric Pitty BARBOUR (1908-09) RHB/LBG University
b. Ashfield, Jan. 27, 1891. d. Darlinghurst, Dec. 7, 1934.
Brother of R.R.P.Barbour (Qld and Oxford U). Author of *The Making of A Cricketer* (1926)

Raymond ('Mick') BARDSLEY (1920-21) RHB University/W.Suburbs
b. Glebe Point, Jan. 19, 1894. Add: 28 Kent Road, Rose Bay.
Tour: New South Wales to New Zealand 1923-24. Brother of W.Bardsley.

Warren BARDSLEY (1903-04) LHB Glebe/W.Suburbs
b. Nevertire, near Warren, Dec. 7, 1882. d.Collaroy, Jan. 20, 1954.
Tests: 41 Tours: England 1909, 1912, 1921, 1926; South Africa 1921-22; New Zealand 1909-10; North America 1913; New South Wales to New Zealand 1923-24.

James **Charles** BARNES (1904-05) RHB/LBG Redfern
b. Sydney, Oct. 16, 1882. Presumed dead.

Sidney George BARNES (1936-37) RHB/LB Petersham/Manly Warringah/N.Sydney
b. Charters Towers, Qld., June 5, 1916. d. Collaroy, Dec. 16, 1973.
Tests: 13 Tours: England 1938, 1948; New Zealand 1945-46.

Barry BATES (1959-60) RHB/RFM Wollongong
b. Wollongong, July 1, 1939. Add: 36 Jacaranda Ave., Figtree.

James Charles BEAL (1855-56) Australian
b. Sydney, May 16, 1833. d. Milton, Qld., Aug. 24, 1904.
Uncle of C.W.Beal, Manager Australian teams in England 1882, 1888.

Graeme Robert BEARD (1975-76) RHB/RM OB Manly-Warringah N.Sydney
b. Auburn, Aug. 19, 1950. Add: 67 Foamcrest Ave., Newport
Tests:3 Tours: Pakistan 1980; Sri Lanka and England 1981.

Neville Ray James ('Bill') BEATH (1946-47) RHB/RFM Randwick
b. Parkes, Nov. 12, 1921. Add: 4/97 Dolphin St., Coogee.

Reginald George BEATTIE (1936-37) RHB Newcastle
b.Wickham, 1913. d. Waratah, May 27, 1957.

Christopher BEATTY (1977-78) RHB Newcastle
b. Newcastle, Oct. 21, 1952. Add: 21 Orchard Road, Cardiff.

John Lievesley BEESTON (1857-58) RHB Australian/Newcastle
b. Lancashire, 1830. d. Newcastle, June 1, 1873.

Samuel Harborne BELCHER (1866-67) Goulburn
b. England, 1834. d. Garroorigang, near Goulburn, Aug. 22, 1920.

John BENAUD (1966-67) RHB/RM Central Cumberland/ Randwick

b. Auburn, May 11, 1944. Add: 24 Singles Ridge Road, Winmalee.
Tests: 3 Tour: West Indies 1973.
Brother of R.Benaud.

Richard ('Richie') BENAUD (1948-49) RHB/LBG Central Cumberland
b. Penrith, October 6, 1930. Add: 178 Beach St., Coogee.
Tests: 63 Tours: England 1953, 1956, 1961; South Africa 1957-58; West Indies 1955; New Zealand 1956-57; Pakistan and India 1956, 1959-60; Cavaliers to South Africa 1960-61; Cavaliers to India, Pakistan and New Zealand 1961-62; Cavaliers to India and South Africa 1962-63; E.W.Swanton to India 1963-64; Commonwealth to Pakistan 1967-68.
Noted cricket journalist, author and television commentator.

Albert BENNETT (1930-31) RHB/LBG Port Kembla
b. St Helens, Lancashire, May 21, 1910.
Lancashire 1932 and 1933.

George Henry BENNETT (1933-34) RHB/RFM Mosman
b. Brookvale, Aug. 16, 1906. Add: 10 Stirgess Ave., Harbord.

Stephen Russell BERNARD (1970-71) RHB/RF Northern District
b. Orange, Dec. 28, 1949. Add: 27 Kitchener St., Maroubra.

Edward Bruce BERRIE (1913-14) /LM Moree
b. Moree, 1886. d. Tamworth, Dec. 8, 1943.

Walter **Lyall** BERRY (1918-19) RHB Glebe
b. Woolwich, April 9, 1893. d. Ettalong Beach, April 20, 1970.

Leslie BEST (1914-15) RHB/RFM University
b. Seven Hills, *circa* 1894. d. Sydney, Aug. 27, 1925.

Brindley Cecil **John** BETTINGTON (1927-28) RHB/LBG Hunter River
b. Parramatta, Sept. 2, 1898. d. Merriwa, Aug. 26, 1931.
Oxford University 1920, 1922.

Reginald Henshall Brindley BETTINGTON (1928-29) RHB/LBG Paddington
b. Parramatta, Feb. 24, 1900. Killed in road accident at Gisborne, New Zealand, June 24, 1969.
Middlesex 1928. Oxford University 1920-23. Gentlemen 1920, 1925,1928.CI.Thornton's XI 1920. Free Foresters 1924, 1925, 1938. Harlequins 1924, 1925, 1928. H.D.G.Leveson-Gower's XI 1925, 1926, 1927, 1928. M.C.C. 1928, 1938.
Brother of B.C.J.Bettington.

Oscar **Wendell** BILL (1929-30) RHB Waverley
b. Waverley, April 8, 1910. Add: 12/31 Elamang Ave., Kirribilli.
Tour: Australia to India and Ceylon 1935-36 (Tarrant).

George **Gordon** BLACK (1903-04) RHB/RAB North Sydney
b. Darling Point, Jan. 19, 1885. d. Orange, Dec. 6, 1954.
London County 1903.

Oswald **Colin** BLACKMAN (1966-67) LHB Petersham-Marrickville
b. Griffith, March 9, 1942. Add: 16 Penrose St., Lower Hutt, Wellington, N.Z.

Marcus Herbert BLAXLAND (1903-04) LHB/LM University/Balmain
b. Callan Park, April 29, 1884. d. Clayfield, Qld., July 31, 1958.
Queensland 1923-24.

James BOGLE (1918-19) LHB University
b Sydney Jan. 4, 1893. d. Southport, Qld., Oct. 19, 1963.
Tour: New Zealand 1920-21.

George John BONNOR (1884-85) RHB /RM Bathurst/Orange
b. Bathurst, Feb. 25, 1855. d. East Orange, June 27, 1912.
Tests: 17 Tours: England 1880, 1882, 1884, 1886, 1888.
Victoria 1881-82 to 1884-85. Non-Smokers (Lord's) 1884.

Brian Charles BOOTH (1954-55) RHB/RM OB St. George
b. Perthville, near Bathurst, Oct. 19, 1933. Add: 5, Dale Crescent, Narwee.
Tests: 29 Tours: England 1961, 1964; West Indies 1965; India and Pakistan 1964; New Zealand 1959-60, 1966-67.

Allan Robert BORDER (1976-77) LHB/SLA Mosman-Mid. Harbour
b. Cremorne, July 27, 1955.
Tests: 33 Tours: England 1980, 1981; India 1979; Pakistan 1980. Sri Lanka 1981.
Gloucestershire 1977. Queensland 1980-81.

Marcus Williams BOSLEY (1924-25) LHB/SLA Central Cumberland
b. Liverpool, Aug. 10, 1897. Add: 53 Bennett St., Harbord.

Albert John BOWDEN (1899-1900) RHB/LBG South Sydney/Glebe
b. Sydney, Sept. 28, 1874. d. Northwood, Aug. 8, 1943.
Brother of S.H.Bowden (Queensland).

Raymond Charles Manning BOYCE (1921-22) RHB University
b. June 28, 1891. d. Northwood, Jan. 20, 1941.

Trevor Joseph BOYD (1966-67) RHB Sydney
b. Nyngan, Oct. 22, 1944. Add: Unit 13, 164 Waterloo Road, Marsfield.

Donald George BRADMAN (1927-28) RHB/LB St.George/N.Sydney
b. Cootamundra, Aug. 27, 1908. Add: 2 Holden St., Kensington Park, S.Aust.
Tests: 52 Tours: England 1930, 1934, 1938, 1948.
South Australia 1935-36 to 1948-49. Chairman Australian Cricket Board 1960-63 and 1969-72. Knighted mainly for his services to cricket in 1949. Author of five books on cricket.

John Sidney BRADRIDGE (1855-56) Australian
b. d. Dulwich Hill, July 14, 1905.

Robert Colin BREWSTER (1893-94) Paddington
b. Aug. 17, 1867. d. Killara, Nov. 8, 1962.

Ronald Edward BRIGGS (1952-53) RHB Bankstown-Canterbury
b. Sept. 22, 1929. Add: 43 Victory Parade, Point Clare.

Thomas Francis BROOKS (1946-47) RHB/RF Manly
b. Paddington, March 28, 1919. Add: 13 St Pauls Road, North Balgowlah.
Test Umpire (24 matches)

**Edward BROWN (1859-60) RHB/WK Albert
b. Uppingham, Kent, Jan. 1837.

Edward K. BROWN (1920-21) RHB Central Cumberland
b. Morpeth, *circa* 1899.

William Alfred BROWN (1932-33) RHB Marrickville
b. Toowoomba, Qld., July 31, 1912. Add: 6 Aspleybank St., Aspley, Qld.
Tests: 22 Tours: England 1934, 1938, 1948; South Africa 1935-36; New Zealand 1945-46; 1949-50. Queensland 1936-37 to 1949-50.

Walter Graham Fairfax BROWN (1919-20) RHB Balmain/North Sydney
b. Five Dock, 1900. d. of septic pneumonia following appendicitis operation at Mosman, May 21, 1931.

Richard BRYANT (1882-83) /WK Newcastle
b. Maitland, 1847. d. Stockton, Oct. 27, 1931.

Ernest Reinhard BUBB (1905-06) RHB Glebe
b. Summer Hill, Dec. 6, 1884. d. Neutral Bay, Nov. 26, 1946.

Roy Alfred BUBB (1924-25) LHB/RF Manly
b. Darlinghurst, June 23, 1900. d. Hamilton, April 4, 1965.
Brother of E.R.Bubb.

Frank ('Sandy') BUCKLE (1913-14) RHB Glebe
b. Pyrmont, Nov. 11, 1891. Add: 10 Centennial Ave., Chatswood.

Eric Alister BULL (1913-14) RHB/RM LB Middle Harbour
b. Bourke, Sept. 28, 1886. d. Mt. Kuring-Gai, May 14, 1954.
Tour: A.I.F. in England and South Africa 1919.

James Wallace BURKE (1948-49) RHB/OB Manly/N. District
b. Mosman, June 12, 1930. d. Manly, Feb. 2, 1979.
Tests: 24 Tours: England, Pakistan and India 1956; South Africa 1957-58; New Zealand 1949-50.

J. BURROWS (1877-78) RHB Warwick

Selby John Wright BURT (1928-29) RHB/OB Western Suburbs
b. Hillgrove, Dec. 12, 1903. d. Camperdown, Feb. 14, 1959.

Frederick James BURTON (1885-86) RHB/WK Carlton/East Sydney
b. 1866? d. Wanganui, New Zealand, Aug. 25, 1929.
Tests: 2 Tour: New South Wales to New Zealand 1895-96.
Victoria 1888-89.

William CAFFYN (1865-66) RHB/RM(r) Warwick
b. Reigate, England, Feb. 2, 1828. d. Reigate, Aug. 28, 1919.
Tours: England to the United States 1859; England to Australia 1861-62, 1863-64.
Surrey 1849 to 1863, 1872, 1873. Players (various matches); All-England XI. United All-England XI. Author of *71 Not Out*.

Tim Charles John CALDWELL (1935-36) RHB/OB Northern District
b. Clayfield, Qld., Oct. 29, 1913. Add: 16 Lord St., Roseville.
Chairman Australian Cricket Board 1972 to 1975.

John Joseph Casimir CALLACHOR (1882-83) RHB/WK Carlton
b. 1859. d.Stanmore, Feb. 20, 1924.

Norman Frank CALLAWAY (1914-15) RHB Waverley
b. Hay, May 1895. Killed in action in France, May 3, 1917.

Sydney Thomas CALLAWAY (1888-89) RHB/RFM Carlton/South Sydney
b.Sydney, Feb.6, 1868. . d. Christchurch, N.Z., Nov. 25, 1923.
Tests: 3 Tours: New South Wales to New Zealand 1889-90, 1895-96.
Canterbury 1900-01 to 1906-07. New Zealand 1902-03, 1904-05, 1906-07. South Island (N.Z.) 1902-03, 1903-04.

James Norval CAMPBELL (1926-27) RHB/LBG Gordon
b. Chatswood, Sept. 21, 1908. d. St Ives, Sept. 11, 1973.

Lyle CAMPBELL (1925-26) RHB/LBG Petersham
b. Petersham, 1902.

William Joseph ('Dodger') CAMPHIN (1892-93) RHB Ivanhoe/East Sydney/Newcastle
b. Nov. 13, 1867. d. Quirindi, Sept. 11, 1942.

Campbell Roy CAMPLING (1922-23) RHB/RM Balmain
b. Burwood, April 3, 1892. d. Harrington, April 21, 1977.

Douglas **Keith** CARMODY (1939-40) RHB Mosman
b. Mosman, Feb. 16, 1919. d. Concord, Oct. 21, 1977.
Tours: Services in England and India 1945.
Western Australia 1947-48 to 1955-56.

Sidney Joseph CARROLL (1945-46) RHB Gordon
b. Willoughby, Nov. 28, 1922. Add: 25 Horsley Ave., Willoughby.

Hanson ('Sammy') CARTER (1897-98) RHB/WK Waverley
b. Halifax, Yorks. March 15, 1878. d. Bellevue Hill, June 8, 1948.
Tests: 28 Tours: England 1902, 1909, 1921; South Africa 1902-03, 1921-22.

William **Jack** Sydney CARTER RHB/LBG Randwick
b. Randwick, Dec. 7, 1907. Add: 3 Kooemba Road, Beverly Hills.

George Arthur Northcote CHAPMAN (1924-25) RHB Gordon
b. Chatswood, April 21, 1904. Add: 16 Kardella Ave., Killara.

Ross Albert CHAPMAN (1972-73) RHB North Sydney
b. New Lambton, Oct. 22, 1952. Add: 48 Wisdom Road, Greenwich.

Trevor Martin CHAPPELL (1979-80) RHB/RM Gordon
b. Unley, S.Aust., Oct. 21, 1952. Add: 35 Fontenoy Road, North Ryde.
Tests: Tours: England 1981; D.H.Robins to South Africa 1975-76.
South Australia 1972-73 to 1975-76. Western Australia 1976-77.
Brother of I.M.Chappell (S.Aust) and G.S.Chappell (S.Aust and Qld.)

David Michael CHARDON (1975-76) RHB/RFM Petersham-Marrickville
b. Newtown, Dec. 12, 1951. Add: 98 Vimiera Road, Eastwood.

Percie Chater CHARLTON (1888-89) RHB/RFM Belvidere/Manly
b. Surry Hills, April 9, 1867. d.Pymble, Sept. 30, 1954.
Tests: 2 Tour: England 1890.

Albert George CHEETHAM (1936-37) RHB/RFM Balmain
b. Ryde, Dec. 7, 1915. Add: 13 Le Fevre St., Sandringham, Victoria.
Tour: Services in England 1945.

John William CHEGWYN (1940-41) RHB Randwick
b. Botany, March 18, 1909. Add: 6 Banksia St., Botany.

Hugh Cecil CHILVERS (1929-30) RHB/LBG Northern District
b. Sawbridgeworth, Herts, Eng., Oct. 26, 1902. Add: 83a The Comenerra Parkway, Turramurra.

Arthur Gordon CHIPPERFIELD (1933-34) RHB/LB Newcastle/W.Suburbs/N.Districts
b. Ashfield, Nov. 17, 1905. Add: 24 Romford Road, Epping.
Tests: 14 Tours: England 1934, 1938; South Africa 1935-36.

John Lawrence CLARK (1953-54) RHB/RFM Paddington
b. Paddington, Oct. 14, 1928. Add: 49 Hancott St., Ryde.
Queensland 1952-53.

Alfred Edward CLARKE (1889-90) Sydney
b. Surry Hills, April 6, 1868. d. *circa* 1940.
Tour: New South Wales to New Zealand 1889-90.
Otago 1893-94 to 1898-99. Wellington 1900-01, 1901-02. New Zealand 1895-96.

Gother Robert Carlisle CLARKE (1899-1900) LHB/LB N.Sydney/University
b. April 27, 1875. Killed in action in Belgium, Oct. 12, 1917.

John CLARKE (1859-60) Albert/National

James CLEEVE (1882-83) /LFM Albert
b. *circa* 1863.

Mark Lindsay CLEWS (1876-77) RHB/RFM Northern District
b. Adelaide, Jan. 13, 1952. Add: 20 The Boulevarde, Cammeray.

Joseph COATES (1867-68) LHB/LM(r) Albert/University
b. Huddersfield, Eng., Nov. 13, 1844? d. Sydney, Sept. 9, 1896.
North (England) 1877.

Leslie **Thomas** COBCROFT (1895-96) RHB/OB Glebe
b. Sydney, Feb 12, 1864 or 1869. d. Wellington, New Zealand, March 9, 1938.
Tours: New South Wales to New Zealand 1895-96; New Zealand to Australia 1898-99.
Canterbury 1897-98 to 1899-00. Wellington 1906-07 to 1909-10.

Leslie Alwyn CODY (1912-13) RHB/LBG Paddington
b. Paddington, Oct. 11, 1890. d. Toorak, Vic. Aug. 10, 1969.
Tours: North America 1913; New Zealand 1913-14.
Victoria 1914-15 to 1921-22.

Morton Barnett COHEN (1939-40) RHB/RM Paddington/Petersham
b. Paddington, Sept. 19, 1913. d. Vaucluse, Jan. 14, 1968.

David John COLLEY (1969-70) RHB/RFM Mosman-Mid. Harbour
b. Mosman, March 15, 1947. Add: 5 Judith St., Seaforth.
Tests: 3 Tour: England 1972.

Herbert Leslie COLLINS (1909-10) RHB/SLA Sydney/Waverley
b. Darlinghurst, Jan. 21, 1889. d. Sydney, May 28, 1959.
Tests: 19 Tours: England 1921, 1926; South Africa 1921-22; New Zealand 1913-14;
North America 1913; A.I.F. in England and South Africa 1919.

Ross Phillip COLLINS (1967-68) RHB/RM Balmain/North Sydney
b. Paddington, Dec. 9, 1945. Add: 40 Darvall St., Crows Nest.
International Cavaliers v Barbados 1969 (Scarborough).

Vincent COLLINS (1941-42) RHB/RM Northern District
b. *circa* 1920.

Bernard Xavier COLREAVY (1899-1900) East Sydney
b. Dripstone, June 30, 1871. d. Wellington, Nov. 30, 1946.

Arthur CONINGHAM (1892-93) LHB/LFM Carlton/South Sydney
b. S.Melbourne, Vic., July 14, 1863. d. Gladesville, June 13, 1939.
Test: 1 Tour: England and North America 1893.
Queensland 1893-94 to 1895-96.

Thomas Christopher CONNELL (1896-97) /LFM Leichardt
b. March 4, 1869. d. Mascot, August 5, 1916.
Wellington 1901-02.

Bruce COOK (1940-41) LHB Manly
b. Orange, Oct. 24, 1914. d. Balgowlah, Jan. 2, 1981.

Allan Ferguson COOPER (1935-36) RHB/RF Balmain
b. March 18, 1916. d. Waverley, Sept. 7, 1970.

Bryce Arnot COOPER (1928-29) RHB/RFM University/Glebe
b. Lewisham, Dec. 19, 1905. Add: 33/45 Cook St., Forestville.

Grahame Edward CORLING (1963-64) RHB/RFM Newcastle/W.Suburbs
b. Newcastle, July 13, 1941. Add: 2/55 Light St., Newcastle.
Tests: 5 Tour: England 1964.

Samuel COSSTICK (1865-66) RHB/RM(r) National
b. Croydon, Surrey, Jan. 1, 1836. d. West Maitland, April 8, 1896.
Victoria 1860-61 to 1875-76
Umpire in second Test Match 1877.

John Thomas COTTAM (1886-87) RHB/LB Warwick/Sydney
b. Strawberry Hill, Sept. 5, 1867. d. of typhoid fever at Coolgardie, Western Australia. Jan. 30, 1897.
Test: 1 Tour: New South Wales to New Zealand 1889-90.

Albert ('Tibby') COTTER (1901-02) RHB/RF Glebe
b. Sydney, Dec. 3, 1883. killed in action at Beersheba, Palestine, Oct. 31, 1917.
Tests: 21 Tours: England 1905, 1909; New Zealand 1904-05.

Edward Kenneth COTTON (1952-53) RHB/RFM Paddington
b. Paddington, Aug. 8, 1929. Add: 30, Turriell Road, Caringbah.

Owen William COWLEY (1893-94) RHB/RAB Redfern
b. Mauritius, Indian Ocean, Feb. 12, 1868.
Played for New South Wales only on tour of New Zealand 1893-94 and for Queensland only on tour of New Zealand 1896-97.

George COWPER (1888-89) RHB Carlton.
Tour: New South Wales to New Zealand 1889-90.

Ian Davis CRAIG (1951-52) RHB Mosman
b. Yass, June 12, 1935. Add: 40 Cowan Road, St. Ives
Tests: 11 Tours: England 1953, 1956; South Africa 1957-58; India and Pakistan 1956; New Zealand 1956-57, 1959-60; Commonwealth to South Africa 1959-60; Commonwealth to New Zealand and India 1961-62.
Free Foresters 1957.

Harold ('Mudgee') CRANNEY (1909-10) RHB Central Cumberland
b. Oct. 23, 1886. d. Sydney, Jan. 29, 1971.

William **Patrick** Anthony CRAWFORD (1954-55) RHB/RF Petersham-Marrickville
b. Sydney, Aug. 3, 1933. Add: 246 Sylvania Road, Miranda.
Tests: 4 Tour: England and India 1956.

Ronald James CRIPPIN (1970-71) RHB Randwick/Waverley/Newcastle
b. Darlinghurst, April 23, 1947. Add: 16/23 Vicar St., Coogee.

Desmond **Robert** CRISTOFANI (1941-42) RHB/RM ,LBG St. George
b. Waverley, Nov. 14, 1920. Add: England
Tour: Services in England, India and Ceylon 1945. Dominions v England 1945.

Ernest Eric CROSSAN (1937-38) RHB/RM W.Suburbs/Newcastle
b. Footscray, Vic., Nov. 3, 1915. Add: Urliup Road, Murwillumbah.

John Alexander CUFFE (1902-03) RHB/SLA Sydney
b. Toowoomba, Qld., June 26, 1880. d.Burton-on-Trent, Eng., May 16, 1931.
Worcestershire 1903 to 1914. South 1905. England XI 1905. H. K.Foster's XI 1913.

Daniel Robert CULLEN (1912-13) RHB /RF Glebe
b. Sydney, 1888 or 1889. d. Concord, July 21, 1971.

William CULLEN (1914-15) RHB/RF Glebe
b. *circa* 1892. d. Sydney, May 7, 1945.
Brother of D.R.Cullen.

Frank Septimus CUMMINS (1925-26) RHB/RM Manly/North Sydney
b. West Maitland, August 8, 1906. d.Lane Cove, April 27, 1966.
Cousin of C.G.Macartney; nephew of L and W.H.Moore.

George Thomas CURTIS (1861-62) Albert
b. Sydney, Aug. 17, 1837. d. Darlinghurst, April 2, 1885.

Norman Lloyd CUSH (1934-35) RHB/RMF Glebe
b. Glebe Point, Oct. 4, 1911. Add: 567 Malabar Road, Maroubra.

D. D'ARCY (1862-63) /Long-stop National

Alan Keith DAVIDSON (1949-50) LHB/LF Northern District
b. Lisarow, near Gosford, June 14, 1929. Add: 48 Churchill Ave., Strathfield.
Tests: 44 Tours: England 1953, 1956, 1961; South Africa 1957-58; West Indies 1955; India and Pakistan 1956 and 1959-60; New Zealand 1949-50.

Hugh Lavery DAVIDSON (1927-28) RHB/WK Waverley
b. May 17, 1907. d. Wamberal, April 22, 1960.

Geoffrey Robert DAVIES (1965-66) RHB/LBG Randwick/ N.Sydney
b. Randwick, July 22, 1946. Add: 74 Whitecross Road, Winmalee.
Tours: New Zealand 1966-67 and 1969-70.

Horace Hyman DAVIS (1911-12) LHB/ Waverley
b. Darlinghurst, Feb. 1, 1889. d. Sydney, Feb. 4, 1960.

Ian Charles DAVIS (1973-74) RHB Gordon
b. North Sydney, June 25, 1953. Add: 110 Flinders Road, Georges Hall.
Tests: 15 Tours: England 1977; New Zealand 1973-74 and 1976-77.
Queensland 1975-76.

Joseph DAVIS (1879-80) Carlton/Warwick
b. May 12, 1859. d. Waverley, May 18, 1911.

Joseph **Coleman** DAVIS (1889-90) Albert
b. 1857. d. Glebe Point, Feb 13, 1922.
Played for New South Wales only on tours of New Zealand 1889-90 and 1893-94.

Oscar Hessel DEAN (1907-08) RHB Central Cumberland
b. April 30, 1886. d. Windsor, May 11, 1962.
scored 412 for Sydney Church of England Grammar School v Newington College in October 1904.

Norman Younger DEANE (1902-03) RHB/RM North Sydney
b. Neutral Bay, Aug 29, 1875. d. Lindfield, Sept. 30, 1950.
Cousin of S.Deane.

Sidney DEANE (1889-90) RHB/WK Sydney
b. March 1, 1866. d. New York? March 20, 1934.

James Harry DE COURCY (1947-48) RHB Newcastle
b. Newcastle, April 18, 1927. Add: 4 Woodstock St., Mayfield.
Tests: 3 Tour: England 1953.

Frank DEVENISH-MEARES (1901-02) Leichardt-Balmain
b. April 25, 1873. d. Sydney, July 4, 1952.
Western Australia 1898-99.

Austin DIAMOND (1899-00) RHB Leichardt/Burwood/Gordon.
b. Huddersfield, Eng., July 10, 1874. d. Roseville, Aug 5, 1966.
Tour: North America 1913.

George D. DICKSON (1859-60) LHB/L-Stop National/Albert

Percy William DIVE (1924-25) RHB/LB Gordon
b. Paddington, July 10, 1881. d. Roseville, Sept. 17, 1965.

Albert Robert DOCKER (1871-72) RHB/RF Albert
b. Thornwaite, near Scone. , June 3, 1848. d. Enfield, Middx, April 8, 1929.
Brother of E.B.Docker; father of G.A.M.Docker (M.C.C.)

Cyril Talbot DOCKER (1909-10) RHB/RFM Burwood
b. Ryde, March 3, 1884. d. Double Bay, March 26, 1975.
Tour: A.I.F. in England and South Africa 1919.

Ernest Brougham DOCKER (1862-63) Albert
b. Thornwaite, near Scone, April 1, 1842. d. Elizabeth Bay, Aug 12, 1923.

Keith Brougham DOCKER (1919-20) RHB Western Suburbs
b. Ryde, Sept. 1, 1888. d. Ashfield, May 16, 1977.
Brother of C.T. and P.W.Docker; nephew of E.B. and A.R.Docker.

Phillip **Wybergh** DOCKER (1910-11) RHB/LM Burwood
b. Ryde, April 8, 1886. d. Concord, Oct. 29, 1978.

Walter Peter James ('Bill') DONALDSON (1945-46) RHB Randwick/Balmain
b. Lilyfield, Oct. 26, 1923. Add: 41, Byron Road, Guildford.

Richard Philip DONE (1978-79) RHB/RFM St. George
b. Ryde, Aug. 5, 1955. Add: 12 Morrissey St., Wanniassa, A.C.T.

Henry ('Harry') DONNAN (1887-88) RHB/RM Carlton/S.Sydney/Burwood
b. Liverpool, Nov. 12, 1864. d. Bexley, Aug. 13, 1956.
Tests: 5 Tour: England and North America 1896.
Brother-in-law of S.E.Gregory.

James Louis DONNELLY (1929-30) LHB Glebe
b. 1908. d. Koorawatha, March 2, 1978.

Francis DOWNES (1881-82) /LM Warwick/Carlton
b. Sydney, June 11, 1864. d. Little Bay, May 20, 1916.

Richard DRIVER (1855-56) Australian
b. Coolah, near Liverpool, Sept. 16, 1829. d. Moore Park, July 8, 1880.

Reginald Alexander DUFF (1898-99) RHB/RM North Sydney
b. Sydney, Aug. 17, 1878. d. North Sydney, Dec. 13, 1911.
Tests: 22 Tours: England 1902, 1905; South Africa 1902; New Zealand 1905.
Brother W.S.Duff.

Walter Scott DUFF (1902-03) RHB Sydney
b. Sydney, April 22, 1875. d. Sydney, Nov. 11, 1921.

William ('Jimmy') DUMMETT (1876-77) RHB /WK Warwick
d. *circa* 1904.

Francois Henri ('Harry') DUPAIN (1927-28) LHB/RFM Western Suburbs
b. Ashfield, June 1, 1887. d. Burradoo, Sept. 29, 1959.

Edmund Alfred ('Chappie') DWYER (1918-19) RHB Paddington/Mosman
b. Mosman, Oct 19, 1893. d. Mosman, Sept. 10, 1975.
Manager Australian team in South Africa 1949-50.

John DYSON (1975-76) RHB Sutherland/Randwick
b. Randwick, June 11, 1954. Add: 103 Carina Road, Oyster Bay.
Tests: 14 Tours: England 1980, 1981. Sri Lanka 1981.

Frank Alexander EASTON (1933-34) RHB/WK Glebe/Petersham
b. Waterloo, Feb. 19, 1910. Add: 44 Dulwich St., Dulwich Hill.

Harry **Ronald** EATON (1928-29) LHB/RFM North Sydney
b. 1909. d. Castlecrag, May 13, 1960.

Norman EBSWORTH (1902-03) RHB Waverley
b. Sydney, Jan. 2, 1878. d. Kirribilli, Nov. 19, 1949.

Ross EDWARDS (1979-80) RHB Northern Districts
b. Cottesloe, Dec. 1, 1942. Add: 65a Kintore St., Wahroonga.
Tests: 20 Tours: England 1972, 1975; West Indies 1973.
Western Australia 1964-65 to 1974-75. Ranji XI (Jamnagar) Sept. 1972.
Son of E.K.Edwards (Western Australia)

Thomas Charles Wills EGAN (1924-25) RHB/LBG King's Sch, Parramatta
b. Warren 1906. d. Double Bay, Nov. 29, 1979.

Leslie George ELLIS (1964-65) /RFM Western Suburbs
b. March 2, 1936. Add: 30 Roslyn Ave., Islington.

Sidney Hand EMERY (1908-09) RHB/LBG Redfern
b. Sydney, Oct. 16, 1886. d. Petersham, Jan. 7, 1967.
Tests: 4 Tours: England and North America 1912; New Zealand 1909-10; North America 1913.

Victor Rupert EMERY (1948-49) RHB/OB North Sydney
b. Redfern, Dec. 20, 1920. Add: 21 Boree Road, Forestville.

Edwin EVANS (1874-75) RHB/RFM Warwick
b. Emu Plains, March 6, 1849. d. Walgett, July 2, 1921.
Tests: 6 Tour: England 1886.

Samuel Charles EVERETT (1921-22) LHB/RF Petersham
b. Sydney, June 17, 1901. d. Sydney, Oct. 10, 1970.
Tours: England 1926; New South Wales to New Zealand 1923-24.

Harold Albert EVERS (1896-97) RHB/WK S.Sydney/Sydney
b. Newcastle, Feb. 28, 1876. d. Perth (W.A.), Feb. 6, 1937.
Western Australia 1905-06 to 1920-21.
Brother-in-law of C.W.Patrick.

Arthur Mervyn FAGAN RHB/RFM Balmain
b. April 24, 1931. Add: Collaroy.

Alan George FAIRFAX (1928-29) RHB/RFM St. George
b. Summer Hill, June 16, 1906. d. Kensington, London, May 17, 1955.
Tests: 10 tour: England 1930.
Gentlemen v Players (Oval) 1934.

Robert John FAIRWEATHER (1868-69) RHB Warwick
b. Pyrmont, 1846. d. Waverley, May 31, 1925.

Henry **Montague** FAITHFULL (1870-71) RHB/RFM (r) University
b. Springfield, near Goulburn, June 16, 1847. d. Elizabeth Bay, Oct. 22, 1908.

Leslie John FALLOWFIELD (1934-35) RHB/RM Northern District
b. North Sydney, March 12, 1916. Add: 12, Eastview Ave., Ryde.

Andrew **William** FARNSWORTH (1908-09) RHB Petersham
b. Sydney 1887. d. Sydney, Oct. 30, 1966.
Lancashire 1919.

Barclay **Wallace** ('Wally') FARQUHAR (1894-95) RHB Central Cumberland/North Sydney
b. Feb. 22, 1873. d. May 31, 1960.

Frank Martindale FARRAR (1914-15) RHB/RM University
b. Rylestone, March 29, 1893. d. Waverley, May 30, 1973.

John James FERRIS (1886-87) LHB/LM, SLA Belvidere
b. Sydney, May 21, 1867. d. Durban, South Africa, Nov. 21, 1900 of enteric fever.
Tests: Australia 8, England 1 Tours: England 1888, 1890; England to South Africa 1891-92.
Gloucestershire 1892 to 1895. South Australia 1895-96. C.I.Thornton's XI 1891, 1892, 1893, 1894. South 1891, 1892, 1893. Gentlemen 1891, 1892, 1893, 1894. M.C.C. 1891, 1892, 1893, 1894. Rest of England 1892. A.J.Webbe 1894.

John Henry Webb FINGLETON (1928-29) RHB Waverley
b. Waverley, April 28, 1908. d. Killara, Nov. 22, 1981.
Tests: 18 Tours: England 1938; South Africa 1935-36.
Author of 10 books on cricket.

Arthur Donnelly Wentworth FISHER (1903-04) RHB/RFM University/N.Sydney
b. Lavender Bay, Dec. 14, 1882. d. Sydney, July 9, 1968.

Jack Herbert FITZPATRICK (1937-38) RHB/LB Central Cumberland
b. Bankstown, Sept. 18, 1915. Add: 35 Columbine Ave., Bankstown.

Raymond George FLOCKTON (1951-52) RHB/RM Paddington/St.George
b. Paddington, March 14, 1930. Add: 87 Carruthers St., Curtin, A.C.T.
Commonwealth XI (Hastings) 1956.

John Paul FLYNN (1914-15) /LFM Waverley
b. Darlinghurst 1890. d. Chatswood, May 28, 1952.

Benjamin James ('Bert') FOLKARD (1910-11) RHB/RM Balmain
b. Gladesville, 1879. d. Leichardt, Jan. 31, 1937.

Douglas Allan FORD (1957-58) RHB/WK Mosman
b. Newcastle, Dec. 12, 1929. Add: 104 Grasmere Road, Cremorne.
Commonwealth to New Zealand 1961-62.

Edward Ernest Brackley FORSSBERG (1920-21) RHB/RFM Waverley
b. Kangaroo Point Brisbane Dec. 10, 1895. d. Bondi, May 23, 1953.
Tour: New Zealand 1920-21.

Thomas Henry FOSTER (1903-04) RHB Redfern
b. Sept. 30, 1883. d. June 27, 1974.

Norman Henry FOX (1926-27) RHB/RFM Gordon
b. Longueville, July 29, 1904. d. Castlecrag, May 7, 1972.

Bruce Colin FRANCIS (1968-69) RHB Waverley
b. Sydney, Feb. 18, 1948. Add: 25, The Avenue, Rose Bay.
Tests: 3 Tours: England 1972; International Wanderers to Rhodesia 1972-73; D.H.Robins to South Africa 1973-74 and 1974-75.
Essex 1971 and 1973.

Keith Raymond FRANCIS (1957-58) LHB/RM St. George
b. Arncliffe, Nov. 14, 1933. Add: 5 Borgah St., Carss Park.

Arthur John FURNESS (1895-96) South Sydney
b. Jan. 11, 1873. d. Strathfield, Oct. 31, 1948.
Played for New South Wales only on tour of New Zealand 1895-96.

George **Leonard** GARNSEY (1904-05) RHB/LB Burwood/Paddington
b. Sydney, Feb. 10, 1881. d. Canberra, April 18, 1951.
Author of *Cricket : its origin and development;* editor of N.S.W.C.A. Coaching Magazine.

Thomas William GARRETT (1876-77) RHB/RFM University
b. Wollongong, July 26, 1858. d. Warrawee, Aug 6, 1943.
Tests: 19 Tours: England 1878, 1882, 1886; North America 1878.

Alfred GEARY (1877-78) RHB/LM Carlton
b. Aug. 8, 1849. d. Brisbane, Oct. 14, 1911.

Daniel Albert GEE (1903-04) RHB Paddington/M.Harbour
b. Dec. 30, 1875. d. Adelaide, 1947.

George Henry Bailey GILBERT (1855-56) RHB/RM(r) Marylebone/Albert
b. Cheltenham, Eng., Sept. 2, 1829. d. Summer Hill, June 16, 1906.
Middlesex 1851. Gentlemen 1851.

Francis Patrick John GILMORE (1938-39) RHB/RFM Northern District
b. 1910. d. Eastwood, April 26, 1955.

Gary John GILMOUR (1971-72) LHB/LFM Western Suburbs/Newcastle
b. Waratah, June 26, 1951. Add: 21 Merinda Close, Adamstown Heights.
Tests: 15 Tours: England 1975; New Zealand 1973-74, 1976-77; International Wanderers to South Africa 1975-76.

John William GLEESON (1966-67) RHB/LBG Balmain/Newcastle
b. Wiangaree, March 14, 1938. Add: 18 McRae St., Tamworth.
Tests: 29 Tours: England 1968, 1972; Ceylon, India and South Africa 1969-70; New Zealand 1966-67; D.H.Robins to South Africa 1973-74.
Eastern Province 1974-75.

Henry ('Harry') GODDARD (1905-06) RHB/LB Sydney/Redfern
b. Nov. 16, 1883?. d. Maroubra, May 13, 1925.

Gordon GOFFET (1965-66) RHB/OB Waverley
b. Speers Point, March 4, 1941. Add: 23 Coronation Ave., Cardiff.

Gamini GOONESEENA (1960-61) RHB/LBG Waverley
b. Colombo, Ceylon, Feb. 16, 1931. Add: 106 Cascade St., Paddington.
Tours: E.W.Swanton to West Indies 1955-56; Cavaliers to West Indies 1964-65; International XI to India, Pakistan and Ceylon 1967-68.
Ceylon 1947-48 Nottinghamshire 1952 to 1959 and 1964. Cambridge University 1954 to 1957.

George Hollinworth GORDON (1866-67) RHB Albert/University
b. Sydney, Sept. 20, 1846. d. Darling Point, May 18, 1923.

Frank O. ('Froggy') GORMAN (1862-63) Albert

Charles Richard GORRY (1907-08) /WK Glebe
b. Auckland, Sept. 18, 1878. d. Petersham, Sept. 13, 1950.
Tour: New Zealand 1909-10.

Reginald Edwin GOSTELOW (1920-21) RHB/WK University/Sydney
b. Darlinghurst, July 26, 1900. Add: 19/2 Eastbourne Road, Darling Point.

John William GOULD (1891-92) RHB/LB Sydney/East Sydney
b. Oct. 1, 1872. d. Lewisham, Dec. 4, 1908.
Tour: New South Wales to New Zealand 1893-94.

Frederick Kingswood GOW (1909-10) RHB Paddington
b. Richmond, Dec. 18, 1882. d. Randwick, Oct. 11, 1961.

Arthur Thomas ('Paddy') GRAY (1922-23) RHB/RM Glebe
b. Glebe, June 12, 1892. d. Glebe, July 19, 1977.

Norman McAlister GREGG (1912-13) RHB University
b. Sydney, March 7, 1892. d. Sydney, July 27, 1966.
World famous ophthalmic surgeon. discovered the effects of rubella on un-born children.

Arthur Herbert GREGORY (1880-81) RHB/LB Albert/Warwick
b. Sydney, July 7, 1861. d. Chatswood, Aug. 17, 1929.
Brother of E.J., C.S. and D.W.Gregory. Noted cricket journalist.

Charles Smith GREGORY (1870-71) RHB Warwick/East Sydney
b. Wollongong, June 5, 1847. d. Chatswood, April 5, 1935.

Charles William GREGORY (1898-99) RHB South Sydney/Waverley
b. Sydney, Sept. 30, 1878. d. of blood poisoning at Darlinghurst, Nov. 14, 1910.
Son of E.J.Gregory; brother of S.E.Gregory.

David William GREGORY (1866-67) RHB/RF(r) National/Warwick/East Sydney/Albert
b. Fairy Meadow, April 15, 1845. d. Turramurra, Aug. 4, 1919.
Tests: 3 Tour: England and North America 1878.

Edward James ('Ned') GREGORY (1862-63) RHB/RM(r) National/East Sydney/Albert
b. Waverley, May 29, 1839. d. Randwick, April 22, 1899.
Test: 1 S.C.G. curator and designer of Australian-style scoreboards.

Jack Morrison GREGORY (1920-21) LHB/RF Sydney/Manly/Paddington/Waverley
b. North Sydney, Aug. 14, 1895. d. Bega, Aug. 7, 1973.
Tests: 24 Tours: England 1921 and 1926; South Africa 1921; A.I.F. in England and South Africa 1919.
Son of C.S.Gregory.

Sydney Edward GREGORY (1889-90) RHB South Sydney/Sydney/Paddington/Waverley
b. Randwick, April 14, 1870. d. Randwick, Aug. 1, 1929.
Tests: 58 Tours: England 1890, 1893, 1896, 1899, 1902, 1905, 1909, 1912; South Africa 1902-03; New Zealand 1905; North America 1893, 1896, 1912.

Kenneth John GRIEVES (1945-46) RHB/LBG Petersham
b. Sydney, Aug 27, 1925.
Tour: Commonwealth to India and Ceylon 1950-51. Lancashire 1949 to 1964.

George Edward GRIFFITHS (1962-63) RHB/OB Glebe-South Sydney Sydney
b. Glebe, April 9, 1938. Add: 7 Manning Parade, Dundas.
South Australia 1965-66 and 1966-67.

John William ('Tim') GROSSER (1968-69) LHB Balmain
b. Gunnedah, Aug. 29, 1942. Add: Dunromin, Carroll Road, Gunnedah.

Bertie GROUNDS (1903-04) LHB/RFM Glebe
b. *circa* 1878. d. Marrickville, July 21, 1950.

Kenneth Charles GULLIVER (1936-37) LHB/LBG Mosman
b. East Maitland, Aug. 14, 1913. Add: 76 Brighton St., Harbord.

Richard Henry GUY (1960-61) RHB/LB Gordon
b. St Leonards, April 4, 1937. Add: 5 Tyagerah Place, Cromer.

Leslie William GWYNNE (1924-25) RHB Manly
b. Homebush, Jan. 26, 1895. d. South Australia, Oct. 25, 1962.

Richard HALL (1880-81) /WK Carlton

Walter Charles HAND (1871-72) RHB Maitland
b. *circa* 1850.

David Walter HANLIN (1948-49) RHB/RF University
b. Ashfield, Dec. 8, 1928. Add: 27, Flannagan St., Garran, A.C.T.

Roger Joseph HARTIGAN (1903-04) RHB North Sydney
b. Chatswood, Dec. 12, 1879. d. Brisbane, June 7, 1958.
Tests: 2 Tour: England 1909
Queensland 1905-06 to 1920-21
Brother of T.J.Hartigan.

Thomas Joseph HARTIGAN (1907-08) RHB North Sydney
b.Chatswood, Dec. 8, 1877. d. Mosman, May 2, 1963.
Manager of N.S.W. team in Brisbane : played only because of injuries to other players.

George G. HARVEY (1909-10) RHB/WK Petersham

Ronald Mason HARVEY (1956-57) RHB Newcastle
b. Newcastle, Oct. 26, 1934. Add: 67, Woodward St., Merewether.

Robert Neil HARVEY (1958-59) LHB/OB Gordon
b. Fitzroy, Vic., Oct. 8, 1928. Add: 3 Whitmont Crescent, St. Ives.
Tests: 79 Tours: England 1948, 1953, 1956, 1961; South Africa 1949-50, 1957-58; West Indies 1955; India and Pakistan 1956, 1959-60; New Zealand 1956-57.
Commonwealth XI 1951-52 (Ceylon). Victoria 1946-47 to 1956-57.
Brother of M.R. (Vic.), C.E. (Vic. and Qld) and Ray Harvey (Vic.)

Gervys Rignold ('Gerry') HAZLITT (1911-12) RHB/RFM Central Cumberland
b. Enfield, Sept. 4, 1888. d. Parramatta, Oct. 30, 1915. of chronic heart disease.
Tests: 9 Tour: England 1912.
Victoria 1905-06 to 1910-11.

Frank HENDERSON (1928-29) RHB Newcastle
b. Tighes Hill, June 1, 1908. d. Heidelberg, Vic., Dec. 6, 1954.

Michael HENDRICKS (1969-70) RHB/WK Corrimal
b. Corrimal, Dec. 12, 1942. Add: 46 The Strand, Reynella, S.Aust.
South Australia 1970-71 to 1974-75.

Hunter Scott Thomas Laurie ('Stork') HENDRY (1918-19) RHB/RFM Paddington/Radwick/Waverley
b. Woollahra, May 24, 1895. Add: 39 Beaumont St., Rose Bay.
Tests: 11 Tours: England 1921, 1926; South Africa 1921-22; Australia to India 1935-36 (Tarrant); New South Wales to New Zealand 1923-24.
Victoria 1924-25 to 1932-33.

Richard Child HEWITT (1865-66) RHB/WK National/Warwick
b. Beverley, Yorkshire, Feb. 13, 1844. d. *circa* 1920.

Robert Newburgh HICKSON (1902-03) RHB North Sydney/Gordon
b. May 2, 1884. d. Armidale, June 21, 1963.

Hugh Charles S. HIDDLESTON (1880-81) RHB Warwick
b. *circa* 1855. d. Coolgardie, W.A., May 14, 1934.

Andrew Mark Jefferson HILDITCH (1976-77) RHB Sutherland
b. North Adelaide, May 20, 1956.
Tests: 9 Tour: India 1979-80.

Clement John HILL (1932-33) LHB/SLA North Sydney
b. Gulgong, July 2, 1904. Add: 9 Golding Ave., Belmont.

Kenneth **Michael** HILL (1964-65) LHB/OB Newcastle
b. Merewether, Jan. 26, 1945. Add: 399 Warners Bay Road, Charlestown.

Stanley ('Solly') HILL (1912-13) RHB North Sydney
b. Adelaide, Aug. 23, 1885. d. Englefield Green, Surrey, May 10, 1970.
South Australia 1909-10 to 1911-12.
Brother of A., C., H.J., L.R., P. and R.J.Hill (South Australia

Henry ('Harry') HILLIARD (1855-56) RHB/RF(u) Marylebone/National
b. Sydney, Nov. 7, 1826. d. Sydney, March 19, 1914.

Sydney Francis HIRD (1931-32) RHB/LBG Balmain
b. Balmain, Jan. 7, 1910. d. Bloemfontein, S.Africa, Dec. 20, 1980.
L.Parkinson's XI 1935. Lancashire 1939. Eastern Province 1945-46 to 1948-49. Border 1950-51.

John HODGKINSON (1908-09) RHB Middle Harbour

Geoffrey Charles Huxtable ('Mick') HOGG (1928-29) RHB University
b. Goulburn, Sept. 28, 1909. d. Coorparoo, Brisbane, Aug. 14, 1959.
Brother of J.E.P.Hogg; grand-nephew of T.Hogg (Tasmania).

James Edgar Phipps HOGG (1926-27) RHB University
b. Goulburn, Oct. 16, 1906. d. West Ryde, Dec. 2, 1975.
Queensland 1931-32.

Thomas Herbert HOGUE (1901-02) RHB Maitland/Burwood
b. Wickham, Oct. 5, 1877. d. Nedlands (W.A.), May 6, 1956.
Western Australia 1906-07 to 1912-13.
Brother of W.W.Hogue (W.A.)

Graeme Blake HOLE (1949-50) RHB/OB St. George
b. Concord West, Jan. 6, 1931. Add: 55 Brigalow Ave, Kensington Gardens, S.Aust.
Tests: 18 Tour: England 1953.
South Australia 1950-51 to 1957-58 Commonwealth XI v M.C.C. (Colombo) 1951-52.

Robert George HOLLAND (1978-79) RHB/LB Newcastle
b. Camperdown, Oct. 19, 1946. Add: 4 Ellis Close, Coal Point, Newcastle.

John Edward **Halford** HOOKER (1924-25) RHB/RFM Mosman/Newcastle
b. Summer Hill, March 6, 1898. Add: 186 Raglan St., Mosman.

Albert John Young ('Bert') HOPKINS (1896-97) RHB/RFM North Sydney
b. Sydney, May 3, 1876. d. North Sydney, April 25, 1931.
Tests: 20 Tours: England 1902, 1905, 1909; South Africa 1902-03; New Zealand 1904-05. and 1909-10.

Herbert Vivian HORDERN (1905-06) RHB/LBG North Sydney
b. North Sydney, Feb. 10, 1884. d. Darlinghurst, June 17, 1938.
Tests: 7 Tours: Philadelphia to England 1908 and to Jamaica 1908-09.
Gents of Philadelphia 1907.

Gordon Cameron HORSFIELD (1934-35) LHB Mosman
b. Balmain, March 24, 1913. Add: 2 Middle Head Road, Mosman.

David William HOURN (1970-71 RHB/SLC Waverley
b. Bondi, Sept. 9, 1949. Add: 4/109 New South Head Road, Vaucluse.

Thomas Harris HOWARD (1899-1900) RHB/OB Waverley
b. May 2, 1877. d. Randwick, Oct. 6, 1965.
Manager Australian team in New Zealand 1920-21.

GEORGE HOWELL (1855-56) RHB/Long- Stop Marylebone
b. Sydney, June 9, 1822. d. Sydney, Nov. 18, 1890.

William Hunter HOWELL (1932-33) LHB/OB Central Cumberland
b. Penrith, Jan. 12, 1902. Add: 24 Burgess Road, South Penrith.
Son of W.P.Howell.

William Peter HOWELL (1894-95) LHB/RM Central Cumberland
b. Penrith, Dec. 29, 1869. d. Castlereagh, near Penrith, July 14, 1940.
Tests: 18 Tours: England 1899, 1902, 1905; South Africa 1902-03; New Zealand 1904-05
Nephew of E.Evans.

Graeme Christopher HUGHES (1975-76) LHB Petersham-Marrickville
b. Stanmore, Dec. 6, 1955. Add: 4 Coolabah St., Beverly Hills.

Andrew Ernest HUME (1895-96) South Sydney
b. Feb. 5, 1869. d. London, June 22, 1912.
Played for New South Wales only on tour of New Zealand 1895-96.

John HUMPHREYS (1875-76) Warwick

William Alfred HUNT (1929-30) LHB/SLA Balmain
b. Balmain, Aug. 26, 1908. Add: 21/3 Gallimore Ave., Balmain.
Test: 1

Lincoln Carruthers ('Bob') HYNES (1935-36) RHB/LFM Gordon
b. Balmain, April 12, 1912. d. Sydney, Aug. 7, 1977.

Thomas Henry ICETON (1877-78) RHB/OB(r) University
b. Sydney, 1850. d. Sydney, May 19, 1908.

Francis Adams ('Noss') IREDALE (1888-89) RHB Albert/Belvidere/N.Sydney/Waverley
b. Surry Hills, June 19, 1867. d. North Sydney, April 15, 1926.
Tests: 14 Tours: England 1896, 1899; North America 1896.
Nephew of F. Adams. Secretary New South Wales Cricket Association from 1922 to 1926. Author of *33 Years of Cricket* (1920)

William Francis IVES (1919-20) RHB/RMF Waverley
b. Glebe, Nov. 14, 1896. d. Newport Beach, March 23, 1975.

Archibald JACKSON (1926-27) RHB Balmain
b. Rutherglen, Scotland, Sept. 5, 1909. d. of tuberculosis in Brisbane, Feb. 16, 1933.
Tests: 8 Tours: England 1930; New Zealand 1927-28.

Victor Edward JACKSON (1936-37) RHB/OB Waverley
b. Sydney, Oct. 25, 1916. d. in a level crossing accident near Manildra, Jan. 30, 1965.
Tour: Cahn to New Zealand 1938-38.
Leicestershire 1938 to 1956. Cahn 1938. Commonwealth XI 1957, 1958 (Torquay).

Ronald Victor JAMES (1938-39) RHB/LM Paddington
b. Paddington, May 23, 1920. Add: 37 Albert Road, Auburn.
South Australia 1946-47, 1947-48.

Ernest William JANSEN (1899-1900) RHB Leichardt-Balmain
b. Ashfield, *circa* 1878. d. Leichardt, May 31, 1945.

Robert Frederick JEFFERY (1978-79) LHB/LM Mosman-M.Harbour
b. Goulburn, Sept. 19, 1953.
Tasmania 1979-80, 1980-81. Brother-in-law of M.B.Pawley.

**Arthur Frederick JEFFREYS (1872-73) RHB/Long- stop
b. London, April 7, 1848. d. Alton, Hampshire, Feb. 4, 1906.
M.C.C. 1872. Hampshire 1876 to 1878.

Francis Barry JOHNSON (1903-04) RHB/LB North Sydney
b. May 21, 1880. d. Longueville, May 28, 1951.

Aubrey Edmund JOHNSTON (1904-05) RHB Burwood
b. Sept. 7, 1883. d. Manly, June 16, 1960.

Clive William ('Sailor') JOHNSTON (1949-50) RHB Petersham-Marrickville
b. Petersham, Aug. 4, 1925. Add: 23, Nield Ave., Rodd Point.

David Alexander Hughes JOHNSTON (1977-78) RHB N.Sydney/Newcastle
b. Maitland, July 10, 1955.

Frank Frederick JOHNSTON (1946-47) RHB/LBG Randwick
b. 1915. d. Sept. 8, 1977.

Sydney JONES (1862-63) RHB Newtown

Samuel Percy JONES (1880-81) RHB/RFM Carlton/University
b. Sydney, Aug. 1, 1861. d. Auckland, July 14, 1951.
Tests: 12 Tours: England 1882, 1886, 1888, 1890; Queensland to New Zealand 1896-97.
Queensland 1896-97 to 1899-1900. Auckland 1904-05 to 1908-09.

Frank Slater JORDAN (1927-28) RHB/RMF Glebe
b. Darlington, Sept. 19, 1905. Add: 75 Kings Road, Vaucluse.

J.JOSEPH (1889-90)
Played for New South Wales only on tour of New Zealand 1889-90.

Charles KELLEWAY (1907-08) RHB/RFM Glebe/Gordon
b. Lismore, April 25, 1889. d. Lindfield, Nov. 16, 1944.
Tests: 26 Tours: England and North America 1912; New Zealand 1909-10; A.I.F. in England 1919. (5 matches).

Charles Moore KELLICK (1865-66) LHB National/Warwick
b. Sydney, Nov. 20, 1842. d. Strathfield, March 27, 1918.
Brother of J.Kellick.

James KELLICK (1868-69) Warwick
b. *circa* 1839. d. Sydney, Aug. 8, 1926.

James Joseph KELLY (1894-95) RHB/WK Paddington
Port Melbourne, Vic., May 10, 1867. d. Bellevue Hill, Aug. 14, 1938.
Tests: 36 Tours: England 1896, 1899, 1902, 1905; South Africa 1902-03; New Zealand 1904-05; North America 1896.

Peter Charles KELLY (1962-63) RHB Mosman
b. Mosman, April 28, 1942. Add: 3 Riverview Terrace, Mt. Pleasant, W.A.
Western Australia 1964-65 to 1966-67.

Alexander KERMODE (1901-02) RHB/RFM Moore Park Juniors
b. Sydney, May 15, 1876. d. Balmain, July 17, 1934.
Lancashire 1902 to 1908. London County 1903.

John Louis KETTLE (1859-60) Union/National
b. Sydney, Dec. 3, 1830. d. Newtown, Oct. 30, 1891.

Percy Macgregor KING (1919-20) RHB North Sydney
Richmond, Vic., Sept. 2, 1889. d. Rose Bay, Dec. 9, 1967.

John KINLOCH (1858-59) RHB/RF(u) University
b. 1833. d. Camperdown, April 9, 1897.

Alan Falconer KIPPAX (1918-19) RHB/LB Waverley
b. Sydney, May 25, 1897. d. Bellevue Hill, Sept. 4, 1972.
Tests: 22 Tours: England 1930, 1934; New Zealand 1920-21; 1927-28; New South Wales to New Zealand 1923-24.

Ronald Keith KISSELL (1946-47) LHB Glebe
b. Camperdown Aug. 9, 1928. Add: 4/18 Burlington St., Monterey.

Oswald LAMBERT (1950-51) LHB/WK Newcastle
b. New Lambton, Aug. 23, 1926. Add: 32 Howitt Drive, Lower Templestowe, Vic.

William Henry Warwick LAMPE (1927-28) RHB/LF Riverina
b. Wagga Wagga, Aug. 29, 1902. Add: 2/14 Small St., Wagga Wagga.

John Bayley ('Paddy') LANE (1907-08) RHB/WK University
b. Petersham, Jan. 7, 1886. d. Manly, Aug. 30, 1937.

Charles Henry Wickham LAWES (1924-25) RHB/OB Paddington
b. Cobar, Dec. 9, 1899. Add: 38 Sublime Point Road, Leura.

Charles LAWRENCE (1862-63) RHB/RM(r) Albert
b. Hoxton, London, Dec. 16, 1828. d. Canterbury, Vic., Dec. 20, 1916.
Surrey 1854, 1857. Middlesex 1861.

Geoffrey Francis LAWSON (1977-78) RHB/RF University of N.S.W.
b. Wagga Wagga, Dec. 7, 1957. Add: 104 Ashmont Ave., Wagga Wagga.
Tests: 4 Tours: England 1981; India 1979-80 (1 match); Pakistan 1980. Sri Lanka 1981.
Lancashire 1979.

Leonard Raymond LEABEATER (1929-30) RHB Central Cumberland
b. Parramatta, July 10, 1906. Add: 10 Cambridge Ave., Vaucluse.

Terance Henry LEE (1962-63) RHB/OB Manly-Warringah
b. Manly, Aug. 31, 1940.
U.S.A. v Canada 1969 *(not first-class)*

Peter Glen LESLIE (1965-66) LHB/LFM St. George
b. Bexley, Feb. 24, 1947. Add: 5/150 Kingscliff St., Kingscliff.

Oswald Hoddle ('Ozzy') LEWIS (1856-57) RHB/RF(u) Australian/Royal Victoria/National
b. Sydney, 1832. d. Darlinghurst, April 28, 1895.
Brother of T.H.Lewis.

Thomas Harvie LEWIS (1856-57) National
b. London, 1828. d. Darlinghurst, June 19, 1901.

Raymond Russell LINDWALL (1941-42) RHB/RF St. George
b. Mascot, Oct. 3, 1921. Add: Endeavour St., Mt. Ommaney, Brisbane.
Tests: 61 Tours: England 1948, 1953, 1956; South Africa 1949-50; West Indies 1955; New Zealand 1945-46; Pakistan and India 1956, 1959-60; E.W.Swanton to West Indies 1960-61; Commonwealth to Rhodesia, India and Pakistan 1961-62.
Queensland 1954-55 to 1959-60. Governor-General's XI v M.C.C. 1960-61 (Auckland)

Raymond Cecil James LITTLE (1934-35) RHB St. George
b. Armidale, Oct. 7, 1915. Add: 33a Lindsay St., Enfield.

Bruce Arthur Lionel LIVINGSTON (1956-57) RHB/RFM Petersham-Marrickville
b. Marrickville, May 11, 1927. Add: 1 Carrington St., Lewisham.

Leonard ('Jock') LIVINGSTON (1941-42) LHB/WK N.Sydney/Randwick
b. Sydney, May 3, 1920. Add: Robertsbridge, Sussex, Eng.
Tours: Commonwealth XI to India, Pakistan and Ceylon 1949-50; Howard's XI to India 1956-57.
Northamptonshire 1950 to 1957. Commonwealth XI 1958. M.C.C. 1964.

Roy W. LODER (1926-27) RHB Northern District

Albert Roy LONERGAN (1935-36) RHB St. George
b. Maylands, W.A., Dec. 6, 1909. d. Adelaide, Oct. 22, 1956.
South Australia 1929-30 to 1934-35.

Edmund James LONG (1911-12) RHB/WK North Sydney
b. Darlinghurst, March 28, 1880. d. Leichardt, Dec. 8, 1947.
A.I.F. in England and South Africa 1919.

W. LOUGH (1906-07) RHB Sydney

Hampden Stanley Bray ('Hammy') LOVE (1920-21) RHB/WK Balmain/Mosman
b. Lilyfield, Aug. 10, 1896. d. Mosman, July 22, 1969.
Test: 1 Tours: A.I.F. in England 1919 (1 match); Australia in India 1935-36 (Tarrant).
Victoria 1922-23 to 1926-27.

Walter David LOVERIDGE (1902-03) RHB/WK Central Cumberland
b. Sydney, Sept. 13, 1867. d. East Brisbane, Jan. 6, 1940.

Eric William LUKEMAN (1946-47) RHB Balmain/St. George
b. Drummoyne, March 11, 1923. Add: 1/57 Prospect Road, Summer Hill.

John Grantley ('Ginty') LUSH (1933-34) RHB/RF Mosman/N.Sydney/Gordon
b. Prahran, Vic., Oct. 14, 1913. Add: 12/1 Coxs Lane, Lane Cove.
Cahn 1938.

Charles George MACARTNEY (1905-06) RHB/SLA Gordon
b. West Maitland, June 27, 1886. d. Sydney, Sept. 9, 1958.
Tests: 35 Tours: England 1909, 1912, 1921, 1926; South Africa 1921-22; North America 1913; New South Wales to New Zealand 1923-24; Australia to India and Ceylon 1935-36 (Tarrant).
Otago 1909-10. Grandson of G.Moore.

Andrew McBE(A)TH (1899-1900) /LFM South Sydney/Sydney
b. June 17, 1876. d. March 17, 1945?
South Australia 1906-07 and 1907-08.

Stanley Joseph McCABE (1928-29) RHB/RM Mosman/North Sydney
b. Grenfell, July 16, 1910. d. Mosman, Aug. 25, 1968.
Tests: 39. Tours: England 1930, 1934, 1938; South Africa 1935-36.

Victor William McCAFFREY (1938-39) RHB Mosman
b.Goulburn, Aug. 11, 1918. Add: 16 Dobson Crescent, Ryde.

Bede Vincent McCAULEY (1937-38) RHB Randwick
b. Coogee, June 11, 1909. Add: 287/3 Darling Point Road, Darling Point.

William Stanley Swain McCLOY (1918-19) RHB Paddington
b. Paddington, Nov. 10, 1886. d. Bateman's Bay, Nov. 10, 1975.
Queensland 1910-11.

Colin Leslie McCOOL (1939-40) RHB/LBG Paddington
b. Paddington, Dec. 9, 1915. Add: 299 Ocean Beach Road, Umina.
Tests: 14 Tours: England 1948; South Africa 1949-50; New Zealand 1945-46; Howard to India 1956-57.
Queensland 1945-46 to 1952-53. Somerset 1956 to 1960. Commonwealth XI 1954, 1955.

Richard Bede McCOSKER (1973-74) RHB Sydney
b. Inverell, Dec. 11, 1946. Add: 80 Algona Road, Charlestown.
Tests: 25 Tours: England 1975, 1977; New Zealand 1976-77.

Bernard Leslie ('Barney') McCOY (1920-21) RHB/LB Balmain
b. Kangaroo Valley, Jan. 1894. d. June 11, 1970.

Percy Stanislaus McDONNELL (1885-86) RHB Carlton
b. Kensington, London, Nov. 13, 1858. d. Brisbane, Sept. 24, 1896.
Tests: 19 Tours: England 1880, 1882, 1884, 1888.
Victoria 1877-78 to 1885-86. Queensland 1894-95 and 1895-96. Smokers 1884.

Frank Eric McELHONE (1910-11) RHB University
b. Sydney, June 27, 1887. d. Sydney, July 21, 1981.
Nephew of W.P.McElhone, Chairman Australian Cricket Board 1911-12.
Brother-in-Law of H.V.Hordern.

Alan David McGILVRAY (1933-34) LHB/RM Paddington
b. Paddington, Dec. 6, 1910. Add: 57 Ocean Ave., Double Bay.
Famous cricket radio commentator.

Walter William McGLINCHY (1885-86) RHB Newcastle
b. Newcastle, Jan. 31, 1866. d. Sydney, July 1, 1946.
Tours: New South Wales to New Zealand 1889-90; Queensland to New Zealand 1896-97.
Queensland 1893-94 to 1899-1900.

Harold Vincent McGUIRK (1926-27) LHB/RM Goulburn
b. Crookwell, Oct. 17, 1906. Add: 106 Wilkes Crescent, Mt. Druitt.

Leo Daniel McGUIRK (1930-31) RHB/RMF Goulburn
b. Crookwell, May 3, 1908. d. Sydney, June 15, 1974.
Brother of H.V.McGuirk.

William H. McINTYRE (1905-06) RHB/WK Middle Harbour
b. Forbes, April 10, 1877.

James Rainey Munro ('Sunny Jim') MACKAY (1902-03) RHB Burwood/W.Suburbs
b. Kentucky, near Uralla, Sept, 9, 1881. d. Walcha, June 13, 1953.
Transvaal 1906-07.

Kerry MACKAY (1970-71) RHB/RM Northern District
b. Brighton-Le-Sands, May 7, 1949. Add: 3 Curra Close, Frenches Forest.

Alexander Cecil Knox ('Alick') MACKENZIE (1888-89) RHB Sydney/Paddington/Waverley
b. Sydney, Aug. 7, 1870. d. Epping, April 11, 1947.
Tour: New South Wales to New Zealand 1893-94.
Manager Australian Team in New Zealand 1909-10.

Cecil George McKEW (1911-12) RHB/WK Balmain/Glebe/Petersham
b. Leichardt, Aug. 12, 1887. d. Lilli Pilli, Oct. 12, 1974.

Thomas Robert McKIBBIN (1894-95) LHB/RM, OB Bathurst/Glebe University
b. Raglan, near Bathurst, Dec. 10, 1870. d. Bathurst, Dec 15, 1939.
Tests: 5 Tours: England and North America 1896.

John James McKONE (1855-56) RHB/RM(u) Marylebone
b. Sydney, 1835. d. Sydney, Aug. 7, 1882.

Raymond Leonard Alphonsus McNAMEE (1926-27) RHB/OB Randwick
b. Waverley, Aug. 26, 1899. d. Sydney, Sept. 18, 1949.
Tour: New Zealand 1927-28

William G. MACNISH (1862-63) National

Herbert James Keele MACPHERSON (1893-94) RHB Mudgee
b. Mudgee, Feb. 20, 1869. d. Mudgee, Nov. 12, 1953.

Keith McPHILLAMY (1904-05)* RHB/LM Bathurst
b. Bathurst, June 20, 1883. d. Bowral, May 3, 1937.

Robert Harold MADDEN (1949-50) RHB/LB Petersham/Glebe/ Bankstown-Canterbury
b. Camperdown, Dec. 12, 1928. Add: 8 Woodbine St., Yagoona.

Arthur Alfred MAILEY (1912-13) RHB/LBG Redfern/Mid. Harbour/ Balmain
b. Waterloo, Jan. 3, 1886. d. Kirrawee, Dec. 31, 1967.
Tests: 21 Tours: England 1921, 1926; South Africa 1921-22; New Zealand 1913-14; North America 1913; New South Wales to New Zealand 1923-24.
Noted cricket author and cartoonist.

Frederick MAIR (1933-34) RHB/RM, LBG Balmain
b. Sydney, April 15, 1901. d. Sydney, Dec. 25, 1959.
Tour: Australia to India and Ceylon 1935-36 (Tarrant).

William MAKIN (1910-11) LHB/LFM Redfern
b. *circa* 1881. d. West Kogarah, Jan. 11, 1962.

Peter Ivan MALONEY (1976-77) RHB/LBG Petersham/Marrickville
b. Ballina, Nov. 5, 1950. Add: 16/13 Riverview St., West Ryde.

Hugh Lynch MARJORIBANKS (1958-59) RHB/LB Newcastle
b. Mackay, Qld., Aug. 12, 1933. Add: 14, Ingall St., Mayfield.

Alexander Edward MARKS (1928-29) LHB/SLA Randwick
b. Toowong, Qld. Dec. 10, 1910. Add: 72 Woonona Ave., Wahroonga.
Brother-in-law of M.J.Ward.

Lynn Alexander MARKS (1962-63) LHB Northern District
b. Randwick, Aug. 15, 1942. Add: 10 Siobhan Place, Mona Vale.
South Australia 1965-66. Son of A.E.Marks; brother of N.G.Marks.

Neil Graham MARKS LHB Northern District
b. Randwick, Sept. 13, 1938. Add: 23 Water St., Wahroonga.

Alfred **Percy** MARR (1882-83) RHB/RM Carlton
b. Pyrmont, March 28, 1862. d. Arncliffe, March 15, 1940.
Test: 1

Jack MARSH /RF Sydney
b. Yugilbar, Clarence River, 1874. d. in a street fight at Orange, May 25, 1916.

Hugh MARTIN (1971-72) RHB/RM Balmain
b. Enkeldoorn, Rhodesia, Aug. 3, 1947. Add: 4 Olsson Close, Hornsby Heights.
Transvaal B 1970-71.

John Frank MARTIN (1966-67) RHB/RFM St.George
b. Alton, Hampshire, May 8, 1942. Add: 395 Shakespeare St., Mackay, Qld.

John Wesley MARTIN (1956-57) LHB/SLC Petersham-Marrickville
b. Wingham, July 28, 1931. Add: Burrel Creek.
Tests: 8 Tours: England and India 1964; South Africa 1966-67; New Zealand 1956-57 and 1959-60; Cavaliers to India and South Africa 1962-63.
South Australia 1958-59.

Hugh Hamon MASSIE (1877-78) RHB Albert
b. near Belfast (now Port Fairy, Vic.,) April 11, 1854. d. Point Piper, Oct. 12, 1938.
Tests: 9 Tour: England 1882.

M.C.C., Gentlemen 1895.

Robert **John** Allright MASSIE (1910-11) LHB/LFM University
b. North Sydney, July 8, 1890. d. Mosman, Feb. 14, 1966.
Son of H.H.Massie.

Adam MATHER (1885-86) RHB Singleton
b. May 1864. d. Singleton, Aug 31, 1917.

Alexander Dunbar Aitken MAYES (1924-25) RHB/RM University
b. Toowoomba, Qld., July 24, 1901. Add: 21 Jethro St., Aspley, Qld.
Queensland 1925-26 to 1927-28.

Frederick Stewart MIDDLETON (1905-06) RHB/RM Sydney/Mid. Harbour
b. Burrola, May 28, 1883. d. Auckland, July 21, 1956.
Auckland 1917-18. Wellington 1919-20 to 1921-22 New Zealand 1920-21.

David Lawson MILLER (1893-94) LHB/LF Bathurst
b. Jan. 30, 1870. d. Brisbane, April 12, 1943.
Tours: New South Wales to New Zealand 1893-94; Queensland to New Zealand 1896-97.
Auckland 1892-93 Queensland 1896-97 to 1905-06.

Keith Ross MILLER (1947-48) RHB/RF North Sydney/Manly-Warringah
b. Sunshine, Vic., Nov. 28, 1919. Add: 47 Nullaburra Road, Newport.
Tests: 55 Tours: England 1948, 1953, 1956; South Africa 1949-50; West Indies 1955; New Zealand 1945-46; Services in England, India and Ceylon 1945; Pakistan 1956.
Victoria 1937-38 to 1946-47; Dominions v England 1945. Commonwealth XI v M.C.C. (Colombo) 1951-52. Nottinghamshire and M.C.C. 1959.
Author or co-author of nine books on cricket.

Noel Keith MILLER (1935-36) RHB Balmain
b. Wyong, July 1, 1913. Add: 99 Ryde Road, Hunters Hill.

**John MILLS (1857-58) Royal Victoria
b. June 1836. d. Dec. 24, 1899.

Leslie Alma MINNETT (1907-08) RHB/RF North Sydney
b. St Leonards, May 19, 1883. d. Collaroy, Aug. 8, 1934.

Roy Baldwin MINNETT (1906-07) RHB/RFM University
b. St. Leonards, June 13, 1888. d. Manly, Oct. 21, 1955.
Tests: 9 Tour: England 1912.
Brother of L.A. and R.V.Minnett.

Rupert Villiers MINNETT (1909-10) RHB North Sydney
b. St. Leonards, Sept. 2, 1884. d. Cremorne, June 24, 1974.
Lionel Robinson's XI 1912.

Eric **James** MINTER (1938-39) RHB Balmain
b. Kempsey, Sept. 13, 1917. Add: 397 Elizabeth Drive, Vincentia.

Francis Michael MISSON (1958-59) RHB/RFM Glebe-South Sydney
b. Darlinghurst, Nov. 19, 1938. Add: 53, Parer St., Maroubra.
Tests: 5 Tours: England 1961; New Zealand 1959-60.

George MOORE (1870-71) RHB/RM(r), RS(r) Maitland
b. Ampthill, Bedfordshire, April 8, 1820. d. West Maitland, Sept. 29, 1916.

George **Stanley** MOORE (1912-13) RHB North Sydney
b. North Sydney, April 18, 1886. d. Bundaberg, Qld., March 22, 1948.
Queensland 1920-21.

James MOORE (1861-62) RHB National
b. Ampthill, Bedfordshire, 1839. d. West Maitland, April 19, 1890.
Brother of G.Moore.

Leon MOORE (1892-93) RHB Maitland
b. West Maitland, Feb. 8, 1871. d. Maitland, Sept 11, 1934.

Tour: New South Wales to New Zealand 1893-94.
Brother of W.H.Moore; son of J.Moore.

William Henry ('Frosty') MOORE (1893-94) RHB/WK Maitland
b. West Maitland, Oct. 16, 1864. d. Lane Cove, Feb. 25, 1956.
Western Australia 1898-99. Son of G.Moore.

George MORGAN (1874-75) RHB Albert
b. Bathurst, 1843. Shot himself on Sydney Domain, July 17, 1896.

John Gordon MORGAN (1921-22) RHB/RM Glebe
b. Camperdown, March 6, 1893. d. Concord, May 7, 1967.

John Rodger? MORONEY (1945-46) RHB Marrickville/Petersham-Marrickville
b. Randwick, Oct. 17, 1919. Add: 7 Jindalee Ave., Dapto.
Tests: 7 Tour: South Africa 1949-50.

Arthur Robert MORRIS (1940-41) LHB/SLC St. George/Paddington
b. Dungog, Jan. 19, 1922. Add: 51 College St., Drummoyne.
Tests: 46 Tours: England 1948, 1953; South Africa 1949-50; West Indies 1955; Cavaliers to India and South Africa 1962-63. Defence Fund Match (India) 1963-64.

John Humphrey MORRIS (1858-59) RHB/Long-stop Marylebone
b. Sydney, June 5, 1831. d. Glebe Point, Dec. 9, 1921.

Norman O'Neil MORRIS (1928-29) RHB/LB Petersham
b. Camperdown, May 9, 1907. Add: 48 Marlborough St., Leichardt.

Charles Vincent ('Tug') MORRISSEY (1924-25) RHB/RFM Newcastle/Singleton
b. Corowa, April 26, 1903. d. Quirindi, Feb. 20, 1938.

Henry MOSES (1881-82) LHB/RAB Albert/Belvidere/Canterbury
b. Windsor, Feb. 13, 1858. d. Strathfield, Dec. 7, 1938.
Tests: 6

Ronald Barber MOSS (1948-49) RHB St. George
b. Alexandria, June 13, 1922. Add: 54 Carabella Road, Caringah.

Harold MUDGE (1935-36) RHB/LBG Glebe/Paddington/Waverley
b. Stanmore, Feb. 14, 1914. Add: 526 Pennant Hills Road, West Pennant Hills.
Tour: Cahn to Ceylon 1936-37. Leicestershire 1937. Cahn 1938.

Desmond Antony MULLARKEY (1923-24) LHB St. George
b. Sept. 19, 1899. d. Sept. 1975.
Tour: New South Wales to New Zealand 1923-24.

R. A. MUNN RHB/WK Paddington

William Lloyd MURDOCH (1875-76) RHB/WK Albert/Cootamundra
b. Sandhurst, Vic., Oct. 18, 1854. d. Melbourne, Feb. 18, 1911.
Tests: Australia 18; England 1 Tours: England 1878, 1880, 1882, 1884, 1890; North America 1878; England to South Africa 1891-92.
Non-Smokers 1884. Sussex 1893 to 1899. London County 1900 to 1904. Thornton's XI 1891, 1892, 1893, 1898. Staffordshire XI 1891. M.C.C. 1891, 1892, 1893, 1896, 1898, 1899, 1901, 1902. South 1891, 1892, 1893, 1894, 1897. Gentlemen 1891, 1892, 1893, 1894, 1895, 1897, 1898, 1904. West 1894. England XI 1895.
Author of *Cricket* (1893).

James Joseph MURPHY (1938-39) /RFM Marrickville
b. 1911. Add: 4/242 William St., Kingsgrove.

Richard MURRAY (1855-56) LHB/WK/ LFM(r) Australian/National

b. Sydney 1831. d. Sydney, Nov. 21, 1861.

Henry Charles Edwin NEWCOMBE (1860-61) Albert/National

b. 1835. d. Randwick, Oct. 26, 1908.

Andrew Livingstone NEWELL (1889-90) RHB/RM, OB Sydney/Glebe/Waverley

b. Nov. 13, 1870. d. Heron's Creek, March 8, 1915.
Tour: New South Wales to New Zealand 1889-90.

Percy NEWTON (1907-08) RHB/LM Petersham

A. J. NICHOLLS (1908-09) RHB Redfern

b. Sept. 3, 188?

Charles Omer NICHOLLS (1925-26) RHB/RFM Central Cumberland

b. Freeman's Reach, near Windsor, Dec. 5, 1901. Add: Blacktown Road, Freeman's Reach.

Edwald George ('Ted') NOBLE (1893-94) RHB Carlton

b. Brickfield Hill, Jan 16, 1865. d. Balmain, May 4, 1941
Tour: New South Wales to New Zealand 1893-94.

Montague Alfred NOBLE (1893-94) RHB/RM, OB Carlton/Paddington

b. Sydney, Jan. 28, 1873. d. Randwick, June 22, 1940.
Tests: 42 Tours: England 1899, 1902, 1905, 1909; South Africa 1902; New Zealand 1904-05, 1913-14; New South Wales to New Zealand 1893-94.
Brother of E.G.Noble. Author of 4 books on Cricket,

David James NOONAN (1895-96) LHB/LAB Waverley

b. Sydney, Jan. 8, 1877. d. Sydney, March 10, 1929.
Played for New South Wales only on tour of New Zealand 1895-96.

Rex NORMAN (1918-19) LHB/LFM Glebe/Paddington

b. *circa* 1892, Presumed dead

Otto Ernst NOTHLING (1922-23) RHB/RFM University

b. Teutoburg, Qld., Aug. 1, 1900. d. Chelmer, Qld., Sept. 26, 1965.
Test: 1 Queensland 1927-28 to 1929-30.

Thomas NUNN (1880-81) RHB Carlton

b. Sevenoaks, Kent, 1846. d. Bexley, May 31, 1889.

Richard Nathaniel NUTT (1931-32) RHB Balmain

b. Balmain, June 25, 1911. Add: 7 Barons Crescent, Gladesville.

James Napoleon OATLEY (1865-66) RHB/Long- stop National/Warwick

b. Aug. 14, 1845. b. Cremorne, Dec. 17, 1925.

Charles O'BRIEN (1945-46) RHB Waverley

b. 1921. Drowned at Port Macquarie, Dec. 15, 1980.
Second cousin of J.H.W.Fingleton.

Ernest Francis ('Cobber') O'BRIEN (1926-27) RHB/LBG Newcastle

b. Paddington, Aug. 26, 1900. d. Newcastle, Nov. 2, 1935.

Leslie John O'BRIEN (1937-38) LHB/RF Marrickville

b. d. 1968.

John Denis Alphonsus O'CONNOR (1904-05) LHB/RM Burwood
b. Sydney, Sept. 9, 1875. d. Lewisham, Aug. 23, 1941.
Tests: 4 Tour: England 1909.
South Australia 1906-07 to 1909-10.

David S. OGILVY (1885-86) Warwick/Carlton

William James O'HANLON (1884-85) RHB/WK Carlton
b. Vic., March 10, 1863. d. Randwick, June 23, 1940.

Francis Aloysius O'KEEFE (1919-20) RHB/OB Paddington
b. Waverley, May 11, 1896. d. of peritonitis at Hampstead, Eng., March 26, 1924.
Victoria 1921-22.

Kerry James O'KEEFFE RHB/LBG St. George/N.Sydney/Newcastle
b. Hurstville, Nov. 25, 1949.
Tests: 24 Tours: England 1977; West Indies 1973; New Zealand 1969-70, 1973-74, 1976-77.
Somerset 1971 and 1972.

William Albert Stanley ('Bert') OLDFIELD (1919-20) RHB/WK Glebe/Gordon
b. Alexandria, Sept. 9, 1894. d. Killara, Aug. 10, 1976.
Tests: 54. Tours: England 1921, 1926, 1930, 1934; South Africa 1921-22, 1935-36; New Zealand 1927-28; A.I.F. to England and South Africa 1919; New South Wales to New Zealand 1923-24.
Author of *Behind The Wicket* and *The Rattle of the Stumps*.

Charles Nicholson Jewel OLIVER (1865-66) RHB National/Warwick/Albert
b. Hobart, April 24, 1848. d. Manly, June 14, 1920.

Norman Clifford O'NEILL (1955-56) RHB/RM, LB St. George Sutherland
b. Carlton, Feb. 19, 1937. Add: Sydney.
Tests: 42 Tours: England 1961, 1964; West Indies 1965; New Zealand 1956-57, 1966-67; Pakistan and India 1959-60; Cavaliers to South Africa 1960-61 and to India and South Africa 1962-63.
Koyna Relief Fund Match (India) 1967-68.
Father of M.D.O'Neill (W.A.).

James Bernard O'REGAN (1957-58) /RMF Paddington
b. 1938.

John William O'REILLY (1953-54) RHB/LB Petersham-Marrickville/St. George
b. Mosman, Nov. 16, 1930. Add: 5/22 Thomas St., Parramatta.

William Joseph O'REILLY (1927-28) LHB/LBG N.Sydney/St.George
b. White Cliffs, Dec. 20, 1905. Add: 94 Hatfield St., Blakehurst.
Tests: 27 Tours: England 1934, 1938; South Africa 1935-36; New Zealand 1945-46.
Cricket Journalist; author of *Cricket Conquest* and *Cricket Task-Force*.

Robert Henry OSBORNE (1924-25) RHB/WK Gordon/N.Sydney
b. Feb. 4, 1898. d. Long Jetty, Feb 21, 1975.

Kerry Alfred OWEN (1965-66) RHB Waverley
b. Bondi Beach, June 23, 1943. Add: 3 Fitzalan St., Kambah, A.C.T.

Alfred Heath PARK (1861-62) RHB/Long-Stop National Warwick
b. Oatlands, Tas., April 15, 1840. d. Liverpool, Jan. 16, 1924.

Thomas Griffith PARSONAGE (1932-33) LHB/RM University
b. Chatswood, Nov. 13, 1910. d. Manly, Feb. 3, 1951.

Leonard Stephen PASCOE (1974-75) RHB/RF Bankstown-Canterbury
b. Bridgetown, W.A. (as *L.S.Durtanovich*), Feb 13, 1950. Add: 114 Mimosa Road, Greenacre,
Tests: 13 Tours: England 1977, 1980.

Charles Wright PATRICK (1893-94) RHB Paddington
b. Sydney, Jan. 13, 1867. d. Coogee, Nov. 29, 1919.
Queensland 1901-02 to 1903-04.

Michael Bernard PAWLEY (1969-70) RHB/SLA Manly-Warringah
b. Glen Innes, March 10, 1944. Add: 27 Stella St., Collaroy Plateau.

Reginald Manus PEARCE (1952-53) RHB/LB Balmain
b. Tumbarumba, April 20, 1918. Add: 59 O'Neill St., Guildford.

Arthur **Percival** PENMAN (1904-05) RHB/RF University
b. Ultimo, Jan. 23, 1885. d. Wahroonga, Sept. 11, 1944.

Cecil George PEPPER (1938-39) RHB/LBG Petersham
b. Forbes, Sept. 15, 1918. Add: 54 Rossall Promenade, Cleveleys, Blackpool, Eng.
Tours: Services in England, India and Ceylon 1945; Commonwealth to India and Pakistan 1949-50.
Dominions v England 1945. Commonwealth XI 1956, 1957.
Test Umpire (England).

Jack PETTIFORD (1946-47) RHB/LBG Gordon
b. Sydney, Nov. 29, 1919. d. North Sydney, Oct. 11, 1964.
Tours: Services in England, India and Ceylon 1945; Commonwealth to India and Pakistan 1949-50.
Kent 1954 to 1959. Dominions v England 1945. Commonwealth XI 1951, 1952, 1953.

Norbert Eugene PHILLIPS (1922-23) RHB/RM Randwick/Gordon
b. July 9, 1896. d. Sydney, Oct. 3, 1961.

Raymond Berry PHILLIPS (1978-79) RHB/WK Waverley
b. Paddington, May 23, 1954. Add: 15 Mondra St., Kenmore. Qld.
Queensland 1979-80, 1980-81.

Peter Ian PHILPOTT (1954-55) RHB/LBG Manly
b. Manly, Nov. 21, 1934. Add: Kings School, Parramatta.
Tests: 8 Tours: West Indies 1965; New Zealand 1966-67; Commonwealth to South Africa 1959-60.
Author of *How to Play Cricket*.

G. **Michael** PIERCE (1892-93) /LB Carlton/Paddington
b. *circa* 1871. d. Sydney, Feb. 4, 1913.
Queensland 1894-95.

Colin John PINCH (1949-50) RHB Paddington
b. Brownsville, June 23, 1921. Add: 23 Marine Ave, Hallett Cove, S.Aust.
South Australia 1950-51 to 1959-60.

Walter Edward PITE (1901-02) RHB/OB Sydney/Waverley
b. Sept. 24, 1877. d. Sydney, May 7, 1955.

William Johnstone POCOCK (1872-73) Warwick
b. Clifton, Eng., 1848. d. East Brighton, Vic., Sept. 27, 1928.
Canterbury 1882-83 and 1883-84.
Cousin of G.H.B.Gilbert, W.G.Rees, W.L.Rees (Vic.) and The Graces.

Leslie Oswald Sheridan POIDEVIN (1895-96) RHB Glebe/Redfern
b. Merrila, Nov. 5, 1876. d. Bondi, Nov. 18, 1931.
Tour: New South Wales to New Zealand 1895-96.
London County 1902 to 1904. Lancashire 1904 to 1908. Leveson-Gower's XI 1903. Gentlemen 1903, 1905, 1906. Grace's XI 1907.
Noted cricket writer for the *Sydney Morning Herald* and *Sydney Mail*.

Roland James POPE (1884-85) RHB University
b. Sydney, Feb. 18, 1864. d. Manly, July 27, 1952.
Test· 1 Assisted Australian teams in England 1886, 1890, 1902. M.C.C. 1889,91.

George POWELL (1941-42) RHB/LB Randwick
b. Newtown, April 12, 1918. Add: 5 Allan Ave., Clovelly.

Theodore ('Jerry') POWELL (1872-73) RHB University
b. Berrima, July 10, 1852. d. Sydney, Sept. 3, 1913.

Herbert Graham ('Bert') PRATTEN (1913-14) RHB Western Suburbs
b. Ashfield, April 22, 1892. d. Neutral Bay, Sept. 11, 1979.

Warden Selby PRENTICE (1912-13) RHB/WK Burwood/W.Suburbs
b. Homebush, July 30, 1886. d.Rosebery, Feb. 26, 1969.

David Godfrey PRYOR (1895-96) RHB Maitland
b. Feb. 3, 1870. d. Gosford, Jan. 3, 1937.
Played for New South Wales only on tour of New Zealand 1895-96.

Austin Thomas Eugene PUNCH (1919-20) RHB/LB North Sydney
b. North Sydney, Aug. 16, 1894. Add: 104 Lady Davidson Crescent, Forestville.
Tour: New South Wales to New Zealand 1923-24.
Tasmania 1927-28.

Leslie Walter PYE (1896-97) RHB/LB Central Cumberland
b. Parramatta, July 6, 1871. d. Parramatta, March 9, 1949.

Karl Hugo QUIST (1899-1900) RHB North Sydney
b. Milsons Point, Aug. 18, 1875. d. Plympton, S.Aust., March 31, 1957.
Western Australia 1905-06. South Australia 1908-09 to 1911-12.
Father of international tennis player Adrian Quist.

James Arthur RANDELL (1909-10) RHB/LBG Middle-Harbour
b. Aug. 4, 1880. d. Balgowlah, Dec. 7, 1952.

Andrew Thomas RATCLIFFE (1913-14) LHB/WK Balmain/Paddington/ St. George
b. Sydney, May 3, 1891. d. Banksia, Aug. 31, 1974.
Tours: New Zealand 1920-21; New South Wales to New Zealand 1923-24.

Sydney John REDGRAVE (1904-05) RHB/RM North Sydney
b. North Sydney, Aug. 5, 1878. d. West End, Qld., Aug 3, 1958.
Queensland 1907-08 to 1921-22.

William Gilbert REES (1856-57) RHB Garrison
b. Haverford West, Pembrokeshire, April 6, 1827. d. Marlborough, New Zealand, Oct. 31, 1898.
Cousin of G.H.B.Gilbert, W.J.Pocock, W.L.Rees and The Graces.

Douglas C. REID (1908-09) RHB Burwood
b. Sept 23, 188?

David Alexander RENNEBERG (1964-65) RHB/RF Balmain
b. Balmain, Sept. 23, 1942. Add: 47 Crampton Drive, Springwood.
Tests: 8 Tours: England 1968; South Africa 1966-67; New Zealand 1969-70.

Brian Leslie RHODES (1971-72) RHB/RFM Western Suburbs
b. Paddington, March 7, 1951. Add: Allawah, Gunnedah Road, Tamworth.

Charles Augustus RICHARDSON (1886-87) RHB Belvidere/E.Sydney
b. Sydney, Feb. 22, 1864. d. Waipara, North Canterbury (New Zealand), Aug. 17, 1949.
New Zealand 1902-03. Wellington 1897-98 to 1906-07.

George Biggs RICHARDSON (1859-60) RHB/OB Bathurst/Albert
b. Bathurst, May 28, 1834. d. Dandaloo, May 1, 1911.

Leonard Martin RICHARDSON (1975-76) RHB Waverley
b. Paddington, May 5, 1950. Add: 192 Paddington St., Paddington.
Queensland 1976-77.

William Alfred RICHARDSON (1887-88) RHB/RFM Belvidere/E.Sydney
b. Sydney, Aug. 22, 1866. d. Mosman, Jan. 3, 1930.
Brother of C.A.Richardson.

Frank Macquarie RIDGE (1895-96) RHB Manly
b. Jan. 10, 1873. d. Manly, May 25, 1959.
Played only on New South Wales tour of New Zealand 1895-96.
Cousin of S.P.Jones.

Stephen John RIXON (1974-75) RHB/WK Waverley/W.Suburbs/Sutherland
b. Albury, Feb. 25, 1954. Add: 10/1 Hamilton St., Allawah.
Tests: 10 Tours: England 1981; West Indies 1978. Sri Lanka 1981.

Anderson Montgomery Everton ROBERTS (1976-77) RHB/RF Sutherland
b. Urlings, Antigua, Jan. 29, 1951.
Tests: 38 for West Indies Tours: West Indies to England 1976, 1980; to Australia 1975-76, 1979-80; to India, Sri Lanka and Pakistan 1974-75. to New Zealand 1979-80.
West Indies (domestic) 1969-70 to date. Hampshire 1973 to 1977. Leicestershire 1981.

William ROBERTS (1880-81) /WK Belvidere/University

Henry Joseph Wickham ROBINSON (1889-90) RHB Sydney
b. South Head 1867. d. Mascot, March 24, 1931.
Tour: New South Wales to New Zealand 1889-90.

Rayford Harold ROBINSON (1934-35) RHB/LBG Gordon
b. Stockton, March 26, 1914. d. Stockton, Aug.10, 1965.
Test: 1
South Australia 1937-38. Otago 1946-47 to 1948-49. South Island (N.Z.) 1947-48.

William Carr ROBISON (1893-94) RHB Canterbury
b. Dec. 14, 1874. d. Sydney, July 5, 1916.

Harry **Owen** ('Tommy') ROCK (1924-25) RHB University
b. Scone, Oct. 18, 1896. d. Manly, March 9, 1978.
Son of C.W.Rock (Cambridge University and Tasmania)

William **John** ROGERS (1968-69) RHB St. George
b. Gosford, May 7, 1943. Add: 24 Pulo Road, Mt. Pleasant, W.Aust.

Arthur William ('Mick') ROPER (1939-40) RHB/RFM Petersham
b. Petersham, Feb. 20, 1917. d. Woy Woy, Sept. 4, 1972.
Tour: Services to England, India and Ceylon 1945.

Gordon Frederick RORKE (1957-58) LHB/RF Mosman
b. Mosman, June 27, 1938. Add: 37 McIntosh St., Gordon.
Tests: 4 Tour: Pakistan and India 1959-60.

Marshall Frederick ROSEN (1971-72) RHB/RM Gordon
b. Paddington, Sept. 17, 1948. Add: 6 Earls Court, Roseville Chase.

Barry Alan ROTHWELL (1963-64) RHB Manly-Warringah/N.District
b. Ryde, Aug. 18, 1939. Add: 85 Cutler Road, Clontarf.

Raymond Curtis ROWE (1932-33) LHB Central Cumberland
b. Harris Park, Dec. 9, 1913. Add: 74 Kliens Road, Northmead.

Frank Walter ROWLAND (1924-25) RHB Mosman
b. March 1, 1893. d. Mosman, Feb. 25, 1957.

Francis ROWLEY (1860-61) RHB/Long-Stop Albert
b. 1836. d. at Woolloomooloo 'of obstinate constipation', June 23, 1862.

Robert Charles ROXBY (1953-54) RHB/LBG Newcastle
b. Newcastle, March 16, 1926. Add: 64 Opey Ave., Hyde Park, S.Aust.
South Australia 1954-55 to 1958-59.

Bernard L. ('Barney') RUSSELL (1920-21) RHB/RFM W,Suburbs/Marrickville
b. Aug. 11, 1892? Presumed dead.

Gregory William RYAN (1934-35) RHB/RFM Newcastle
b. Wallsend, March 13, 1913. Add: 26 Burbong St., Kingsford.

Edward SADDLER (1855-56) /Long-stop Marylebone/National
b. d. Oct. 28, 1874.

Ronald Arthur SAGGERS (1939-40) RHB/WK Marrickville
b. Sydenham, May 15, 1917. Add: 65 Brighton Road, Harbord.
Tests: 6 Tours: England 1948; South Africa 1949-50.

Benjamin Melville SALMON (1924-25) LHB Sydney Church of Eng. Gram. Sch./Mosman
b. Footscray, Vic., Jan. 9, 1906. d. Mosman, Jan. 24, 1979.

Edward SAMUELS (1859-60) National

Warren Joseph SAUNDERS (1955-56) RHB St. George
b. Arncliffe, July 18, 1934. Add: 11 Junction Road, Peakhurst.

Harold SAVAGE (1921-22) /WK Waverley

Albert Edward SCANES (1921-22) RHB Petersham/St.George
b. Aug. 6, 1900. d. Nov. 1969.

Edmund ('Ted') SCANLAN (1877-78) RHB Newtown
b. *circa* 1850. d. Newtown, Jan. 9, 1916.

John Drake SCOTT (1908-09) RHB/RF Petersham/Marrickville
b. Sydney, Jan. 31, 1888. d. Springbank, S.Aust., April 7, 1964.
South Australia 1925-26 to 1928-29.
Test Umpire (10 matches)

Robert Barrington ('Barry') SCOTT (1940-41) RHB/RF University
b. Middle Park, Vic., Oct. 9, 1916. Add: 6 Barnsbury Road, South Yarra, Vic.
Victoria 1935-36 to 1939-40.

E. **Joseph** SEALE (1877-78) Warwick

James SEARLE (1888-89) RHB/WK Sydney
b. Surry Hills, Aug 8, 1861. d. Manly, Dec. 28, 1936.
Tour: New South Wales to New Zealand 1893-94.

Dudley Cecil ('Snowy') SEDDON (1926-27) RHB Petersham
b. July 3, 1902. d. Dulwich Hill, April 18, 1978.

Morris SHEA (1895-96) East Sydney
Played for New South Wales only on tour of New Zealand 1895-96

James SHEPHERD (1889-90) Albert
b. May 24, 186?
Played for New South Wales only on tour of New Zealand 1889-90.

Edward Orwell ('Ned') SHERIDAN (1867-68) RHB/RM(r) Albert/Warwick
b. Sydney, Jan. 3, 1842. d. West End, Qld, Nov. 30, 1923.

B. J. ('Bert') SHORTLAND (1911-12) /LB Gordon

Arthur Harry SIMMONS (1934-35) RHB/RFM Western Suburbs
b. Croydon, Nov. 13, 1909 Add: 77 Grand Parade, Bonnells Bay.

Charles Edward SIMPSON (1909-10) RHB/OB Lismore
b. March 27, 1882. d. Sydney, June 26, 1956.
Tour: New Zealand 1909-10. Queensland 1906-07 to 1908-09.

Robert Baddeley SIMPSON (1952-53) RHB/LBG Petersham-Marrickville W.Suburbs
b. Marrickville, Feb. 3, 1936. Add: 10A Wonga St., Strathfield.
Tests: 62 Tours: England 1961, 1964; South Africa 1957-58, 1966-67; West Indies 1965, 1978; India and Pakistan 1964; New Zealand 1956-57, 1959-60; Commonwealth to South Africa 1959-60; Cavaliers to South Africa 1960-61; Commonwealth to India, Pakistan and New Zealand 1961-62.
Western Australia 1956-57 to 1960-61. Rest of World v England 1966 (Scarborough).
Author of 3 books on cricket.

Arthur SINCLAIR (1867-68) Albert
b. d. Sydney, Nov. 29, 1869.

Clive Vallack SINGLE (1912-13) RHB/RM University
b. Penrith, Sept. 17, 1888. d. Woollahra, July 10, 1931.

Stanley George SISMEY (1938-39) RHB/WK Western Suburbs
b. Junee, July 15, 1916. Add: 5 Avona Crescent, Seaforth.
Tour: Services to England, India and Ceylon 1945. Scotland 1952.

Stephen Mark SMALL (1978-79) LHB Penrith
b. Canterbury, March 2, 1955.

James SMITH (1909-10) Burwood

Cyril Moss SOLOMON (1931-32) RHB Petersham/Waverley
b. Cootamundra, March 11, 1911. Add: 1/12 Woods Parade, Fairlight.

Frederick Robert SPOFFORTH (1874-75) RHB/RFM Warwick
b. Balmain, Sept. 9, 1853. d. Ditton Hill, Surbiton, Eng., June 4, 1926.
Tests: 18 Tours: England 1878, 1880, 1882, 1884, 1886; North America 1878.
Victoria 1885-86 to 1887-88. Smokers 1884. Scarborough Festival 1888, 1890, 1892, 1893, 1894, 1895, 1896, 1897.

George Bagot STACK (1866-67) Albert
b. West Maitland, March 12, 1846. d. Orange, Oct. 7, 1930.

Walter Jaques STACK (1909-10) RHB/LBG University
b. Croydon, Oct. 31, 1884. d. Bathurst, March 26, 1972.
Son of G.B.Stack.

Harold Vincent STAPLETON (1940-41) LHB/LM St. George
b. Kyogle, Jan. 7, 1915. Add: 28 Hopewood Crescent, Fairy Meadow.

Harry Cornwall ('Bob') STEELE (1926-27) LHB Marrickville
b. East Sydney, April 22, 1901. Add: 20 Blandford Ave., Waverley.

John Anthony STEELE (1968-69) RHB Balmain
b. Waverley, Nov. 13, 1942.
Tour: New Zealand 1969-70.

John STEVENS (1970-71) RHB Central Cumberland
b. Feb. 22, 1947. Add:

Gordon Lionel STEWART (1930-31) RHB/RFM Northern District
b. Petersham, June 16, 1906. Add: 41, Toulon Ave., Wentworth Falls.

William Cathcart STILL (1856-57) RHB Royal Victoria
b. in N.S.W. 1820. d. July 5, 1910.
Brother of R.S.Still (Tasmania).

Alfred Ernest ('Magic') SULLIVAN (1904-05) LHB/SLA Balmain
b. Balmain, Dec. 10, 1872. d. Balmain, Sept. 25, 1942.

James Thomas SUPPEL (1946-47) RHB/LB Glebe
b. Warren, Oct. 19, 1914. Add: 109 Francis St., Lidcombe.

Hedley Brian TABER (1964-65) RHB/WK Gordon
b. Wagga Wagga, April 29, 1940. Add: 91 Buffalo Road, Ryde.
Tests: 16 Tours: England 1968, 1972; South Africa 1966-67, 1970; India 1969.

David TAYLOR (1907-08) RHB Glebe
b. Sydney, May 2, 1881.

John Morris TAYLOR (1913-14) RHB Petersham/University
b. Stanmore, Oct. 10, 1895. d. Turramurra, May 12, 1971.
Tests: 20 Tours: England 1921, 1926; South Africa 1921; A.I.F. to England and South Africa 1919.

Joseph Stanley TAYLOR (1911-12) RHB Burwood
b. Nov. 1, 1887.
Wellington 1927-28.

Ross Simeon TAYLOR (1959-60) RHB/RFM Manly-Warringah
b. Tamworth, May 8, 1938. Add: RMB/211 Hallsville.

Allen Norman THATCHER (1920-21) RHB/LBG Marrickville
b. Sydney, April 1899. d. of quinsy at Dulwich Hill, Feb. 12, 1932.

Henry John Thomas THEAK (1929-30) LHB/RF St. George
b. Pyrmont, March 19, 1909. d. Narwee, Sept. 14, 1979.

Grahame THOMAS (1957-58) RHB Bankstown-Canterbury
b. Croydon Park, March 21, 1938. Add: 89 Carthage St., Tamworth.
Tests: 8 Tours: South Africa 1966-67; West Indies 1965; New Zealand 1959-60. Rest of World v England 1966 (Scarborough).

G. A. ('Goldie') THOMAS (1909-10) RHB Sydney
b. April 30, 188?

C. D. THOMPSON (1869-70) /Long-stop

Kerry William THOMPSON (1977-78) RHB/WK Newcastle
b. Wallsend, Dec. 12, 1949. Add: 18 Arkana Close, New Lambton Heights.

Nathaniel THOMPSON (1857-58) RHB/RM(r)/WK Union/National/Warwick/Albert
b. Birmingham, Eng., April 21, 1838. d. Burwood, Sept. 2, 1896.
Tests: 2

Jeffrey Robert THOMSON (1972-73) RHB/RF Bankstown/Canterbury
b. Greenacre, Aug. 16, 1950. Add: Bulimba, Qld.
Tests: 34 Tours: England 1975, 1977, 1980; West Indies 1978.
Queensland 1974-75 to 1980-81.

Edwin TINDALL (1874-75) RHB/RM Newtown/Albert
b. March 31, 1851. d. Marrickville, Jan. 16, 1926.

John Andrew TOOHER (1875-76) RHB East Sydney
b. Nov. 18, 1846. d. Neutral Bay, May 23, 1941.
Umpired 2nd Test 1891-92.

Peter Michael TOOHEY (1974-75) RHB Western Suburbs/Mosman-Mid. Harbour
b. Blayney, April 20, 1954.
Tests: 15 Tour: West Indies 1978.

Ernest Raymond Herbert TOSHACK (1945-46) RHB/LM Marrickville/Randwick
b. Cobar, Dec. 15, 1914. Add: 27 Havilah Ave., Wahroonga.
Tests: 12 Tours: England 1948; New Zealand 1945-46.

Claude John TOZER (1910-11) RHB University/Gordon
b. Sydney, Sept. 27, 1890. Shot himself at Lindfield, Dec. 21, 1920.
Nephew of P.C.Charlton.

John Cassimar TREANOR (1954-55) LHB/LBG Central Cumberland
b. Darlinghurst, Aug. 17, 1922. Add: 7 Frederick Ave., Granville.

Edwin ('Ted') TRENERRY (1919-20) RHB/RFM University/Paddington
b. Queanbeyan, Feb. 24, 1897. Add: 8 Fullarton St., Woollahra.
Brother of W.L.Trenerry.

William Leo TRENERRY (1920-21) RHB/LB Paddington/Mosman Glebe
b. Queanbeyan, Nov. 29, 1892. d. Mosman, Sept. 4, 1975.
Tour: A.I.F. to England and South Africa 1919.

Geoffrey Stanley TRUEMAN (1951-52) RHB/WK Balmain
b. Double Bay, Jan. 7, 1926. d. Sydney, June 28, 1981.

Victor TRUMPER (1940-41) LHB/RFM Manly
b. Chatswood, Oct. 14, 1913. d. Sydney, Aug. 31, 1981.
Son of V.T.Trumper.

Victor Thomas TRUMPER (1894-95) RHB/RM South Sydney/Paddington/Gordon
b. Darlinghurst, Nov. 2, 1877. d. Darlinghurst, June 28, 1915.
Tests: 48 Tours: England 1899, 1902, 1905, 1909; South Africa 1902; New Zealand 1904-05, 1913-14.

William TUNKS (1855-56) Marylebone
b. Nepean River district, April 8, 1816. d. St Leonards, April 12, 1883.

Alan TURNER (1968-69) LHB Randwick
b. Camperdown, July 23, 1950. Add: 1 Larose Ave., Matraville.
Tests: 14 Tours: England 1975; New Zealand 1969-70, 1976-77.

Charles Thomas Biass TURNER (1882-83) RHB/RMF Carlton/East Sydney/Goulburn
b. Bathurst, Nov. 16, 1862. d. Manly, Jan. 1, 1944.
Tests: 17 Tours: England 1888, 1890, 1893.
Author of *The Quest For Bowlers*; co.editor of *Australian Cricket : A Weekly Record (1896)*.
Brother-in-law of A.E.A.Goldman (Queensland)

Ernest Richard TWEEDDALE (1925-26) RHB/RF Western Suburbs
b. Newtown, Aug. 23, 1895. d. Dover Heights, May 28, 1956.

TWOPENNY (Murrumgunarriman) (1869-70) /RF(r) Newtown
b. *circa* 1845 d. West Maitland, March 12, 1883.

Leonard VAUGHAN (1925-26) RHB St. George
b. 1907 d. 1960 or 1961.

Robert VAUGHAN (1855-56) Australian
b. in Aust. *circa* 1834. d. July 12, 1865 following an epileptic fit on board the barque *Novelty* en route from New Zealand to Australia.

Robert Trevor VIDLER (1977-78) RHB Bankstown-Canterbury
b. Feb. 5, 1957. Add: 61 Temple St., Greenacre.

Ernest Frederick ('Mick') WADDY (1902-03) RHB University/Central Cumberland/Hunter River
b. Morpeth, Oct. 5, 1880. d. Evesham, Eng., Sept 23, 1958.
Warwickshire 1919-1922. Brother of E.L.Waddy and P.S.Waddy (O.U.)

Edgar Lloyd ('Gar') WADDY (1896-97) RHB/RM Central Cumberland/Newcastle/Gordon
b. Morpeth, Dec. 3, 1878. d. Collaroy, Aug. 2, 1963.
Tours: New Zealand 1913-14, 1920-21.

Frank H. WADE (1895-96) North Sydney
b. Sept. 1, 1871. d. Lindfield, Oct. 4, 1940.
Played for New South Wales only on tour of New Zealand 1895-96.

Isaac F. ('Ike') WALES (1886-87) /WK Warwick/Carlton
b. *circa* 1868. d. *circa* 1942.

Sydney Rundle WALFORD (1892-93) RHB I Zingari/ Central Cumberland
b. Darlinghurst, Nov. 19, 1859. d. Woollahra, July 2, 1949.
Tours: New South Wales to New Zealand 1893-94, 1895-96.

Alan Keith WALKER (1948-49) RHB/LF Manly
b. Manly, Oct. 4, 1925. Add: 40 Curban St., Balgowlah.
Tour: South Africa 1949-50. Nottinghamshire 1954 to 1958.

John Lyall WALL (1914-15) LHB/LFM Sydney/Paddington/Waverley/Balmain/St. George
b. Birchgrove, Oct. 25, 1891. d. West Pymble, June 9, 1969.

Walter Thomas WALMSLEY (1945-46) RHB/LBG Western Suburbs
b. Homebush, March 16, 1916. d. Hamilton, New Zealand, Feb. 25, 1978.
Tasmania 1947-48. Queensland 1954-55 to 1958-59. Northern Districts (N.Z.) 1958-59 1959-60. Commonwealth XI 1953. (Kingston upon Thames)

John Edward WALSH (1939-40) LHB/SLC Petersham
b. Sydney, Dec. 4, 1912. d. Wallsend, May 20, 1980.
Tours: Cahn to Ceylon 1936-37 and New Zealand 1938-39.
Leicestershire 1937 to 1956. Cahn 1938.

Francis Henry WALTERS (1895-96) RHB/RM South Sydney
b. East Melbourne, Vic., Feb. 9, 1860. d. at sea near Bombay, June 1, 1922.
Test: 1 Tour: England 1890.
Victoria 1880-81 to 1893-94.

Kevin **Douglas** WALTERS (1962-63) RHB/RM Central Cumberland
b. Dungog, Dec. 21, 1945. Add: 13 Lanceley Ave., Carlingford.
Tests: 74 Tours: England 1968, 1972, 1975, 1977; Ceylon, India and South Africa 1969-70; West Indies 1973; New Zealand 1973-74 and 1976-77.
Governor General's XI v West Indies (Auckland) 1968-69.

Edward Wolstenholme WARD (1856-57) RHB/LF(r) Garrison/Royal Victoria/Albert
b. Calcutta, Aug. 17, 1823. d. Cannes, France, Feb. 5, 1890.

Maxwell John WARD (1936-37) LHB Randwick
b. Randwick, Feb. 3, 1907. Add: 20 Ambrose St., Toronto.

John Russell WATKINS (1971-72) RHB/LBG Newcastle
b. Newcastle, April 16, 1943. Add: 207 Kemp St., Hamilton.
Test: 1 Tour: West Indies 1973.

Bertie Francis WATSON (1927-28) RHB Gordon
b. March 13, 1898.

Graeme Donald WATSON (1976-77) RHB/RM Gordon
b. Kew, Vic., March 8, 1945. Add: 7a/74 Shirley Road, Wollstonecraft.
Tests: 5 Tours: England 1972; South Africa 1966-67; New Zealand 1969-70.
Victoria 1964-65 to 1970-71. Western Australia 1971-72 to 1974-75.

Gregory George WATSON (1977-78) RHB/RFM University of N.S.W.
b. Mudgee, Jan. 29, 1955. Add: 81 Newport Road, Stafford, England.
Worcestershire 1978, 1979. Western Australia 1979-80.

William WATSON (1910-11) LHB Glebe
b. Nov. 10, 1881. d. North Sydney, Feb. 12, 1926.

William James WATSON (1953-54) RHB St. George
b. Randwick, Jan. 31, 1931. Add: 35 Wakefield Road, Strathfield.
Tests: 4 Tours: West Indies 1955; New Zealand 1956-57.

Russell Frederick WAUGH (1960-61) RHB Petersham-Marrickville
b. Sydney, Sept. 29, 1941. Add: 92 Swanview Road, Greenmount, W.A.
Western Australia 1961-62 to 1963-64.

W. **Stewart** WEARNE (1880-81) /LM Carlton/Albert
b. Liverpool, *circa* 1860.

Stuart Edward WEBSTER (1972-73) RHB W.Suburb/Balmain
b. Orange, June 11, 1946. Add: 26 Ashfield Ave., Castle Hill.

Dirk MacDonald WELLHAM (1980-81) RHB Western Suburbs
b. Summer Hill, March 13, 1959. Add: 36 Claremont Road, Enfield.
Test: 1 Tour: England 1981.
Nephew of W.A.Wellham.

Walter Arthur WELLHAM (1959-60) LHB/SLA Western Suburbs
b. Belmont, Sept. 17, 1932. Add: 30 Alexandra St., Concord.

Arthur Phillip ('Billy') WELLS (1920-21) RHB/RM Paddington
b. Paddington, Sept. 4, 1900. d. South Coogee, Dec. 27, 1964.

Henry ('Harry') WHIDDON (1907-08) RHB/LB Middle Harbour
b. 1878. d. Manly, Dec. 19, 1935.

Alfred Becher Stewart WHITE (1905-06) RHB North Sydney
b. Mudgee, Oct. 4, 1879. d. Karuah, Dec. 15, 1962.

Alfred Henry Ebsworth ('Jim') WHITE (1925-26) RHB/RFM Scone
b. Scone, Oct. 18, 1901. d. Darling Point, March 6, 1964.
Cambridge University 1922 to 1924.

Edward Clive Stewart WHITE (1934-35) RHB/LM North Sydney
b. Mosman, April 17, 1913. Add: 5 Garden Square, Gordon.
Tour: England 1938.
Son of A.B.S.White.

John WHITING (1886-87) Carthona

Michael Roy WHITNEY (1980-81) RHB/LFM Randwick
b. Surry Hills, Feb. 24, 1959.
Tests: 2
Assisted Australian Team in England 1981 (3 matches). Gloucester 1981.

Willam Charles WHITTING (1905-06) RHB/SLA Balmain
b. Drummoyne, July 9, 1884. d. Bellevue Hill, Oct. 26, 1936.

William James WHITTY (1907-08) RHB/LFM Newtown Footballers
b. Sydney, Aug. 15, 1886. d. Tantanoola, S.Aust., Jan. 30, 1974.
Tests: 14 Tours: England 1909, 1912; New Zealand 1909-10; North America 1912.
South Australia 1908-09 to 1925-26. Leveson-Gower's XI 1912.

** John Carandini WILSON (1891-92) LHB/LAB Belvidere
b. Feb. 11, 1869. Died of wounds at Alexandria, Egypt, May 21, 1915.

John Warwick WILSON (1968-69) RHB St. George
b. Paddington, Sept. 1, 1947. Add: 65 Castlereagh Rd, Richmond.

John Robert WOOD (1887-88) RHB/RM University
b. Newcastle, April 11, 1865. d. Putney, Eng., Feb 14, 1928.

William WOODS (1874-75) Albert

Gordon Rae WOOLMER (1945-46) RHB/RFM Newcastle
b. Hamilton, Feb. 24, 1917. Add: 194 Ware St., Fairfield.

Charles WORDSWORTH (1907-08) /RM Redfern
Otago 1908-09 to 1909-10.

Alan Edward WYATT (1956-57) LHB/RFM) Western Suburbs
b. Annandale, April 4, 1935. Add: 17 Barnby St., Murwillumbah.

George Walter Carrington YEATES (1949-50) LHB/LB St. George
b. Erskineville, May 5, 1918. d. Kogarah Bay, April 8, 1967.

George Joseph YOUILL (1889-90) RHB Carlton/Glebe
b. Sydney, Oct. 2, 1871. d. Glebe, Dec. 21, 1936.
Tour: New South Wales to New Zealand 1889-90.

CAREER RECORDS

In the details set out below, the first line against each player's name shews his career record in first-class matches for New South Wales; players who appeared in first-class matches other than for New South Wales have two lines of statistics, the second of which shews the player's career record in all first-class matches.

Career records are complete to the end of the 1981 English season.

Name	*From*	*To*	*M*	*I*	*NO*	*Runs*	*HS*	*Avge*	*100*	*Runs*	*Wkts*	*Avge*	*BB*	*5wi*	*10wm*	*c*	*s*
Achurch, C.S.	1921-22		2	4	0	64	37	16.00	-	did	not	bowl				1	
Adams, E.W.	1919-20		1	1	1	18	18*	-	-	53	0					-	
Adams, F.	1858-59		1	2	0	18	14	9.00	-	did	not	bowl				1	
Allen, H.D.	1871-72		1	2	0	3	3	1.50	-	did	not	bowl				-	
Allen, R.C.	1878-79	1887-88	14	28	3	289	41	11.56	-	99	2	49.50	1/4	-	-	6	
	1878-79	1887-88	17	34	3	382	41	12.32	-	117	2	58.50	1/4	-	-	9	
Alley, W.E.	1945-46	1947-48	12	17	3	597	129*	42.64	3	219	5	43.80	2/21	-	-	3	
	1945-46	1968	400	682	67	19612	221*	31.88	31	17421	768	22.68	8/65	30	1	293	
Alleyne, J.P.	1927-28		1	2	0	1	1	0.50	-	did	not	bowl				-	
Allsopp, A.H.	1929-30	1930-31	11	17	1	774	136	48.37	2	6	0					5	2
	1929-30	1935-36	21	34	2	1469	146	45.90	5	25	0					11	2
Amos, G.S.	1926-27	1931-32	5	7	1	54	24	9.00	-	284	8	35.50	5/22	1	-	-	
	1926-27	1936-37	25	45	4	560	93	13.65	-	1936	49	39.51	5/22	3	-	22	
Anderson, A.D.	1971-72	1972-73	3	6	0	49	28	8.16	-	did	not	bowl				2	
Anderson, P.G.	1966-67		8	12	2	98	24	9.80	-	did	not	bowl				16	7
Andrews, C.W.	1928-29	1930-31	8	14	1	302	87	23.23	-	10	0					5	
	1928-29	1936-37	39	73	2	2246	253*	31.63	3	191	6	31.83	2/37	-	-	17	
Andrews, T.J.E.	1912-13	1928-29	74	115	6	4869	247*	44.66	11	2413	82	29.42	5/41	2	-	35	
	1912-13	1930-31	151	222	17	8095	247*	39.48	14	3050	95	32.10	6/109	3	-	85	
Arnott, P.S.	1911-12	1912-13	6	11	2	280	80*	31.11	-	153	3	51.00	2/27	-	-	3	
	1911-12	1913	10	16	3	391	80*	30.07	-	153	3	51.00	2/27	-	-	5	
Asher, O.P	1919-20	1925-26	8	11	3	181	41	22.62	-	609	23	26.47	4/28	-	-	7	
	1919-20	1925-26	14	17	3	230	41	16.42	-	900	39	23.07	4/28	-	-	10	
Atkins, A.A.	1896-97		1	1	0	0	0	0.00	-	did	not	bowl				-	
Austin, S.W.	1892-93	1893-94	8	12	0	176	43	14.66	-	620	53	11.69	8/14	6	1	2	
	1892-93	1894-95	10	16	2	188	43	13.42	-	709	60	11.81	8/14	6	1	4	
Baker, C.R.	1968-69		2	4	1	156	123	52.00	1	did	not	bowl				-	
Bannerman, A.C.	1876-77	1893-94	46	83	5	1942	117	24.89	2	206	8	25.75	3/12	-	-	38	
	1876-77	1893-94	219	381	28	7816	134	22.14	5	656	22	29.81	3/12	-	-	154	
Bannerman, C.	1870-71	1887-88	23	44	3	747	83*	18.21	-	44	0					6	
	1870-71	1887-88	44	84	6	1687	165*	21.62	1	44	0					20	
Barbour, E.P.	1908-09	1914-15	21	34	4	1540	160	51.33	5	361	9	40.11	2/32	-	-	10	
	1908-09	1924-25	23	38	4	1577	160	46.38	5	475	10	47.50	2/32	-	-	11	

Name	From	To	M	I	NO	runs	HS	Avge	100	Runs	Wkts	Avge	BB	5wi	10wm	c	s
Bardsley, R.	1920-21	1925-26	11	14	1	410	87	31.53	-	did	not	bowl				3	
Bardsley, W.	1903-04	1925-26	83	132	11	6419	235	53.04	20	did	not	bowl				48	
	1903-04	1926-27	250	376	35	17025	264	49.92	53	41	0					112	
Barnes, J.C.	1904-05	1912-13	24	40	2	916	82	24.10	-	1150	36	31.94	6/59	4	1	11	1
	1904-05	1912-13	27	46	3	1077	82	25.04	-	1408	41	34.34	6/59	4	1	13	1
Barnes, S.G.	1936-37	1952-53	56	91	4	4733	200	54.40	19	1239	39	31.76	3/20	-	-	32	
	1936-37	1952-53	110	164	10	8333	234	54.11	26	1836	57	32.21	3/0	-	-	80	4
Bates, B.	1959-60	1960-61	10	9	3	52	16	8.66	-	750	26	28.84	4/50	-	-	7	
Beal, J.C.	1855-56		1	1	0	0	0	0.00	-	did	not	bowl				-	
Beard, G.R.	1975-76	1980-81	29	38	5	713	75	21.60	-	1935	78	24.80	5/33	5	1	18	
	1975-76	1981	44	58	8	1063	75	21.26	-	2777	103	26.96	5/33	6	1	19	
Beath, N.R.J.	1946-47	1947-48	7	7	0	44	17	6.28	-	477	11	43.36	2/20	-	-	3	
Beattie, R.G.	1936-37		4	8	0	170	60	21.25	-	did	not	bowl				4	
Beatty, C.	1977-78	1978-79	9	15	1	322	68	23.00	-	did	not	bowl				6	
Beeston, J.L.	1857-58	1860-61	3	6	1	40	18	8.00	-	16	1	16.00	1/16	-	-	-	
Belcher, S.H.	1866-67		1	1	0	9	9	9.00	-	did	not	bowl				1	
Benaud, J.	1966-67	1972-73	34	60	4	2042	134	36.46	3	100	2	50.00	1/5	-	-	20	
	1966-67	1972-73	47	85	6	2888	142	36.55	4	176	5	35.20	2/12	-	-	30	
Benaud, R.	1948-49	1963-64	86	121	10	4116	158	37.08	9	8376	322	26.01	7/18	17	4	106	
	1948-49	1967-68	259	365	44	11719	187	36.50	23	23370	945	24.73	7/18	56	9	255	
Bennett, A.	1930-31		1	2	0	16	16	8.00	-	41	0					-	
	1930-31	1933	17	16	1	254	51	16.93	-	906	24	37.75	4/49	-	-	12	
Bennett, G.H.	1933-34		1	1	0	2	2	2.00	-	62	4	15.50	4/62	-	-	-	
Bernard, S.R.	1970-71	1978-79	29	28	10	122	21	6.77	-	2833	85	33.32	7/85	2	-	4	
Berrie, E.B.	1913-14		1	1	0	0	0	0.00	-	66	4	16.50	3/45	-	-	-	
Berry, W.L.	1918-19	1919-20	3	5	0	98	37	19.60	-	did	not	bowl				2	
Best, L.	1914-15		1	2	1	31	24*	31.00	-	14	1	14.00	1/12	-	-	-	
Bettington, B.C.J.	1927-28		1	2	1	98	69	98.00	-	69	3	23.00	3/35	-	-	-	
	1920	1927-28	4	7	2	153	69	30.60	-	229	8	28.62	3/35	-	-	1	
Bettington, R.H.B.	1928-29	1931-32	5	8	0	152	42	19.00	-	506	10	50.60	3/56	-	-	2	
	1920	1938	86	142	21	3314	127	27.38	4	8496	357	23.79	8/66	21	5	60	
Bill, O.W.	1929-30	1934-35	23	39	3	1308	153	36.33	3	did	not	bowl				13	
	1929-30	1935-36	35	57	6	1931	153	37.86	6	did	not	bowl				20	
Black, G.G.	1903-04		1	2	0	103	72	51.50	-	73	2	36.50	2/41	-	-	1	
	1903	1903-04	2	3	0	104	72	34.66	-	143	2	71.50	2/41	-	-	1	
Blackman, O.C.	1966-67	1968-69	11	21	0	488	88	23.23	-	did	not	bowl				4	
Blaxland, M.H.	1903-04	1907-08	10	15	0	494	94	32.93	-	91	4	22.75	1/4	-	-	10	
	1903-04	1923-24	11	16	0	495	94	30.93	-	91	4	22.75	1/4	-	-	11	
Bogle, J.	1918-19	1920-21	7	12	0	600	200	50.00	3	did	not	bowl				4	
	1918-19	1920-21	15	21	1	911	200	45.55	3	32	3	10.66	2/27	-	-	5	
Bonnor, G.J.	1884-85	1890-91	5	9	0	235	84	26.11	-	32	0					5	
	1880	1890-91	148	244	17	4820	128	21.23	5	470	12	39.16	3/34	-	-	127	1
Booth, B.C.	1954-55	1968-69	93	146	18	5577	177	43.57	11	433	6	72.16	2/53	-	-	63	
	1954-55	1968-69	183	283	35	11265	214*	45.42	26	956	16	59.75	2/29	-	-	119	
Border, A.R.	1976-77	1979-80	25	44	2	1791	200	42.64	4	669	19	35.21	3/32	-	-	19	
	1976-77	1981	84	146	21	6059	200	48.47	16	1371	38	36.07	4/61	-	-	77	

Name	From	To	M	I	NO	Runs	HS	Avge	100	Runs	Wkts	Avge	BB	5wi	10wm	c	s
Bosley, M.W.	1924-25		1	2	0	10	9	5.00	-	82	0					-	
Bowden, A.J.	1899-00	1907-08	10	14	3	462	149	42.00	1	1175	49	23.97	5/70	1	-	9	
	1899-00	1907-08	11	15	3	496	149	41.33	1	1232	51	24.15	5/70	1	-	13	
Boyce, R.C.M.	1921-22		2	4	0	126	50	31.50	-	did	not	bowl				1	
Boyd, T.J.	1966-67	1969-70	4	7	0	107	46	15.28	-	did	not	bowl				2	
Bradman, D.G.	1927-28	1933-34	41	69	10	5813	452*	98.52	21	712	15	47.46	3/54	-	-	17	
	1927-28	1948-49	234	338	43	28067	452*	95.14	117	1367	36	37.97	3/35	-	-	131	1
Bradridge, J.S.	1855-56		1	2	0	4	2	2.00	-	did	not	bowl				1	
Brewster, R.C.	1893-94		1	2	0	7	7	3.50	-	11	0					-	
Briggs, R.E.	1952-53	1954-55	14	23	1	1041	136	47.31	3	13	0					12	
	1952-53	1954-55	15	24	1	1089	136	47.34	3	13	0					12	
Brooks, T.F.	1946-47	1952-53	16	22	10	192	26*	16.00	-	1463	65	22.50	6/54	3	-	10	
Brown, E.	1859-60		1	2	1	10	9*	10.00	-	did	not	bowl				3	-
Brown, E.K.	1920-21		1	2	0	40	25	20.00	-	0	0					1	
Brown, W.A.	1932-33	1934-35	22	35	2	1527	205	46.27	4	17	1	17.00	1/8	-	-	11	
	1932-33	1949-50	189	284	15	13838	265*	51.44	39	110	6	18.33	4/16	-	-	110	1
Brown, W.G.F.	1919-20	1925-26	9	13	3	390	168	39.00	1	15	0					1	
Bryant, R.	1882-83	1884-85	2	4	2	2	2	1.00	-	did	not	bowl				1	-
Bubb, E.R.	1905-06	1908-09	5	10	2	330	77	41.25	-	did	not	bowl				1	
Bubb, R.A.	1924-25		2	3	1	47	24*	23.50	-	179	6	29.83	2/36	-	-	1	
Buckle, F.	1913-14		1	1	0	10	10	10.00	-	did	not	bowl				1	
Bull, E.A.	1913-14	1914-15	3	4	0	111	42	27.75	-	73	4	18.25	2/8	-	-	1	
	1913-14	1919-20	23	33	2	595	42	19.19	-	100	4	25.00	2/8	-	-	8	
Burke, J.W.	1948-49	1958-59	67	105	19	3901	220	45.36	9	1948	60	32.46	6/60	2	-	27	
	1948-49	1958-59	130	204	36	7563	220	45.01	21	2941	101	29.11	6/40	3	-	59	
Burrows, J.	1877-78		1	1	0	0	0	0.00	-	did	not	bowl				-	
Burt, S.J.W.	1928-29	1929-30	2	2	1	52	42*	52.00	-	54	1	54.00	1/22	-	-	-	
Burton, F.J.	1885-86	1895-96	17	28	8	310	47	15.50	-	did	not	bowl				23	6
	1885-86	1895-96	22	38	10	376	47	13.42	-	did	not	bowl				25	7
Caffyn, W.	1865-66	1870-71	5	9	0	114	38	12.66	-	77	2	38.50	2/33	-	-	5	
	1849	1873	200	350	23	5885	103	17.99	2	7772	577	13.46	9/29	49	12	149	
Caldwell, T.C.J.	1935-36	1936-37	3	5	0	48	26	9.60	-	162	3	54.00	2/55	-	-	5	
Callachor, J.J.	1882-83		1	2	1	11	11*	11.00	-	did	not	bowl				-	-
Callaway, N.F.	1914-15		1	1	0	207	207	207.00	1	did	not	bowl				2	
Callaway, S.T.	1888-89	1895-96	33	56	5	931	86	18.25	-	2414	139	17.36	8/98	14	4	26	
	1888-89	1906-07	62	112	8	1747	86	16.79	-	5460	320	17.06	8/33	33	12	48	
Campbell, J.N.	1926-27	1934-35	11	14	1	127	48	9.76	-	1192	29	41.20	6/118	1	1	7	
Campbell, L.	1925-26		2	2	1	28	16*	28.00	-	255	6	42.50	5/132	1	-	2	
Camphin, W.J.	1892-93	1894-95	2	4	0	22	13	5.50	-	did	not	bowl				-	
Campling, C.R.	1922-23		3	5	0	49	19	9.80	-	146	1	146.00	1/62	-	-	2	
Carmody, D.K.	1939-40	1946-47	13	25	0	695	93	27.80	-	65	1	65.00	1/24	-	-	6	
	1939-40	1955-56	65	123	2	3496	198	28.89	2	187	3	62.33	1/0	-	-	39	3
Carroll, S.J.	1945-46	1958-59	43	68	3	2627	126	40.41	6	22	0					20	
	1945-46	1958-59	46	74	3	2811	126	39.59	6	22	0					21	

Name	From	To	M	I	NO	Runs	HS	Avge	100	Runs	Wkts	Avge	BB	5wi	10wm	c	s
Carter, H.	1897-98	1924-25	44	64	10	1262	149	23.37	2	did	not	bowl				81	40
	1897-98	1924-25	128	175	31	2897	149	20.11	2	did	not	bowl				182	89
Carter, W.J.S.	1928-29		1	1	0	0	0	0.00	-	78	1	78.00	1/31	-	-	1	
Chapman, G.A.N.	1924-25		1	2	0	34	28	17.00	-	did	not	bowl				-	
Chapman, R.A.	1972-73		1	2	1	4	3*	4.00	-	did	not	bowl				1	
Chappell, T.M.	1979-80	1980-81	20	34	3	1300	150	41.93	4	283	14	20.21	3/22	-	-	12	
	1972-73	1981	57	96	8	2668	150	30.31	4	426	15	28.40	3/22	-	-	29	
Chardon, D.M.	1975-76		1	2	0	16	16	8.00	-	119	2	59.50	1/47	-	-	1	
Charlton, P.C.	1888-89	1897-98	14	22	4	198	50	11.00	-	1165	55	21.18	7/44	3	1	16	
	1888-89	1897-98	40	65	13	648	50	12.46	-	1937	97	19.96	7/44	6	1	38	
Cheetham, A.G.	1936-37	1939-40	20	38	2	850	85	23.61	-	1254	35	35.82	4/75	-	-	6	
	1936-37	1945-46	24	46	3	899	85	20.90	-	1517	42	36.11	4/75	-	-	7	
Chegwyn, J.W.	1940-41	1941-42	5	8	0	375	103	46.87	1	did	not	bowl				3	
Chilvers, H.C.	1929-30	1936-37	32	41	10	524	52	16.90	-	3604	142	25.38	6/62	11	3	17	
	1929-30	1936-37	34	45	11	548	52	16.11	-	3985	151	26.39	6/62	11	3	17	
Chipperfield, A.G.	1933-34	1939-40	30	51	3	1766	154	36.79	2	1005	22	45.68	4/72	-	-	33	
	1933-34	1939-40	96	129	17	4295	175	38.34	9	2582	65	39.72	8/66	1	1	91	
Clark, J.L.	1953-54		1	1	0	23	23	23.00	-	56	0					1	
	1952-53	1953-54	3	4	2	36	23	18.00	-	169	5	33.80	5/61	1	-	1	
Clarke, A.E.	1889-90	1891-92	8	13	0	166	43	12.76	-	39	2	19.50	2/12	-	-	5	
	1889-90	1901-02	25	44	1	808	76	18.79	-	223	14	15.92	4/25	-	-	12	
Clarke, G.R.C.	1899-00	1901-02	7	12	1	140	25	12.72	-	874	28	31.21	6/133	1	1	13	
Clarke, J.	1859-60	1862-63	3	6	0	14	8	2.33	-	did	not	bowl				1	
Cleeve, J.	1882-83	1883-84	3	5	2	17	8*	5.66	-	238	7	34.00	6/95	1	-	3	
Clews, M.L.	1976-77	1978-79	17	28	4	484	62	20.16	-	1482	41	36.14	6/41	1	-	2	
Coates, J.	1867-68	1879-80	13	22	5	141	36*	8.29	-	784	65	12.06	7/40	4	-	3	
	1867-68	1879-80	15	26	6	158	36*	7.90	-	885	76	11.64	7/39	5	1	3	
Cobcroft, L.T.	1895-96		5	10	1	160	85*	17.77	-	77	2	38.50	2/15	-	-	-	
	1895-96	1909-10	23	42	2	868	85*	21.70	-	652	37	17.62	6/23	2	-	18	
Cody, L.A.	1912-13	1913-14	10	13	1	374	84	31.16	-	did	not	bowl				6	
	1912-13	1921-22	30	41	5	1230	107	34.16	1	112	4	28.00	2/22	-	-	15	
Cohen, M.B.	1939-40	1940-41	10	18	0	574	118	31.88	1	119	5	23.80	4/25	-	-	3	
Colley, D.J.	1969-70	1977-78	71	107	20	2106	101	24.20	1	6513	203	32.08	6/30	6	-	39	
	1969-70	1977-78	87	123	23	2374	101	23.74	1	7459	236	31.60	6/30	8	-	44	
Collins, H.L.	1909-10	1925-26	52	86	5	3622	282	44.71	14	550	16	34.37	2/21	-	-	37	
	1909-10	1926	168	258	10	9924	282	40.01	32	3871	181	21.38	8/31	8	2	115	
Collins, R.P.	1967-68	1975-76	22	41	3	975	88*	25.65	-	910	31	29.35	5/54	1	-	19	
	1967-68	1975-76	23	43	3	1061	88*	26.52	-	910	31	29.35	5/54	1	-	20	
Collins, V.	1941-42	1947-48	2	3	1	76	29*	38.00	-	116	2	58.00	2/33	-	-	2	
Colreavy, B.X.	1899-00		1	1	0	0	0	0.00	-	125	4	31.25	3/93	-	-	1	
Coningham, A.	1892-93	1898-99	13	21	0	235	51	11.19	-	1074	45	23.86	6/38	3	-	17	
	1892-93	1898-99	35	59	2	896	151	15.71	1	2603	112	23.24	6/38	7	-	27	
Connell, T.C.	1896-97		1	1	0	2	2	2.00	-	24	0					-	
	1896-97	1901-02	3	4	1	9	4	3.00	-	133	5	26.60	4/65	-	-	1	
Cook, B.	1940-41		1	2	0	16	15	8.00	-	did	not	bowl				1	

Name	From	To	M	I	NO	Runs	HS	Avge	100	Runs	Wkts	Avge	BB	5wi	10wm	c	s
Cooper, A.F.	1935-36		7	10	5	38	19	7.60	-	613	18	34.05	6/128	1	-	1	
Cooper, B.A.	1928-29	1929-30	2	3	1	35	14*	17.50	-	88	2	44.00	1/9	-	-	2	
Corling, G.E.	1963-64	1968-69	46	65	26	441	42*	11.30	-	4165	129	32.28	5/44	5	-	9	
	1963-64	1968-69	65	78	32	484	42*	10.52	-	5546	173	32.05	5/44	6	-	11	
Cosstick, S.	1865-66		1	2	0	23	21	11.50	-	109	8	13.62	8/109	1	-	2	
	1860-61	1875-76	18	32	0	315	36	9.84	-	998	106	9.41	9/61	11	5	14	
Cottam, J.T.	1886-87	1889-90	6	11	1	269	62	26.90	-	98	3	32.66	2/48	-	-	3	
	1886-87	1889-90	7	13	1	273	62	22.75	-	98	3	32.66	2/48	-	-	4	
Cotter, A.	1901-02	1913-14	38	53	5	947	82*	19.72	-	4005	171	23.42	7/77	10	1	25	
	1901-02	1913-14	113	157	10	2484	82	16.89	-	10730	442	24.27	7/15	31	4	63	
Cotton, E.K.	1952-53	1954-55	6	9	2	191	49*	27.28	-	175	2	87.50	1/26	-	-	3	
Cowley, O.W.	1893-94		7	12	1	266	55	24.18	-	78	6	13.00	3/14	-	-	5	
	1893-94	1896-97	11	17	1	432	135	27.00	1	103	6	17.16	3/14	-	-	7	
Cowper, G.	1888-89	1889-90	6	10	2	211	54	26.37	-	54	3	18.00	3/7	-	-	2	
Craig, I.D.	1951-52	1961-62	55	83	5	3379	213*	43.32	7	53	0					22	
	1951-52	1961-62	144	208	15	7328	213*	37.96	15	127	1	127.00	1/3	-	-	70	
Cranney, H.	1909-10	1921-22	15	29	2	856	144	31.70	1	118	2	59.00	1/19	-	-	7	
Crawford, W.P.A.	1954-55	1957-58	14	21	10	241	86	21.90	-	1325	70	18.92	6/55	5	1	9	
	1954-55	1957-58	37	42	20	424	86	19.27	-	2313	110	21.02	6/55	5	1	18	
Crippin, R.J.	1970-71	1978-79	19	38	3	899	80	25.68	-	3	0					15	
Cristofani, D.R.	1941-42	1946-47	3	6	0	101	31	16.83	-	390	9	43.33	4/97	-	-	3	
	1941-42	1946-47	18	30	2	749	110*	26.75	1	1581	48	32.93	5/49	2	-	13	
Crossan, E.E.	1937-38	1945-46	4	8	1	103	35*	14.71	-	96	1	96.00	1/20	-	-	2	
Cuffe, J.A.	1902-03		1	2	0	30	25	15.00	-	62	1	62.00	1/39	-	-	1	
	1902-03	1914	221	368	32	7476	145	22.25	4	18798	738	25.47	9/38	33	7	126	
Cullen, D.R.	1912-13	1913-14	2	3	1	20	8	10.00	-	254	5	50.80	3/79	-	-	2	
Cullen, W.	1914-15		1	1	0	11	11	11.00	-	39	5	7.80	4/20	-	-	-	
Cummins, F.S.	1925-26	1932-33	11	16	0	264	78	16.50	-	203	2	101.50	1/17	-	-	5	
Curtis, G.T.	1861-62	1865-66	2	4	1	27	14	9.00	-	did	not	bowl				-	
Cush, N.L.	1934-35		1	1	1	0	0*	-	-	50	2	25.00	1/24	-	-	-	
D'Arcy, D.	1862-63		1	2	1	51	34*	51.00	-	did	not	bowl				-	
Davidson, A.K.	1949-50	1962-63	72	100	17	2753	122*	33.16	4	5858	273	21.45	7/31	10	-	54	
	1949-50	1962-63	193	246	39	6804	129	32.86	9	14048	672	20.90	7/31	33	2	168	
Davidson, H.L.	1927-28	1930-31	11	16	0	398	109	24.87	1	did	not	bowl				32	8
Davies, G.R.	1965-66	1971-72	57	101	11	3065	127	34.05	5	2908	86	33.81	6/43	2	-	59	
	1965-66	1971-72	73	121	13	3903	127	36.13	6	3444	107	32.18	6/43	2	-	70	
Davis, H.H.	1911-12	1924-25	12	16	0	393	77	24.56	-	102	2	51.00	1/6	-	-	3	
Davis, I.C.	1973-74	1980-81	34	59	7	1869	156	35.94	4	7	0					17	
	1973-74	1980-81	76	128	9	3985	156	33.48	5	7	0					36	
Davis, J.	1879-80	1887-88	8	14	2	234	85	29.50	-	did	not	bowl				3	
Davis, J.C.	1889-90	1893-94	12	19	5	409	57	29.21	-	did	not	bowl				6	2
Dean, O.H.	1907-08		1	2	0	23	23	11.50	-	did	not	bowl				-	
Deane, N.Y.	1902-03	1908-09	4	6	0	105	54	17.50	-	319	10	31.90	3/58	-	-	1	
Deane. S.	1889-90		2	2	1	26	23*	26.00	-	did	not	bowl				7	-

Name	From	To	M	I	NO	Runs	HS	Avge	100	Runs	Wkts	Avge	BB	5wi	10wm	c	s
De Courcy, J.H.	1947-48	1957-58	50	74	8	2362	114	35.78	2	27	0					36	
	1947-48	1957-58	79	113	11	3778	204	37.03	6	67	0					51	
Devenish-Meares, F.	1901-02		2	4	0	69	55	17.25	-	did	not	bowl				1	
	1898-99	1901-02	3	6	0	101	55	16.83	-	9	0					2	
Diamond, A.	1899-00	1918-19	30	51	5	1608	210*	34.95	4	did	not	bowl				30	
	1899-00	1918-19	35	56	5	1681	210*	32.96	4	did	not	bowl				35	
Dickson, G.D.	1859-60	1871-72	2	4	1	0	0*	0.00	-	did	not	bowl				2	
Dive, P.W.	1924-25		1	1	0	2	2	2.00	-	90	1	90.00	1/90	-	-	2	
Docker, A.R.	1871-72		1	2	0	5	5	2.50	-	24	2	12.00	2/24	-	-	-	
Docker, C.T.	1909-10		1	1	0	15	15	15.00	-	132	9	14.66	5/67	1	-	-	
	1909-10	1919-20	24	32	10	371	52*	16.86	-	1091	58	18.81	5/20	5	-	17	
Docker, E.B.	1862-63		1	2	1	1	1	1.00	-	3	0					-	
Docker, K.B.	1919-20		2	4	0	43	27	10.75	-	did	not	bowl				-	
Docker, P.W.	1910-11		2	3	1	42	41*	21.00	-	79	5	15.80	3/47	-	-	-	
Donaldson, W.P.J.	1945-46	1949-50	20	31	2	875	105	30.17	2	27	1	27.00	1/10	-	-	3	
Done, R.P.	1978-79	1980-81	6	5	0	40	13	8.00	-	453	13	34.84	4/93	-	-	5	
Donnan, H.	1887-88	1900-01	58	102	10	3019	160*	32.81	5	889	24	37.04	3/14	-	-	21	
	1887-88	1900-01	94	160	14	4262	167	29.19	6	1191	29	41.06	3/14	-	-	37	
Donnelly, J.L.	1929-30	1931-32	3	5	0	96	57	19.20	-	did	not	bowl				1	
Downes, F	1881-82	1890-91	6	11	4	40	12	5.71	-	447	13	34.38	4/49	-	-	5	
Driver, R.	1855-56		1	2	0	18	18	9.00	-	did	not	bowl				-	
Duff, R.A.	1898-99	1907-08	38	64	1	2692	271	42.73	6	98	2	49.00	2/29	-	-	19	
	1898-99	1907-08	121	197	9	6589	271	35.04	10	478	14	34.14	2/17	-	-	73	
Duff, W.S.	1902-03		3	6	0	204	67	34.00	-	did	not	bowl				2	
Dummett, W.	1876-77	1877-78	3	4	1	14	6*	4.66	-	did	not	bowl				4	
Dupain, F.H.	1927-28	1929-30	3	4	0	24	10	6.00	-	289	11	26.27	5/44	1	-	2	
Dwyer, E.A.	1918-19	1928-29	3	5	1	65	23*	16.25	-	did	not	bowl				-	
Dyson, J.	1975-76	1980-81	44	80	8	3091	197	42.93	7	0	0					24	
	1975-76	1981	70	125	12	4143	197	36.66	8	2	0					28	
Easton, F.A.	1933-34	1938-39	17	29	6	547	83	23.78	-	did	not	bowl				27	14
	1933-34	1938-39	18	31	7	619	83	25.79	-	did	not	bowl				28	16
Eaton, H.R.	1928-29		1	1	0	7	7	7.00	-	69	6	11.50	4/39	-	-	1	
Ebsworth, N.	1902-03		3	6	0	48	19	8.00	-	did	not	bowl				-	
Edwards, R.	1979-80		5	10	2	324	91	40.50	-	did	not	bowl				4	
	1964-65	1979-80	126	212	25	7345	170*	39.28	14	75	1	75.00	1/24	-	-	111	11
Egan, T.C.W.	1924-25		1	2	1	7	7	7.00	-	54	0					-	
Ellis, L.G.	1964-65		3	2	0	0	0	0.00	-	267	5	53.40	2/31	-	-	-	
Emery, S.H.	1908-09	1912-13	20	34	5	625	80*	21.55	-	2015	72	27.98	7/28	3	1	10	
	1908-09	1913	58	80	15	1192	80*	18.33	-	4355	183	23.79	7/28	11	3	30	
Emery, V.R.	1948-49		5	5	2	42	17	14.00	-	327	6	54.50	4/77	-	-	5	
Evans, E.	1874-75	1887-88	27	47	4	505	51	11.74	-	2169	145	14.95	7/16	15	4	32	
	1874-75	1887-88	65	105	23	1006	74*	12.26	-	3356	201	16.69	7/16	18	4	63	
Everett, S.C.	1921-22	1929-30	28	36	8	363	62	12.96	-	2724	103	26.44	6/23	8	-	14	
	1921-22	1929-30	45	51	9	617	77	14.69	-	3634	134	27.11	6/23	8	-	26	

Name	From	To	M	I	NO	Runs	HS	Avge	100	Runs	Wkts	Avge	BB	5wi	10wm	c	s
Evers, H.A.	1896-97	1901-02	5	8	0	307	138	38.37	1	8	0					5	4
	1896-97	1920-21	19	30	2	624	138	22.28	1	8	0					22	16
Fagan, A.M.	1953-54	1956-57	4	5	1	34	14*	8.50	-	321	10	32.10	3/49	-	-	1	
Fairfax, A.G.	1928-29	1931-32	21	34	2	922	104	28.81	1	1730	71	24.36	5/104	1	-	6	
	1928-29	1934	55	76	10	1910	104	28.93	1	3735	134	27.87	6/54	2	-	41	
Fairweather, R.J.	1868-69		1	2	0	1	1	0.50	-	did	not	bowl				-	
Faithfull, H.M.	1870-71	1874-75	2	4	0	32	24	8.00	-	59	4	14.75	3/16	-	-	1	
Fallowfield, L.J.	1934-35	1941-42	11	19	2	756	101*	44.47	1	71	0	-				2	
Farnsworth, A.W.	1908-09		1	2	0	75	69	37.50	-	did	not	bowl				-	
	1908-09	1919	2	4	0	78	69	19.50	-	did	not	bowl				-	
Farquhar, B.W.	1894-95	1903-04	11	16	1	466	110	31.06	1	83	2	41.50	1/4	-	-	8	
Farrar, F.M.	1914-15		2	3	0	62	27	20.66	-	39	2	19.50	2/16	-	-	5	
Ferris, J.J.	1886-87	1897-98	19	29	3	231	51	8.88	-	1755	102	17.20	8/84	7	1	13	
	1886-87	1897-98	198	328	56	4264	106	15.67	1	14260	813	17.53	8/41	63	11	90	
Fingleton, J.H.W.	1928-29	1939-40	49	80	6	3178	160	42.94	8	30	1	30.00	1/6	-	-	32	1
	1928-29	1939-40	108	166	13	6816	167	44.54	22	54	2	27.00	1/6	-	-	81	4
Fisher, A.D.W.	1903-04	1907-08	3	6	1	94	63	18.80	-	236	6	39.33	2/41	-	-	4	
Fitzpatrick, J.H.	1937-38	1938-39	5	10	0	180	61	18.00	-	132	4	33.00	2/47	-	-	1	
Flockton, R.G.	1951-52	1962-63	34	49	9	1692	264*	42.30	2	1027	27	38.03	4/33	-	-	11	
	1951-52	1962-63	35	50	9	1695	264*	41.34	2	1027	27	38.03	4/33	-	-	11	
Flynn, J.P.	1914-15		2	4	1	27	16*	9.00	-	140	4	35.00	2/43	-	-	2	
Folkard, B.J.	1910-11	1920-21	15	22	1	280	61	13.33	-	1214	45	26.97	7/65	2	-	9	
Ford, D.A.	1957-58	1963-64	63	65	23	545	36*	12.97	-	did	not	bowl				120	57
	1957-58	1963-64	65	67	24	575	36*	13.37	-	did	not	bowl				122	57
Forssberg, E.E.B.	1920-21	1921-22	3	5	0	223	143	44.60	1	142	6	23.66	2/41	-	-	-	
	1920-21	1921-22	8	10	0	298	143	29.80	1	267	11	24.27	2/41	-	-	-	
Foster, T.H.	1903-04		1	2	0	8	8	4.00	-	did	not	bowl				-	
Fox, N.H.	1926-27		2	3	0	10	8	3.33	-	195	6	32.50	2/17	-	-	2	
Francis, B.C.	1968-69	1972-73	32	59	0	1700	132	28.81	3	did	not	bowl				24	
	1968-69	1974-75	109	192	10	6183	210	33.97	13	15	1	15.00	1/10	-	-	42	
Francis, K.R.	1957-58		2	3	1	17	6*	8.50	-	99	4	24.25	2/11	-	-	1	
Furness, A.J.	1895-96		4	6	2	74	43*	18.50	-	did	not	bowl				3	
Garnsey, G.L.	1904-05	1906-07	18	25	3	319	37	14.50	-	1782	80	22.27	6/35	5	2	25	
Garrett, T.W.	1876-77	1897-98	56	98	8	1952	163	21.68	2	2912	124	23.48	6/55	9	2	38	
	1876-77	1897-98	160	256	29	3673	163	16.18	2	8353	445	18.77	7/38	29	5	80	
Geary, A.	1877-78	1882-83	5	9	0	58	22	6.44	-	86	2	43.00	1/9	-	-	1	
Gee, D.A.	1903-04	1913-14	2	3	0	74	43	24.66	-	44	1	44.00	1/17	-	-	1	
Gilbert, G.H.B.	1855-56	1874-75	12	23	0	220	31	9.56	-	160	16	10.00	6/65	2	1	10	
	1851	1874-75	18	34	0	283	31	8.32	-	160	16(12)	10.00	6/65	2	1	13	
Gilmore, F.P.J.	1938-39	1939-40	2	3	2	23	21*	23.00	-	202	5	40.40	3/50	-	-	2	
Gilmour, G.J.	1971-72	1979-80	42	72	10	1913	122	30.85	3	4671	140	33.36	5/59	3	-	44	
	1971-72	1979-80	75	120	18	3126	122	30.64	5	7345	233	31.52	6/85	6	-	68	

Name	From	To	M	I	NO	Runs	HS	Avge	100	Runs	Wkts	Avge	BB	5wi	10wm	c	s
Gleeson, J.W.	1966-67	1972-73	35	46	13	277	25	8.39	-	3230	126	25.63	7/52	7	1	20	
	1966-67	1974-75	116	137	38	1095	59	11.06	-	10729	430	24.95	7/52	22	2	58	
Goddard, H.	1905-06	1910-11	6	9	3	320	108*	53.33	1	215	10	21.50	4/49	-	-	2	
Goffet, G.	1965-66	1968-69	17	32	1	1036	122	33.41	1	76	2	38.00	1/1	-	-	6	
Goonesena, G.	1960-61	1963-64	7	9	1	147	47	18.37	-	662	20	33.10	3/21	-	-	-	
	1947-48	1968	194	304	37	5751	211	21.53	3	16430	674	24.37	8/39	41	8	108	
Gordon, G.H.	1866-67	1867-68	2	3	0	51	31	17.00	-	did	not	bowl				-	
Gorman, F.O.	1862-63		1	2	0	24	19	12.00	-	did	not	bowl				-	
Gorry, C.R.	1907-08	1910-11	11	20	9	84	16	7.63	-	did	not	bowl				20	10
	1907-08	1910-11	19	31	13	143	16	7.94	-	did	not	bowl				26	19
Gostelow, R.E.	1920-21	1924-25	3	6	1	49	28	9.80	-	did	not	bowl				6	1
Gould, J.W.	1891-92	1895-96	11	19	0	346	53	18.21	-	611	24	25.45	4/30	-	-	7	
Gow, F.K.	1909-10	1910-11	6	12	0	186	67	15.50	-	did	not	bowl				2	
	1909-10	1910-11	7	14	0	233	67	16.64	-	did	not	bowl				2	
Gray, A.T.	1922-23	1924-25	7	10	0	146	51	14.60	-	403	13	31.00	3/33	-	-	-	
Gregg, N.M.	1912-13	1914-15	3	4	0	116	79	29.00	-	16	0					3	
Gregory, A.H.	1880-81	1888-89	5	8	0	45	12	5.62	-	24	0					2	
	1880-81	1888-89	6	10	0	45	12	4.50	-	24	0					3	
Gregory, C.S.	1870-71	1871-72	2	4	0	14	9	3.50	-	did	not	bowl				-	
Gregory, C.W.	1898-99	1907-08	30	46	1	1535	383	34.11	2	13	0					10	
	1898-99	1907-08	31	48	1	1546	383	32.89	2	13	0					11	
Gregory, D.W.	1866-67	1882-83	19	34	4	520	85	17.33	-	513	29	17.68	5/55	1	-	18	
	1866-67	1882-83	41	68	7	889	85	14.57	-	553	29	19.06	5/55	1	-	35	
Gregory, E.J.	1862-63	1877-78	14	25	2	409	65*	17.78	-	99	5	19.80	2/14	-	-	10	
	1862-63	1877-78	16	29	2	470	65*	17.40	-	106	5	21.20	2/14	-	-	11	
Gregory, J.M.	1920-21	1928-29	17	24	2	752	152	34.18	2	1644	57	28.84	7/88	2	-	31	
	1919	1928-29	129	173	18	5661	152	36.52	13	10580	504	20.99	9/32	33	8	195	
Gregory, S.E.	1889-90	1911-12	80	136	8	5340	201	41.71	11	107	0					50	
	1889-90	1912	368	587	55	15192	201	28.55	25	394	2	197.00	1/8	-	-	174	
Grieves, K.J.	1945-46	1946-47	10	10	2	330	102*	41.25	1	140	2	70.00	1/10	-	-	14	
	1945-46	1964	490	746	79	22454	224	33.66	29	7209	242	29.78	6/60	8	-	610	4
Griffiths, G.E.	1962-63	1967-68	9	13	0	279	57	21.46	-	544	10	54.40	2/38	-	-	9	
	1962-63	1967-68	19	31	2	649	67	22.37	-	1203	24	50.12	2/28	-	-	14	
Grosser, J.W.	1968-69		2	4	0	68	48	17.00	-	did	not	bowl				2	
Grounds, B.	1903-04	1905-06	2	2	2	5	5*	-	-	31	6	5.16	3/1	-	-	1	
Gulliver, K.C.	1936-37	1945-46	12	16	3	451	72*	34.69	-	883	22	40.13	5/80	1	-	10	
Guy, R.H.	1960-61	1968-69	8	12	2	92	19	9.20	-	697	25	27.88	4/64	-	-	3	
Gwynne, L.W.	1924-25	1926-27	4	8	1	290	138	41.42	1	did	not	bowl				-	
	1924-25	1926-27	5	10	2	333	138	41.62	1	did	not	bowl				1	
Hall, R.	1880-81	1883-84	2	4	1	8	6	2.66	-	did	not	bowl				2	-
Hand, W.C.	1871-72		1	2	0	1	1	0.50	-	did	not	bowl				-	
Hanlin, D.W.	1948-49	1949-50	3	5	1	46	19	11.50	-	190	8	23.75	3/26	-	-	1	
Hartigan, R.J.	1903-04		1	2	1	13	9*	13.00	-	did	not	bowl				-	
	1903-04	1920-21	45	80	4	1901	116	25.01	2	361	9	40.11	3/27	-	-	36	

Name	From	To	M	I	NO	Runs	HS	Avge	100	Runs	Wkts	Avge	BB	5wi	10wm	c	s
Hartigan, T.J.	1907-08		1	2	1	4	4	4.00	-	15	0					1	
Harvey, G.G.	1909-10	1911-12	7	12	1	68	12	6.18	-	did	not	bowl				9	5
Harvey, R.M.	1956-57		1	2	0	27	24	13.50	-	did	not	bowl				1	
Harvey, R.N.	1958-59	1962-63	30	43	2	2263	231*	55.19	7	69	1	69.00	1/22	-	-	30	
	1946-47	1962-63	306	461	35	21699	231*	50.93	67	1106	30	36.86	4/8	-	-	228	
Hazlitt, G.R.	1911-12	1912-13	6	8	1	39	12	5.57	-	574	26	22.07	7/95	2	-	6	
	1905-06	1913-14	57	83	14	876	82*	12.69	-	4906	188	26.09	7/25	8	-	31	
Henderson, F.	1928-29	1929-30	2	2	0	141	101	70.50	1	did	not	bowl				-	
Hendricks, M.	1969-70		9	14	4	143	32	14.30	-	did	not	bowl				31	9
	1969-70	1974-75	41	66	19	799	66	17.00	-	did	not	bowl				99	20
Hendry, H.S.T.L.	1918-19	1923-24	38	57	7	1998	146	39.96	3	2743	105	26.12	8/33	4	1	49	
	1918-19	1935-36	140	206	25	6799	325*	37.56	14	6647	229	29.02	8/33	6	1	152	
Hewitt, R.C.	1865-66	1872-73	7	13	0	133	60	10.23	-	130	8	16.25	3/5	-	-	7	4
	1865-66	1872-73	8	15	0	142	60	9.46	-	139	8	17.37	3/5	-	-	7	5
Hickson, R.N.	1902-03	1907-08	14	22	2	480	89*	24.00	-	44	1	44.00	1/10	-	-	3	
Hiddleston, H.C.S.	1880-81	1888-89	15	25	3	220	37	10.00	-	85	3	28.33	3/39	-	-	8	
Hilditch, A.M.J.	1976-77	1980-81	21	37	0	1352	124	36.54	1	4	0					14	
	1976-77	1980-81	34	62	1	1998	124	32.75	1	4	0					29	
Hill, C.J.	1932-33	1934-35	14	19	4	291	91	19.40	-	913	45	20.28	7/18	2	1	6	
	1932-33	1934-35	15	21	5	304	91	19.00	-	992	45	22.04	7/18	2	1	7	
Hill, K.M.	1964-65	1974-75	14	25	4	388	61	18.47	-	332	11	30.18	3/34	-	-	6	
Hill, S.	1912-13		1	2	0	29	17	14.50	-	did	not	bowl				-	
	1909-10	1912-13	12	22	0	372	62	16.90	-	did	not	bowl				3	
Hilliard, H.	1855-56	1859-60	5	10	1	42	20	4.66	-	27	2	13.50	2/27	-	-	4	1
Hird, S.F.	1931-32	1932-33	14	21	0	697	106	33.19	2	948	31	30.58	6/56	2	-	7	
	1931-32	1950-51	32	49	5	1453	130	33.02	5	1684	59	28.54	6/56	3	-	8	
Hodgkinson, J.	1908-09	1909-10	3	5	0	121	62	24.20	-	did	not	bowl				1	
Hogg, G.C.H.	1928-29		1	1	0	26	26	26.00	-	did	not	bowl				-	
Hogg, J.E.P.	1926-27	1929-30	4	7	2	168	57	33.60	-	did	not	bowl				3	
	1926-27	1931-32	9	17	2	427	71	28.46	-	2	0					6	
Hogue, T.H.	1901-02	1902-03	2	4	1	124	75*	41.33	-	did	not	bowl				-	
	1901-02	1912-13	17	31	2	939	119	32.37	1	806	36	22.38	4/26	-	-	7	
Hole, G.B.	1949-50		1	2	0	29	23	14.50	-	61	6	10.16	3/26	-	-	1	
	1949-50	1957-58	98	166	12	5647	226	36.66	11	2686	61	44.03	5/109	1	-	82	
Holland, R.G.	1978-79	1980-81	15	14	7	37	6	5.28	-	1806	56	32.25	5/82	1	-	10	
Hooker, J.E.H.	1924-25	1931-32	22	28	9	418	62	22.00	-	2097	75	27.96	6/42	4	1	12	
	1924-25	1931-32	23	30	9	421	62	20.04	-	2223	78	28.50	6/42	4	1	12	
Hopkins, A.J.	1896-97	1914-15	52	85	5	2437	218	30.46	6	3235	126	25.67	5/17	6	-	30	
	1896-97	1914-15	162	240	21	5563	218	25.40	8	6613	271	24.40	7/10	10	-	87	
Hordern, H.V.	1905-06	1912-13	10	13	2	168	64	15.27	-	1085	71	15.28	8/81	7	3	9	
	1905-06	1912-13	33	53	9	721	64	16.38	-	3644	217	16.79	8/31	23	9	39	
Horsfield, G.C.	1934-35	1941-42	5	8	1	172	43	24.57	-	1	0					2	
Hourn, D.W.	1970-71	1980-81	41	52	21	196	27	6.32	-	4423	161	27.47	9/77	11	2	12	
Howard, T.H.	1899-00	1902-03	7	11	3	129	64	16.12	-	499	22	22.68	6/59	2	-	2	
Howell, G.	1855-56	1858-59	4	8	0	38	16	4.75	-	did	not	bowl				2	

Name	From	To	M	I	NO	Runs	HS	Avge	100	Runs	Wkts	Avge	BB	5wi	10wm	c	s
Howell, W.H.	1932-33	1935-36	14	19	4	100	20	6.66	-	1216	32	38.00	5/31	2	-	5	
Howell, W.P.	1894-95	1904-05	48	78	17	1350	128	22.13	1	4698	196	23.96	9/52	11	1	47	
	1894-95	1905-06	141	201	51	2228	128	14.85	1	11157	520	21.45	10/28	30	5	124	
Hughes, G.C.	1975-76	1978-79	20	32	5	604	65	22.37	-	did	not	bowl				19	
Hume, A.E.	1895-96		5	8	1	88	36*	12.57	-	381	17	22.41	5/34	1	-	1	
Humphreys, J.	1875-76		1	2	1	5	4	5.00	-	did	not	bowl				-	
Hunt, W.A.	1929-30	1931-32	17	24	4	301	45	15.05	-	1387	62	22.37	5/36	2	-	11	
	1929-30	1931-32	18	25	4	301	45	14.33	-	1426	62	23.00	5/36	2	-	12	
Hynes, L.C.	1935-36	1938-39	16	26	2	430	63*	17.91	-	1277	46	27.76	6/25	1	-	7	
	1935-36	1938-39	17	27	2	436	63*	17.44	-	1359	48	28.31	6/25	1	-	7	
Iceton, T.H.	1877-78		1	1	0	1	1	1.00	-	10	0					-	
Iredale, F.A.	1888-89	1901-02	56	95	4	3359	196	36.91	5	179	5	35.80	3/1	-	-	41	
	1888-89	1901-02	133	214	12	6794	196	33.63	12	211	6	35.16	3/1	-	-	111	
Ives, W.F.	1919-20	1921-22	7	10	4	176	41*	29.33	-	433	21	20.61	4/31	-	-	6	
Jackson, A.	1926-27	1930-31	28	47	6	2303	168*	56.17	8	41	0					6	
	1926-27	1930-31	70	107	11	4383	182	45.65	11	49	0					26	
Jackson, V.E.	1936-37	1940-41	20	35	3	929	88	29.03	-	912	21	43.42	3/30	-	-	7	
	1936-37	1958	354	605	53	15698	170	28.43	21	23874	965	24.73	8/43	43	6	250	
James, R.V.	1938-39	1950-51	29	43	5	1415	111*	37.23	3	126	1	126.00	1/65	-	-	20	
	1938-39	1950-51	45	70	6	2582	210	40.34	4	199	1	199.00	1/65	-	-	23	
Jansen, E.W.	1899-00	1903-04	3	4	0	167	105	41.75	1	6	0					1	
Jeffery, R.F.	1978-79		1	2	0	31	31	15.50	-	26	0					-	
	1978-79	1980-81	14	27	2	854	198	34.16	2	682	15	45.46	4/37	-	-	5	
Jeffreys, A.F.	1872-73		1	2	0	7	4	3.50	-	did	not	bowl				1	
	1872	1879	26	44	3	587	44	14.31	-	did	not	bowl				9	1
Johnson, F.B.	1903-04	1908-09	17	27	11	179	29	11.18	-	1806	64	28.21	5/93	1	-	10	
Johnston, A.E.	1904-05		2	3	0	9	9	3.00	-	did	not	bowl				1	
Johnston, C.W.	1949-50	1957-58	11	20	2	418	68	23.22	-	did	not	bowl				1	
Johnston, D.A.H.	1977-78	1979-80	13	22	2	446	81	22.30	-	did	not	bowl				10	
Johnston, F.F.	1946-47	1950-51	35	43	10	408	46	12.36	-	3623	123	29.45	6/100	5	-	24	
	1946-47	1950-51	36	45	11	423	46	12.44	-	3824	125	30.59	6/100	5	-	25	
Jones, S.	1862-63	1869-70	3	6	0	54	20	9.00	-	48	2	24.00	1/16	-	-	-	
Jones, S.P.	1880-81	1894-95	31	57	2	1268	109	23.05	2	687	19	36.15	5/54	1	-	18	
	1880-81	1908-09	151	259	13	5193	151	21.10	5	1844	55	33.52	5/54	1	-	82	
Jordan, F.S.	1927-28	1928-29	6	11	2	244	65	27.11	-	473	20	23.65	4/18	-	-	4	
Joseph, J.	1889-90		5	6	0	12	7	2.00	-	did	not	bowl				-	
Kelleway, C.	1907-08	1928-29	57	90	10	3031	168	37.88	10	5137	215	23.89	7/35	7	1	43	
	1907-08	1928-29	132	205	23	6389	168	35.10	15	8925	339	26.32	7/35	10	1	103	
Kellick, C.M.	1865-66	1872-73	2	4	0	52	23	13.00	-	did	not	bowl				2	
Kellick, J.	1868-69		1	2	1	0	0*	0.00	-	10	1	10.00	1/10	-	-	-	
Kelly, J.J.	1894-95	1904-05	53	84	17	1521	108	22.70	1	did	not	bowl				81	45
	1894-95	1906-07	185	266	60	4108	108	19.94	3	16	0					243	112

Name	From	To	M	I	NO	Runs	HS	Avge	100	Runs	Wkts	Avge	BB	5wi	10wm	c	s
Kelly, P.C.	1962-63		1	2	0	7	5	3.50	-	did	not	bowl				-	
	1962-63	1966-67	23	43	3	1611	132	40.27	4	47	0					10	
Kermode, A.	1901-02		2	4	2	18	7*	9.00	-	261	9	29.00	4/49	-	-	-	
	1901-02	1908	80	109	24	680	64*	8.00	-	7825	340	23.01	7/44	21	3	33	
Kettle, J.L.	1859-60	1861-62	3	6	1	41	13*	8.20	-	did	not	bowl				-	
King, P.M.	1919-20		1	1	0	72	72	72.00	-	did	not	bowl				-	
Kinloch, J.	1858-59	1861-62	3	6	2	5	3	1.25	-	134	12	11.16	4/14	-	-	2	
Kippax, A.F.	1918-19	1935-36	87	135	16	8005	315*	67.26	32	831	13	63.92	4/66	-	-	35	
	1918-19	1935-36	175	256	33	12762	315*	57.22	43	1099	21	52.33	4/66	-	-	73	
Kissell, R.K.	1946-47	1951-52	11	16	4	372	80*	31.00	-	did	not	bowl				4	
Lambert, O.	1950-51	1956-57	24	29	10	101	15	5.31	-	5	0					50	14
Lampe, W.H.W.	1927-28	1928-29	2	4	0	29	17	7.25	-	185	5	37.00	2/24	-	-	1	
Lane, J.B.	1907-08	1912-13	3	5	0	51	27	10.20	-	did	not	bowl				1	4
Lawes, C.H.W.	1924-25		1	2	0	1	1	0.50	-	129	2	64.50	2/82	-	-	-	
Lawrence, C.	1862-63	1869-70	5	9	0	92	24	10.22	-	261	25	10.44	7/25	2	1	5	
	1854	1869-70	8	13	0	212	78	16.31	-	382	37	10.32	7/25	4	2	6	
Lawson, G.F.	1977-78	1980-81	31	38	8	313	39	10.43	-	2779	106	26.21	5/50	3	-	19	
	1977-78	1981	47	56	14	521	39	12.40	-	3728	152	24.52	7/81	5	-	26	
Leabeater, L.R.	1929-30	1931-32	4	7	0	315	128	45.00	1	did	not	bowl				1	
Lee, T.H.	1962-63	1967-68	26	42	4	756	68	19.89	-	1286	36	35.72	4/19	-	-	20	
	1962-63	1967-68	27	44	4	758	68	18.95	-	1368	38	36.00	4/19	-	-	20	
Leslie, P.G.	1965-66	1968-69	7	11	3	79	30	9.87	-	395	9	43.88	2/17	-	-	-	
Lewis, O.H.	1856-57	1860-61	4	8	0	71	40	8.87	-	119	11	10.81	4/13	-	-	3	
Lewis, T.H.	1856-57	1859-60	3	6	0	21	13	3.50	-	did	not	bowl				2	
Lindwall, R.R.	1941-42	1953-54	50	61	7	1140	134*	21.11	1	4451	196	22.70	7/45	7	1	32	
	1941-42	1961-62	228	270	39	5042	134*	21.82	5	16956	794	21.35	7/20	34	2	123	
Little, R.C.J.	1934-35	1935-36	8	15	0	360	78	24.00	-	45	1	45.00	1/7	-	-	11	
Livingston, B.A.L.	1956-57		1	2	0	8	4	4.00	-	85	5	17.00	4/43	-	-	-	
Livingston, L.	1941-42	1946-47	5	10	2	256	100*	32.00	1	did	not	bowl				2	1
	1941-42	1964	236	384	45	15269	210	45.04	34	50	4	12.50	2/22	-	-	149	23
Loder, R.W.	1926-27	1928-29	2	4	0	54	49	13.50	-	did	not	bowl				1	
Lonergan, A.R.	1935-36		3	6	1	102	39	20.40	-	did	not	bowl				2	
	1929-30	1935-36	43	80	4	3137	159	41.27	9	12	0					14	
Long, E.J.	1911-12		1	2	0	24	24	12.00	-	did	not	bowl				1	-
	1911-12	1919-20	18	22	10	135	24	11.25	-	did	not	bowl				20	12
Lough, W.	1906-07		1	2	1	5	3*	5.00	-	did	not	bowl				1	
Love, H.S.B.	1920-21	1932-33	21	36	3	1018	102	30.84	1	did	not	bowl				26	12
	1919	1935-36	54	90	7	2906	192	35.01	7	19	0					73	29
Loveridge, W.D.	1902-03		1	2	0	10	10	5.00	-	did	not	bowl				3	-
Lukeman, E.W.	1946-47	1949-50	16	29	1	1125	118	40.17	1	did	not	bowl				10	
Lush, J.G.	1933-34	1946-47	18	30	5	522	54	20.88	-	1227	50	24.54	7/72	3	1	8	
	1933-34	1946-47	20	33	5	554	54	19.78	-	1346	50	26.92	7/72	3	1	10	

Name	From	To	M	I	NO	Runs	HS	Avge	100	Runs	Wkts	Avge	BB	5wi	10wm	c	s
Macartney, C.G.	1905-06	1926-27	81	123	13	5581	221	50.73	22	3465	148	23.41	7/85	3	-	32	
	1905-06	1935-36	249	360	32	15019	345	45.78	49	8781	419	20.95	7/58	17	1	102	
McBeth, A.	1899-00	1903-04	22	34	13	125	15*	5.95	-	2168	95	22.82	6/36	4	1	9	
	1899-00	1907-08	28	46	16	215	36	7.16	-	2768	111	24.93	6/36	4	1	13	
McCabe, S.J.	1928-29	1941-42	55	89	5	4556	229*	54.23	9	1732	60	28.86	5/36	1	-	38	
	1928-29	1941-42	182	262	20	11951	240	49.38	29	5362	159	33.72	5/36	1	-	139	
McCaffrey, V.W.	1938-39		5	9	0	124	40	13.77	-	9	0					-	
McCauley, B.V.	1937-38	1938-39	4	8	1	228	76	32.57	-	did	not	bowl				-	
McCloy, W.S.S.	1918-19		1	1	0	0	0	0.00	-	did	not	bowl				2	
	1910-11	1918-19	5	9	0	67	17	7.44	-	216	5	43.20	2/92	-	-	10	
McCool, C.L.	1939-40	1940-41	7	13	3	450	100	45.00	1	615	25	24.60	5/65	1	-	10	
	1939-40	1960	251	412	34	12420	172	32.85	18	16542	602	27.47	8/74	34	2	262	2
McCosker, R.B.	1973-74	1980-81	46	81	10	3326	168	46.84	11	31	0					59	
	1973-74	1980-81	94	169	17	6311	168	41.51	19	36	0					98	
McCoy, B.L.	1920-21	1923-24	2	4	0	46	21	11.50	-	57	2	28.50	1/23			-	
McDonnell, P.S.	1885-86	1891-92	17	33	2	895	239	28.87	2	did	not	bowl				19	
	1877-78	1895-96	166	285	10	6470	239	23.52	7	247	2	123.50	1/7	-	-	99	
McElhone, F.E.	1910-11	1911-12	6	9	0	369	101	41.00	1	did	not	bowl				6	
	1910-11	1911-12	7	10	0	385	101	38.50	1	did	not	bowl				6	
McGilvray, A.D.	1933-34	1936-37	18	28	3	618	68	24.72	-	1037	19	54.57	3/35	-	-	17	
	1933-34	1936-37	20	31	3	684	68	24.42	-	1135	20	56.75	3/35	-	-	20	
McGlinchy, W.W.	1885-86	1892-93	8	15	2	162	34	12.46	-	348	30	11.60	6/62	2	1	2	
	1885-86	1899-00	20	36	2	475	45	13.97	-	1345	71	18.94	6/62	4	2	6	
McGuirk, H.V.	1926-27		2	3	0	0	0	0.00	-	207	4	51.75	3/20	-	-	2	
McGuirk, L.D.	1930-31		1	2	0	17	15	8.50	-	116	2	58.00	1/44	-	-	-	
McIntyre, W.H.	1905-06	1906-07	4	6	1	123	55	24.60	-	did	not	bowl				5	2
Mackay, J.R.M.	1902-03	1905-06	16	26	2	1309	203	54.54	6	did	not	bowl				3	
	1902-03	1906-07	20	33	2	1556	203	50.19	6	did	not	bowl				5	
Mackay, K.	1970-71	1974-75	18	30	2	917	117	32.75	1	196	3	65.33	2/20	-	-	16	
Mackenzie, A.C.K.	1888-89	1906-07	46	82	3	2115	130	26.77	1	did	not	bowl				38	
	1888-89	1906-07	48	86	3	2150	130	25.90	1	did	not	bowl				40	
McKew, C.G.	1911-12	1913-14	12	16	3	72	29	5.53	-	did	not	bowl				17	11
McKibbin, T.R.	1894-95	1898-99	25	40	9	397	75	12.80	-	3822	181	21.11	9/68	17	7	27	
	1894-95	1898-99	57	92	24	683	75	10.04	-	6297	319	19.73	9/68	28	11	46	
McKone, J.J.	1855-56	1857-58	3	6	2	20	18*	5.00	-	93	12	7.75	5/11	2	1	3	
McNamee, R.L.A.	1926-27	1928-29	14	21	11	45	8*	4.50	-	1765	52	33.94	7/21	4	1	5	
	1926-27	1928-29	19	26	11	87	14	5.80	-	2180	72	30.27	7/21	5	1	9	
MacNish, W.G.	1862-63		1	2	0	13	12	6.50	-	did	not	bowl				1	
Macpherson, H.J.K.	1893-94	1894-95	3	5	1	66	32	16.50	-	did	not	bowl				2	
McPhillamy, K.	1904-05		1	1	0	11	11	11.00	-	116	3	38.66	3/51	-	-	-	
Madden, R.H.	1949-50	1959-60	7	11	0	372	100	33.81	1	138	6	23.00	3/24	-	-	3	
Mailey, A.A.	1912-13	1929-30	67	89	32	835	66	14.64	-	9246	334	27.68	8/81	28	6	74	
	1912-13	1930-31	158	186	62	1529	66	12.33	-	18778	779	24.10	10/66	61	16	157	
Mair, F.	1933-34	1937-38	7	7	0	64	39	9.14	-	533	18	29.61	4/69	-	-	1	
	1933-34	1937-38	22	27	5	336	48	15.27	-	1719	76	22.61	5/43	3	-	7	

Name	From	To	M	I	NO	Runs	HS	Avge	100	Runs	Wkts	Avge	BB	5wi	10wm	c	s
Makin, W.	1910-11		2	3	0	102	71	34.00	-	6	0					1	
Maloney, P.I.	1976-77		1	did		not		bat		did	not	bowl				1	
Marjoribanks, H.L.	1958-59		4	6	0	28	11	4.66	-	374	8	46.75	3/38	-	-	1	
Marks, A.E.	1928-29	1936-37	33	53	2	1837	201	36.01	3	283	5	56.60	1/6	-	-	17	
	1928-29	1936-37	35	57	2	2038	201	37.05	3	354	5	70.80	1/6	-	-	17	
Marks, L.A.	1962-63	1968-69	24	44	1	1318	185	30.65	1	0	0					19	
	1962-63	1968-69	33	62	1	1873	185	30.70	2	0	0					22	
Marks, N.G.	1958-59	1959-60	10	15	3	568	180*	47.33	2	did	not	bowl				6	
Marr, A.P.	1882-83	1890-91	12	23	0	294	69	12.78	-	390	11	35.45	3/75	-	-	8	
	1882-83	1890-91	14	27	0	304	69	11.25	-	454	14	32.42	3/50	-	-	8	
Marsh, J.	1900-01	1902-03	6	10	2	40	9*	5.00	-	730	34	21.47	5/34	3	1	2	
Martin, H.	1971-72		5	7	0	202	64	28.85	-	81	0					9	
	1970-71	1971-72	10	13	0	392	64	30.15	-	81	0					14	
Martin, J.F.	1966-67	1969-70	8	12	1	57	14	5.18	-	702	19	36.94	4/63	-	-	6	
Martin, J.W.	1956-57	1967-68	78	111	14	2582	101	26.61	1	8987	293	30.67	8/97	12	-	83	
	1956-57	1967-68	135	193	26	3970	101	23.77	1	13872	445	31.17	8/97	17	1	114	
Massie, H.H.	1877-78	1887-88	17	32	1	664	78*	21.41	-	3	0					11	
	1877-78	1895	64	113	5	2485	206	23.00	1	60	2	30.00	2/39	-	-	35	
Massie, R.J.A.	1910-11	1913-14	16	22	3	199	50*	10.47	-	1820	99	18.38	7/110	7	4	14	
Mather, A.	1885-86	1886-87	3	6	0	71	49	11.83	-	11	0					2	
Mayes, A.D.A.	1924-25		3	6	2	49	29*	12.25	-	196	4	49.00	2/34	-	-	2	
	1924-25	1927-28	10	19	4	297	70	19.80	-	933	21	44.42	4/53	-	-	6	
Middleton, F.S.	1905-06	1909-10	3	6	1	44	22	8.80	-	128	4	32.00	2/24	-	-	2	
	1905-06	1921-22	14	24	1	355	70	15.43	-	911	56	16.26	7/36	5	2	6	
Miller, D.L.	1893-94		7	11	2	86	18	9.55	-	482	30	16.06	4/25	-	-	5	
	1892-93	1905-06	15	25	5	162	21	8.10	-	1045	55	19.00	5/38	2	-	11	
Miller, K.R.	1947-48	1955-56	50	68	6	3538	214	57.06	10	3019	119	25.36	7/12	3	-	29	
	1937-38	1959	226	326	36	14183	281*	48.90	41	11087	497	22.30	7/12	16	1	136	
Miller, N.K.	1935-36		1	2	0	30	12	15.00	-	did	not	bowl				-	
Mills, J.	1857-58		1	2	1	1	1	1.00	-	did	not	bowl				5	
Minnett, L.A.	1907-08	1914-15	9	18	4	196	37	14.00	-	996	37	26.91	7/131	2	-	8	
	1907-08	1914-15	10	20	4	202	37	12.62	-	1107	37	29.91	7/131	2	-	8	
Minnett, R.B.	1906-07	1914-15	20	32	4	1048	216*	37.42	2	889	39	22.79	8/50	1	1	12	
	1906-07	1914-15	55	85	9	2203	216*	28.98	2	2152	86	25.02	8/50	3	1	18	
Minnett, R.V.	1909-10		4	6	0	262	169	43.66	1	did	not	bowl				2	
	1909-10	1912	5	8	1	270	169	38.57	1	did	not	bowl				3	
Minter, E.J.	1938-39		1	2	0	33	33	16.50	-	did	not	bowl				1	
Misson, F.M.	1958-59	1963-64	42	48	9	753	51*	19.30	-	3207	85	37.72	4/35	-	-	28	
	1958-59	1963-64	71	77	17	1052	51*	17.53	-	5511	177	31.13	6/75	1	-	58	
Moore, G.	1870-71	1872-73	3	6	3	22	8*	7.33	-	184	15	12.26	6/56	1	-	5	
Moore, G.S.	1912-13		4	7	1	208	52	34.66	-	81	3	27.00	2/27	-	-	4	
	1912-13	1920-21	8	14	1	343	85	26.38	-	81	3	27.00	2/27	-	-	5	
Moore, J.	1861-62		1	2	0	30	21	15.00	-	26	2	13.00	2/20	-	-	-	
	1861-62		2	3	0	30	21	10.00	-	26	2	13.00	2/20	-	-	-	
Moore, L.	1892-93	1894-95	11	18	1	292	68	17.17	-	23	0					7	

Name	From	To	M	I	NO	Runs	HS	Avge	100	Runs	Wkts	Avge	BB	5wi	10wm	c	s
Moore, W.H.	1893-94		*4*	*7*	*1*	*91*	*31**	15.16	-	did	not	bowl				3	3
	1893-94	1898-99	5	9	1	109	31*	13.62	-	did	not	bowl				4	4
Morgan, G.	1874-75		1	1	0	0	0	0.00	-	did	not	bowl				-	
Morgan, J.G.	1921-22	1928-29	25	40	2	1151	121	30.28	3	1314	30	43.80	4/60	-	-	21	
	1921-22	1928-29	27	44	2	1337	121	31.83	3	1385	30	46.16	4/60	-	-	22	
Moroney, J.R.	1945-46	1951-52	36	60	13	2419	166*	51.46	5	15	0					14	
	1945-46	1951-52	57	93	16	4023	217	52.24	12	15	0					19	1
Morris, A.R.	1940-41	1954-55	50	77	4	4660	253	63.83	17	200	1	200.00	1/5	-	-	30	
	1940-41	1963-64	162	250	15	12614	290	53.67	46	592	12	49.33	3/36	-	-	73	
Morris, J.H.	1858-59		1	2	0	0	0	0.00	-	did	not	bowl				-	
Morris, N.O.	1928-29		4	5	4	15	8*	15.00	-	430	5	86.00	2/27	-	-	2	
Morrissey, C.V.	1924-25	1925-26	6	9	1	85	32	10.62	-	626	19	32.94	6/30	1	-	2	
Moses, H.	1881-82	1894-95	38	71	8	2593	297*	41.15	4	44	1	44.00	1/19	-	-	21	
	1881-82	1894-95	48	89	8	2898	297*	35.77	4	52	1	52.00	1/19	-	-	25	
Moss, R.B.	1948-49		3	5	0	78	52	15.60	-	did	not	bowl				2	
Mudge, H.	1935-36	1939-40	14	26	2	835	94	34.79	-	865	24	36.04	6/42	2	-	12	
	1935-36	1939-40	18	34	2	1060	118	33.12	1	1106	25	44.24	6/42	2	-	15	
Mullarkey, D.A.	1923-24		7	9	0	290	130	32.22	1	did	not	bowl				2	
Munn, R.A.	1912-13	1913-14	2	3	1	62	32*	31.00	-	did	not	bowl				1	2
Murdoch, W.L.	1875-76	1893-94	19	34	3	1346	321	43.41	2	did	not	bowl				17	4
	1875-76	1904	391	679	48	16953	321	26.86	19	430	10	43.00	2/11	-	-	218	25
Murphy, J.J.	1938-39		4	8	5	43	10	14.33	-	469	7	67.00	3/143	-	-	-	
Murray, R.	1855-56	1859-60	4	8	0	47	12	5.87	-	69	9	7.66	5/13	1	-	3	
Newcombe, H.C.E.	1860-61	1862-63	3	6	1	47	23*	9.40	-	did	not	bowl				-	
Newell, A.L.	1889-90	1899-00	25	43	13	477	68*	15.90	-	1662	82	20.26	8/56	4	2	15	
Newton, P.	1907-08		2	3	1	47	27*	23.50	-	211	4	52.75	3/52	-	-	-	
Nicholls, A.J.	1908-09		2	4	0	84	58	21.00	-	did	not	bowl				3	
Nicholls, C.O.	1925-26	1928-29	11	16	1	322	110	21.46	1	1316	35	37.60	5/97	2	-	15	
	1925-26	1928-29	12	18	1	369	110	21.70	1	1388	37	37.51	5/97	2	-	16	
Noble, E.G.	1893-94		7	11	2	215	51	23.88	-	did	not	bowl				9	
Noble, M.A.	1893-94	1919-20	77	124	10	5653	281	49.58	19	5379	230	23.38	7/44	13	2	67	
	1893-94	1919-20	248	377	34	13975	284	40.74	37	14445	625	23.11	8/48	33	7	191	
Noonan, D.J.	1895-96		5	9	3	213	57	35.50	-	329	20	16.45	7/95	2	1	-	
Norman, R.	1918-19	1919-20	7	10	0	128	28	12.80	-	832	31	26.83	5/61	1	-	5	
Nothling, O.E.	1922-23	1924-25	5	8	0	70	25	8.75	-	259	4	64.75	1/26	-	-	3	
	1922-23	1929-30	21	38	2	882	121	24.50	1	1478	36	41.05	5/39	2	-	15	
Nunn, T.	1880-81	1884-85	4	8	1	81	24	11.57	-	19	0	-				2	
	1880-81	1884-85	5	10	1	91	24	10.11	-	19	0	-				2	
Nutt, R.N.	1931-32	1932-33	6	12	1	351	102	31.90	1	did	not	bowl				2	
Oatley, J.N.	1865-66	1868-69	2	4	2	10	4	5.00	-	did	not	bowl				-	
O'Brien, C.	1945-46		1	2	0	22	17	11.00	-	did	not	bowl				1	
O'Brien, E.F.	1926-27	1927-28	3	5	1	19	7	4.75	-	370	7	52.85	5/99	1	-	3	

Name	From	To	M	I	NO	Runs	HS	Avge	100	Runs	Wkts	Avge	BB	5wi	10wm	c	s
O'Brien, L.J.	1937-38	1938-39	7	10	3	76	24	10.85	-	647	19	34.05	3/44	-	-	5	
	1937-38	1938-39	8	12	5	76	24	10.85	-	724	20	36.20	3/44	-	-	6	
O'Connor, J.D.A.	1904-05	1905-06	8	11	3	109	54	13.62	-	820	46	17.82	6/50	4	2	5	
	1904-05	1909-10	50	77	18	695	54	11.77	-	5255	224	23.45	7/36	18	5	32	
Ogilvy, D.S.	1885-86	1886-87	2	3	0	22	19	7.33	-	42	0					-	
O'Hanlon, W.J.	1884-85	1888-89	4	7	1	25	11	4.16	-	did	not	bowl				3	-
O'Keefe, F.A.	1919-20	1920-21	5	7	0	218	83	31.14	-	52	2	26.00	2/17	-	-	3	
	1919-20	1921-22	9	13	0	926	180	71.23	3	230	12	19.16	5/45	1	-	5	
O'Keeffe, K.J.	1968-69	1979-80	65	99	30	1880	81*	27.24	-	5708	211	27.05	6/49	12	1	53	
	1968-69	1979-80	169	233	73	4169	99*	26.05	-	13382	476	28.11	7/38	24	5	113	
Oldfield, W.A.S.	1919-20	1937-38	82	115	12	2393	129	23.23	3	did	not	bowl				165	106
	1919	1937-38	245	315	57	6135	137	23.77	6	did	not	bowl				399	262
Oliver, C.N.J.	1865-66	1872-73	3	6	1	54	29	10.80	-	did	not	bowl				-	
O'Neill, N.C.	1955-56	1966-67	70	115	12	5419	233	52.61	18	1617	46	35.15	4/40	-	-	40	
	1955-56	1967-68	188	306	34	13859	284	50.95	45	4060	99	41.01	4/40	-	-	104	
O'Regan, J.B.	1957-58		6	6	2	42	29*	10.50	-	432	10	43.20	2/32	-	-	-	
O'Reilly, J.W.	1953-54	1959-60	7	8	3	190	41*	38.00	-	346	13	26.61	3/62	-	-	-	
O'Reilly, W.J.	1927-28	1945-46	54	81	20	746	47	12.22	-	5369	325	16.52	9/41	26	7	38	
	1927-28	1945-46	135	167	41	1655	56*	13.13	-	12850	774	16.60	9/38	63	17	65	
Osborne, R.H.	1924-25	1926-27	3	6	0	38	19	6.33	-	did	not	bowl				7	-
Owen, K.A.	1965-66		1	2	0	14	8	7.00	-	did	not	bowl				2	
Park, A.H.	1861-62	1868-69	3	5	0	30	15	6.00	-	did	not	bowl				-	
Parsonage, T.G.	1932-33									15	0					2	
Pascoe, L.S.	1974-75	1980-81	34	37	12	212	51*	8.48	-	3233	137	23.59	7/18	5	1	14	
	1974-75	1980-81	58	61	22	337	51*	8.64	-	5566	236	23.58	7/18	8	1	17	
Patrick, C.W.	1893-94		1	2	0	13	12	6.50	-	did	not	bowl				2	
	1893-94	1903-04	6	12	0	216	61	18.60	-	did	not	bowl				3	
Pawley, M.B.	1969-70	1973-74	11	17	4	153	50	11.76	-	748	20	37.40	4/67	-	-	5	
Pearce, R.M.	1952-53		3	3	2	7	7*	7.00	-	379	15	25.26	5/57	2	1	-	
Penman, A.P.	1904-05	1905-06	5	7	4	45	15*	15.00	-	395	18	21.94	5/48	1	-	-	
Pepper, C.G.	1938-39	1940-41	16	29	5	648	81	27.00	-	1932	57	33.89	6/57	4	-	10	
Pettiford, J.	1938-39	1957	44	72	7	1927	168	29.64	1	5019	171	29.35	6/33	7	-	41	
	1946-47	1947-48	16	28	2	738	87	28.38	-	1558	40	38.95	5/49	2	1	13	
	1945	1959	201	324	48	7077	133	25.64	4	9259	295	31.38	6/134	7	1	99	
Phillips, N.E.	1922-23	1929-30	17	30	2	962	144	34.35	3	770	14	55.00	4/26	-	-	6	
Phillips, R.B.	1978-79		3	5	0	127	57	25.40	-	did	not	bowl				7	-
	1978-79	1980-81	22	31	5	698	85	26.84	-	did	not	bowl				65	5
Philpott, P.I.	1954-55	1966-67	52	79	12	2309	156	34.46	4	4755	153	31.07	7/53	7	2	42	
	1954-55	1966-67	76	109	17	2886	156	31.36	4	7427	245	30.31	7/53	12	2	55	
Pierce, G.M.	1892-93	1893-94	7	12	3	80	32	8.88	-	729	28	26.03	8/111	3	1	5	
	1892-93	1894-95	8	14	4	87	32	8.70	-	838	30	27.93	8/111	3	1	7	
Pinch, C.J.	1949-50		2	3	0	116	54	38.66	-	did	not	bowl				3	
	1949-50	1959-60	63	113	7	4206	146*	39.67	12	242	8	30.25	2/1	-	-	26	
Pite, W.E.	1901-02	1914-15	2	3	0	77	56	25.66	-	did	not	bowl				1	

Name	From	To	M	I	NO	Runs	HS	Avge	100	Runs	Wkts	Avge	BB	5wi	10wm	c	s
Pocock, W.J.	1872-73		1	2	0	6	6	3.00	-	24	4	6.00	3/10	-	-	1	
	1872-73	1883-84	8	15	1	96	28	6.85	-	408	43	9.48	6/18	3	-	3	
Poidevin, L.O.S.	1895-96	1904-05	13	22	3	1097	179	57.73	3	6	0					8	
	1895-96	1908	149	234	21	7022	179	32.96	14	1927	46	41.89	8/66	2	-	160	
Pope, R.J.	1884-85		3	6	0	67	47	11.16	-	did	not	bowl				1	
	1884-85	1902	20	33	7	318	47	12.23	-	19	0					13	
Powell, G.	1941-42	1948-49	4	5	0	63	47	12.60	-	162	1	162.00	1/71	-	-	1	
Powell, T.	1872-73	1884-85	14	25	5	332	32*	16.60	-	40	1	40.00	1/32	-	-	2	
	1872-73	1884-85	15	27	5	335	32*	15.22	-	40	1	40.00	1/32	-	-	3	
Pratten, H.G.	1913-14	1914-15	5	9	0	221	53	24.55	-	did	not	bowl				1	
Prentice, W.S.	1912-13	1920-21	2	2	0	0	0	0.00	-	did	not	bowl				2	-
Pryor, D.G.	1895-96		5	10	0	136	35	13.60	-	did	not	bowl				4	
Punch, A.T.E.	1919-20	1928-29	31	48	2	1665	176	36.19	1	1001	35	28.60	5/33	1	-	22	
	1919-20	1928-29	33	51	2	1717	176	35.04	1	1044	35	29.82	5/33	1	-	23	
Pye, L.W.	1896-97	1905-06	28	45	6	1157	166	29.66	2	1547	62	24.95	5/29	1	-	18	
	1896-97	1905-06	29	47	6	1189	166	29.00	2	1651	62	26.62	5/29	1	-	20	
Quist, K.H.	1899-00		1	2	1	28	25	28.00	-	18	0					-	
	1899-00	1911-12	10	18	2	296	56	18.50	-	300	12	25.00	4/33	-	-	7	
Randell, J.A.	1909-10	1924-25	9	15	2	91	17	7.00	-	827	31	26.67	5/97	1	-	8	
Ratcliffe, A.T.	1913-14	1928-29	35	56	6	1553	128	31.06	3	did	not	bowl				43	26
	1913-14	1928-29	43	65	6	1899	161	32.18	4	did	not	bowl				45	30
Redgrave, S.J.	1904-05	1906-07	7	8	0	259	94	32.37	-	225	4	56.25	3/33	-	-	5	
	1904-05	1921-22	26	45	0	940	107	20.88	1	1540	41	37.56	4/19	-	-	19	
Rees, W.G.	1856-57		1	2	0	31	28	15.50	-	did	not	bowl				-	
Reid, D.C.	1908-09	1909-10	3	6	0	110	38	18.33	-	did	not	bowl				1	
Renneberg, D.A.	1964-65	1970-71	54	71	26	380	26	8.44	-	5793	190	30.48	7/33	8	1	23	
	1964-65	1970-71	90	109	43	466	26	7.06	-	8527	291	29.30	8/72	13	1	35	
Rhodes, B.L.	1971-72		1	2	1	2	2	2.00	-	100	2	50.00	1/40	-	-	1	
Richardson, C.A.	1886-87	1894-95	15	26	5	473	75*	22.52	-	39	0					9	
	1886-87	1906-07	30	50	7	1079	113	25.09	1	193	3	64.33	2/12	-	-	21	
Richardson, G.B.	1859-60	1860-61	2	4	1	8	8	2.66	-	105	15	7.00	6/42	1	-	1	
Richardson, L.M.	1975-76		2	3	1	89	87*	44.50	-	did	not	bowl				1	
	1975-76	1976-77	8	13	1	261	87*	21.75	-	did	not	bowl				4	
Richardson, W.A.	1887-88	1895-96	11	18	4	215	76	15.35	-	577	22	26.22	4/18	-	-	11	
	1887-88	1895-96	12	20	4	237	76	14.81	-	577	22	26.22	4/18	-	-	13	
Ridge, F.M.	1895-96		4	6	0	98	46	16.33	-	25	0					-	
Rixon, S.J.	1974-75	1980-81	62	89	16	1565	128	21.43	3	did	not	bowl				162	22
	1974-75	1981	86	128	21	2192	128	20.48	3	20	0					228	33
Roberts, A.M.E.	1976-77		2	2	1	12	8*	12.00	-	87	3	29.00	2/56	-	-	-	
	1969-70	1981	172	215	52	2396	63	14.69	-	13987	662	21.12	8/47	31	4	39	
Roberts, W.	1880-81		1	2	0	10	10	5.00	-	did	not	bowl				1	1
Robinson, H.J.W.	1889-90	1892-93	6	9	2	118	61*	16.85	-	did	not	bowl				1	

Name	From	To	M	I	NO	Runs	HS	Avge	100	Runs	Wkts	Avge	BB	5wi	10wm	c	s
Robinson, R.H.	1934-35	1939-40	22	39	3	1513	163	42.02	4	618	15	41.20	2/37	-	-	14	
	1934-35	1948-49	46	81	4	2441	163	31.70	4	1654	44	37.59	4/45	-	-	24	
Robison, W.C.	1893-94		1	2	0	15	15	7.50	-	8	0					1	
Rock, H.O.	1924-25	1925-26	5	7	1	711	235	118.50	3	did	not	bowl				1	
	1924-25	1925-26	6	9	1	758	235	94.75	3	did	not	bowl				1	
Rogers, W.J.	1968-69	1969-70	4	8	0	183	65	22.87	-	did	not	bowl				2	
Roper, A.W.	1939-40		2	4	0	15	15	3.75	-	131	2	65.50	1/26	-	-	-	
	1939-40	1945-46	11	15	0	102	28	6.80	-	503	13	38.69	2/9	-	-	11	
Rorke, G.F.	1957-58	1963-64	30	29	9	233	35	11.65	-	1873	67	27.95	6/52	2	-	8	
	1957-58	1963-64	36	35	12	248	35	10.78	-	2165	88	24.60	6/52	3	-	10	
Rosen, M.F.	1971-72	1974-75	21	41	1	1220	97	30.50	-	25	1	25.00	1/21	-	-	13	
Rothwell, B.A.	1963-64	1968-69	36	61	7	1685	125	31.20	1	39	2	19.50	1/2	-	-	10	
Rowe, R.C.	1932-33	1933-34	10	15	3	411	70	34.25	-	61	1	61.00	1/36	-	-	6	
Rowland, F.W.	1924-25		1	2	1	42	22	42.00	-	did	not	bowl				1	
Rowley, F.	1860-61	1861-62	2	4	0	10	5	2.50	-	did	not	bowl				-	
Roxby, R.C.	1953-54		4	5	0	72	38	14.40	-	462	15	30.80	5/84	1	-	2	
	1953-54	1958-59	16	25	4	322	41	15.33	-	1315	26	50.57	5/84	1	-	10	
Russell, B.L.	1920-21	1921-22	3	5	0	63	34	12.60	-	236	7	33.71	4/59	-	-	3	
Ryan, G.W.	1934-35		1	1	0	1	1	1.00	-	31	0					-	
Saddler, E.	1855-56	1861-62	3	5	1	17	7	4.25	-	did	not	bowl				1	
Saggers, R.A.	1939-40	1950-51	40	61	6	1427	90	25.94	-	did	not	bowl				85	30
	1939-40	1950-51	77	93	14	1888	104*	23.89	1	did	not	bowl				147	74
Salmon, B.M.	1924-25	1931-32	5	10	1	323	94	35.88	-	10	1	10.00	1/10	-	-	1	
Samuels, E.	1859-60		1	2	0	7	5	3.50	-	did	not	bowl				-	
Saunders, W.J.	1955-56	1964-65	35	55	3	1701	98	32.71	-	14	0					19	1
Savage, H.	1921-22		1	1	0	2	2	2.00	-	did	not	bowl				3	1
Scanes, A.E.	1921-22	1927-28	10	18	1	434	94	25.52	-	did	not	bowl				5	
Scanlan, E.	1877-78		1	1	0	25	25	25.00	-	did	not	bowl				2	
Scott, J.D.	1908-09	1924-25	35	50	7	634	100	14.74	1	3364	150	22.42	6/48	9	1	19	
	1908-09	1928-29	59	91	15	1113	100	14.64	1	6427	227	28.31	6/48	12	1	34	
Scott, R.B.	1940-41		3	5	2	27	11*	9.00	-	167	5	33.40	2/10	-	-	2	
	1935-36	1940-41	22	33	10	318	49	13.82	-	2137	59	36.22	7/33	3	1	9	
Seale, E.J.	1877-78	1878-79	2	3	0	22	19	7.33	-	did	not	bowl				2	
Searle, J.	1888-89	1893-94	9	15	6	222	45*	24.66	-	did	not	bowl				11	6
Seddon, D.C.	1926-27	1928-29	6	11	1	361	134	36.10	1	did	not	bowl				-	
Shea, M.	1895-96		4	7	1	90	25	15.00	-	99	4	24.75	3/6	-	-	-	
Shepherd, J.	1889-90		5	6	2	61	19*	15.25	-	did	not	bowl				2	1
Sheridan, E.O.	1867-68	1878-79	10	19	1	230	43	12.77	-	82	4	20.50	2/12	-	-	3	
Shortland, B.J.	1911-12		1	1	0	14	14	14.00	-	44	0					-	
Simmons, A.H.	1934-35		2	3	0	47	41	15.66	-	76	1	76.00	1/16	-	-	1	
Simpson, C.E.	1909-10	1910-11	2	4	0	79	55	19.75	-	31	1	31.00	1/17	-	-	3	
	1906-07	1910-11	15	28	2	719	102	27.65	1	566	18	31.44	5/50	1	-	15	
Simpson, R.B.	1952-53	1977-78	67	116	16	5317	359	53.17	15	3355	79	42.46	5/37	2	-	102	
	1952-53	1977-78	257	436	62	21029	359	56.22	60	13287	349	38.07	5/33	6	-	383	

Name	From	To	M	I	NO	Runs	HS	Avge	100	Runs	Wkts	Avge	BB	5wi	10wm	c	s
Sinclair, A.	1867-68		1	2	0	19	12	9.50	-	did	not	bowl				2	
Single, C.V.	1912-13		2	4	0	138	72	34.50	-	96	0					-	
Sismey, S.G.	1938-39	1950-51	20	29	10	227	30	11.94	-	did	not	bowl				64	4
	1938-39	1952	35	52	11	725	78	17.68	-	did	not	bowl				88	18
Small, S.M.	1978-79	1980-81	3	4	0	64	24	16.00	-	did	not	bowl				2	
Smith, J.	1909-10		2	3	1	10	7*	5.00	-	256	6	42.66	2/36	-	-	1	
Solomon, C.M.	1931-32	1939-40	13	24	0	787	131	32.79	1	9	0					5	
Spofforth, F.R.	1874-75	1884-85	12	20	1	163	36	8.57	-	1215	55	22.09	6/122	5	-	10	
	1874-75	1897	155	236	41	1928	56	9.88	-	12759	853	14.95	9/18	84	32	83	
Stack, G.B.	1866-67	1868-69	2	3	1	4	4*	2.00	-	did	not	bowl				-	
Stack, W.J.	1909-10	1912-13	7	13	2	142	58*	12.90	-	746	24	31.08	4/53	-	-	1	
Stapleton, H.V.	1940-41		1	1	0	1	1	1.00	-	38	0					2	
Steele, H.C.	1926-27	1927-28	5	10	0	449	130	44.90	2	16	0					3	
Steele, J.A.	1968-69	1970-71	15	28	3	943	158	37.72	3	23	0					20	
	1968-69	1970-71	22	36	4	1168	158	36.50	3	23	0					27	2
Stevens, J.	1970-71		2	3	0	32	17	10.66	-	did	not	bowl				-	
Stewart, G.L.	1930-31	1932-33	10	14	9	31	7*	6.20	-	701	22	31.86	4/58	-	-	10	
Still, W.C.	1856-57	1858-59	2	4	0	21	9	5.25	-	did	not	bowl				1	
Sullivan, A.E.	1904-05	1906-07	3	5	1	103	38	25.75	-	166	5	33.20	3/67	-	-	5	
Suppel, J.T.	1946-47		1	1	1	29	29*	-	-	129	1	129.00	1/95	-	-	-	
Taber, H.B.	1964-65	1973-74	73	111	21	1489	109	16.54	1	did	not	bowl				207	35
	1964-65	1973-74	129	182	35	2648	109	18.01	1	6	0					345	50
Taylor, D.	1907-08		1	2	0	11	11	5.50	-	did	not	bowl				-	
Taylor, J.M.	1913-14	1926-27	27	42	2	1806	180	45.15	5	did	not	bowl				14	
	1913-14	1926-27	135	195	7	6274	180	33.37	11	53	1	53.00	1/25	-	-	68	
Taylor, J.S.	1911-12	1913-14	2	3	1	46	19	23.00	-	did	not	bowl				1	
	1911-12	1927-28	3	5	1	108	61	27.00	-	18	0					1	
Taylor, R.S.	1959-60		1	1	0	0	0	0.00	-	91	1	91.00	1/59	-	-	1	
Thatcher, A.N.	1920-21	1923-24	3	6	2	93	31*	23.25	-	318	7	45.42	3/76	-	-	-	
Theak, H.J.T.	1929-30	1934-35	23	31	12	196	39	10.31	-	2148	65	33.04	5/41	1	-	10	
Thomas, G.	1957-58	1965-66	68	105	7	4351	229	44.39	15	12	0					61	
	1957-58	1966-67	100	154	12	5726	229	40.32	17	30	0					92	2
Thomas, G.A.	1909-10		2	4	1	176	96	58.66	-	did	not	bowl				1	
Thompson, C.D.	1869-70		1	2	2	3	3*	-	-	did	not	bowl				-	
Thompson, K.W.	1977-78		4	8	0	78	24	9.75	-	did	not	bowl				13	-
Thompson, N.	1857-58	1879-80	24	45	1	621	73	14.11	-	479	22	21.77	3/13	-	-	20	7
	1857-58	1879-80	27	51	1	705	73	14.10	-	512	23	22.26	3/13	-	-	23	7
Thomson, J.R.	1972-73	1973-74	7	9	5	65	30*	16.25	-	664	27	24.59	7/85	1	-	2	
	1972-73	1981	115	138	32	1420	61	13.39	-	10851	452	24.00	7/33	20	3	45	
Tindall, E.	1874-75	1880-81	10	16	3	146	52	11.23	-	567	25	22.68	6/31	2	-	11	
	1874-75	1880-81	11	18	4	148	52	10.57	-	577	25	23.08	6/31	2	-	11	
Tooher, J.A.	1875-76		1	1	1	0	0*	-	-	did	not	bowl				-	
Toohey, P.M.	1974-75	1980-81	51	86	6	3235	158	40.43	9	4	0					34	
	1974-75	1980-81	69	121	7	4398	158	38.57	10	8	0					48	

Name	From	To	M	I	NO	Runs	HS	Avge	100	Runs	Wkts	Avge	BB	5wi	10wm	c	s
Toshack, E.R.H.	1945-46	1949-50	21	24	7	77	14	4.52	-	2010	90	22.33	6/38	3	-	3	
	1945-46	1949-50	48	45	13	185	20*	5.78	-	3973	195	20.37	7/81	12	1	10	
Tozer, C.J.	1910-11	1919-20	6	10	1	410	103	45.55	1	did	not	bowl				4	
	1910-11	1920-21	7	12	1	514	103	46.72	1	did	not	bowl				4	
Treanor, J.C.	1954-55	1956-57	16	23	7	158	21	9.87	-	1633	62	26.33	5/36	4	-	3	
	1954-55	1956-57	17	25	8	197	33*	11.58	-	1746	63	27.71	5/36	4	-	3	
Trenerry, E.	1919-20	1920-21	4	5	1	29	15*	7.25	-	373	16	23.31	6/19	2	1	3	
	1919-20	1920-21	5	7	2	37	15*	7.40	-	451	18	25.05	6/19	2	1	4	
Trenerry, W.L.	1920-21	1924-25	3	5	0	90	70	18.00	-	52	0					4	
	1919	1924-25	38	61	3	1547	82	26.67	-	337	10	33.70	3/28	-	-	22	
Trueman, G.S.	1951-52	1953-54	24	26	9	135	16	7.94	-	did	not	bowl				63	19
Trumper, V.T.	1894-95	1913-14	73	123	9	5823	292*	51.07	15	1154	33	34.96	4/32	-	-	51	
	1894-95	1913-14	255	401	21	16939	300*	44.57	42	2031	64	31.73	5/19	2	-	171	
Trumper, V. jun.	1940-41		6	11	2	73	18	8.11	-	373	12	31.08	3/37	-	-	3	
	1940-41		7	13	3	74	18	7.40	-	433	12	36.08	3/37	-	-	3	
Tunks, W.	1855-56		1	2	0	1	1	0.50	-	did	not	bowl				-	
Turner, A.	1968-69	1977-78	76	142	8	4171	127	31.12	4	10	1	10.00	1/6	-	-	57	
	1968-69	1977-78	105	196	10	5744	156	30.88	7	10	1	10.00	1/6	-	-	80	
Turner, C.T.B.	1882-83	1909-10	43	75	2	1138	70	15.58	-	4256	263	16.18	8/32	29	11	28	
	1882-83	1909-10	155	261	13	3856	103	15.54	2	14147	993	14.24	9/15	102	35	85	
Tweeddale, E.R.	1925-26		3	3	2	3	2	3.00	-	285	6	47.50	4/36	-	-	1	
Twopenny	1869-70		1	2	0	8	8	4.00	-	56	0					-	
Vaughan, L.	1925-26		2	3	0	29	15	9.66	-	did	not	bowl				2	
Vaughan, R.	1855-56	1857-58	2	4	2	14	13*	7.00	-	did	not	bowl				-	
Vidler, R.T.	1977-78	1978-79	4	7	1	184	48	30.66	-	1	0					4	
Waddy, E.F.	1902-03	1910-11	28	44	3	1359	129*	33.14	3	did	not	bowl				29	
	1902-03	1922	55	87	5	2326	129*	28.36	4	23	0					43	
Waddy, E.L.	1896-97	1920-21	41	70	4	2031	133	30.77	4	4	1	4.00	1/4	-	-	29	1
	1896-97	1920-21	58	92	7	2775	140	32.64	6	96	2	48.00	1/4	-	-	41	5
Wade, F.H.	1895-96		5	10	1	145	40*	16.11	-	68	2	34.00	2/46	-	-	3	
Wales, I.F.	1886-87	1893-94	16	28	6	121	21	5.50	-	did	not	bowl				28	5
Walford, S.R.	1892-93	1895-96	13	22	0	351	122	15.95	1	did	not	bowl				5	
Walker, A.K.	1948-49	1952-53	26	28	6	316	42	14.36	-	2238	97	23.07	6/20	5	-	7	
	1948-49	1958	94	118	26	1603	73	17.42	-	6072	221	27.47	7/56	9	-	37	
Wall, J.L.	1914-15	1924-25	11	17	5	153	61	12.75	-	1059	41	25.82	7/133	1	1	14	
Walmsley, W.T.	1945-46		1	2	0	30	16	15.00	-	63	2	31.50	1/20	-	-	-	
	1945-46	1959-60	37	50	11	1064	180*	27.28	2	3861	122	31.64	6/56	3	-	8	
Walsh, J.E.	1939-40		2	3	2	11	10*	11.00	-	131	2	65.50	1/26	-	-	-	
	1936-37	1956	296	460	52	7247	106	17.76	2	29226	1190	24.56	9/101	98	26	209	
Walters, F.H.	1895-96		5	8	2	336	150	56.00	1	11	0					-	
	1880-81	1895-96	56	96	9	1755	150	20.17	4	81	1	81.00	1/17	-	-	31	
Walters, K.D.	1962-63	1980-81	103	279	21	6612	253	41.84	19	4166	119	35.00	7/63	5	-	54	
	1962-63	1980-81	258	179 426	57	16180	253	43.84	45	6782	190	35.69	7/63	6	-	149	

Name	From	To	M	I	NO	Runs	HS	Avge	100	Runs	Wkts	Avge	BB	5wi	10wm	c	s
Ward, E.W.	1856-57	1861-62	4	8	0	27	13	3.37	-	207	27	7.66	6/24	3	1	4	
Ward, M.J.	1936-37		2	4	0	114	68	28.50	-	did	not	bowl				-	
Watkins, J.R.	1971-72	1972-73	5	7	3	12	11*	3.00	-	369	10	36.90	4/72	-	-	6	
	1971-72	1972-73	10	15	8	70	36	10.00	-	726	20	36.30	4/72	-	-	10	
Watson, B.F.	1927-28		2	3	0	88	46	29.33	-	did	not	bowl				1	
Watson, G.D.	1976-77		5	7	0	188	70	26.85	-	180	8	22.50	3/42	-	-	1	
	1964-65	1976-77	107	162	19	4674	176	32.68	7	4709	186	25.31	6/61	8	-	73	
Watson, G.G.	1977-78	1978-79	14	23	9	211	30*	15.07	-	1337	30	44.56	4/98	-	-	4	
	1977-78	1979-80	45	58	15	552	38	12.83	-	3832	102	37.56	6/45	1	-	12	
Watson, W.	1910-11		2	3	0	84	38	28.00	-	41	0					-	
Watson, W.J.	1953-54	1960-61	29	45	4	1418	206	34.58	5	18	0					22	
	1953-54	1960-61	41	66	5	1958	206	32.09	6	40	0					26	
Waugh, R.F.	1960-61		1	2	0	10	10	5.00	-	did	not	bowl				-	
	1960-61	1963-64	14	27	3	569	87	23.70	-	69	1	69.00	1/12	-	-	4	
Wearne, W.S.	1880-81	1887-88	3	6	1	24	11	4.80	-	150	3	50.00	1/35	-	-	1	
Webster, S.E.	1972-73	1977-78	23	44	2	1215	112*	28.92	1	29	0					21	
Wellham, D.M.	1980-81		5	8	2	408	128*	68.00	2	0	0					5	
	1980-81	1981	14	21	6	905	135*	60.33	4	11	1	11.00	1/11	-	-	8	
Wellham, W.A.	1959-60		7	7	3	64	21	16.00	-	442	19	23.26	6/43	1	-	2	
Wells, A.P.	1920-21	1924-25	9	15	2	320	70	24.61	-	did	not	bowl				1	
Whiddon, H.	1907-08		3	5	0	33	11	6.60	-	420	16	26.25	4/53	-	-	1	
White, A.B.S.	1905-06	1908-09	4	7	1	291	147	48.50	1	did	not	bowl				4	
White, A.H.E.	1925-26		1	1	0	11	11	11.00	-	72	1	72.00	1/72	-	-	-	
	1922	1925-26	20	25	6	279	53*	14.68	-	1299	45	28.86	5/66	1	-	9	
White, E.C.S.	1934-35	1938-39	32	55	14	927	108*	22.60	-	2061	73	28.23	8/31	1	-	19	
	1934-35	1938-39	56	81	22	1316	108*	22.30	1	3072	115	26.71	8/31	2	-	37	
Whiting, J.	1886-87		1	1	0	5	5	5.00	-	did	not	bowl				-	
Whitney, M.R.	1980-81		4	2	0	4	3	2.00	-	347	11	31.54	4/62	-	-	6	
	1980-81	1981	11	9	0	9	4	1.00	-	1073	35	30.65	5/60	1	-	9	
Whitting, W.C.	1905-06		1	2	0	1	1	0.50	-	21	0					-	
Whitty, W.J.	1907-08		1	1	0	1	1	1.00	-	145	3	48.33	3/86	-	-	-	
	1907-08	1925-26	119	171	44	1464	81	11.52	-	11488	491	23.39	8/27	26	4	35	
Wilson, J.C.	1891-92		1	2	1	17	15*	17.00	-	21	0					2	
Wilson, J.W.	1968-69	1971-72	12	22	1	619	114	29.47	1	did	not	bowl				7	
Wood, J.R.	1887-88		1	1	0	81	81	81.00	-	97	4	24.25	3/65	-	-	1	
	1887-88		2	3	0	87	81	29.00	-	150	4	37.50	3/65	-	-	1	
Woods, W.	1874-75		2	3	0	18	9	6.00	-	did	not	bowl				3	
Woolmer, G.R.	1945-46		1	2	0	24	15	12.00	-	18	0					-	
Wordsworth, C.	1907-08		1	2	1	16	12*	16.00	-	72	4	18.00	3/24	-	-	-	
	1907-08	1909-10	5	10	1	72	19	8.00	-	407	16	25.43	3/24	-	-	1	
Wyatt, A.E.	1956-57	1958-59	20	23	10	179	40	13.76	-	1338	40	33.45	5/36	2	-	7	
Yeates, G.W.C.	1949-50		6	11	1	299	93	29.90	-	233	6	38.83	2/52	-	-	3	
Youill, G.J.	1889-90	1895-96	14	22	1	372	40	17.71	-	44	0					7	

NOTES ON CAREER RECORDS

1. The career records are compiled from the matches set out in *A Guide to First-class Cricket Matches played in Australia,* published by the A.C.S.
2. E.F.Waddy's N.S.W. XI v Ceylon (Colombo) January 1914 is not included as first-class.
3. R.H.B.Bettington : The last two runs of his innings of 101 not out for Oxford University v H.D.G.Leveson-Gower's XI in 1920 were scored after the winning hit had been made. He is therefore credited herein with a score of 99 not out (see *3Cricket Statistician* No.24 p.4).
4. F.Devenish-Meares : He was known as F.D.Meares during his playing career.
5. D.J.Noonan (N.S.W. 1895-96) and D.Noonan (Victoria 1900-01 and 1902-03) : It has been established beyond any doubt that two players were involved.
6. C.T.B.Turner : His first class career effectively ended in 1896-97. He played only one match thereafter : his own benefit in 1909-10.

ERRATA, CORRIGENDA AND ADDENDA TO VICTORIAN CRICKETERS

Page 5 H.M.Austin: d. Timboon, July 31, 1981.
Page 9 B.M.Campbell: second name Maesmore, not Maismore.
Page 14 J.W.Egglestone: b. July 7, 1847.
D.M.J.Fitzmaurice: d. Prahran, Jan. 19, 1981.
Page 16 R.A.Gaunt: b. Yarloop, Western Australia, not Yarlu.
Page 17 C.V.Grimmett: b. Caversham, near Dunedin; d Adelaide, May 2, 1980.
B.Grinrod: d. May 23, 1895.
Page 21 H.J.Jennings: b. Launceston, April 9, 1849.
Page 22 Henry Frederick Lorenz Kortlang, always known as B.J.Kortlang.
Page 28 T.F.Morres: b. Sept. 12, 1829.
S.Morris: b. June 22, 1855. (Not Sept 15, 1856)
Page 29 D.J.Noonan: not the N.S.W. player.
Page N.M.Osborne: b. England 1844.
R.L.Park: WK (v Western Australia, Jan. 1913)
Page 31 W.Philpott: b. circa 1819; d. Linton, near Maidstone, England, Nov. 4, 1891.
J.Potter: b. Coburg.
Page 32 F.Richards: LHB
Page 34 H.C.Schrader: d. East Kew, June 10, 1980.
C.A.H.Sindrey: d. Vermont, June 26, 1981.
Page 35 W.Slight: d. Adelaide, Dec. 22, 1941.
Page 41 O.C.Williams: b. Impression Bay, Tasman Peninsula, June 20, 1847 (not June 24).
Page 42 F.W.Wingrove: d. 1939.
F.Wright: b. 1875.
L.A.Wynne: d. Melbourne, Nov. 29, 1980.
Page 46 T.A.Carlton: batting(all matches) 103 inns, 1153 runs, av.15.37.
W.Carlton : batting(all matches) 38 inns, 727 runs, av. 23. 45; Bowling(all matches) conceded 552 runs, av.20.44
A.H.Christian: 10wm (all matches) 2.
Page 47 J.Conway: bowling(all matches) conceded 424 runs, av. 13.25.
W.H.Cooper: best bowling (Victoria and all matches) 7/37; 5wi(Victoria) 4; (all matches) 5.
Page 48 G.Elliott: 10wm (Victoria and all matches) 1.
Page 50 C.V.Grimmett: 5wi (all matches) 127.
W.J.Hammersley: delete correction in Queensland booklet p. 38. To bring his career figures into conformity with the matches listed in the pre-1864 match booklet, his record in all matches should now read: 32-57-5-571-46-10.98. 42-9 (plus 41 wickets with no analysis) - 4.66-6/?-2-1. 20/1.
R.N.Harvey: catches (all matches) 228.
Page 51 J.D.Higgs: bowling (all matches) conceded 6157 runs.
I.W.Johnson: bowling (all matches) conceded 14423 runs, av 23.30.
Page 52 J.L.Keating: best Bowling (Victoria) 6/72.
A.J.W.Lansdown: best bowling (Victoria) 4/53.
Page 53 C.C.McDonald: catches (all matches) 54.
P.S.McDonnell: catches (all matches) 98.
Page 54: I.Meckiff: bowling (all matches) conceded 6283 runs.
Page 55 F.A.O'Keefe: best bowling (Victoria and all matches) 5/45.
Page 57 E.R.Rowlands: highest score (Victoria) 2*.
Page 61 W.M.Woodfull: matches (all matches) 174.
Page 62 Notes on overseas matches: (2) W.J.Hammersley 27 matches 1847 to 1854 (not 22).

ERRATA, CORRIGENDA AND ADDENDA TO QUEENSLAND CRICKETERS

Page 3 P.J.Allan: b. 1935 (not 1936)
Thorpe Allen: b. Oxley.
James William Anderson: b. Feb.25, 18?

Page 4 R.S.Ayres: b. Clayfield
S.W.Ayres: b. Enmore, N.S.W.
G.G.Baker: Name registered at birth as Glen William but always known as Glen George.
E.C.Bensted: d. Brisbane, Jan. 1980.

Page 5 John Macdonald Blackstock: b Drum, near Thornhill, Dumfries-shire, Scotland, Jan. 16, 1871. Delete John Price Blackstock.
J.T.Bolton: b. Oct. 3, 18?
G.A.L.Brown: b. July 31, 1884. RHB.
W.C.Browne: d. Southport, Oct. 25, 1980.

Page 6 P.J.P.Burge: Toured West Indies 1955, not 1965.
Thomas Byrnes: d. Brisbane, Dec. 20, 1951. Delete J. - no second name.
J.Carew: b. Pine Mountain; d. Kelvin Grove, Sept. 1, 1950.
P.Carew: SRA; b. Pine Mountain; d. Queanbeyan, N.S.W., March 31, 1942.

Page 7 J.P.Clark: b. March 14, 1871; d. Coolangatta, June 6, 1941.
Gordon Rex Clem: b. Milora, July 5, 1909; d. Melbourne, March 3, 1970. LHB
C.J.Cook: should be Cooke.

Page 8 E.W.Currie: Otago 1893-94, 1894-95.
Joseph Aloyius Downey: RHB; b. Feb. 4, 1895; d. Kangaroo Point, April 16, 1934.
W.L.Druery: underline Lance.
William Duncan

Page 9 M.M.F.Dunn: b. May 10, 1883. RHB.
W.T.Evans: b. Indooroopilly; d. Buranda.
T.B.Faunce: d. Greenslopes.
S.J.Fennelly: b. March 22, 1887.
H.Fewin: d. Bongarie, Bribie Island, Aug. 25, 1980.
A.Fisher: b. March 14, 1908; d. October 6, 1968.
B.Fisher: d. Inverell, N.S.W., April 6, 1980.
W.T.Fisher: b. Aug. 31, 1868; d. Brisbane, June 1, 1945.
J.W.Fletcher: b. Jan. 25, 1884.

Page 10 F.J.Gough: d. Sandgate, Jan. 30, 1980.
J.M.Govan: b. Coorparoo.
N.F.Grant: b. Jan. 15, 1891.

Page 11 Harold Bickerton Griffith
Charles Samuel Griffiths, b. Townsville, May 28, 1889.
C.E.Harvey: also played for Valley.
W.B.Hayes: RHB; b. Oct. 16, 1883, not as shewn, at Surry Hills.

Page 12 H.V.Hewitt: b. Jan. 12, 1868.
O.C.Hitchcock: b. Sept. 9, 1859.
E.F.Hubbard: b. June 27, 18?
A.Hurwood: Tests - 2; Tour - England 1930.
J.S.Hutcheon: RFM; d. Albion Heights.

Page 13 H.Ironmonger: b. 1881 (not 1883).
A.H.Jones: b. Dec. 17, 1874; d. in camp, Salisbury Plain, Eng., in World War 1. RHB/LB.
A.R.Jones: second name Robert, not Ross; b. Greenslopes; add: 17 Moriac St., Moorooka.

Page 14 J.D.Leary: LM; d. Jan. 16, 1940.
W.J.Lewis: RFM; d. 1939 or 1940.

Page 15 John William McAndrew: b. Nov. 4, 1889; d. Ipswich, April 10, 1960.
R.Macdonald: b. Feb. 14 (not 28). Frank Michael McCaffrey: b c.1878.

Page 16 J.A.Maclean: Tour - New Zealand 1969-70.
A.Marshall: d. Tintaria Hospital, Malta.
D.C.Mengel: underline Charles.

Page 17 D.G.Muddle: b. The Grange; add: Bollon.
R.O'Brien: RHB/RM.

Page 18 L.E.Oxenham: d. Clayfield.
R.K.Oxenham: d. Nundah.
George Augustus Poeppel: b. Bundaberg, Nov. 1893; d. Feb. 2, 1917 in a German prisoner-of-war camp.
H.R.G.Poon: d. Greenslopes, Jan. 25, 1980.
H.A.Price: underline Alexander.

Page 19 H.W.Rahmann: RHB; b. Maryborough; d. Nundah.
M.F.Ramsay : not Ramsey.

Page 20 S.A.Schreiber: b. April 7, 1873.
J.F.Sheppard: b. Jan. 16, 1888 or 1889.

Page 21 C.G.R.Stibe: Reinzi (not Reinsi).
D.Tallon: also played for South Brisbane and Valley.
William J.Thompson.
J.Thomson: b. May 26, 1877; d. circa 1954.

Page 22 F.R.V.Timbury: d. Sydney (not Roma).
B.L.Webb: played for Valley, not Northern Suburbs.
H.S.Weir: Underline Stanley.

Page 23 G.K.Whyte: also played for Northern Suburbs.
Richard Wilson: LB; b. 1870.

Page 24 **G.S.Amos: batting (Queensland) 506 runs, av. 14.45; (all matches) 560 runs, av. 13.65.**
C.B.Barstow: bowling (Queensland) conceded 2124 runs, av. 27.58; (all matches) conceded 2194 runs, av. 28.12.

Page 25 W.S.Bradley: catches (Queensland) 9; (all matches) 10.
F.M.Brew: bowling - conceded 2172 runs, av. 54.30.
W.A.Brown: batting (Queensland) 4565 runs, av. 53.08; (all matches) 13838 runs.

Page 26 E.R.Crouch and G.S.Crouch: batting - there is doubt over their first innings scores v Victoria (Brisbane) 1905-06. Some sources give E.R.C. 1 and G.S.C. 7; others give E.R.C. 7 and G.S.C. 1. If the latter is in fact the case then their figures should be amended to E.R.Crouch 557 runs, av. 17.96 and G.S.Crouch 258 runs, av 25.80.
E.W.Currie: insert second line (all matches)
7-12-2-97-42-9.70. did not bowl. 3/0
J.A.Downey: batting - 66 runs, av. 6.00.

Page 27 T.B.Faunce: catches - 2 (no stumpings)

Page 28 R.J.Hartigan: bowling (Queensland) conceded 329 runs, av. 36.55; (all matches) conceded 361 runs, av 40.11.
O.C.Hitchcock: catches/stumpings - 2/5.
W.S.Hoare: batting (Queensland and all matches) 289 runs, av. 13.13.
A.Hurwood: bowling (Queensland) conceded 2060 runs, av. 30.74; (all matches) conceded 3122 runs, av 27.62.

Page 29 M.J.Khan: all matches figures omit his performances on the 1978-79 Pakistan tour of New Zealand and Australia
J.N.Langley: catches (all matches) 18.

Page 30 P.S.McDonnell: catches (Queensland) 6; (all matches) 98.
W.W.McGlinchy: batting (Queensland) 314 runs, av. 14.95; (all matches) 476 runs, av 14.00; bowling (Queensland) conceded 998 runs, av. 24.34; (all matches) conceded 1346 runs, av. 18.95.
J.W.McLaren: bowling (Queensland) conceded 1890 runs, av. 29.07; (all matches) conceded 2859 runs, av. 26.71; catches (Queensland) 4; (all matches) 7.
J.N.Maguire: batting - 15 innings, 7 not outs.
D.L.Miller: amend all matches career figures to :-
15-25-5-162-21-8.10. 1045-55-19.00-5/38-2-0. 11.
C.F.Morgan: catches - 3.

Page 31 A.D.Ogilvie: catches (Queensland) 29; (all matches) 39.
R.G.Paulsen: catches (all matches) 46.

Page 32 W.Sullivan: catches - 1.
R.F.Surti: batting (all matches) 8066 runs, av. 30.90.
F.C.Thompson: bowling (Queensland) conceded 1256 runs, av. 40.51; (all matches) conceded 1269 runs, av. 40.93.
J.Thomson: bowling - conceded 503 runs, av. 71.85; catches - 7.

Page 33 J.R.Thomson: bowling (all matches) conceded 8016 runs, av. 23.85.

N.B. for new details on C.W.Andrews, S.W.Austin, A.Coningham, O.W.Cowley, R.J.Hartigan, J.E.P.Hogg, C.L.McCool, W.S.S.McCloy, P.S.Macdonnell, W.W.McGlinchy, D.L.Miller, G.M.Pierce, L.M.Richardson, C.E.Simpson, J.R.Thomson and W.T.Walmsley, who also appeared for New South Wales, see main body of text.

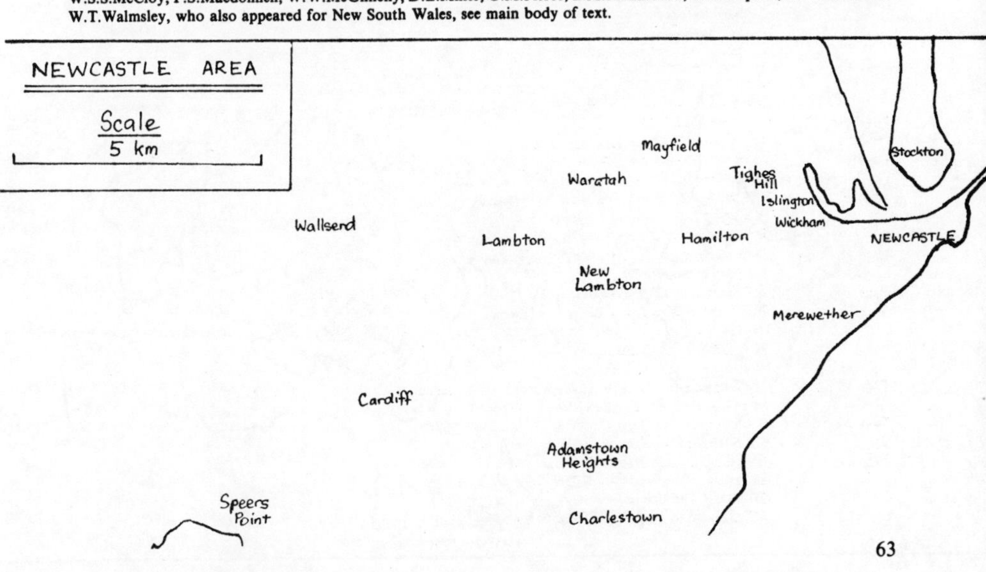

SYDNEY AND SUBURBS
Scale
5 km
Newport Beach
Mona Vale
Hornsby
Wahroonga
Castle Hill
Turramurra
St. Ives
Pennant Hills
Pymble
Frenches Forest
Cromer
Collaroy
Gordon
Marsfield
Killara
Forestville
Brookvale
Seven Hills
Epping
Lindfield
Harbord
Northmead
Eastwood
Roseville
Castle Cove
Balgowlah
Manly
Chatswood
Seaforth
Fairlight
Castlecrag
Dundas
Willoughby
Clontarf
Parramatta
Ryde
Lane Cove
Cammeray
Harris Park
St. Leonards
Mosman
Gladesville
Longueville
Cremorne
Granville
Wollstonecraft
Greenwich
North Sydney
Neutral Bay
Woolwich
Waverton
Crows Nest
Lavender Bay
Milsons Pt.
Kirribilli
JACKSON
Guildford
Auburn
Drummoyne
Birchgrove
Vaucluse
Balmain
PORT
Rodd Pt.
SYDNEY
Concord
Elizabeth Bay
Darling Point
Point Piper
Dover Heights
Homebush
Five Dock
Lilyfield
Pyrmont
Burwood
Croydon
Leichardt
Glebe
Ultimo
Darlinghurst
Double Bay
Rose Bay
Bellevue Hill
Strathfield
Annandale
Ashfield
Surry Hills
Paddington
Petersham
Camperdown
Redfern
Woollahra
Croydon Park
Stanmore
Darlington
Moore Park
Summer Hill
Lewisham
Newtown
Waterloo
Bondi
Enfield
Erskineville
Waverley
Dulwich Hill
Georges Hall
Greenacre
Alexandria
Randwick
Marrickville
Clovelly
Canterbury
Liverpool
Bankstown
Sydenham
Rosebery
Coogee
Mascot
Arncliffe
Beverly Hills
Bexley
Banksia
Maroubra
PACIFIC
Botany
Narwee
Matraville
Brighton-Le-Sands
OCEAN
Hurstville
Kogarah
Carlton
Allawah
BOTANY BAY
Little Bay
Blakehurst
Oyster Bay
Kirrawee
Miranda
Caringbah
NORTH
Lilli Pilli
PORT HACKING

BARBADOS CRICKETERS

1865-1990

By

PHILIP THORN

Published by The Association of Cricket Statisticians, West Bridgford, Nottingham and printed by Peartree Printers of Derby.

BARBADOS
PIE CORNER
ST. LUCY
BOSCOBEL
ALLEYNEDALE
CHECKER HALL
CASTLE
MAYNARDS
MILE AND A QUARTER
GREENLAND
ST. PETER
BELLE PLAINE
ASHTON HALL
ST. ANDREW
DOUGLAS
SPEIGHTSTOWN
RICHMOND HILL
HAGGATTS
CAMBRIDGE
JOE'S RIVER
BLACK BESS
PARKS
FOSTER HALL
ST MARGARETS
FARMERS
WESTMORELAND
ST. JOSEPH
POREY'S SPRING
THE GARDEN
WATER HALL
WELCHMAN HALL
NEWCASTLE
MOUNT STANDFAST
INDUSTRY
ST. JAMES
MOUNT TABOR
BATH
ST. THOMAS
SOCIETY
COLLEGE
BAYFIELD
VAUCLUSE
ST. JOHN
LODGE SCHOOL
PORTERS
TRENTS
REEDS HILL
GLENDALE
WAKEFIELD
POOL
STEWART HILL
EAST POINT
THICKET
BAYLEYS
GREENS
BOWMANSTON
HOLE TOWN
LOCUST HALL
RIVER
MERRICKS
THORPE
KENDAL
HOLDERS HILL
HALLS
AIREYHILL
GLEBELAND
DRAX HALL
HILL VIEW
SANDFORD
CANE WOOD
ST. GEORGE
WHITEHALL
MOUNT
EDGECUMBE
BLACK ROCK
WAVERLEY COT
ST. PHILIP
ST. MICHAEL
BULKELEY
BLADES
KIRTONS
BRERETON
SALTERS
BRIGHTON
FOUR SQUARE BOTTOM
BUTTALS
BENTLEY
BANK HALL
FOUL BAY
HOWELLS
PACKERS VALLEY
LOWER GREYS
BRIDGETOWN
WILDEY
ST DAVID'S
FAIRVIEW
BAYVILLE
PINE
CHRIST CHURCH
CLAPHAM
LOWLANDS
BALLS
GARRISON
ABERDARE
LODGE ROAD
PROVIDENCE
HASTINGS
ROCKLEY
CHRISTCHURCH
MAXWELL
WORTHING
ENTERPRISE
SILVER SANDS

INTRODUCTION

The Easternmost Island of the West Indies, Barbados is 21 miles long and 14 miles wide with an area of about 166 square miles and is slightly larger than the Isle of Wight.

It is said to have been first visited by the Portugese about 1536 who found it to be uninhabited and named the Island 'Los Barbudos' meaning 'the bearded ones' and thought to refer to the beardlike hanging roots of the banyan trees which grew in profusion.

The Portugese made no formal claim to the Island which was nominally taken possession by the English Ship Olive Blossom perhaps in 1605 and a grant of the Island was given to the Earl of Marlborough by James I. In 1625 a ship was fitted out by Sir William Courteen, a London Merchant, and a party of 30 people landed on the leeward side of the Island forming the town of James' or Hole Town and appointed Captain William Deane as the first Governor.

In February 1627 (or perhaps 1628) a further 64 settlers arrived aboard the vessel William and John in Carlisle Bay named after the Earl of Carlisle who had been granted the Island after the death of James I in 1625. The settlers built a number of houses and a bridge across the river which intersected the ground and thus laid the foundations of Bridgetown.

Sugar cane was introduced from Brazil in the 1630s and many slaves were brought from Africa to work on the plantations. Other early colonizers were from English prisons transported for forced labour supplemented by many Royalist captives of Cromwell and later by political prisoners who supported the Duke of Monmouth's rebellion against James II. Prior to the introduction of sugar cane, which took some time to develop, the main production was of indigo, cotton-wool, ginger, aloes and various types of wood.

The House of Assembly first met in 1639 and the Island remained a British Colony until 1966 when it became an independent nation within the Commonwealth with the Queen as the head of state. Whilst the sugar industry has declined in recent years it is an important export and about 60% of the Island is under sugar cultivation with over 70 Plantations. The mainstay of the economy is tourism with nearly 400,000 visitors each year mainly going to the west coast resorts.

The Island is divided into eleven Parishes named St. Andrew, St. George, St. James, St. John, St. Joseph, St. Lucy, St. Michael, St. Peter, St. Philip, St. Thomas and Christ Church with Bridgetown taking up a good part of St. Michael.

Turning to cricket on the Island the first mention of this is on May 10th 1806 in the *'Barbados Mercury'* which announced that a meeting of the St. Anne's Cricket Club was to take place on May 12th. After that there is no further word until May 1838 when the *'Barbadian'* announced a match between the Garrison and the 78th Regiment.

There are accounts of other matches in the years that followed but the first full score is that of the St. Michael's Club versus The Lodge School in early 1861 with nine of those taking part later representing the Island.

The first match of First-class status was played between Barbados and Demerara on the 15th and 16th February 1865 and resulted in an easy win for Barbados by 138 runs and Demerara were in fact dismissed in their first innings for just 22 runs which remained a record lowest score in the West Indies until 1942 when

Trinidad were dismissed for 16 runs again against Barbados. One of the Demerara side, E.C.Beete, was later quoted on the match as follows:

> 'On the Friday morning we went to the Garrison and practised on the pitch there. Consequently the islanders had to prepare a pitch on the Savannah. And such a pitch! The outfield was very high with grass, you could not run after a ball. The pitch itself was so studded with small pieces of corral that the ball had to be changed twice in an innings which lasted about two hours and mangled balls were brought back as a memento. We practised on Saturday and the match was fixed for the Monday and Tuesday following but was postponed until the Wednesday and Thursday'.

One of the problems in playing First-class matches in the West Indies was the time required by the visiting team to be away from home and to some extent the strength of the team depended more on this factor than ability and it is recorded that the Demerara team in the first match were away for a period of three weeks to play a match lasting two days.

It was arranged that Barbados would visit Georgetown for a return match in September 1865 and this time the home team won by two wickets in an exciting game. After the match there were various social events planned including a boat trip to the Penal Settlement in the interior which involved sailing up the Massarani River and shooting the Koestabraek Falls. One of the three boats involved capsized on the falls and seven people were drowned including two of the Demerara team, H.C.Beresford and R.D.Stewart, and it was later revealed the boat had been overloaded and that this was the main cause of the tragedy.

Barbados played First-class matches at irregular intervals against Demerara in 1871, 1883, and 1887 until in September 1891 the first Inter-Colonial Tournament took place, to include Trinidad, at the Bay Pasture in Bridgetown. Barbados met Jamaica for the first time in September 1896 at the Kensington Oval although it was 1925 before a further meeting took place and 1947 until the next match when Barbados visited Jamaica for the first time. The Inter-Colonial Tournament was played on a regular basis up to 1938/39 and the Shell Shield was introduced in 1965/66 which has continued to the present day and now known as the Red Stripe Cup.

Many Barbados cricketers, especially of the earlier period, were well known in other fields and a brief mention of some of these may be of interest. Very few First-class cricketers have become the leader of their Country but Sir Grantley Adams, after an earlier career as a Barrister, was the Premier of Barbados from 1954 to 1958 and then Prime Minister of the West Indies Federation from 1958 to 1962.

A good number of cricketers became members of the House of Assembly including Sir Grantley Adams, Sir Harold Austin, Sir John Carrington, Sir Allan Collymore, Sir Aubrey Goodman, E.A.Hinkson, E.C.Jackman and Sir George Pile.

In the legal world both E.C.Jackman and H.S.Thorne were Judges of the Court of Appeal and Sir Allan Collymore was the Attorney-General and later the Chief Justice. Sir Aubrey Goodman was the Solicitor-General and then the Attorney-General. T.W.Roberts joined the Colonial Service and was for many years a Judge at Galle in Ceylon and when I wrote to the Public Library there asking if anyone remembered him they replied it would be very difficult not to as there was a large portrait of him hung on the Library wall!

Of those who joined the teaching profession T.L.Speed and G.B.Y.Cox were Headmasters of Combermere School and P.A.Goodman was for many years

Headmaster of the Christ Church Foundation School. A.Somers-Cocks was Headmaster of Harrison College and L.A.Walcott the deputy Headmaster at The Lodge School.

A.E.Smith became the Archdeacon of Trinidad and A.M.B.Jemmott after a period in British Guiana became the 'foremost Anglo-Catholic in the Colony' on his return to Barbados. Thomas Clarke held posts in England and Tobago before his last at Brockenhurst in Hampshire and F.B.Speed was a Curate in the City of London. Charles Webb was for many years Vicar of Mansfield Woodhouse in Nottinghamshire and would have christened, married or buried a good many First-class Cricketers of the County.

The Medical professional accounts for nine Barbados cricketers four of these (R.H.Alleyne, R.E.Batson, J.E.Phillips and E.M.Skeete) having attended Edinburgh University and Batson and Phillips remained in the UK and played cricket for Scotland. Doctor Alleyne practised in Barbados after his return from Edinburgh but it is recorded that he 'left for the United States about 1880 owing to a love affair'. He settled in the small Iowa town of Wesley living in a Hotel and not communicating with his relatives in Barbados. He was 'very popular in Wesley and regarded as a very clever physician' and died there unmarried at the age of 39. Of the other Doctors, H.W.Barnes was in practice at Bickley in Kent and C.B.Clarke in London whilst W.O.Gibbs, L.C.Hutson and H.E.Skeete remained in Barbados it being said of the latter 'he was a very fast bowler but his Hippocratic Oath debarred him from trying to lay the batsmen out!'

In more recent times both Garry Sobers and Frank Worrell were knighted and Wes Hall was a Member of the House of Assembly, with C.B.Williams as Ambassador to the USA and later High Commissioner in the UK.

Readers will see from the biographical details that many of the cricketers left their native Island to pursue a career overseas and of surviving cricketers a good many no longer live in Barbados. In England will be found C.B.Clarke (London), C.C.Depeiaza (Manchester), J.B. de C.Emtage (Essex), M.C.Frederick (Kent) and R.E.Marshall (Somerset).

Canada is the home of G.M.Foster, J.H.Lucas, J.L.Parris and G.R.Sealy whilst E.L.Foster, A.A.Harris and N.G.Proverbs are in New Zealand. In the USA are R.Bradshaw (New York), C.C.Hunte (Atlanta), and J.B.Newton. Others overseas are C.F.Blades (Bermuda), Sir Clifford Inniss (Belize), E.A.Norris (St. Lucia), F.C.Lobo (Trinidad), A.C.Medford (Trinidad), F.G.Thomas (St. Vincent) and A.W.White (Venezuela).

Our Association has since 1973 produced similar booklets on the seventeen English First-class Counties plus Ireland and Scotland and our colleagues in Australia have completed works on the six Australian States. It was thought a booklet on Barbados, Jamaica or Trinidad would prove a challenge and I came to the conclusion that of these Barbados would be the best choice with perhaps more local enthusiasm for the project and the possibility that some of our members might visit the Island whilst on holiday.

Since 1865 a total of 324 cricketers have played for Barbados and obtaining biographical details was clearly not going to be easy as of these no information of any sort was known about 164 of them. It also became clear at an early stage that such information as had been published was either incomplete or incorrect in many cases and that everything needed to be re-checked.

Many of the cricketers themselves were contacted and asked to complete a form giving their own biographical details and also to give information on other cricketers with whom they played. Relatives of cricketers who had died were traced and many copies of birth or death certificates were obtained from the Registration Office in Bridgetown and there were very many other sources of information.

Of the cricketers who kindly assisted I would especially like to thank Denis Atkinson, Lionel Birkett, Rawle Brancker, Chester Cumberbatch, Richard Edwards, Bernard Emtage, Ted Hoad, Erskine King, Peter Lashley, James Parris, Kenneth Warren and Clyde Walcott. Relatives who were very helpful included Steve Camacho, George M.Challenor, F.R.B.Howell, H.R.Packer, H.N.Rogers and Stephen Worme.

Others who have greatly helped are Kit Bartlett, Lionel King, John Medford, Basil Matthews (Barbados Cricket Association), Mike Spurrier, Mervyn Wong (Trinidad) and Peter Wynne-Thomas. My particular thanks to Mick Pope, Lynda Miles, Norman Oley and Ian Whyte who visited Harrison College whilst on holiday on the Island and extracted valuable information from the pupil entry records.

Three people have made an outstanding contribution to the completion of the booklet and they are:

Philip Bailey for completing the career records and record section and, as ever, for much other research and support.

Patrick Frost, a Master at The Lodge School, for tracing many cricketers and their relatives in Barbados.

Bill Lane for his tireless work at the Colindale Newspaper Library and in examining the Mormon (Church of Jesus Christ of Latter-day Saints) Genealogical records in London in which were found many previously unknown details of the earlier Barbados cricketers.

Philip Thorn,
Colsterworth, Lincs.
May 1991

CRICKETERS WHO HAVE APPEARED IN A FIRST-CLASS MATCH FOR BARBADOS BETWEEN FEBRUARY 1865 AND APRIL 1990

ADAMS, Sir Grantley Herbert. b 28.4.1898 Government Hill, Bridgetown. d 28.11.1971 Queen Elizabeth Hospital, Bridgetown. rhb, wkt. ed; Harrison College.

ALLAN, David Walter. b 5.11.1937 Hastings, Christ Church. rhb, wkt. ed; The Lodge School. Tours (2). West Indies (5).

ALLEYNE, Hartley Leroy. b 28.2.1957 Derricks, St. James. rhb, rf. Worcestershire, Kent, Natal. Tour (1). West Indies to South Africa (1).

ALLEYNE, Marven Athelston. b 21.10.1949 Maynards, St. Joseph. rhb.

ALLEYNE, Peter Jeremy Clark. b 31.5.1965 Queen Elizabeth Hospital, Bridgetown. rhb, rm. ed; The Lodge School and Harrison College.

ALLEYNE, Doctor Robert Harbin. b 25.3.1847 Hothersal Plantation, St. John. d 25.7.1886 Wesley, Kossuth County, Iowa, USA. ed; The Lodge School. Cousin of W.N.Alleyne.

ALLEYNE, William Newton. b 25.12.1860 Alleynedale Hall, St. Lucy. d 5.9.1910 Sedge Pond Plantation, St. Andrew. rhb. ed; The Lodge School and Malvern. Cousin of R.H.Alleyne. Brother in Law of K.Mason and Sir G.L.Pile.

ARCHER, Frederick Leslie. b 21.11.1888 Hastings, Christ Church. d 12.5.1937 Woodlands, St. George, Grenada. rhb. ed; King's College, Taunton.

ARCHER, Nichollas Riggleby Sheffield. b 23.7.1887 Checker Hall, St. Lucy.

ARMSTRONG, Gregory De Lisle. b 11.5.1950 Bank Hall, St Michael. rhb. rf. Glamorgan.

ARTHUR, Robert. b 23.7.1866 Richmond, Christ Church. d 1948.

ASHBY, Winslow Edwin. b 13.5.1953 Clarkes Land, Deacons Road, St Michael. rhb. ed; Combermere School.

ATKINS, Cyril Anthony. b 23.11.1929 Sobers Lane, St. Michael. rhb, sra.

ATKINSON, Denis St. Eval. b 9.8.1926 Rockley, Christ Church. rhb, rm/ob. ed; Combermere School. Tours (5). West Indies (22). Trinidad. Brother of E.St.E.Atkinson.

ATKINSON, Eric St. Eval. b 6.11.1927 Rockley, Christ Church. rhb, rmf. ed; Combermere School. Tour (1). West Indies (8). Brother of D.St.E.Atkinson.

AUSTIN, Francis Elwin Wilday Gardiner. b 10.4.1882 Enmore, St. Michael. d 23.1.1938 Wildey, St. Michael. lhb, lfm. ed; Harrison College. British Guiana. Brother of A.P.G. Austin (British Guiana), H.B.G.Austin, J.G.Austin, M.B.G.Austin (British Guiana).

AUSTIN, Sir Harold Bruce Gardiner. b 15.7.1877 Enmore, St Michael. d 27.7.1943 Collymore Rock, St. Michael. rhb. ed; Harrison College. Tours (2). Brother of A.P.G.Austin (British Guiana), J.G.Austin, F.E.W.G.Austin and M.B.G.Austin (British Guiana).

AUSTIN, Henry Fitzherbert. b 1.9.1874 Salters Plantation, St. George, d 18.1.1957 Hastings, Christ Church. rhb. ed; Combermere School. Grandfather of M.R.Bynoe.

AUSTIN, Brigadier General John Gardiner. b 20.6.1871 The Farm, St. Philip. d 2.11.1956 Victoria, British Columbia, Canada. ed; Harrison College. Brother of A.P.G.Austin (British Guiana). F.E.W.G.Austin, H.B.G.Austin, and M.B.G.Austin (British Guiana).

BAILEY, Herbert Packer. b 5.12.1889 River Road, St. Michael. Killed in action 31.7.1917 Hollebeke, France. ed; Harrison College.

BANCROFT, Claude Keith. b 30.10.1885 Fontabelle, St. Michael. d 12.1.1919 Toronto, Canada. rhb, wkt. ed; Harrison College. Tour (1).

BARKER, Hughley Woodbine. b 27.6.1925 Jackman's, St.Michael. rhb, rf. ed; Combermere School.

BARNES, Doctor Howell Wood. b 3.9.1887 Whitehall, St. Michael. d 31.8.1959 Colchester, Essex. rhb, sra. ed; Harrison College. Brother in Law of N.F.Norman (Essex).

BARROW, Luther Challenor Marshall. b 19.5.1876 Baxter Road, St. Michael. d 15.2.1933 Bay Street, St. Michael.

BARTLETT, Edward Lawson. b 10.3.1906 Flint Hall, St. Michael. d 21.12.1976 Bayville, St.Michael. rhb. ed; Harrison College. Tours (2). West Indies (5).

BATSON, Doctor Richard Erstine. b 11.6.1891 Belleville, St. Michael. d 25.1.1971 Islington, London. rhb. ed; Harrison College. Scotland.

BECKLES, Clyde Samuel. b 14.8.1948 Hill View, Marley Vale, St. Philip. rhb, rm.

BENN, Alick Jerome. b 15.6.1875 Green Park Lane, St Michael. lhb, lm.

BEST Carlisle Alonza. b 14.5.1959 Richmond Gap, St. Michael. rhb, rm/ob. Tour (1). Rest of World in England. West Indies (6).

BETHELL, John Arthur Lionel. b 18.12.1940 Bowmanston, St. John. lhb, lmf. Barbados to England.

BIRKETT, Lionel Sydney. b 14.4.1905 Strathclyde, St. Michael. rhb, rm. ed; Harrison College. Tour (1). West Indies (4). British Guiana, Trinidad. Brother of T.S.Birkett.

BIRKETT, Theodore Sydney. b 14.4.1918 Fontabelle, St. Michael. rhb, rmf. ed; Harrison College. Brother of L.S.Birkett.

BLACKMAN, Roger George. b 4.4.1915 Parks House, St. Joseph. rhb, rm. ed; Harrison College and The Lodge School.

BLADES, Charles Elliott. b 4.9.1883 Ruby Plantation, St. Philip. d 25.11.1914 Brooklyn, USA. lhb, sla.| ed; The Lodge School.

BLADES, Colin Francis. b 13.8.1944 Clarkes Hill, St. Philip. rhb, rm. ed; The Lodge School. Barbados to England.

BOURNE, Charles Lincoln. b 13.10.1910 New Orleans, St. Michael. d 26.8.1975 Crown Point on the Bay, Tobago. rhb, wkt. Son of C.L.C.Bourne (British Guiana).

BOURNE, William Anderson. b 15.11.1952 Clapham, St. Michael. rhb, rmf. ed; Harrison College. Warwickshire.

BOWRING, William. b 14.11.1874 St. John's, Newfoundland. d 12.8.1945 Bay, St. Michael. rhb. Tours (1-not First-class). ed; Sherborne and Marlborough. Brother in Law of D.C.C.C. Da Costa.

BOXILL, Darnley Da Costa. b 2.10.1944 Christchurch, Christ Church. rhb, wkt. Barbados to England.

BOYCE, Keith David. b 11.10.1943 Castle, St. Peter. rhb, rfm. Essex. Tours (3). Commonwealth to Pakistan. Rest of the World to Pakistan. West Indies (21).

BRADSHAW, Cecil St. Clair. b 2.7.1928 Cambridge, St. Joseph. rhb, rf.

BRADSHAW, Rudolph. b 26.6.1939 Parish Land, Christ Church. rhb,

BRANCKER, Rawle Cecil. b 19.11.1937 Emmerton, St. Michael. lhb, sla. ed; Combermere School. Tour (1). Barbados to England.

BRANKER, Kenneth Augustus. b 23.10.1932 Howells Cross Road, St. Michael. rhb, ob/lb. ed; Combermere School.

BRATHWAITE, Hubert Arlington. b 6.6.1950 Victoria Tenantry, St. John. rhb.

BRATHWAITE, John Mowbury McClure. b 24.2.1872 College Estate, St. John. ed; Harrison College.

BROOME, Oliver Alphonzo. b 6.2.1937 Six Men's, St. Peter. rhb, wkt.

BROOMES, Noel Da Costa. b 23.12.1956 Water Hall, St. James. lhb, sla.

BROWNE, Alfred. b 22.2.1860 Pleasant Hall, Christ Church. d 12.9.1940 Bridgetown. ed; Harrison College. Brother of Clement Browne and Robert Browne. Uncle of C.F.Browne.

BROWNE, Clement. b 28.7.1865 Pleasant Hall, Christ Church. d 24.6.1927 Douglas, St. Peter. rhb, wkt. ed; Harrison College. Brother of Alfred Browne and Robert Browne. Father of C.F.Browne.

BROWNE, Chester Allan. b 20.7.1888 Robert's Tenantry, St. Michael. d 12.10.1941. Collymore Rock, St. Michael. rhb, rm. ed; Harrison College. Brother of C.R.Browne.

BROWNE, Clement Fraser. b 8.1.1892 Hastings, Christ Church. d 15.11.1975 Ashton Hall, St. Peter. rhb, rm. Son of Clement Browne. Nephew of Alfred Browne and Robert Browne.

BROWNE, Cyril Rutherford. b 8.10.1890 Robert's Tenantry, St. Michael. d 12.1.1964 Georgetown, British Guiana. rhb, rmlb. ed; Harrison College. Tours (2). West Indies (4). British Guiana. Brother of C.A.Browne.

BROWNE, Robert. b 3.7.1863 Pleasant Hall, Christ Church. rhb, wkt. ed; Harrison College. Brother of Alfred Browne and Clement Browne. Uncle of C.F.Browne.

BROWNE, Samuel. c 3.8.1844 Lightfoots Plantation, St. Philip.

BURKE, Irwin Lincoln. b 23.7.1916 Bayville, St. Michael. rhb, ob.

BURNETT, Henry Thomas. c 20.7.1851 Boscobel, St. Peter. ed; The Lodge School.

BURNHAM, Chetwyn Gideon. b 7.9.1945 Mount Standfast, St James. rhb, rmf. ed; Harrison College.

BUTCHER, Roland Orlando. b 14.10.1953 East Point, St. Philip. rhb, rm. England Tour (1). Middlesex to Zimbabwe. International XI to Pakistan. International XI to Jamaica. England (3). Middlesex. Tasmania. Cousin of B.F.Butcher (British Guiana).

BYER, John Walter. b 20.9.1903 Charles Rowe Bridge, St. George. d 11.8.1988 The Garden, St. James. rhb, rmf.

BYNOE, Michael Robin. b 23.2.1941. Alleynedale, Black Rock, St. Michael. rhb, sla. ed; Harrison College. Tours (2). Barbados to England. West Indies (4). Grandson of H.F.Austin. Cousin of M.C.Frederick.

CAMPBELL, Trevor Douglas Anderson. b 15.11.1950 Station Hill, St. Michael. rhb. ed; Harrison College.

CAREW, George McDonald. b 4.6.1910 Halls Road, Belmont, St. Michael. d 9.12.1974 Holetown, St. James. rhb, sla. ed; Combermere School. Tours (1). West Indies (4).

CARRINGTON, Sir John Worrell. b 29.5.1847 Industry Plantation, St. Joseph. d 11.2.1913 Reading, Berkshire. ed; The Lodge School. Father in Law of C.H.Clarke.

CARTER, Duncan. b 6.11.1939 Vauxhall, Christ Church. rhb, rf.

CHALLENOR, Brigadier General Edward Lacy. b 10.3.1873 Speightstown, St. Peter. d 15.9.1935 Hampstead Garden Suburb, London. rhb. ed; Harrison College. Natal. Western Province. Leicestershire. Brother of George Challenor, Robert Challenor and V.C.Challenor. Nephew of G.D.Whitehall. Great Uncle of M.L.Sealy.

CHALLENOR, George. b 28.6.1888 Waterloo, St. Michael. d 30.7.1947 Collymore Rock, St. Michael. rhb, rm. ed; Harrison College. Tours (3). West Indies (3). Brother of E.L. Challenor. Robert Challenor and V.C.Challenor. Nephew of G.D.Whitehall. Grandfather of M.L.Sealy.

CHALLENOR, Robert. b 25.6.1884 Belmont, St. Michael. d 26.6.1977 Upper Collymore Rock, St. Michael. rhb, wkt. ed; Harrison College. Brother of E.L.Challenor, George Challenor and V.C.Challenor. Nephew of G.D.Whitehall. Great Uncle of M.L.Sealy.

CHALLENOR, Vicary Clive. b 15.5.1883 Belmont, St. Michael. d 25.3.1973 Vegreville, Alberta, Canada. lhb. ed; Harrison College. Brother of E.L.Challenor, George Challenor and Robert Challenor. Nephew of G.D.Whitehall. Great Uncle of M.L.Sealy.

CLAIRMONTE, Frederick Archibald Conrad. b 25.5.1886 Constitution, St. Michael. d 20.9.1960 Worthing, Christ Church. rhb, rfm. ed; Harrison College.

CLARKE, Doctor Carlos Bertram. b 7.4.1918 Lakes Folly, Cats Castle, St. Michael, rhb, lbg. ed; Harrison College. Tour (1). West Indies (3). Northants. Essex.

CLARKE, Carleton Howell. b 28.8.1875 Corrale House, St. Michael. d 13.12.1961 Pine Hill, St Michael. rhb. ob. ed; HarrisonCollege. Son of W.C.Clarke. Nephew of Thomas Clarke and Theodore Clarke.

CLARKE, Martin Ian Coleridge. b 21.9.1913 Strathclyde, St. Michael. d 10.11.1982 Bay Street, St. Michael. rhb, rfm.

CLARKE, Mitchell Wilkinson. b 5.1.1901 Weymouth, St. Michael. d 9.7.1988 Weymouth, St. Michael. rhb, rm.

CLARKE, Nolan Ewatt. b 22.6.1948 Lower Westbury Road, St. Michael. rhb, lbg.

CLARKE, Sylvester Theophilus. b 11.12.1954 Lead Vale, Christ Church. rhb, rf. Tours (3). West Indies to South Africa (2). West Indies (11). Surrey. Transvaal. Northern Transvaal. Orange Free State. Half Brother of R.O.Estwick.

CLARKE, Rev Thomas. b 17.10.1839 The Rectory, Christ Church. d 8.8.1892 Brockenhurst, Hants. ed; Bury St. Edmunds. Brother of Theodore Clarke and W.C.Clarke. Uncle of C.H.Clarke.

CLARKE, Theodore Gordon. b 29.4.1860 St. Michaels Row, St. Michael. d USA (New Jersey?) date unknown. rhb, wkt. ed; Harrison College. Brother of Thomas Clarke and W.C.Clarke. Uncle of C.H.Clarke.

CLARKE, William Coleridge. b May 1841 Bridgetown. d 17.7.1907 The Garrison, St. Michael. rhb. wkt. Brother of Thomas Clarke and Theodore Clarke. Father of C.H. Clarke.

COLE, Hallam Adolphus FitzLaurie. b 1.6.1874 Weymouth, St Michael. d 15.3.1932 Maxwell, Christ Church. rhb. ed; Harrison College.

COLLYMORE, Sir Ernest Allan. b 4.2.1893 Country Road, St. Michael. d 23.6.1962 Bannister Land, St. Michael. rhb. ed; Harrison College.

COLLYMORE, Walter Osmond. b 30.8.1856 Fontabelle, St. Michael. d 23.7.1907 Bridgetown.

CONNELL, Valance Richard. b 9.2.1944 Fontabelle, St. Michael. rhb. wkt.

CONSTANTINE, Sir Leslie Nicholas. (Baron Constantine of Maraval and Nelson). b 21.9.1901 Petit Valley, Diego Martin, Trinidad. d 1.7.1971 Brondesbury, Hampstead, London. rhb, rf/rm. Tours (5). West Indies (18). Trinidad. Son of L.S.Constantine (Trinidad). Brother in Law of V.S.Pascall (Trinidad). Brother of E.Constantine (Trinidad).

COX, Allan Pile. b 11.11.1873 Foster Hall Plantation, St. Joseph. d 5.1.1896 Joe's River, St. Joseph. ed; The Lodge School. Brother of Percy Cox and H.T.Cox.

COX, Gustavus Blagrove Young. b 30.5.1870 Grand View, St. Michael. d 9.9.1958 Port of Spain, Trinidad. rhb. ed; Harrison College.

COX, Hampden Tudor. b 3.4.1866 Haggatts Plantation, St. Andrew. d 1940 Naparima, Trinidad. rhb. ed; The Lodge School. Brother of A.P.Cox and Percy Cox.

COX, Percy Ince. b 16.9.1878 Foster Hall Plantation, St. Joseph. d 1918 Princes Town, Trinidad. rhb. ed; The Lodge School. Tour (1-not First-class). Trinidad. Brother of A.P.Cox and H.T.Cox.

CRICK, Cuthbert O'Brien. b 24.10.1920. ed; Combermere School.

CUMBERBATCH, Chester St. Clair. b 12.12.1913 Wesley Hall, St. Michael. rhb, wkt. ed; Harrison College. Son of J. St. C. Cumberbatch.

CUMBERBATCH, Dave Anton. b 26.9.1964 Maynards, St. Peter. rhb, sla.

CUMBERBATCH, Julian St. Clair. b 10.5.1877 near Canewood, St. Michael. d 16.3.1944 Bank Hall, St. Michael. rhb, wkt. ed; Harrison College. Father of C. St. C.Cumberbatch.

CUMMINS, Anderson Cleophas. b 7.5.1966 Packers Valley, Christ Church. rhb, rfm.

DA COSTA, Darnley Clements Campbell Clairmonte. b 30.3.1877 Palm Villa, St. Michael. d 9.7.1966 Dalkeith, St. Michael. rhb, wkt. ed; Harrison College and Harrow. Nephew of D.M.McAuley. Brother in Law of W.Bowring.

DANIEL, Wayne Wendell. b 16.1.1956 Brereton Village, St. Philip. rhb, rf. Tours (3). West Indies (10). Middlesex. Western Australia.

DEPEIAZA, Cyril Clairmonte. b 10.10.1928 Mount Standfast, St. James. rhb, wkt. Tour (1). West Indies (5).

DOWNES, Othneil D'Arcy. b 1.9.1934 Carrington Village, St. Michael. rhb. rfm.

DOYLE, Hillard Hartley. b 15.11.1935 Brittons Hill, St. Michael. rhb, wkt.

EDWARDS, John Ralph. b 15.8.1909 Hastings, Christ Church. d 12.7.1976 Beckles Road, St. Michael. rhb, lb. ed; Harrsion College.

EDWARDS, Richard Martin. b 3.6.1940 Garden Gap, Worthing, Christ Church. rhb, rf. ed; The Lodge School. Tour (1). Barbados to England. West Indies (5).

ELLCOCK, Dale Everson. b 16.11.1967 Bridgetown. rhb. rfm. Brother of R.M.Ellcock.

ELLCOCK, Ricardo McDonald. b 17.6.1965 Bridgetown.rhb, rf. ed; Combermere School and Malvern. Worcestershire. Middlesex. Brother of D.E.Ellcock.

ELLIOTT, Greenidge. b 21.10.1861 River Side, St. Michael. rhb, wkt. ed; Harrison College. Brother of Gilbert Elliott (Priestley to West Indies).

EMTAGE, James Bernard de Courcey. b 14.2.1902 The Lodge School, St. John. rhb. lb/rm. ed; The Lodge School.

ESTWICK, Roderick Orville. b 28.6.1961 Christchurch, Christ Church. rhb, rfm. Transvaal. Tour (1). D.B.Close's XI. Half brother of S.T.Clarke.

EVELYN, Edward Ernest. b 27.12.1864 Harmony Hall, Christ Church. ed; Harrison College.

FARMER, Stephen Wilfred. b 23.5.1950 Garrison, St. Michael. rhb, rm. ed; The Lodge School. Son of W.A.Farmer.

FARMER, Wilfred Arthur. b 7.10.1921 Clifden, St. John. d 25.2.1975 Bridgetown. rhb, rf. Father of S.W.Farmer.

FIELDS, Walter Sydney Herbert. b 16.3.1879 White Park Road, St. Michael. d 7.2.1942 Kensington New Road, St. Michael.

FOSTER, Campbell Seymore. b 2.11.1914 The Garrison, St. Michael. d 17.12.1978 Bridgetown. Brother of N.L.Foster. Cousin of W.M.Foster.

FOSTER, Geoffrey Michael. b 4.5.1935 Bayville, St. Michael. lhb, sla. ed; Harrison College.

FOSTER, Neville Leon. b 9.6.1913 The Garrison, St. Michael. rhb, rm. Brother of C.S.Foster. Cousin of W.M.Foster.

FOSTER, Teddy Fernando. b 5.5.1955 Chase Land, Tweedside Road, St. Michael. rhb, sla. ed; The Lodge School.

FOSTER, Walter Michael. b 24.5.1915 Beckles Road, Bayville, St. Michael. rhb, rf. ed; Harrison College. Cousin of C.S.Foster and N.L.Foster.

FRANCIS, George Nathaniel, (birth recorded as John Nathaniel). b 11.12.1897 Trents, St. James. d 7.1.1942 Black Rock, St. Michael. rhb, rf. Tours (4). West Indies (10).

FREDERICK, Michael Campbell. b 6.5.1927 Mile and a Quarter, St. Peter. rhb. rm. ed; The Lodge School. West Indies (1). Jamaica. Derbyshire. Cousin of M.R.Bynoe.

GARNER, Joel. b 16.12.1952 Enterprise, Christ Church. rhb. rf. Tours (7). West Indies (58). Somerset. South Australia.

GIBBS, Doctor Will O'Brian. b 19.9.1885 Bridgetown. d 29.1.1949 Black Rock, St. Michael. rhb. rm.

GILKES, Arnold Sylvester. b 26.2.1958 Porey's Spring, St. Thomas. rhb, wkt.

GILKES, Benjamin Irvine. b 16.3.1893 d December 1967 Belleville, St. Michael. rhb, rmf.

GILKES, Oswell Hutson. b 25.2.1892 Bank Hall Road, St. Michael.

GILL, Shirley Samuel. b 19.11.1918 St. Michael. ed; Harrison College.

GITTENS, Stanton O'Connor. b 4.5.1911 Weymouth, St. Michael. rhb, wkt.

GODDARD, John Douglas Claude. b 21.4.1919 Fontabelle, St. Michael. d 26.8.1987 Paddington, London. lhb, rm. ed; The Lodge School and Harrison College. Tours (5). West Indies (27).

GODDARD, Kenneth. b 1918 d 18.12.1978 Westbury, St. Michael. rhb, ob. ed; The Lodge School.

GOODMAN, Clifford Everard. b 20.11.1869 College View, St. Philip. d 1.2.1911 Belleville, St. Michael. rhb. rf. ed; The Lodge School. Brother of G.A.Goodman, P.A.Goodman and W.E.Goodman.

GOODMAN, Sir Gerald Aubrey. b 6.9.1862 College View, St. Philip. d 20.1.1921 Bath, England. rhb. ed; Harrison College. Brother of C.E.Goodman, P.A.Goodman and W.E.Goodman.

GOODMAN, Percy Arnold. b 3.10.1874 Sandford, St. Philip. d 25.4.1935 Elbank, St. Lawrence, Christ Church. rhb, rm. ed; The Lodge School. Tours (2-1 not First-class). Brother of C.E.Goodman, G.A.Goodman and W.E.Goodman.

GOODMAN, Walter Evans. b 29.9.1872 College View, St. Philip. d 13.4.1910 Georgetown, Penang Island, Malaya. rhb, wkt. ed; The Lodge School. British Guiana. Brother of C.E.Goodman, G.A.Goodman and P.A.Goodman.

GRAHAM, Ormond St. Elmo. b 31.5.1918 Carrington Village, St. Michael. d 18.1.1989 Bridgetown. rhb, rf.

GRANT, Adrian Llewellyn. b 16.6.1961 Bridgetown. rhb, ob.

GREAVES, Herbert Francis Kenneth. b 13.10.1898 Edmonton, London. d 17.11.1953 Hastings, Christ Church. rhb, sla. ed; Harrison College.

GREAVES, Sherlon Ricardo. b 26.4.1962 Belleplaine, St. Andrew. rhb, lbg.

GREENE, Edmund. b 20.4.1921 Glebe Land, St. George, rhb, rmf.

GREENE, Victor Sylvester. b 24.9.1960 Lodge Road, Christ Church. rhb, rfm. Tour (1). Gloucestershire.

GREENIDGE, Alvin Ethelbert. b 20.8.1956 Bath Village, Christ Church. rhb, rm. Tours (1). West Indies to South Africa (2). West Indies (6).

GREENIDGE, Cuthbert Gordon. b 1.5.1951 Black Bess, St. Peter. rhb, rm. Tours (15). West Indies (100). Hampshire.

GREENIDGE, Geoffrey Alan. b 26.5.1948 Fontabelle, St. Michael. rhb, lb. ed; Harrison College. Robins to South Africa. International XI to South Africa. West Indies (5). Sussex.

GREENIDGE, John Winston. b 15.3.1929 Brighton Beach, Black Rock, St. Michael. rhb, ob.

GREENIDGE, Malcolm Fiddis. b 25.8.1860 Belle Farm, St. George. d 8.9.1926 Haynes Hill, St. John. rhb. rm. ed; The Lodge School.

GREENIDGE, Witney Tyrone. b 16.5.1965 Westmoreland, St. James. rhb, rfm.

GRIFFITH, Charles Christopher. b 14.12.1938 Pie Corner, St. Lucy. rhb, rf. Tours (4). President's XI to India. Commonwealth XI to Pakistan. West Indies (28).

GRIFFITH, Edward Hallam Cosmo. b 18.3.1936 Brittons Cross Road, St. Michael. lhb, rm. ed; Harrison College. Jamaica. Son of H.C.Griffith. Brother of G.H.C.Griffith (Cambridge Univ) and H.L.V.Griffith.

GRIFFITH, Herman Clarence. b 1.12.1893 Arima, Trinidad. d 18.3.1980 Queen Elizabeth Hospital, Bridgetown. rhb, rf. ed; Combermere School. Tours (3). West Indies (13). Father of E.H.C.Griffith, G.H.C.Griffith (Cambridge Univ) and H.L.V.Griffith.

GRIFFITH, Harold Lloyd Vincent. b 21.6.1921 Brittons Cross Road, St. Michael. rhb, ob. ed; Harrison College. Son of H.C.Griffith. Brother of E.H.C.Griffith and G.H.C. Griffith (Cambridge Univ).

GRIFFITHS, Russell Fayne. b 19.7.1909 The Garrison, St. Michael. rhb, ob. ed; Combermere School.

HALL, Wesley Winfield. b 12.9.1937 Glebe Land, Station Hill, St. Michael. rhb, rf. ed; Combermere School. Tours (7). Commonwealth to Rhodesia. Rest of the World to England (2). Barbados to England. West Indies (48). Trinidad. Queensland.

HARDING, Gerry. b 1.11.1943 St. Christopher, Christ Church. rhb, ob.

HARRIS, Arnott Austin. b 10.12.1909 Clement Rock, St. Joseph. rhb, rmf. ed; Combermere School.

HARRIS, Joseph Vikram. b 16.8.1965. rhb, ob.

HARRIS, Leslie Fitzroy. b 9.10.1920 Laynes Gap, Brittons Hill, St. Michael. rhb, lbg. ed; Harrison College. Half Brother of F.G.Thomas.

HASSELL, Albert Eric Elisha. b 19.3.1936 Bridgetown. rhb, wkt. ed; Harrison College.

HAYNES, Desmond Leo. b 15.2.1956 Holders Hill, St. James. rhb, lbg. Tours (13). West Indies (89). Middlesex. Rest of the World in England.

HAYNES, Henry Husbands. c 20.9.1834 Bath Plantation, St. John. d February 1892 Bridgetown. Uncle of C.Haynes (Glos).

HINDS, Delmont Cameron St. Clair. b 1.6.1880 Westbury Road, St. Michael. Tour (1-not First-class).

HINDS, Hilton Deane. b 13.11.1889 Retreat, St. George. lhb, lm.

HINKSON, Ernest Augustus. b 24.8.1870 Lightfoot, St. Michael. d 10.6.1936 Worthing, Christ Church. ed; Harrison College.

HINKSON, Ernest Stephen. b 4.1.1942 Bridgetown. lhb, rf. ed; The Lodge School. Barbados to England (did not play in a First-class match).

HOAD, Edwin. b 17.9.1870 Fontabelle, St. Michael. d 1946 St. Michael. Cousin of E.L.G.Hoad, E.L.G.Hoad Jnr, J.J.S.Hoad and W.C.Hoad.

HOAD, Edward Lisle Goldsworthy. b 29.1.1896 Richmond, St. Michael. d 5.3.1986 Bridgetown. rhb, lbg. ed; Harrison College. Tours (2). West Indies (4). Father of E.L.G.Hoad Jnr. Brother of J.J.S.Hoad and W.C.Hoad. Cousin of Edwin Hoad.

HOAD, Edward Lisle Goldsworthy. b 4.9.1925 Vaucluse, St. Thomas. rhb, lbg. ed; Harrison College. Son of E.L.G.Hoad Snr. Nephew of J.J.S.Hoad and W.C.Hoad. Cousin of Edwin Hoad.

HOAD, John Julian Sebert. b 9.10.1891 Richmond, St. Michael. d 1.12.1971 Bridgetown. rhb, lb. ed; Combermere School. Brother of E.L.G.Hoad and W.C.Hoad. Uncle of E.L.G.Hoad Jnr. Cousin of Edwin Hoad.

HOAD, William Cyril. b 7.10.1885 Fontabelle, St. Michael. d 24.1.1920 Bridgetown. rhb, lb. ed; Harrison College. Trinidad. Brother of E.L.G.Hoad and J.J.S.Hoad. Uncle of E.L.G.Hoad Jnr. Cousin of Edwin Hoad.

HOLDER, Adzil Harcourt. b 22.10.1931 Joe's River, St. Joseph. rhb, sla.

HOLDER, Roland Irwin Christopher. b 22.12.1967 Port of Spain, Trinidad. rhb, rm. ed; Combermere School.

HOLDER, Vanburn Alonzo. b 10.10.1945 Deans Village, St. Michael. rhb, rfm. Tours (6). Rest of World to Pakistan. West Indies (40). Worcestershire. Orange Free State.

HOLFORD, David Anthony Jerome. b 16.4.1940 Upper Collymore Rock, St. Michael. rhb, lb. ed; Harrison College. Tours (3). Barbados to England. West Indies (24). Trinidad. Cousin of G. St. A.Sobers.

HORNE, Leonard Montague. b 14.9.1878 Wallingford, Oxfordshire. d Jamaica date unknown but after 1925. rhb, rf.

HOWARD, Anthony Bourne. b 27.8.1946 Lower Collymore Rock, St. Michael lhb, ob. West Indies (1).

HOWELL, William Murray. b 9.8.1866 Erdiston, Pine Hill, St. Michael. d 11.11.1958 St. John's, Antigua. lhb, lf. ed; Harrison College.

HOYTE, Ricardo Lawrence. b 15.10.1969 Bridgetown. lhb, wkt. Son of D.A.Murray.

HUNTE, Conrad Cleophas. b 9.5.1932 Greenland Plantation, Shorey, St. Andrew. rhb, rm. Tours (5). Commonwealth in England. West Indies (44).

HUNTE, Terence Anderson. b 4.4.1962 Thickets, St. Philip. rhb, rm.

HUTCHINSON, Geoffrey. b 29.8.1933 Perry Gap, St. Michael. rhb, rm. ed; Harrison College and The Lodge School.

HUTCHINSON, Leo Richard. b 9.10.1896 Tamarind Hall, St. Joseph. d 27.3.1977 Bank Hall, St. Michael. lhb, lfm. ed; Combermere School.

HUTSON, Doctor Lionel Charles. b 27.10.1891 Wakefield, Belmont, St. Michael. d 28.7.1941 White Park, St. Michael. rhb. ed; Harrison College.

INCE, Harry Wakefield. b [illegible] Christ Church. d 11.5.1978 Bayville, St Michael. lhb, sra. ed; H[illegible] (1). Cousin of R.M. Jones.

INNISS, Bruce de Lisle. b 8.2.1912 [illegible] St. Michael. d 10.12.1976 Enterprise Road, Christ Church. rhb. ed; Harrison College and The Lodge School. Brother of Sir Clifford Inniss.

INNISS, Sir Clifford de Lisle. b 26.10.19[illegible] Michael. rhb, sra. ed; Harrison College. Tour [illegible] matches whilst at Oxford University). Brother of B. de L. Inniss.

INNISS, Michael Henderson [illegible] Hall, St. Michael. lhb. ed; The Lodge School.

JACKMAN, Edward [illegible] St. Michael. d [illegible] 1956 Bayville, St. Michael. rhb. [illegible] Harrison College.

JEMMOTT, Reverend [illegible] 1868 Society Plantation, St. John. d 14.3.19[illegible]5 USA [illegible]

JOHNSON, An[illegible] Hill, St. [illegible]es. rhb, rf.

JOHNSON, Nigel Anderson [illegible] St. George. rh[illegible]

JOHNSON, Wesley. b 2.9.1[illegible] rhb, rf. ed; Harrison College.

JONES, Robert Martin. b [illegible] Michael. d 20.5.1951 Two Mile Hill, St. Michael. lhb, lm. ed; [illegible] of H.W. [illegible]

JORDAN, Emmerson Leroy [illegible] Country, St. Peter. rhb, rf.

JORDAN, Harold Radcliffe. b [illegible] on Bridge House, St. Michael. rhb, lmf. ed; Harrison College.

KIDNEY, John McCall. b 29.10.18[illegible] St. Michael. d 18.10.1962 Bayville, St. Michael. rhb.

KING, Anthony St. Elmo. b 19[illegible] Village, [illegible] St. Michael. rhb, [illegible] ed: Harrison College. Brother of H.A. King.

KING, Collis Llewellyn. b 11.6.1951 F[illegible] Christ Church. [illegible] (3). International XI to Pakistan. [illegible] South Africa (2). West Indies [illegible] Glamorgan. Worcestershire. Natal.

KING, Earnest. b 21.5.184[illegible] St. Michael. lhb, [illegible] ed; The Lodge School.

KING, Erskine Henderson. [illegible] Christ Church. rhb, w[illegible]

KING, Frank McDonald. b 8.12.192[illegible] Lane, Brighton, St. Michael. d 23.12.1990 Bescot, Walsall, Staffs. [illegible] West Indies (14). Trinidad.

KING, Horace Arlington. b 1[illegible] Village, Green Hill, St. Michael. lhb, sla. ed; Combermere School and [illegible] Brother of A St. E. King.

LABORDE, Arthur [illegible] 1875 Kingstown, St. Vincent. d 25.8.1951 Highgate, London [illegible] College.

LASHLEY, Patrick Douglas [illegible] Lashley). b 11.2.1937 St. Matthias Gap, Christ Church. lhb, rm. ed: [illegible] (2). Barbados to England. West Indies (4).

LAYNE, Oliver Hoff[illegible] Michael. d 16.8.1932 Bellevue Hospital, New York. rhb, rm. [illegible]

LEARMOND, George C[illegible] b 4.7.1875 [illegible] British Guiana. d 2.3.1918 St. Vincent. rhb, wkt. ed; Co[illegible] First-class). British Guiana, Trinidad. Father of [illegible] of G.S.C[illegible]

LINTON, George Le[illegible] St. George. [illegible]

L[illegible]**, Frank Clement** [illegible] rhb, rm. ed: [illegible] and Harrison College.

LUCAS, John Herman [illegible] Michael. rhb, [illegible] School. Tour [illegible]

LUCAS, Noel Stephen. b 15.12.1926 Weym[illegible] [illegible] Combermere School. Brother of [illegible] Lucas.

McAULEY, Donald Musson. b 25.4.1867 [illegible], St. Michael. d 27.1.1912 Dalkeith, St. Michael. Uncle of D.C.C.C. Da Costa.

McCLEAN, William Young. b 2[illegible].1842 [illegible]

MARSHALL, Malcolm Denzil. b [illegible] Bridgetown. rhb. rf. Tours (1[illegible]). West Indies (68). Hampshire [illegible]

MARSHALL, Norman Edgar. b 27.[illegible].1924 [illegible] St. Thomas. rhb, ob. West Indies [illegible] Trinidad. Brother of R.[illegible] Warren.

MARSHALL, Roy Edwin. b [illegible].1930 Farmers [illegible] [illegible]as. rhb, ob. ed; The Lodge School. Tours (2). [illegible] XI [illegible] Jamaica. Cavaliers to West Indies. Commonwealth to India [illegible], New Zealand and Rhodesia. Commonwealth to South Africa (2). W[illegible] Hampshire. Brother of N.E.Marshall. Cousin of K.B.Warren.

MARTINDALE, Emmanuel Alfred. b 25.11.1[illegible] Joseph Hospital near Ashton Hall, St. Peter. rhb, [illegible]. Tours ([illegible]). West Indies [illegible]

MASON, Kenneth. b 18.9.1881 Bulkeley Plantation, St. George. [illegible] Nov. 1974 Garrison, St. Michael. rhb, ob. ed; Harrison College. Brother in law [illegible] Alleyne and Sir G.L.Pile.

MAXWELL, Lawrence Evan. b [illegible]7.1.1941 Bayfield, St. Philip. [illegible], ob. Barbados to England.

MAYERS, Anthony Cecil. b 1[illegible].7.1937 Newcastle, St. John. [illegible] ed; The Lodge School.

MAYERS, Michael Spencer. b 2[illegible].9.1884 Super [illegible], Worthing, Christ Church. d 26.7.1925 The Garrison, St. Michael. rhb. ed; The Lodge School.

MEDFORD, Avelyn Clyde. b 12.9.1912 St. David's, Christ Church. rhb. rf.

MILLINGTON, Errol Lamont. b 29.8.1914 Weymouth, St. Michael. d 29.4.1991 Queen Elizabeth Hospital, Bridgetown. lhb, lf[illegible]

MOORE, Joseph Seifert. b 15.11.1880 Watts, St. George[illegible]

MOSELEY, Ezra Alphonsa. b [illegible].1958 Walronds, Christ Church. rhb, rfm. West Indies to South Africa (2). West Indies (2). Glamorgan [illegible] Province. Cousin of H.R.Moseley.

MOSELEY, Hallam Reynold. b 28.[illegible].1948 Providence, Christ Church. rhb, rfm. Barbados to England. Somerset. Cousin of [illegible].Moseley.

MULLINS, Carl Seymour. b 6.3.1925 Peterkin [illegible] Hill, St. Michael. rhb, rf.

MURRAY, David Anthony. b 29.5.1950 Murr[illegible] Gap, Westbury Road, St. Michael. rhb, wkt. Tours [illegible]. West Indies to South Africa (2). West Indies [illegible]. Father of R.L Hoyte.

NESFIELD, [illegible] Augustus. b [illegible]s. rhb, ob.

NEWTON, Joseph Benjamin. b [illegible].1950 Thyme Bottom, Christ Church. rhb.

NORRIS, [illegible] Anton. b [illegible] Kirtons, [illegible]

NURSE, Seymour MacDonald. b [illegible] Black Rock, St. Michael rhb, ob. Tours [illegible] England (2). Barbados to England. West Indies (2[illegible]).

OUTRAM, Barton Henry Vernon. b 1[illegible] Bowmanston, St. John. d 5.4.1974. Queen Elizabeth Hospital, Bridgetown. rhb, [illegible] ed; The Lodge School. Nephew of W.E. Out(t)ram.

OUT(T)RAM, Walter Evelyn. [illegible].6.1855 [illegible] The Lodge School. Uncle of B.H.V.Outram.

PACKER, Charles Henry. b 29.1[illegible] d 2[illegible].1958 Trinidad. Ed: The Lodge School and Bradfield [illegible] Packer.

PACKER, Edward Fielding. b [illegible]9.7.185[illegible] [illegible] 1937 Hastings, Christ Church. ed: [illegible]. Brother of J.G.Packer. [illegible]

PACKER, James Grant. b 2.12.1847 Walmer, St. Michael. Brother of E.F.Packer. Uncle of C.H.Packer.

PADMORE, Albert Leroy. b 17.12.1946 Halls Village, St. James. rhb, ob. Tours (3). West Indies to South Africa (1). West Indies (2).

PARRIS, James Lambert. b 15.12.1905 Weymouth, St Michael. rhb, sra. ed; Combermere School and Harrison College.

PAR(R)IS, Richard. c 13.12.1845 Glendale Plantation, St. Thomas. ed; The Lodge School.

PAYNE, Elrick Colin. b 17.11.1945 Carrington Village, St. Michael. rhb, rf.

PAYNE, Thelston Rodney O'Neale. b 13.2.1957 Foul Bay, St. Philip. lhb, wkt. Tours (5). West Indies (1).

PEIRCE, Thomas Noel Malcolm. b 26.12.1916 Rock Dale, St Lawrence, Christ Church. d 15.11.1988 Crane Gardens, St. Philip. rhb, lb. ed; Harrison College.

PHILLIPS, Doctor Joseph Evelyn. b 28.7.1891 Kendal Plantation, St. John. d 10.12.1958 Edinburgh, Scotland. rhb, rm. ed; The Lodge School. Scotland.

PHILLIPS, Neal Anderson. b 20.1.1956 Holders Hill, St. James. rhb, rm.

PHILLIPS, Roy Wycliffe. b 8.4.1941 Holders Hill, St. James. rhb, lb. Gloucestershire.

PILE, Sir George Laurie. b 8.7.1858 Mount Plantation, St. George. d 15.3.1948 Bulkeley, St. George. rhb. rf. ed; Clifton. Brother in Law of W.N.Alleyne and K.Mason.

PILGRIM, John Frere. b 24.9.1860 Spencer Hall, St. John. d 11.3.1925 Porters, St. James. ed; The Lodge School.

PILGRIM, Owen Alexander. b 1.10.1893 Mount Tabor, St. John. d 13.1.1972 Queen Elzabeth Hospital, Bridgetown. rhb, rmlb. ed; The Lodge School.

PROVERBS, Elbert Anthony. b 1.7.1957 Merricks, St. Philip. rhb, ob.

PROVERBS, Nigel Gordon. b 22.5.1924 Flint Hall, St. Michael. rhb, wkt. ed; Harrison College.

PROVERBS, Stanton Nathaniel. b 6.3.1968 Bridgetown. rhb, rm.

PUCKERIN, Livingstone Kenneth. b 19.6.1969 Rosegate, St. John. rhb. wkt.

REECE, Courtenay Walton. b 4.12.1899 Selman's, St. Thomas. d 16.4.1984 Hong Kong. rhb, rm. ed; Harrison College. Oxford Univ.

REED, Clinton Austin. b 12.9.1876 Fontabelle, St. Michael. d 14.7.1954 Rockley, Christ Church. ed; Harrison College.

REID, Winston Emmerson. b 29.9.1962 Bank Hall, St. Michael. lhb, sla.

REIFER, Elvis Leroy. b 21.3.1961 Airy Hill, St. George. lhb, lfm. Hampshire. Brother of G.N.Reifer and L.N.Reifer.

REIFER, George Nathaniel. b 21.3.1961 Airy Hill, St. George. rhb, lm. Brother of E.L.Reifer and L.N.Reifer.

REIFER, Leslie Norman. b 1.12.1958 Airy Hill, St. George. rhb, ob. Brother of E.L.Reifer and G.N.Reifer.

ROBERTS, Thomas Webb. b 27.4.1880 Black Rock, St. Michael. d 13.7.1976 Lambeth, London. rhb. ed; Harrison College.

ROBINSON, Oscar Merton. b 2.7.1916 Four Square Bottom, St. Philip. rhb, wkt.

ROCK, George Barton. b 24.5.1936 Branchbury, St. Joseph. rhb, rf.

ROGERS, Cecil Carlton. b 11.11.1907 Government Hill, St. Michael. d 26.1.1970 Navy Gardens, Christ Church. rhb, rmf. ed; Combermere School. Brother of H.M.Rogers.

ROGERS, Herbert Mitchell. b 17.4.1906 Government Hill, St. Michael. d 19.1.1976 Queen Elizabeth Hospital, Bridgetown. rhb, rf. ed; Combermere School. Brother of C.C.Rogers.

RUDDER, Stephen Albert Best. b 7.12.1872 Stafford House, Garrison, St. Michael. d June 1954 River Road. St. Michael. rhb, rmf. ed; Harrison College. Trinidad.

ST. HILL, Clinton Dalton. b 2.5.1961 Howells, St. Michael. rhb. ed; The Lodge School.

SEAL(E)Y, James Edward Derrick. b 11.9.1912 Collymore Rock, St. Michael. d 3.1.1982 Palo Seco, Trinidad. rhb, rm. ed; Combermere School. Tours (2). West Indies (11). Trinidad.

SEALY, Glenroy Ricardo. b 11.6.1940 Chase Land, Tweedside, St. Michael. rhb, rm.

SEALY, Mark Laurie. b 24.8.1961 Belleville, St. Michael. rhb, ob. ed; Harrow. Grandson of G.Challenor. Great Nephew of E.L./R./V.C.Challenor.

SELMAN, Courtenay Anthony. b 13.6.1945 St. Helens, St. George. rhb, rfm.

SHEPHERD, John Neil. b 9.11.1943 Belleplaine, St. Andrew. rhb. rm. Tour (1). Robins to South Africa (2). International XI to South Africa (2). West Indies (5). Kent. Rhodesia. Gloucestershire.

SHEPHERD, William C. b c 1873 Trinidad. d c 1955 Barbados. Trinidad.

SIMMONS, Henderson McDonald. b 14.12.1941 Constance Gap, St. Michael. rhb, rm. ed; Combermere School.

SIMMONS, Henry Peter Carter. (later Simmons-Anderson). b 16.11.1871 Hastings, Christ Church. d 11.7.1934 Worthing, Christ Church. rhb, rf.

SKEETE, Doctor Ernest Murray. b 4.6.1865 Edgecumbe Plantation, St. Philip. d 14.8.1939 St. Andrew. ed; Harrison College. Brother of T.S.Skeete. Uncle of H.E.Skeete.

SKEETE, Doctor Harold Edward. b 13.12.1892 Balls Plantation, Christ Church. d 18.8.1972 Dalkeith, St. Michael. rhb, rf. ed; Harrison College and The Lodge School. Son of T.S.Skeete. Nephew of E.M.Skeete.

SKEETE John Brathwaite. b 16.6.1848 St. Clement Vicarage, St. Lucy. d July 1889 Supers Land, Barbados. ed; The Lodge School.

SKEETE, Ricardo Langley. b 14.9.1952 Holders Hill, St. James. rhb, wkt.

SKEETE, Samuel McDonald. b 19.1.1967 St. Michael. rhb, rf.

SKEETE, Torrance Seymour. b 17.5.1852 Bayleys Plantation, St. Philip. d 5.7.1945 Bentley, Christ Church. ed; The Lodge School. Father of H.E.Skeete. Brother of E.M.Skeete.

SKELTON, Eric George. b 13.4.1881. d 11.6.1942 Chelsea, London. wkt.

SKINNER, Clarence Irving. b 13.10.1900 Richmond Hill, St. Peter. d 2.2.1969 Strathclyde, St. Michael. rhb.

SKINNER, Henry Anthony O'Neal. b 8.9.1921 St. Peter. rhb, lb. ed; The Lodge School.

SMALL, Milton Aster. b 12.2.1964 Blades Point, St. Philip. rhb, rf. Tour (1). West Indies (2). Cousin of G.C.Small (Warwickshire).

SMITH, Reverend Augustus Elder. c 17.10.1844 Codrington College, St. Michael. d 8.1.1916 West Kensington, London. ed; The Lodge School. Brother of F.B.Smith. Uncle of S.G.Smith (Trinidad/Northants).

SMITH, A.W.L. d circa 1903. rhb.

SMITH, Cameron Wilberforce. b 29.7.1933 Upper Dayrells Road, St. Michael. rhb, wkt. Tour (1). West Indian XI to England. Commonwealth to India. West Indies (5).

SMITH, Eustace Harte. b 14.8.1877 Drax Hall Plantation, St. George. rhb, wkt. ed; The Lodge School. Brother of R.H.Smith.

SMITH, Frederick Bonham. b 31.3.1837 Codrington College, St. Michael. d 27.3.1923 Tweedside, St. Michael. rhb, rf. ed; The Lodge School. Brother of A.E.Smith. Uncle of S.G.Smith (Trinidad/Northants).

SMITH, Richard Henry. b 2.2.1873 Drax Hall Plantation, St. George. d 10.6.1954 Pine Road, St. Michael. ed; The Lodge School. Brother of E.H.Smith.

SOBERS, Sir Garfield St. Aubrun. b 28.7.1936 Chelsea Road, Bay Land, St. Michael. lhb, lfm/sla. Tours (10). Rest of World to Pakistan. Rest of World to Australia. Swanton to India. Cavaliers to West Indies/India. West Indies (93). South Australia. Nottinghamshire. Cousin of D.A.J.Holford.

SOMERS-COCKS, Arthur. b 19.5.1870 Bredbury, Stockport, Cheshire. d 9.2.1923. Harrison College, St. Michael. rhb, rf. ed; Manchester GS.

SPEED, Reverend Francis Bentinck. b 13.11.1849 Pool Factory, St. John. d 5.3.1906 Stone, Dartford, Kent. ed; The Lodge School. Brother of T.L.Speed.

SPEED, Thomas Lyall. c 7.4.1843 Locust Hall Plantation, St. George. d July 1896 Waterford, St. Michael. ed; The Lodge School. Brother of F.B.Speed.

SPOONER, Charles Daniel. b 23.7.1909 Flint Hall, St. Michael. d 21.11.1988 Bridgetown. rhb, rf. ed; Combermere School. Trinidad.

SPRINGER, Henderson Winfield Da Costa. b 27.4.1964 Bishop's Road, St. Lucy. rhb, ob. ed; Combermere School.

STEPHENSON, Franklyn Da Costa. b 8.4.1959 Halls, St. James. rhb, rf. West Indies to South Africa (2). Gloucestershire. Tasmania. Nottinghamshire.

STRAKER, Richard Anthony Oliver. b 4.8.1951 St. Lawrence, Christ Church. rhb, rm.

TARILTON, Percy Hamilton. b 8.2.1885 St. Margaret's, St. John. d 18.2.1953 Bayville, St. Michael. rhb, sra, wkt. ed; The Lodge School. Tour (1). Brother of A.Tarilton (Jamaica).

TAYLOR, Alfred MacDonald. b 5.4.1918 Swan Street, St. Michael. rhb, wkt. Father of A.M.Taylor Jnr.

TAYLOR, Alfred Maurice b 14.5.1944 Collymore Rock, St. Michael. rhb, wkt. ed; The Lodge School. Son of A.M.Taylor Snr.

THOMAS, Frank Gilbert. b 6.3.1924 Harmony Hall, St. Michael. rhb, rfm. ed; Combermere School. Half Brother of L.F.Harris.

THORNE, Herbert Sandford. b 1.8.1865 Wakefield, St. John. d 12.12.1956 Stewart Hill, St. John.

TROTMAN, Emmerson Nathaniel. b 10.11.1954 Paradise Village. Christ Church. rhb, rm, wkt. West Indies to South Africa (1). Border.

TROTMAN, Henry. c 19.7.1837 Bulkeley Plantation, St. George. Brother of J.H.Trotman. Cousin of R.B.T.S.Payne (Somerset).

TROTMAN, John Hamilton. c 14.4.1834 Bulkeley Plantation, St. George. Brother of H.Trotman. Cousin of R.B.T.S.Payne (Somerset).

WAITHE, Gladstone. b 1902. d 17.6.1979 Port of Spain, Trinidad. rhb.

WALCOTT, Clyde Leopold. b 17.1.1926 New Orleans, St. Michael. rhb, rfm, wkt. ed: Combermere School and Harrison College. Tours (4). West Indies (44). British Guiana. Brother of K.E.Walcott. Father of M.A.C.Walcott.

WALCOTT, Keith Eyre. b 8.3.1924 New Orleans, St. Michael. rhb, sra. ed; Harrison College. Brother of C.L.Walcott. Uncle of M.A.C.Walcott.

WALCOTT, Leslie Arthur. b 19.1.1894 Fontabelle, St. Michael. d 27.2.1984 Flint Hall, St. Michael. rhb. ob. ed; Harrison College. West Indies (1).

WALCOTT, Michael Alex Clyde. b 22.3.1952 Bridgetown. rhb, lm. ed; Harrison College. Son of C.L.Walcott. Nephew of K.E.Walcott.

WALCOTT, Victor De Courcey. b 12.4.1962 Lower Greys, Christ Church. rhb, rf.

WALLACE, Philo Alphonzo. b 2.8.1970 Around-The-Town, St. Peter. rhb. rm.

WARD, Edward Louis. b 11.7.1896 St. John. d 10.8.1966 Bank Hall, St. Michael. rhb, sra.

WARREN, Kenneth Byron. b 23.6.1926 New Orleans, St. Michael. rhb. ob. ed; Combermere School. Cousin of N.E.Marshall and R.E.Marshall.

WEBB, Reverend Charles b 1830 England. d 16.3.1917 Cambridge, England. lhb, lobs.

WEEKES, Everton de Courcy. b 26.2.1925 Westbury, St. Michael. rhb, rm. Tours (5). Swanton to West Indies. International XI to India, Pakistan, New Zealand and Rhodesia. West Indies (48). Cousin of K.H.Weekes (Jamaica).

WHITE, Anthony Wilbur. b 20.11.1938 Brighton, St. Michael. rhb, ob. Tour (1). West Indies (2).

WHITE, William Nicholas. b 10.9.1879 St. Pancras, London. d 27.12.1951 Poltimore, Devon, England. rhb. ed; Malvern. Hampshire. Father of G.W.White (Army).

WHITEHALL, George Donovan. b 29.3.1843 Fairview, Christ Church. d 24.8.1882 Lowlands Plantation, Christ Church. rhb, rf. Uncle of E.L.Challenor, G.Challenor, R.Challenor and V.C.Challenor.

WILLIAMS, Cecil Beaumont. b 8.3.1926 Cats Castle, St. Michael. rhb, lbg. ed; Harrison College. Tour (1).

WILLIAMS, Ernest Albert Vivian. b 10.4.1914 Bank Hall, St Michael. rhb, rfm. ed; Combermere School. Tour (1). West Indies (4).

WILLIAMS, Lionel Leon. b 26.11.1937 Mason Hall, St. Michael. rhb. rfm. ed; Combermere School.

WOOD, Gerald Lear. b 7.[illegible].1926 Vaucluse Plantation, St. Thomas. rhb, wkt. ed; Harrison College. Son of L.O.Wood.

WOOD, Lear Oderic. b 12.11.1885 Buttals Plantation, St. George. d 31.12.[illegible] St. Joseph Hospital near Ashton Hall, St. Peter. rhb, rmf. ed; The Lodge School. Father of G.L.Wood.

WOOD, Rupert Clement. b 12.11.1917 Bayleys Plantation, St. Philip. d 5.1.1968 Montreal, Canada. rhb, rm. ed; The Lodge School.

WORM(E), Clarence Aubrey. b 10.3.1883 River Plantation, St. Philip. d 19.2.1935 Buffalo, New York State, USA. ed; The Lodge School. Brother of S.M.Worme.

WORM(E), Stanley Mills. b 26.10.1887 River Plantation, St. Philip. d 1942 Buffalo, New York State, USA. rhb, rf. ed; The Lodge School. Brother of C.A.Worme.

WORRELL, Sir Frank Mortimer Maglinne. b 1.8.1924 Bank Hall, St. Michael. d 13.3.1967 Mona, Kingston, Jamaica. rhb, lm/sla. ed; Combermere School. Tours (5). Commonwealth to India/Pakistan. Commonwealth to India/Ceylon. West Indian XI to England. West Indies (51). Jamaica. Cousin of L.R.Worrell (Hampshire).

WORRELL, Michael Christopher. b 14.6.1958 Around-The-Town, St. Peter. rhb, wkt. Tour (1).

YARDE, M[illegible]. b 26.4.1944 Silver Sands, Christ Church. rhb.

YEARWOOD, Lawrence Timothy. b 25.6.1884 Holders Hill, St. James. d 18.1.1942 Maxwell's Coast, Christ Church. rhb, wkt. ed; The Lodge School.

Notes:

1. The date of birth, christening or death is represented by b, c and d.
2. The School is shown if educated in England and Combermere School, Harrison College and The Lodge School if educated in Barbados.
3. Official West Indies tours are shown as (Tours) all playing First-class matches except the 1900 tour to England.
4. English Counties (or overseas equivalents) are shown if the player appeared in a First-class match.
5. The match Barbados Born v Rest of West Indies in 1928 is regarded as a First-class match but not as a Barbados island match.

BARBADOS RECORDS

Highest Team Total	for:	753 v Jamaica (Bridgetown) 1951-52
	against:	692-9 dec by British Guiana (Georgetown) 1951-52
Lowest Team Total	for:	47 v Demerara (Georgetown) 1887-88
	against:	16 by Trinidad (Bridgetown) 1942-43
Highest Individual Score	for:	314* C.L.Walcott v Trinidad (Port of Spain) 1945-46
	against:	281* W.R.Hammond for MCC (Bridgetown) 1934-35
Best Bowling (Innings)	for:	8-8 J.E.D.Sealey v Trinidad (Bridgetown) 1942-43
	against:	8-17 O.E.Weber for British Guiana (Bridgetown) 1891-92
Best Bowling (Match)	for:	14-57 C.E.Goodman v British Guiana (Bridgetown) 1891-92
	against:	13-135 C.R.Browne for British Guiana (Georgetown) 1925-26

HIGHEST PARTNERSHIPS FOR EACH WICKET

1st	292	G.Challenor & P.H.Tarilton v Trinidad (Bridgetown)	1926-27
2nd	318	C.W.Smith & S.M.Nurse v Trinidad (Bridgetown)	1962-63
3rd	306	S.M.Nurse & G.S.Sobers v MCC (Bridgetown)	1959-60
4th	574*	C.L.Walcott & F.M.M.Worrell v Trinidad (Port of Spain)	1945-46
5th	214	G.S.Sobers & R.C.Brancker v British Guiana (Bridgetown)	1965-66
6th	187	E.N.Trotman & D.A.Murray v Combined Islands (Bridgetown)	1980-81
7th	224	C.F.Browne & K.Mason v Trinidad (Bridgetown)	1919-20
8th	255	E.A.V.Williams & E.A.Martindale v Trinidad (Bridgetown)	1935-36
9th	125	A.M.Taylor & E.A.V.Williams v British Guiana (Georgetown)	1946-47
10th	100	P.H.Tarilton & H.W.Ince v MCC (Bridgetown)	1912-13

Note: Two Barbados batsmen shared the world 7th wicket record of 347: D.S.Atkinson & C.C.Depeiaza West Indies v Australia (Bridgetown) 1954-55

Most Catches in Innings:	5	T.N.M.Peirce v Trinidad (Bridgetown)	1942-43
Most Catches in Match:	7	T.N.M.Peirce v Trinidad (Bridgetown)	1942-43
Most Dismissals in Innings:	6	(6ct) M.C.Worrell v Leeward Islands (Bridgetown) 1984-85	
	6	(5ct 1st) T.R.O.Payne v England (Bridgetown)	1985-86
Most Dismissals in Match:	7	(7ct) M.C.Worrell v Leeward Islands (Bridgetown) 1984-85	
Most Runs in Career	3,994	(av 48.70) P.D.Lashley 1957-58 to 1974-75	
Most Wickets in Career	158	(av 17.79) M.D.Marshall 1977-78 to 1989-90	
Most Catches in Career	59	C.A.Best 1979-80 to 1989-90	
Most Dismissals in Career	114	(104ct 10st) D.A.Murray 1970-71 to 1981-82	

PLAYING RECORD AGAINST EACH OPPONENT

	First Played	Played	*Won*	*Lost*	*Drawn*
v Demerara/British Guiana/Guyana	1864-65	62	27	13	22
v Trinidad	1891-92	70	35	21	14
v Jamaica	1896-97	37	14	4	19
v Combined Islands	1965-66	13	9	1	3
v Leeward Islands	1966-67	10	5	2	3
v Windward Islands	1981-82	9	4	2	3
v English Touring Teams	1894-95	35	14	7	14
v Indian Touring Teams	1952-53	5	3	0	2
v Australian Touring Teams	1954-55	5	0	2	3
v Pakistan Touring Teams	1957-58	2	0	0	2
v New Zealand Touring Teams	1971-72	1	0	0	1
v Rest of the World	1966-67	1	0	1	0
West Indies Total		250	111	53	86
(figures v English teams include 2 draws v International Cavaliers in 1964-65)					
v Nottinghamshire	1969	1	0	0	1
v International Cavaliers	1969	1	0	1	0
Overall total		252	111	54	87

CAREER RECORDS

	First	Last	M	I	NO	R	HS	Av	100	R	W	Av	BB	5i	10m	ct	st
Adams,G.H.	1925/26	1925/26	1	2	0	15	14	7.50	0							0	1
Allan,D.W.	1955/56	1965/66	19	22	4	268	45	14.88	0							34	5
	1955/56	1966	54	64	12	764	56	14.69	0							117	24
Alleyne,H.L.	1978/79	1982/83	8	8	3	58	24	11.60	0	689	31	22.22	6-63	1	0	2	
	1978/79	1989/90	85	96	25	709	72	9.98	0	7028	254	27.66	8-43	9	2	17	
Alleyne,M.A.	1974/75	1974/75	1	2	0	38	34	19.00	0							0	
Alleyne,P.J.C.	1987/88	1987/88	3	5	0	19	10	3.80	0							1	
Alleyne,R.H.	1871/72	1871/72	1	1	0	26	26	26.00	0	79	7	11.28	5-52	1	0	0	
Alleyne,W.N.	1891/92	1894/95	7	11	1	173	82	17.30	0		+1		1-?	0	0	4	
Archer,F.L.	1907/08	1925/26	11	13	3	197	63	19.70	0							12	
	1907/08	1925/26	13	17	3	225	63	16.07	0							13	
Archer,N.R.S.	1912/13	1912/13	1	1	0	6	6	6.00	0	128	7	18.28	4-21	0	0	3	
Armstrong,G.D.	1973/74	1977/78	9	10	1	204	93	22.66	0	655	19	34.47	4-45	0	0	3	
	1973/74	1977/78	40	54	12	642	93	15.28	0	3199	91	35.15	6-91	2	0	13	
Arthur,R.	1896/97	1896/97	1	2	0	6	4	3.00	0							1	
Ashby,W.E.	1970/71	1974/75	11	19	1	268	61	14.88	0							6	
Atkins,C.A.	1958/59	1958/59	4	8	1	234	119	33.42	1	211	7	30.14	4-28	0	0	1	
Atkinson,D.S.	1946/47	1960/61	19	31	2	1101	151	37.96	3	1357	45	30.15	4-43	0	0	12	
	1946/47	1960/61	78	115	16	2812	219	28.40	5	5291	200	26.45	8-58	6	2	39	
Atkinson,E.S.	1949/50	1957/58	12	18	3	453	77	30.20	0	564	9	62.66	4-70	0	0	6	
	1949/50	1958/59	29	38	6	696	77	21.75	0	1630	61	26.72	6-10	4	0	14	
Austin,F.E.W.G.	1910/11	1912/13	7	6	0	7	4	1.16	0	318	18	17.66	5-29	1	0	10	
	1904/05	1912/13	10	12	0	25	12	2.08	0	524	25	20.96	5-29	1	0	13	
Austin,H.B.G.	1894/95	1925/26	30	44	3	1318	129	32.14	1	280	15	18.66	3-7	0	0	29	3
	1894/95	1927/28	65	100	7	2643	129	28.42	1	302	15	20.13	3-7	0	0	45	3
Austin,H.F.	1897/98	1903/04	6	9	1	114	36*	14.25	0							3	
	1897/98	1903/04	8	13	1	121	36*	10.08	0							3	
Austin,J.G.	1905/06	1905/06	2	4	0	24	18	6.00	0	2	0					5	
Bailey,H.P.	1908/09	1910/11	3	3	0	26	13	8.66	0	66	8	8.25	6-12	1	0	1	
Bancroft,C.K.	1904/05	1904/05	2	3	1	22	11	11.00	0							2	1
	1904/05	1906	14	27	7	293	53	14.65	0							14	6
Barker,H.W.	1951/52	1955/56	4	3	1	4	2	2.00	0	368	12	30.66	3-22	0	0	2	
Barnes,H.W.	1903/04	1904/05	4	7	0	105	59	15.00	0	12	0					1	
Barrow,L.C.M.	1904/05	1905/06	3	6	1	50	27	10.00	0	136	8	17.00	4-8	0	0	3	
Bartlett,E.L.	1923/24	1938/39	17	30	0	639	88	21.30	0							5	
	1923/24	1938/39	42	72	4	1581	109	23.25	1							8	
Batson,R.E.	1909/10	1911/12	4	7	0	174	111	24.85	1							2	
	1909/10	1923	6	10	0	260	111	26.00	1							2	
Beckles,C.S.	1977/78	1978/79	4	6	0	168	83	28.00	0	69	2	34.50	1-16	0	0	1	
Benn,A.J.	1901/02	1901/02	1	2	0	40	31	20.00	0	38	0					0	
Best,C.A.	1979/80	1989/90	47	78	3	3278	179	43.70	10	346	11	31.45	2-17	0	0	59	
	1979/80	1989/90	64	106	9	4289	179	44.21	12	382	11	34.72	2-17	0	0	84	
Bethell,J.A.L.	1963/64	1969/70	16	25	6	496	84*	26.10	0	391	10	39.10	2-16	0	0	7	

	First	Last	M	I	NO	R	HS	Av	100	R	W	Av	BB	5i	10m	ct	st
Birkett,L.S.	1924/25	1928/29	6	7	1	190	62*	31.66	0	134	7	19.14	2-6	0	0	8	
	1924/25	1944/45	26	42	3	1295	253	33.20	3	504	9	56.00	2-6	0	0	22	
Birkett,T.S.	1942/43	1956/57	2	2	0	74	57	37.00	0							0	
Blackman,R.G.	1940/41	1941/42	4	8	0	405	140	50.62	1	58	0					2	
Blades,C.E.	1905/06	1905/06	2	4	1	73	40	24.33	0	64	6	10.66	3-9	0	0	0	
Blades,C.F.	1963/64	1969/70	12	22	0	406	75	18.45	0	21	0					11	
Bourne,C.L.	1931/32	1942/43	12	23	1	543	75	24.68	0							16	4
	1931/32	1942/43	13	25	1	553	75	23.04	0							16	4
Bourne,W.A.	1970/71	1970/71	1	2	2	25	19*		0	90	2	45.00	2-54	0	0	1	
	1970/71	1977	60	78	15	1325	107	21.03	1	4164	128	32.53	6-47	2	0	39	
Bowring,W.	1899/00	1901/02	2	3	0	9	7	3.00	0							3	
	1898/99	1904/05	5	8	0	38	17	4.75	0							8	
Boxill,D.D.	1898/99	1971/72	15	19	1	149	38	8.27	0							28	14
Boyce,K.D.	1964/65	1974/75	22	34	3	795	112	25.64	1	1506	58	25.96	5-56	1	0	17	
	1964/65	1977	285	420	27	8800	147*	22.39	4	21324	857	25.02	9-61	35	7	215	
Bradshaw,C.S.	1951/52	1951/52	1	2	0	13	12	6.50	0	66		33.00	2-66	0	0	0	
Bradshaw,R.	1964/65	1964/65	1	2	0	59	57	29.50	0							0	
Brancker,R.C.	1955/56	1969/70	31	49	6	1337	135*	31.09	5	2035	73	27.87	6-39	2	0	11	
	1955/56	1969/70	47	68	7	1666	135*	27.31	5	2895	106	27.31	7-77	4	0	21	
Branker,K.A.	1951/52	1955/56	2	4	1	2	2*	0.66	0	119	1	119.00	1-24	0	0	0	
Brathwaite,H.A.	1978/79	1983/84	6	11	1	245	86	24.50	0	10	0					4	
Brathwaite,J.M.M.	1891/92	1891/92	3	2	0	31	23	15.50	0							0	
Broome,O.A.	1964/65	1964/65	1	2	0	24	22	12.00	0							0	
Broomes,N.D.	1982/83	1986/87	8	9	4	71	18	14.20	0	416	5	83.20	2-74	0	0	5	
Browne,A.	1883/84	1887/88	3	5	2	12	5*	4.00	0	119	10	11.90	4-27	0	0	2	
Browne,C.	1891/92	1899/00	14	21	0	317	74	15.09	0							20	1
Browne,C.A.	1907/08	1929/30	20	25	2	816	131*	35.47	1	188	9	20.88	5-33	1	0	10	
	1907/08	1929/30	23	30	2	950	131*	33.92	1	188	9	20.88	5-33	1	0	11	
Browne,C.F.	1919/20	1926/27	11	13	1	459	137	38.25	1	427	14	30.50	2-1	0	0	13	
Browne,C.R.	1908/09	1910/11	7	9	1	73	19	9.12	0	584	44	13.27	6-60	2	1	10	
	1908/09	1938/39	74	115	11	2077	103	19.97	3	6228	278	22.40	8-58	17	6	59	
Browne,R.	1883/84	1896/97	2	4	1	8	5*	2.66	0							1	
Browne,S.	1864/65	1871/72	3	6	0	69	33	11.50	0							0	
Burke,I.L.	1938/39	1938/39	1	1	0	0	0	0.00	0	37	3	12.33	3-24	0	0	2	
Burnett,H.T.	1871/72	1871/72	1	1	0	2	2	2.00	0	11	1	11.00	1-11	0	0	0	
Burnham,C.G. G.	1964/65	1964/65	1	1	1	11	11*		0	19	0					0	
Butcher,R.O.	1974/75	1974/75	1	2	0	67	38	33.50	0							0	
	1974	1990	277	428	43	12021	197	31.22	17	182	4	45.50	2-37	0	0	290	1
Byer,J.W.	1929/30	1935/36	6	11	5	132	47*	22.00	0	537	17	31.58	4-28	0	0	3	
Bynoe,M.R.	1957/58	1971/72	37	64	5	2676	190	45.35	6	117	2	58.50	2-7	0	0	26	
	1957/58	1971/72	56	97	10	3572	190	41.05	6	246	9	27.33	2-7	0	0	45	
Campbell,T.D.A.	1969/70	1969/70	1	2	0	13	7	6.50	0							0	
Carew,G.M.	1934/35	1947/48	27	42	4	1288	100	33.89	1	485	9	53.88	2-26	0	0	13	
	1934/35	1948/49	39	69	7	2131	107	34.27	3	600	13	46.15	2-6	0	0	17	
Carrington,J.W.	1865/66	1865/66	1	2	1	3	3	3.00	0	7	0					1	
Carter,D.	1964/65	1964/65	1	1	1	7	7*		0	88	3	29.33	2-46	0	0	0	

	First	Last	M	I	NO	R	HS	Av	100	R	W	Av	BB	5i	10m	ct	st
Challenor,E.L.	1894/95	1895/96	3	6	1	92	30	18.40	0							0	
	1894/95	1914	29	52	1	1106	111	21.68	1	15	0					23	
Challenor,G.	1905/06	1929/30	24	33	2	1713	237*	55.25	8	954	45	21.20	4-16	0	0	10	
	1905/06	1929/30	95	160	9	5822	237*	38.55	15	1290	54	23.88	4-16	0	0	25	
Challenor,R.	1904/05	1924/25	11	16	1	296	73	19.73	0							16	
	1904/05	1924/25	13	20	1	413	77	21.73	0							19	
Challenor,V.C.	1901/02	1903/04	5	9	0	239	67	26.55	0							0	
	1900/01	1903/04	10	18	0	344	67	19.11	0							3	
Clairmonte,F.A.C.	1909/10	1909/10	1	2	1	0	0*	0.00	0	55	0					0	
Clarke,C.B.	1937/38	1938/39	3	5	2	43	17*	14.33	0	362	12	30.16	5-62	1	0	0	
	1937/38	1961	97	145	40	1292	86	12.30	0	8782	333	26.37	7-75	20	1	42	
Clarke,C.H.	1893/94	1893/94	2	2	0	16	12	8.00	0	17	4+4	4.25	4-?	0	0	1	
Clarke,M.I.C.	1940/41	1940/41	2	4	0	212	153	53.00	1	73	1	73.00	1-29	0	0	2	
Clarke,M.W.	1928/29	1928/29	1	2	0	1	1	0.50	0							1	
Clarke,N.E.	1969/70	1976/77	26	46	4	1331	159	31.69	2	54	0					27	
Clarke,S.T.	1977/78	1981/82	20	22	6	204	36	12.75	0	1898	68	27.91	6-39	1	1	14	
	1977/78	1989/90	238	265	44	3269	100*	14.79	1	18397	942	19.52	8-62	59	10	146	
Clarke,T.	1871/72	1871/72	1	2	1	3	3*	3.00	0	56	8	7.00	4-27	0	0	1	
Clarke,T.G.	1883/84	1887/88	3	5	0	59	21	11.80	0	39	4	9.75	2-15	0	0	2	
Clarke,W.C.	1864/65	1887/88	4	7	0	30	20	4.28	0							4	
Cole,H.A.F.	1894/95	1907/08	22	38	2	909	78	25.25	0	36	0					21	
Collymore,E.A.	1922/23	1922/23	1	1	0	30	30	30.00	0							0	
Collymore,W.O.	1883/84	1883/84	1	1	0	6	6	6.00	0							1	
Connell,V.R.	1969/70	1969/70	1	2	0	40	26	20.00	0							0	1
Constantine,L.N.	1938/39	1938/39	1	2	0	12	11	6.00	0	69	4	17.25	4-41	0	0	0	
	1921/22	1945	119	197	11	4475	133	24.05	5	8991	439	20.48	8-38	25	4	133	
Cox,A.P.	1895/96	1895/96	1	2	0	27	24	13.50	0	1	0					0	
Cox,G.B.Y.	1893/94	1903/04	15	23	1	619	161	28.13	2	17	0					16	
	1893/94	1904/05	18	29	1	767	161	27.39	2	17	0					16	
Cox,H.T.	1887/88	1887/88	2	4	1	19	16	6.33	0	1	0					0	
Cox,P.I.	1896/97	1899/00	8	12	0	256	74	21.33	0	75	10	7.50	4-17	0	0	4	
	1896/97	1905/06	19	30	0	417	74	13.90	0	277	17	16.29	4-17	0	0	21	
Crick,C.O.	1940/41	1940/41	2	3	1	22	13*	11.00	0	227	10	22.70	4-84	0	0	0	
Cumberbatch,C.S.	1933/34	1938/39	5	8	0	170	59	21.25	0							3	
Cumberbatch,D.A.	1983/84	1984/85	6	10	0	146	45	14.60	0	563	13	43.30	3-67	0	0	5	
Cumberbatch,J.S.	1907/08	1907/08	1	2	2	18	17*		0							0	
Cummins,A.C.	1988/89	1988/89	2	3	0	29	20	9.66	0	164	4	41.00	2-41	0	0	1	
Da Costa,D.C.C.C.	1899/00	1899/00	1	1	1	6	6*		0							0	
	1898/99	1900/01	5	8	2	23	15*	3.83	0							5	2
Daniel,W.W.	1975/76	1984/85	23	28	12	265	53*	16.56	0	2182	92	23.71	7-33	6	2	3	
	1975/76	1988	266	241	106	1551	53*	11.48	0	19490	867	22.47	9-61	31	7	63	
Depeiaza,C.C.	1951/52	1956/57	8	13	3	319	65	31.90	0							18	3
	1951/52	1956/57	16	24	5	623	122	32.78	1	15	0					31	9
Downes,O.D.	1958/59	1958/59	4	5	3	8	6*	4.00	0	448	13	34.46	5-24	1	0	0	
Doyle,H.H.	1961/62	1961/62	1	2	0	8	7	4.00	0							2	

	First	Last	M	I	NO	R	HS	Av	100	R	W	Av	BB	5i	10m	ct	st
Edwards,J.R.	1931/32	1937/38	5	10	0	154	51	15.40	0	290	5	58.00	3-83	0	0	5	
	1931/32	1937/38	6	11	0	178	51	16.18	0	290	5	58.00	3-83	0	0	5	
Edwards,R.M.	1961/62	1969/70	20	23	6	199	31*	11.70	0	1395	42	33.21	6-45	2	0	11	
	1961/62	1969/70	35	43	10	389	34	11.78	0	2831	78	36.29	6-45	3	0	15	
Ellcock,D.E.	1986/87	1986/87	4	5	1	102	52	25.50	0	246	8	30.75	3-49	0	0	1	
Ellcock,R.M.	1983/84	1983/84	3	5	0	36	18	7.20	0	185	6	30.83	2-31	0	0	1	
	1982	1989	42	46	12	398	45*	11.70	0	3191	109	29.27	5-35	1	0	8	
Elliott,G.	1883/84	1883/84	1	2	0	20	15	10.00	0							0	
Emtage,J.B.D	1921/22	1921/22	1	1	0	2	2	2.00	0	52	1	52.00	1-28	0	0	0	
Estwick,R.O.	1982/83	1986/87	19	31	7	182	34*	7.58	0	1716	67	25.61	6-68	3	0	8	
	1982/83	1989/90	37	49	12	376	43*	10.16	0	3088	141	21.90	6-88	6	0	16	
Evelyn,E.E.	1883/84	1883/84	1	1	0	1	1	1.00	0	8	1	8.00	1-8	0	0	0	
Farmer,S.W.	1969/70	1976/77	17	27	4	551	58	23.95	0	769	16	48.06	4-55	0	0	10	
Farmer,W.A.	1946/47	1958/59	9	14	1	663	275	51.00	2							3	
Fields,W.S.H.	1907/08	1912/13	3	3	0	33	25	11.00	0	232	7	33.14	5-58	1	0	3	
Foster,C.S.	1936/37	1937/38	2	4	1	38	34*	12.66	0							0	
Foster,G.M.	1958/59	1961/62	6	9	1	86	28*	10.75	0	442	14	31.57	4-31	0	0	6	
Foster,N.L.	1931/32	1935/36	2	4	0	44	43	11.00	0							0	
Foster,T.F.	1975/76	1980/81	11	18	5	276	62	21.23	0	501	13	38.53	3-27	0	0	7	
Foster,W.M.	1941/42	1941/42	1	2	0	15	13	7.50	0	31	0					0	
Francis,G.N.	1924/25	1929/30	4	2	0	86	47	43.00	0	360	24	15.00	7-50	2	0	1	
	1923	1933	62	91	23	874	61	12.85	0	5159	223	23.13	7-50	8	2	42	
Frederick,M.C.	1944/45	1944/45	1	1	0	8	8	8.00	0							0	
	1944/45	1953/54	6	10	0	294	84	29.40	0							3	
Garner,J.	1976/77	1987/88	29	36	7	656	67	22.62	0	2491	136	18.31	6-28	10	0	20	
	1976/77	1987/88	214	231	54	2964	104	16.74	1	16333	881	18.53	8-31	48	7	129	
Gibbs,W.O.	1907/08	1926/27	13	18	2	465	129*	29.06	1	435	17	25.58	5-62	1	0	10	
	1907/08	1926/27	18	27	2	634	129*	25.36	1	622	21	29.61	5-62	1	0	12	
Gilkes,A.S.	1983/84	1987/88	11	22	1	654	104	31.14	1							5	
Gilkes,B.I.	1919/20	1929/30	4	4	0	2	2	0.50	0	294	6	49.00	4-83	0	0	1	
Gilkes,O.H.	1919/20	1919/20	1	1	0	6	6	6.00	0	20	1	20.00	1-20	0	0	1	
Gill,S.S.	1940/41	1940/41	1	2	0	6	5	3.00	0	71	0					0	
Gittens,S.O.	1935/36	1944/45	11	21	0	459	105	21.85	1							16	4
Goddard,J.D.C.	1936/37	1957/58	32	53	13	2102	218*	52.55	5	1376	51	26.98	5-43	2	0	27	
	1936/37	1957/58	111	145	32	3769	218*	33.35	5	3845	146	26.33	5-20	4	0	94	
Goddard,K.	1948/49	1948/49	1	2	1	7	4*	7.00	0	57	1	57.00	1-37	0	0	1	
Goodman,C.E.	1891/92	1896/97	14	21	6	260	68	17.33	0	1202	115 + 2	10.45	8-40	14	6	12	
	1891/92	1896/97	15	22	6	274	68	17.12	0	1327	124 + 2	10.70	8-40	15	6	14	
Goodman,G.A.	1893/94	1893/94	2	2	0	1	1	0.50	0							2	
Goodman,P.A.	1891/92	1912/13	28	42	4	1170	180	30.78	3	903	74 + 3	12.20	7-18	5	1	31	
	1891/92	1912/13	40	66	7	1824	180	30.91	5	1155	85 + 3	13.58	7-18	5	1	47	
Goodman,W.E.	1891/92	1893/94	5	7	1	122	41	20.33	0							8	
	1891/92	1901/02	15	24	1	398	65	17.30	0							12	
Graham,O.S.	1942/43	1942/43	2	3	0	26	12	8.66	0	105	2	52.50	2-55	0	0	0	

	First	Last	M	I	NO	R	HS	Av	100	R	W	Av	BB	5i	10m	ct	st
Grant,A.L.	1986/87	1988/89	12	15	2	463	89	35.61	0	10	0					12	
Greaves,H.F.K.	1923/24	1929/30	8	9	4	72	19	14.40	0	487	8	60.87	5-18	1	0	3	
Greaves,S.R.	1983/84	1985/86	7	12	0	229	67	19.08	0	235	4	58.75	2-27	0	0	0	
Greene,E.	1943/44	1945/46	8	9	3	64	22	10.66	0	768	20	38.40	4-82	0	0	2	
Greene,V.S.	1985/86	1987/88	8	10	1	78	18	8.66	0	632	29	21.79	5-72	1	0	3	
	1985/86	1989	28	35	8	332	62*	12.29	0	2273	93	24.44	7-96	4	1	11	
Greenidge,A.E.	1974/75	1981/82	24	38	4	1455	172	42.79	4	99	3	33.00	2-52	0	0	18	
	1974/75	1983/84	48	81	5	2319	172	30.51	4	147	5	29.40	2-52	0	0	32	
Greenidge,C.G.	1972/73	1989/90	45	76	6	3297	237	47.10	8	31	0					36	
	1970	1990	506	860	72	36434	273*	46.23	90	472	17	27.76	5-49	1	0	508	
Greenidge,G.A.	1966/67	1973/74	22	37	3	1237	205	36.38	3	398	8	49.75	7-124	1	0	8	
	1966/67	1975/76	182	332	22	9112	205	29.39	16	948	13	72.92	7-124	1	0	95	
Greenidge,J.W.	1951/52	1960/61	6	10	1	90	25*	10.00	0	249	4	62.25	4-174	0	0	3	
Greenidge,M.F.	1895/96	1895/96	1	2	1	13	13*	13.00	0	53	1	53.00	1-48	0	0	0	
Greenidge,W.T.	1985/86	1986/87	5	7	4	28	10	9.33	0	346	12	28.83	2-25	0	0	3	
Griffith,C.C.	1959/60	1966/67	18	18	5	161	38	12.38	0	1509	69	21.86	5-50	3	0	7	
	1959/60	1968/69	96	119	32	1502	98	17.26	0	7172	332	21.60	8-23	17	1	39	
Griffith,E.H.C.	1953/54	1955/56	2	3	0	57	31	19.00	0	22	0					0	
	1953/54	1966/67	25	48	1	1690	150	35.95	3	1159	24 + 1	48.29	3-64	0	0	11	
Griffith,H.C.	1921/22	1940/41	18	23	3	328	60	16.40	0	1826	87	20.98	7-38	5	1	11	
	1921/22	1940/41	79	108	28	1204	84	15.05	0	7294	258	28.27	7-38	12	2	36	
Griffith,H.L.V.	1943/44	1946/47	9	13	0	347	64	24.78	0	239	3	79.66	1-12	0	0	6	
Griffiths,R.F.	1933/34	1933/34	1	2	0	10	8	5.00	0	10	0					0	
Hall,W.W.	1955/56	1970/71	13	18	4	258	88	18.42	0	1238	41	30.19	6-75	1	0	6	
	1955/56	1970/71	170	215	38	2673	102*	15.10	1	14273	546	26.14	7-51	19	2	58	
Harding,G.	1974/75	1974/75	2	4	1	27	14	9.00	0	108	4	27.00	2-28	0	0	1	
Harris,A.A.	1934/35	1934/35	1	1	0	24	24	24.00	0	44	0					0	
Harris,J.V.	1988/89	1988/89	2	1	0	4	4	4.00	0	76	0					1	
Harris,L.F.	1942/43	1944/45	5	6	4	65	27*	32.50	0	313	12	26.08	4-55	0	0	2	
Hassell,A.E.E.	1955/56	1955/56	1	1	1	2	2*		0							2	1
Haynes,D.L.	1976/77	1989/90	47	79	5	3037	160	41.04	6	22	1	22.00	1-2	0	0	20	
	1976/77	1990	247	421	46	17126	255*	45.66	38	196	6	32.66	1-2	0	0	145	1
Haynes,H.H.	1864/65	1864/65	1	2	0	6	6	3.00	0							0	
Hinds,D.C.S.	1901/02	1904/05	7	13	3	243	55	24.30	0	352	17	20.70	5-41	1	0	7	
	1900/01	1904/05	12	22	4	366	55	20.33	0	435	29	15.00	10-36	2	1	10	
Hinds,H.D.	1907/08	1907/08	1	2	0	11	11	5.50	0	40	0					0	
Hinkson,E.A.	1887/88	1887/88	2	4	1	23	16*	7.66	0							1	
Hinkson,E.S.	1973/74	1973/74	1	1	0	0	0	0.00	0	61	1	61.00	1-61	0	0	0	
Hoad,E.	1896/97	1896/97	1	1	0	0	0	0.00	0							0	
Hoad,E.L.G.	1921/22	1937/38	20	30	5	1425	174*	57.00	4	1425	46	30.97	5-84	1	0	16	
	1921/22	1937/38	63	104	13	3502	174*	38.48	8	1923	53	36.28	5-84	1	0	26	
Hoad,E.L.G.	1944/45	1953/54	9	15	3	303	74	25.25	0	669	15	44.60	3-98	0	0	3	
Hoad,J.J.S.	1919/20	1919/20	2	1	1	16	16*		0	113	2	56.50	1-36	0	0	2	
Hoad,W.C.	1901/02	1901/02	1	1	0	2	2	2.00	0							1	
	1901/02	1905/06	6	9	0	53	14	5.88	0	258	11	23.45	4-95	0	0	7	

	First	Last	M	I	NO	R	HS	Av	100	R	W	Av	BB	5i	10m	ct	st
Holder,A.H.	1951/52	1958/59	11	14	2	251	52	20.91	0	908	26	34.92	7-38	3	0	5	
Holder,R.I.C.	1985/86	1989/90	15	23	4	652	124	34.31	2							7	
	1985/86	1989/90	16	25	4	687	124	32.71	2							7	
Holder,V.A.	1966/67	1977/78	43	57	11	742	122	16.13	1	3140	134	23.43	7-44	3	1	17	
	1966/67	1985/86	313	358	81	3593	122	12.97	1	23300	950	24.52	7-40	38	3	99	
Holford,D.A.J.	1960/61	1978/79	46	68	13	1993	111	36.23	1	3683	130	28.33	6-61	4	1	46	
	1960/61	1978/79	99	149	27	3821	111	31.31	3	8096	253	32.00	8-52	8	2	83	
Horne,L.M.	1901/02	1901/02	2	3	2	18	18*	18.00	0	142	11	12.90	8-39	1	0	0	
Howard,A.B.	1965/66	1974/75	30	38	7	310	42*	10.00	0	2181	83	26.27	5-46	2	0	10	
	1965/66	1974/75	31	38	7	310	42*	10.00	0	2321	85	27.30	5-46	2	0	10	
Howell,W.M.	1883/84	1894/95	5	9	0	36	19	4.00	0	214	18	11.88	7-29	1	0	4	
Hoyte,R.L.	1989/90	1989/90	6	10	2	74	46	9.25	0							8	3
Hunte,C.C.	1950/51	1966/67	27	43	4	2004	263	51.38	3	89	0					12	1
	1950/51	1967	132	222	19	8916	263	43.92	16	644	17	37.88	3-5	0	0	68	1
Hunte,T.A.	1893/84	1987/88	13	24	0	516	72	21.50	0	46	0					9	
	1983/84	1987/88	14	25	0	585	72	23.40	0	46	0					9	
Hutchinson,G.	1955/56	1955/56	2	3	0	63	35	21.00	0	9	0					1	
Hutchinson,L.R.	1925/26	1929/30	2	4	0	30	22	7.50	0	184	1	184.00	1-105	0	0	0	
Hutson,L.C.	1922/23	1924/25	2	2	0	57	45	28.50	0	4	0					0	
Ince,H.W.	1912/13	1929/30	15	19	3	754	151	47.12	2	175	3	58.33	3-34	0	0	10	
	1912/13	1929/30	35	52	6	1352	167	29.39	3	242	5	48.40	3-34	0	0	13	
Inniss,B.D.	1942/43	1942/43	1	1	0	33	33	33.00	0	36	0					0	
Inniss,C.D.	1928/29	1938/39	7	13	0	351	80	27.00	0	50	1	50.00	1-17	0	0	3	
	1927/28	1938/39	10	18	1	474	80	27.88	0	50	1	50.00	1-17	0	0	4	
Inniss,M.H.W.	1985/86	1988/89	4	7	2	251	68*	50.20	0							4	
Jackman,E.C.	1887/88	1897/88	7	10	4	95	28	15.83	0	37	5	7.40	3-18	0	0	2	
Jemmott,A.M.B.	1891/92	1891/92	3	4	1	92	43	30.66	0	6	0					0	
Johnson,A.L.	1988/89	1989/90	6	8	1	43	13	6.14	0	379	11	34.35	3-42	0	0	3	
Johnson,N.A.	1978/79	1986/87	12	18	0	502	98	27.88	0							3	
Johnson,W.	1896/97	1896/97	1	1	1	0	0*			0						1	
Jones,R.M.	1911/12	1911/12	1	1	0	12	12	12.00	0	8	0					0	
Jordan,E.L.	1988/89	1988/89	4	3	2	26	24*	26.00	0	264	8	33.00	4-53	0	0	1	
Jordan,H.R.	1936/37	1936/37	1	2	0	7	7	3.50	0	95	3	31.66	3-64	0	0	1	
Kidney,J.M.	1908/09	1931/32	10	15	2	203	73	15.61	0							4	
	1908/09	1931/32	11	17	2	229	73	15.26	0							4	
King,A.S.	1960/61	1970/71	9	14	1	360	89	27.69	0							7	
King,C.L.	1972/73	1981/82	35	55	6	2173	156	44.34	4	1130	46	24.56	5-91	1	0	34	
	1972/73	1986/87	125	202	25	6770	163	38.24	14	4379	128	34.21	5-91	1	0	98	
King,E.	1864/65	1865/66	2	4	0	23	18	5.75	0							0	
King,E.H.	1966/67	1968/69	2	2	0	2	2	1.00	0							3	2
King,F.M.	1947/48	1956/57	12	11	3	78	30*	9.75	0	1050	49	21.42	5-35	1	0	9	
	1947/48	1956/57	31	34	8	237	30*	9.11	0	2588	90	28.75	5-35	2	0	17	

	First	Last	M	I	NO	R	HS	Av	100	R	W	Av	BB	5i	10m	ct	st
King,H.A.	1948/49	1952/53	3	3	1	27	19*	13.50	0	171	4	42.75	1-15	0	0	2	
Laborde,A.L.C.	1895/96	1895/96	1	2	0	4	4	2.00	0							0	
Lashley,P.D.	1957/58	1974/75	58	93	11	3994	204	48.70	8	551	13	42.38	2-10	0	0	45	
	1957/58	1974/75	85	132	13	4932	204	41.44	8	958	27	35.48	3-15	0	0	66	
Layne,O.H.	1901/02	1904/05	3	4	0	121	43	30.25	0	314	16	19.62	5-54	1	0	3	
	1901/02	1912/13	27	48	2	1023	106	22.23	1	2035	91	22.36	9-19	6	2	19	
Learmond,G.C.	1894/95	1895/96	3	6	0	164	86	27.33	0							4	
	1894/95	1910/11	45	78	3	1700	120	22.66	1	69	2	34.50	1-4	0	0	27	2
Linton,G.L.L.	1981/82	1989/90	26	38	9	734	83	25.31	0	2321	78	29.75	5-35	5	0	11	
Lobo,F.C.	1933/34	1933/34	1	2	0	3	3	1.50	0	7	0					2	
Lucas,J.H.	1945/46	1949/50	12	20	4	1030	216*	64.37	2	437	13	33.61	4-88	0	0	9	
	1945/46	1954	15	25	5	1074	216*	53.70	2	484	15	32.26	4-88	0	0	11	
Lucas,N.S.	1953/54	1954/55	3	5	0	138	91	27.60	0							3	
McAuley,D.M.	1887/88	1897/98	18	29	3	397	37	15.26	0	372	20	18.60	7-40	1	0	12	
	1887/88	1897/98	19	31	4	413	37	15.29	0	413	22	18.77	7-40	1	0	12	
McClean,W.Y.	1864/65	1864/65	1	2	1	0	0*	0.00	0							0	
Marshall,M.D.	1977/78	1989/90	33	44	6	1110	89	29.21	0	2811	158	17.79	6-38	8	1	19	
	1977/78	1990	324	411	53	8757	117	24.46	6	25443	1396	18.22	8-71	82	13	118	
Marshall,N.E.	1940/41	1955/56	27	40	6	1125	134	33.08	2	2426	70	34.65	6-117	1	0	5	
	1940/41	1958/59	33	50	6	1337	134	30.38	2	2855	90	31.72	6-117	2	0	6	
Marshall,R.E.	1945/46	1952/53	8	12	0	695	191	57.91	3	501	16	31.31	3-25	0	0	6	
	1945/46	1972	602	1053	59	35725	228*	35.94	68	5092	176	28.93	6-36	5	0	294	
Martindale,E.A.	1929/30	1935/36	9	15	2	355	134	27.30	1	1149	30	38.30	5-106	1	0	8	
	1929/30	1939	59	84	20	972	134	15.18	1	5205	203	25.64	8-32	11	1	29	
Mason,K.	1903/04	1925/26	17	23	7	277	113	17.31	1	1402	50	28.04	7-82	2	0	21	
Maxwell,L.E.	1968/69	1978/79	16	23	11	90	19	7.50	0	1261	34	37.08	5-73	1	0	2	
Mayers,A.C.	1954/55	1954/55	2	3	0	17	10	5.66	0	204	2	102.00	1-90	0	0	0	
Mayers,M.S.	1905/06	1908/09	4	8	0	55	16	6.87	0							2	
Medford,A.C.	1938/39	1938/39	1	2	0	35	21	17.50	0	52	1	52.00	1-52	0	0	0	
Millington,E.L.	1946/47	1950/51	3	5	1	36	23	9.00	0	204	5	40.80	2-67	0	0	1	
Moore,J.S.	1904/05	1904/05	1	1	0	0	0	0.00	0	29	2	14.50	1-1	0	0	0	
	1904/05	1909/10	5	9	0	55	29	6.11	0	125	5	25.00	1-1	0	0	2	
Moseley,E.A.	1981/82	1989/90	10	13	2	257	48	23.26	0	1018	40	23.36	5-89	1	0	5	
	1980	1990	64	83	15	1259	70*	18.51	0	5440	223	24.39	6-23	7	0	17	
Moseley,H.R.	1969	1971/72	8	10	8	31	17*	15.50	0	484	10	48.40	2-28	0	0	2	
	1969	1982	213	217	94	1533	67	12.46	0	13668	557	24.53	6-34	16	1	78	
Mullins,C.S.	1950/51	1953/54	3	5	2	28	22	9.33	0	348	7	49.71	3-68	0	0	1	
Murray,D.A.	1970/71	1981/82	42	68	12	2136	143	38.14	4							104	10
	1970/71	1983/84	114	176	30	4503	206*	30.84	7	11	0					292	31
Nesfield,G.A.	1964/65	1964/65	1							78	3	26.00	2-16	0	0	1	
Newton,J.B.	1975/76	1976/77	2	4	1	113	84	37.66	0							0	

	First	Last	M	I	NO	R	HS	Av	100	R	W	Av	BB	5i	10m	ct	st
Norris,E.A.	1962/63	1962/63	1	2	2	10	10*		0	44	0					0	
Nurse,S.M.	1958/59	1971/72	41	66	7	3049	213	51.67	10	51	2	25.50	1-0	0	0	43	
	1958/59	1971/72	141	235	19	9489	258	43.93	26	389	12	32.41	3-36	0	0	116	
Outram,B.H.V.	1903/04	1903/04	2	4	2	16	6	8.00	0	199	12	16.58	5-52	2	1	5	
Outtram,W.E.	1871/72	1871/72	1	2	2	54	42*		0							0	
Packer,C.H.	1896/97	1897/98	8	12	0	123	34	10.25	0							6	
	1896/97	1901/02	13	22	1	312	82	14.85	0	5	0					7	
Packer,E.F.	1883/84	1887/88	3	6	0	40	25	6.66	0							1	
Packer,J.G.	1865/66	1865/66	1	2	1	11	11*	11.00	0							0	
Padmore,A.L.	1972/73	1981/82	34	36	12	369	79	15.37	0	2441	82	29.76	5-42	2	0	16	
	1972/73	1983/84	68	66	23	562	79	13.06	0	5780	193	29.94	6-69	8	2	29	
Parris,J.L.	1925/26	1946/47	14	20	4	376	65	23.50	0	1194	26	45.92	4-34	0	0	10	
	1925/26	1946/47	15	22	4	390	65	21.66	0	1205	27	44.62	4-34	0	0	12	
Parris,R.	1864/65	1865/66	2	4	0	30	18	7.50	0							0	
Payne,E.C.	1971/72	1972/73	2	3	1	14	11	7.00	0	142	2	71.00	1-25	0	0	1	
Payne,T.R.O.	1978/79	1989/90	49	79	10	2862	140	41.47	6							74	7
	1978/79	1989/90	68	106	14	3391	140	36.85	6							103	8
Peirce,T.N.M.	1941/42	1948/49	16	23	6	261	45*	15.35	0	1095	29	37.75	5-54	1	0	16	
Phillips,J.E.	1919/20	1919/20	2	2	0	2	2	1.00	0	44	1	44.00	1-32	0	0	2	
	1919/20	1923	4	6	0	52	25	8.66	0	118	2	59.00	1-15	0	0	4	
Phillips,N.A.	1982/83	1984/85	15	24	3	370	51	17.61	0	1144	39	29.33	4-35	0	0	8	
Phillips,R.W.	1966/67	1966/67	2	3	0	98	92	32.66	0							1	
	1966/67	1970	18	28	0	529	92	18.89	0	6	0					11	
Pile,G.L.	1883/84	1891/92	4	5	1	67	40*	16.75	0	93	11	8.45	4-21	0	0	3	
Pilgrim,J.F.	1891/92	1891/92	3	2	1	8	6	8.00	0	5	0					1	
Pilgrim,O.A.	1919/20	1925/26	4	2	1	11	11	11.00	0	359	15	23.93	5-45	1	0	2	
Proverbs,E.A.	1984/85	1984/85	1	2	1	24	16*	24.00	0	4	0					0	
Proverbs,N.G.	1948/49	1954/55	6	10	0	268	84	26.80	0							2	
Proverbs,S.N.	1989/90	1989/90	3	6	0	96	58	16.00	0							0	
Puckerin,L.K.	1988/89	1988/89	4	3	0	113	79	37.66	0							12	1
Reece,C.W.	1926/27	1929/30	3	3	0	3	3	1.00	0	354	10	35.40	4-72	0	0	2	
	1925	1929/30	4	5	1	4	3	1.00	0	433	13	33.30	4-72	0	0	4	
Reed,C.A.	1899/00	1899/00	1	2	0	23	17	11.50	0							0	
Reid,W.E.	1985/86	1987/88	9	15	3	160	31	13.33	0	454	20	22.70	4-46	0	0	5	
Reifer,E.L.	1985/86	1985/86	1	1	1	51	51*		0	50	0					0	
	1984	1985/86	21	27	9	408	51*	22.66	0	1811	49	36.95	4-43	0	0	6	
Reifer,G.N.	1979/80	1984/85	12	20	1	388	71	20.42	0	28	0					6	
Reifer,L.N.	1977/78	1987/88	25	42	3	765	153*	19.61	1	26	1	26.00	1-18	0	0	22	
Roberts,T.W.	1896/97	1897/98	4	6	0	72	24	12.00	0							1	
Robinson,O.M.	1943/44	1946/47	5	9	0	285	148	31.66	1							2	4
Rock,G.B.	1960/61	1968/69	8	12	3	59	19	6.55	0	748	40	18.70	6-18	3	0	3	
Rogers,C.C.	1935/36	1936/37	2	4	1	6	2*	2.00	0	215	8	26.87	3-68	0	0	1	

	First	Last	M	I	NO	R	HS	Av	100	R	W	Av	BB	5i	10m	ct	st
Rogers,H.M.	1926/27	1928/29	3	3	3	3	2*		0	337	8	42.12	4-93	0	0	1	
Rudder,S.A.B.	1895/96	1901/02	5	8	0	106	29	13.25	0	357	32	11.15	6-43	4	0	6	
	1895/96	1901/02	9	13	1	183	53	15.25	0	441	37	11.91	6-43	4	0	10	
St.Hill,C.D.	1986/87	1986/87	1	2	0	31	25	15.50	0							1	
Sealey,J.E.D.	1928/29	1942/43	22	41	0	1135	107	27.68	2	771	33	23.36	8-8	1	1	15	
	1928/29	1948/49	80	134	8	3831	181	30.40	8	1802	63	28.60	8-8	2	1	67	13
Sealy,G.R.	1964/65	1964/65	1	1	1	10	10*		0	20	1	20.00	1-17	0	0	0	
Sealy,M.L.	1988/89	1988/89	2	2	0	11	6	5.50	0							0	
Selman,C.A.	1970/71	1973/74	3	5	1	56	27*	14.00	0	217	6	36.16	3-49	0	0	0	
Shepherd,J.N.	1964/65	1970/71	10	17	1	357	73	22.31	0	592	19	31.15	4-40	0	0	12	
	1964/65	1987	423	613	106	13359	170	26.34	10	32068	1157	27.71	8-40	54	2	292	
Shepherd,W.C.	1901/02	1904/05	3	4	0	19	9	4.75	0	201	16	12.56	5-39	2	0	1	
	1896/97	1909/10	15	26	3	126	18	5.47	0	748	38	19.68	5-32	3	0	12	
Simmons,H.M.	1970/71	1970/71	1	2	0	22	12	11.00	0	87	5	17.40	4-58	0	0	0	
Simmons,H.P.C.	1899/00	1907/08	8	15	2	155	43*	11.92	0	377	19	19.84	5-41	1	0	5	
	1898/99	1907/08	11	21	3	196	43*	10.88	0	421	20	21.05	5-41	1	0	5	
Skeete,E.M.	1883/84	1887/88	3	6	1	59	24	11.80	0							1	
Skeete,H.E.	1924/25	1928/29	2	3	0	42	24	14.00	0	167	6	27.83	5-33	1	0	2	
Skeete,J.B.	1865/66	1865/66	1	2	0	0	0	0.00	0							0	
Skeete,R.L.	1975/76	1984/85	25	37	5	774	80	24.18	0	16	0					38	2
Skeete,S.M.	1989/90	1989/90	3	3	0	20	19	6.66	0	213	5	42.60	2-24	0	0	0	
Skeete,T.S.	1871/72	1887/88	4	7	0	25	10	3.57	0	81	8	10.12	4-28	0	0	1	
Skelton,E.G.	1901/02	1901/02	1	2	1	2	2	2.00	0							2	1
Skinner,C.I.	1935/36	1935/36	1	2	0	56	30	28.00	0	47	0					0	
Skinner,H.A.O.	1941/42	1944/45	2	4	0	27	13	6.75	0	19	0					2	
Small,M.A.	1983/84	1988/89	11	13	3	44	15	4.40	0	1058	42	25.19	6-55	2	0	4	
	1983/84	1988/89	17	16	5	50	15	4.54	0	1454	56	25.96	6-55	2	0	5	
Smith,A.E.	1864/65	1871/72	3	6	0	69	15	11.50	0	40	8+8	5.00	5-26	2	0	2	
Smith,A.W.L.	1896/97	1896/97	1	1	0	35	35	35.00	0							0	
Smith,C.W.	1951/52	1962/63	20	32	2	1434	140	47.80	5	73	1	73.00	1-8	0	0	22	
	1951/52	1964/65	37	64	3	2277	140	37.32	5	97	3	32.33	2-24	0	0	32	3
Smith,E.H.	1897/98	1897/98	2	2	1	13	13	13.00	0							2	2
Smith,F.B.	1864/65	1871/72	3	5	1	95	50*	23.75	0	75	6+10	12.50	6-?	1	1	1	
Smith,R.H.	1893/94	1893/94	2	3	2	35	17*	35.00	0							0	
Sobers,G.S.	1952/53	1973/74	30	40	9	2355	204	75.96	8	2133	71	30.04	6-56	2	0	22	
	1952/53	1974	383	609	93	28315	365*	54.87	86	28941	1043	27.74	9-49	36	1	406	
Somers-Cocks,A.	1894/95	1901/02	10	17	4	200	62*	15.38	0	1002	53	18.90	8-99	2	1	4	
Speed,F.B.	1871/72	1871/72	1	2	1	17	17*	17.00	0							1	
Speed,T.L.	1864/65	1864/65	1	2	0	5	5	2.50	0							0	
Spooner,C.D.	1933/34	1934/35	4	7	4	25	12*	8.33	0	529	11	48.09	4-48	0	0	3	
	1933/34	1937/38	5	9	4	26	12*	5.20	0	647	12	53.91	4-48	0	0	3	
Springer,H.W.D.	1987/88	1989/90	13	17	8	162	32*	18.00	0	825	33	25.00	4-40	0	0	12	
Stephenson,F.D.	1981/82	1989/90	8	10	2	367	165	45.87	1	510	21	24.28	3-27	0	0	3	
	1981/82	1990	96	154	17	3575	165	26.09	4	9011	393	22.92	8-47	25	6	43	

	First	Last	M	I	NO	R	HS	Av	100	R	W	Av	BB	5i	10m	ct	st
Straker,R.A.O.	1976/77	1978/79	8	11	1	327	95	32.70	0	31	1	31.00	1-15	0	0	9	
Tarilton,P.H.	1905/06	1929/30	28	39	4	1885	304*	53.85	7	0	1	0.00	1-0	0	0	28	3
	1905/06	1929/30	51	79	7	2777	304*	38.56	8	0	1	0.00	1-0	0	0	33	5
Taylor,A.M.	1941/42	1951/52	16	26	1	860	168	34.40	4	12	0					9	3
Taylor,A.M.	1966/67	1966/67	4	7	0	79	46	11.28	0							11	
Thomas,F.G.	1944/45	1944/45	1	2	1	31	21	31.00	0	70	1	70.00	1-45	0	0	1	
Thorne,H.S.	1891/92	1891/92	3	2	0	8	7	4.00	0	45	4	11.25	3-19	0	0	3	
Trotman,E.N.	1975/76	1981/82	21	30	1	1088	167	37.52	2							22	
	1975/76	1989/90	71	119	6	4245	173	37.56	9	1153	34	33.91	5-30	1	0	85	15
Trotman,H.	1865/66	1865/66	1	2	0	4	4	2.00	0							0	
Trotman,J.H.	1864/65	1864/65	1	2	0	24	15	12.00	0							0	
Waithe,G.	1928/29	1940/41	9	18	0	391	112	21.72	1							4	
Walcott,C.L.	1941/42	1955/56	25	43	3	2328	314*	58.20	7	409	16	25.56	4-26	0	0	21	4
	1941/42	1963/64	146	238	29	11820	314*	56.55	40	1269	35	36.25	5-41	1	0	174	33
Walcott,K.E.	1940/41	1951/52	15	24	4	536	72	26.80	0	109	0					11	
Walcott,L.A.	1928/29	1940/41	11	19	2	515	73*	30.29	0	440	15	29.33	3-30	0	0	8	1
	1928/29	1940/41	12	21	3	555	73*	30.83	0	472	16	29.50	3-30	0	0	8	1
Walcott,M.A.C.	1974/75	1974/75	1	2	0	33	24	16.50	0							0	
Walcott,V.D.	1987/88	1989/90	8	8	3	28	11	5.60	0	705	19	37.10	3-25	0	0	2	
Wallace,P.A.	1989/90	1989/90	1	2	0	20	18	10.00	0							0	
Ward,E.L.	1928/29	1928/29	1	2	0	16	16	8.00	0	10	0					0	
Warren,K.B.	1954/55	1954/55	1	1	0	0	0	0.00	0	99	0					0	
Webb,C.	1865/66	1865/66	1	2	0	42	28	21.00	0	19	0					0	
Weekes,E.D.	1944/45	1963/64	32	53	6	2518	253	53.57	8	297	7	42.42	4-38	0	0	16	
	1944/45	1963/64	152	241	24	12010	304*	55.34	36	731	17	43.00	4-38	0	0	125	1
White,A.W.	1958/59	1965/66	18	25	3	584	75	26.54	0	1656	60	27.60	6-80	1	0	21	
	1958/59	1965/66	31	46	7	996	75	25.53	0	2665	95	28.05	6-80	1	0	32	
White,W.N.	1903/04	1905/06	6	12	1	241	51	21.90	0	24	0					5	
	1903	1922	72	128	5	3225	160*	26.21	2	39	0					42	
Whitehall,G.D.	1864/65	1871/72	3	5	0	25	21	5.00	0	36	4	9.00	4-16	0	0	2	
Williams,C.B.	1947/48	1956/57	16	20	1	788	133	41.47	2	1288	43	29.95	6-28	2	0	11	
	1947/48	1956/57	37	39	5	987	133	29.02	2	2183	75	29.10	7-55	4	0	27	
Williams,E.A.V.	1934/35	1948/49	27	42	5	969	131*	26.18	1	2602	89	29.23	5-73	1	0	12	
	1934/35	1948/49	42	63	8	1479	131*	26.89	2	3387	116	29.19	5-73	1	0	19	
Williams,L.L.	1956/57	1964/65	2	3	0	51	41	17.00	0	55	0					0	
Wood,G.L.	1948/49	1958/59	7	6	0	158	53	26.33	0							10	5
Wood,L.O.	1924/25	1924/25	1	1	0	24	24	24.00	0							0	
Wood,R.C.	1933/34	1938/39	4	8	0	97	25	12.12	0	206	9	22.88	4-73	0	0	0	
	1933/34	1938/39	5	9	0	132	35	14.66	0	208	9	23.11	4-73	0	0	0	
Worme,C.A.	1899/00	1899/00	1	1	0	2	2	2.00	0	22	0					1	
Worme,S.M.	1908/09	1912/13	9	9	4	82	33	16.40	0	745	36	20.69	6-18	2	0	7	
	1908/09	1912/13	10	10	4	82	33	13.66	0	784	36	21.77	6-18	2	0	7	
Worrell.F.M.M.	1941/42	1946/47	15	27	6	1547	308*	73.66	4	1148	43	26.69	5-32	2	0	15	
	1941/42	1964	208	326	49	15025	308*	54.24	39	10115	349	28.98	7-70	13	0	139	

	First	Last	M	I	NO	R	HS	Av	100	R	W	Av	BB	5i	10m	ct	st
Worrell,M.C.	1982/83	1986/87	14	23	6	478	105	28.11	1							48	5
	1982/83	1986/87	16	27	6	526	105	25.04	1							59	6
Yarde,M.	1969/70	1969/70	1	2	0	41	36	20.50	0							0	
Yearwood,L.T.	1910/11	1910/11	3	3	0	20	12	6.66	0							3	2

NOTES: 1. Where two lines are shown, the first is for Barbados matches only and the second for all First-class matches.

2. The match Barbados Born v Rest in 1927/28 is not included as a Barbados match, but is included where relevant in the figures for all First-class matches.

3. The two matches played by Barbados in England in 1969 are included in the Barbados figures.

4. There are no bowling analyses for the match v Demerara in 1864-65, nor for the second innings v Trinidad in 1893/94 (second match)—these wickets are shown as (eg) + 1.

5. Figures are complete to the end of 1990 English season.